MEDIEVAL
AND
RENAISSANCE
DRAMA
IN ENGLAND

Editorial Board

MEDIEVAL
AND
RENAISSANCE
DRAMA
IN ENGLAND

Volume 15

Edited by
John Pitcher

Associate Editor
Robert Lindsey

Book Review Editor
Susan Cerasano

Madison • Teaneck
Fairleigh Dickinson University Press
London: Associated University Presses

Associated University Presses
2010 Eastpark Boulevard
Cranbury, NJ 08512

Associated University Presses
16 Barter Street
London WC1A 2AH, England

Associated University Presses
P.O. Box 338, Port Credit
Mississauga, Ontario
Canada L5G 4L8

The paper used in this publication meets the requirements of the American National Standard for Permanence of Paper for Printed Library Materials Z39.48-1984.

International Standard Book Number 0-8386-3963-1 (vol. 15)
International Standard Serial Number 0731-3403

All editorial correspondence concerning *Medieval and Renaissance Drama in England* should be addressed to Dr. John Pitcher, St. John's College, Oxford OX1 3JP, United Kingdom. Orders and subscriptions should be directed to Associated University Presses, 2010 Eastpark Boulevard, Cranbury, New Jersey 08512.

Medieval and Renaissance Drama in England disclaims responsibility for statements, either of fact or opinion, made by contributors.

Contents

Foreword   7

Contributors   9

Articles

Mankind and the Fifteenth-Century Preaching Controversy   17
    LYNN FOREST-HILL

The Theatrical Rhetoric of *Edward III*   43
    LESLIE THOMSON

Filling Fare: The Appetite for Current Issues and Traditional Forms
in the Repertory of the Chamberlain's Men   57
    ROSLYN L. KNUTSON

Dramatic Authorship and Publication in Early Modern England   77
    DOUGLAS A. BROOKS

Printing Conventions and the Early Modern Play   98
    PAUL J. VOSS

The Crone in English Renaissance Drama   116
    JEANNE ADDISON ROBERTS

Prostitution in Late Elizabethan London: The Case of Mary
Newborough   138
    GUSTAV UNGERER

Leaning Too Hard Upon the Pen: Suburb Wenches and City Wives
in *Westward Ho*   224
    MICHELLE M. DOWD

Songs by Aurelian Townshend, in the Hand of Sir Henry Herbert, for
an Unrecorded Masque by the Merchant Adventurers   243
    PETER BEAL

Reviews

Mary Bly, *Queer Virgins and Virgin Queans on the Early Modern
Stage*   263
    PATRICIA CAHILL

Martin Butler, ed., *Re-Presenting Ben Jonson: Text, History,*
Performance   268
RICHARD FINKELSTEIN

R. P. Draper, *Shakespeare: The Comedies*   274
ANNETTE DREW-BEAR

John Forrest, *The History of Morris Dancing, 1458–1750*   276
SKILES HOWARD

Andrew Gurr and Mariko Ichikawa, *Staging in Shakespeare's*
Theatres   281
ROSLYN L. KNUTSON

Jay Halio, ed., *Henry VIII or All is True by William Shakespeare and*
John Fletcher   286
MICHAEL A. WINKELMAN

Grace Ioppolo, ed., *Shakespeare Performed: Essays in Honor of*
R. A. Foakes   294
ARTHUR F. KINNEY

Ann Rosalind Jones and Peter Stallybrass, *Renaissance Clothing and*
the Materials of Memory   300
JEAN MACINTYRE

Joan Pong Linton, *The Romance of the New World: Gender and the*
Literary Formations of English Colonialism   306
NAOMI C. LIEBLER

Kathleen McKluskie and David Bevington, eds. *Plays on Women*   313
ALISON FINDLAY

Leah S. Marcus, Janel Mueller, and Mary Beth Rose, *Elizabeth I:*
Collected Works, and Carole Levin, Debra Barrett-Graves, Jo
Eldridge Carney, W. M. Spellman, Gwynne Kennedy, and Stephanie
Witham, *Extraordinary Women of the Medieval and Renaissance*
World. A Biographical Dictionary   317
MARGUERITE A. TASSI

Bruce R. Smith, *Shakespeare and Masculinity*   326
CHARLES R. FORKER

John Southworth, *Shakespeare the Player: A Life in the Theatre*   330
MICHAEL TAYLOR

Frederick Turner, *Shakespeare's Twenty-First Century Economics*   333
SCOTT CUTLER SHERSHOW

Index   341

Foreword

Volume 15 offers articles devoted to the historical contexts for drama in six-teenth-century England. One of these is a substantial discussion of prostitu-tion in Elizabethan London, based on archival research. Another piece is focused on the efforts of the Chamberlain's Men to satisfy the tastes of their audiences for political and other topical issues of the day. The volume also contains essays on genre and rhetoric in early modern plays, and on the con-vention for representing character types on the Renaissance stage (with spe-cial reference to the figures of the crone and of the city wife). Further essays concentrate on dramatic authorship, and the publication and printing of plays, and on the connections between *Mankind* and the fifteenth-century contro-versy over preaching. The final article is given over to the texts and contexts of newly discovered songs by Aurelian Townsend, intended for an unre-corded 1630s masque by the Merchant Adventurers.

JOHN PITCHER

Contributors

PETER BEAL is English Manuscript Expert and a Director at Sotheby's, London. He is author of *Index of English Literary Manuscripts, 1450–1700* and *In Praise of Scribes: Manuscripts and their Makers in Seventeenth-Century England.*

DOUGLAS A. BROOKS is Assistant Professor of English at Texas A&M University. He is the author of *From Playhouse to Printing House: Drama and Authorship in Early Modern England.*

PATRICIA CAHILL is Assistant Professor of English at Emory University and is completing a book entitled *Tales of Iron Wars: Martial Bodies and Manly Economics in Elizabethan Culture.*

MICHELLE M. DOWD is writing a dissertation at Columbia University on representations of women and work in early modern drama and in early modern writing.

ANNETTE DREW-BEAR is Professor of English at Washington and Jefferson College in Washington, Pennsylvania. Her most recent publication is *Painted Faces on the Renaissance Stage: The Moral Significance of Face-Painting Conventions.*

ALISON FINDLAY teaches at Lancaster University and is the author of *Illegitimate Power: Bastards in Renaissance Drama* and *A Feminist Perspective on Renaissance Drama.*

RICHARD FINKELSTEIN, Professor of English at SUNY-Geneseo, has written articles on Shakespeare, Jonson, and other early modern dramatists.

LYNN FOREST-HILL is a Fellow of the Wessex Medieval Centre at the University of Southampton. Her most recent book is *Transgressive Language in Medieval English Drama.*

CHARLES R. FORKER, Emeritus Professor of English at Indiana University, is the author of *The Critical Tradition: Richard II.*

9

SKILES HOWARD teaches at Rutgers University and is the author of *The Politics of Courtly Dancing in Early Modern England.*

ARTHUR F. KINNEY is the Thomas W. Copeland Professor of Literary History and Director of the Massachusetts Center for Renaissance Studies at the University of Massachusetts, Amherst. He has written *Shakespeare, "Macbeth" and the Cultural Moment,* and has edited books of essays on *Hamlet.*

ROSLYN L. KNUTSON, Professor of English at the University of Arkansas at Little Rock, is the author of *The Repertory of Shakespeare's Company, 1594–1613* and *Playing Companies and Commerce in Shakespeare's Time.*

NAOMI C. LIEBLER, Professor of English at Montclair State University, is the author of *Shakespeare's Festive Tragedy: The Ritual Foundations of Genre.* She is working on a critical edition of Richard Johnson's *Most Famous History of the Seven Champions of Christendom.*

JEAN MACINTYRE is Professor Emerita of English at the University of Alberta. She has published *Costumes and Script in the Elizabethan Theatre* as well as many related articles.

JEANNE ADDISON ROBERTS is Professor Emerita at the American University, Washington DC, and author of *The Shakespearean Wild: Geography, Genus, and Gender.*

SCOTT CUTLER SHERSHOW is Associate Professor of English at Miami University in Oxford, Ohio. He is the author of *Puppets and "Popular" Culture* and the co-editor of *Marxist Shakespeare.*

MARGUERITE TASSI is Assistant Professor at the University of Nebraska at Kearney. Her current work analyzes Elizabethan dramatists' ambivalence toward the painter's art.

MICHAEL TAYLOR, formerly Professor of English at the University of New Brunswick, is the author of *Shakespeare Criticism in the Twentieth Century.* He is currently working on an edition of *Henry VI, Part I.*

LESLIE THOMSON teaches English at the University of Toronto. She has published articles on English Renaissance staging and stage directions and has edited *Anything for a Quiet Life* in the forthcoming Oxford edition of Middleton's works.

GUSTAV UNGERER, retired Professor of English Literature at the University of Berne, is the author of *A Spaniard in Elizabethan England: The Correspon-*

dence of Antonio Pérez's Exile. He is currently working on the political and cultural background of *The Merchant of Venice.*

PAUL J. VOSS is an Associate Professor of English at Georgia State University. He has recently published *Elizabethan News Pamphlets: Shakespeare, Spenser, Marlowe, and the Birth of Journalism.*

MICHAEL WINKELMAN, Assistant Professor of English at Earlham in Richmond Indiana, is currently writing a book-length study on marriage relationships in Tudor political drama.

MEDIEVAL
AND
RENAISSANCE
DRAMA
IN ENGLAND

Articles

Mankind and the Fifteenth-Century Preaching Controversy

LYNN FOREST-HILL

THE purpose of this essay is to consider the language of preaching as it is represented in the fifteenth-century East Anglian morality play *Mankind*. The language of this metalinguistic play has been the subject of a number of studies, and the play has been interpreted as offering a range of general instructions against the misuse of language. Kathleen Ashley, in her discussion of the battle between good and evil words in the play, refers to "*Mankind*'s demonstrable contrast between doctrine and idle speech,"[1] and she addresses the mocking and parodying of the character Mercy's preaching style as part of the battle of words. Joerg O. Fichte suggests that the play teaches against all forms of *"otiosum verbum"*[2] and indeed this is made explicit in the play when Mercy warns the three Worldlings "Thys ydyll language ȝe xall repent."[3] Paula Neuss links idle language with physical idleness or sloth.[4] Idle speech, words or language are variously defined by these critics. Ashley suggests, "The idle tongue sins in five ways which recall the activities of the Worldlings . . . by telling jokes full of filth; by telling lies or foolish things; by telling tales; and by scorning good men" (149). Fichte refers to "idle words taking such forms as verbal horse-play, dirty jokes, and exaggeration" (43), and Neuss selects "chattering in church" (45), gossiping (49), anticlerical satire (54), and lies (62). Medieval sermons are more helpful in identifying the scope of "idle" language, speech or words as these were understood by contemporary commentators. John Mirk wrote, "Seynt Poule . . . forbedyth yche cristen man not to speke all maner ydull speche, and rybaudy, and harlatry, *and all othyr speches þat turnyth to foly and noght.*"[5] The author of the sermon cycle *Jacob's Well* describes five aspects of "ydel speche":

> Þe first is outrage in here woordys, as a clapp of a melle, þat neuere wyll be stylle. Þe secunde is veyn woordys, male-apert, in iangeling, in tellyng of thynges, & often þei are false & lyerys. Þe iij manere, summe vsyn veyn woordys in sotyll speche to plesyn þe hererys. . . . Þe iiij manere, summe vsyn veyne woordys in lesynges & bourdys. Þe v manere, summe vsen veyn speche in scornyng of gode men þat don wel, for þei wolde drawyn hem fro þat vse of goodnes.[6]

The author of *A Myrour to Lewde Men and Women* gives a long and extremely detailed commentary on "Idel speche men clepeþ ydel wordes" He asserts that "in fyue maneres men may synne in ydel speche or ydel wordes." The five categories can be identified, like the *Jacob's Well* definitions, in *Mankind,* but perhaps the *Myrour* writer's most significant observation is that

> þe ferþe manere is foule wordes and lesynges . . . whiche men clepeþ ydel wordes; but al ydel, as noþing doynge, beþ þei noght, for þei doo ofte moche harme, boþ to þe spekers and to the hyreres.[7]

Physical sloth is not, then, the same as linguistic "idleness." The idleness of the body or the mind is its inactivity which, according to medieval opinion led to sin, but the idleness of language actively produces harm. These careful definitions of "idle language" are not, however, quite sufficient to define all the forms included in *Mankind.*

Although the modern critics associate idle speech or idle words primarily with the wicked characters in the play, when Mercy's preaching and instruction are shown to be ineffective they too may be described as "idle language" according to the definition provided by the fifteenth-century theologian Reginald Pecock. In his book *The Folower to the Donet,* this controversial churchman asserts that

> parauenture wel nyȝ ech kynde or spice of deede which may be maad vertuose may be doon ydeli and may be maad ydel, fforwhi ech deede is doon ydeli whanne it is doon and not for þe eend and entent for which bi doom of resoun he ouȝte be don; wherfore ech idil speche, ech ydil seyng and heeryng, and ech ydil deede . . . is synne.[8]

These epistemological opinions shed light on the moral function of language, but other contexts are vital for appreciating the scope and sophistication of the relationship between language and the complex web of moral, cultural, and political issues it addresses in the play.

The language of *Mankind* has been addressed most recently by Janette Dillon in her article "*Mankind* and the Politics of 'Englysch Laten'" where she considers the treatment of language in the play in its cultural and political contexts, arguing that it represents the dramatist's careful negotiation between orthodoxy and sympathy for Lollard views. She suggests that "at a time of polarized responses to English and Latin in theological contexts, the play might be seen as striving to moderate such polarity."[9] As part of this process, Dillon suggests that the "capacity of latinate English to command automatic reverence" is challenged, and the play "insists that the audience consider it *as one possible mode of discourse,* rather than as the necessary, or natural discourse of the church."[10] While Dillon's views are persuasive, her reading of *Mankind*'s language in the context of Lollardy does not fully address the subtlety with which the playwright treats language, nor the relationship between this subtlety and the play's message of mercy. The playwright's technique, as well as the play's argument, are illuminated by fifteenth-century didactic texts written to counter Lollardy, including those considered in their own time to be culturally, doctrinally, and politically contentious, but earlier texts shed light on the complex problems associated with preaching in the fifteenth century.

In this essay I will argue that while *Mankind* can, itself, be seen to preach a universal message of avoiding the sin of idle language which would be appropriate for any audience, it offers a much more specific message of particular relevance in the cultural and religious climate of the fifteenth century, and especially in East Anglia where the play originated, that those who err may be saved, and that in the process of dramatizing this reminder, the play offers comments which reflect on a number of complex contemporary issues surrounding language.

In the fifteenth century those who erred most problematically were the Lollards, whose activities appear to have been particularly problematic in East Anglia. The play's message is not aimed at an audience of those who have erred, but takes the form of a dramatization of specific, or perhaps allegorical, contexts in which error may occur. This is bracketed by statements and reminders of Christian charity and mercy.[11] The language in which these statements and reminders are constructed is vividly contrasted to unequivocally sinful language, but is itself problematic when it is seen to be ineffective.

The *Mankind* playwright provides a detailed treatment of the effect of language, firstly in his dramatization of the Mankind character's particular orientation toward aureate preaching language, and his subsequent sudden fall into sin and eventual recuperation. Secondly, the playwright makes distinctions between the attitudes of troublemakers and those who err. Thirdly, he places emphasis in the play on contextualizing language according to the character who uses it and the intention that motivates that use. The centrality of the preaching of mercy and forgiveness for those who repent of their errors reflects opinions and distinctions found in the extant works of fifteenth-century orthodox and didactic writers such as Nicholas Love and Reginald Pecock.

At the start of the fifteenth century Nicholas Love's *The Mirrour of the Blessed Lyf of Jesus Christ Oure Lord* had been authorized for publication by Archbishop Thomas Arundel, who regarded the book as *"ad fidelium edificacionem, & hereticum sive lollardorum confutacionem"* [for the instruction of the faithful and the confutation of heretics or Lollards].[12] Love himself declared that he wrote "to confusion of alle fals lollardes & heritykes."[13] In the middle years of the century Reginald Pecock asserted his determination to point out to the heretics the extent to which they erred in their opinions and beliefs. Both Love and Pecock intended to confute error using the vernacular, and while Love's *Mirrour* emphasizes mercy, Pecock's books emphasize reasoned debate.

As part of his argument, Love sets out in lively detail the archangel Gabriel's petition to God on behalf of mankind in which Gabriel repeatedly refers to mercy. He pleads eloquently

> Where to lord be þei born to such grete myschefe? For þough it be done after ȝour riȝtwisnesse, neuerles lorde it is now tyme of mercy. Haue in mynde þat ȝhe made þaim after ȝour awne liknesse, & þough hire formfadres folily & wrecchedly breken ȝour our maundment neuereles ȝour mercy is aboue alle þinge. Wherefore alle hir eyen ben sett vpon ȝow . . . til ȝe haue mercy and help hem with a spedeful & heleful remedye.[14]

There follows a conventional debate between the four daughters of God over the fate of sinful mankind. The result of the debate is that Christ is incarnated and suffers death to redeem sinners. In *Mankind,* Mercy's opening speech on devotion to Christ the Redeemer, in which he reminds the audience of the Passion and its redemptive purpose, is in the spirit of Love's narration of the debate and Passion.

The East Anglian morality play, *The Castle of Perseverance,* which predates *Mankind,* actually dramatizes the debate between the four daughters of God, in which Misericordia argues on behalf of the character Humanum Genus,[15] so Love's work may have provided an orthodox source for the *Mankind* playwright's approach to Lollardy. It seems less likely at first glance that Reginald Pecock could have influenced *Mankind.* The play is conventionally dated sometime between 1465 and 1470,[16] some ten years after Pecock's death in ca. 1460, but in 1457 Pecock had been charged with heresy arising from his English books.[17] He had declared that his purpose in writing his books as he did, in English, was to challenge the heretical opinions of the Lollards in the language they themselves favored.[18] After his death, his most profound opponent, Thomas Gascoigne, in his book *Loci et Libro Veritatum,* asserted that although Pecock's many books contained theological views and opinions which were in error, he was tried, forced to recant, and to burn his books, not because of those unorthodox views but because he wrote them in English.[19] Anne Hudson notes, however, that the friar John Bury ignored Pecock's use of English in his violent condemnation of the bishop's unorthodoxy.[20] Whichever aspect offended individuals most, taken as a whole, Pecock's works gave rise to considerable hegemonic anxiety which continued even after his death. A letter from Edward IV to Pope Sixtus IV, dated 1475–76, suggests that Pecock's books were still being widely disseminated. The King wrote:

After the death of the said Reginald, the writings and treatises composed by him multiplied in such wise that not only the laity but churchmen and scholastic graduates scarcely studied anything else.[21]

Given the intense concern provoked by Lollardy throughout the fifteenth century the letter may overstate the case,[22] but it testifies to a continuing interest in Pecock's work. The *Mankind* playwright may have been unsympathetic toward much of the work of this controversial contemporary figure, but anyone as interested in language as the playwright appears to be could hardly have escaped knowledge of his opinions and his method of expressing them. This is not to suggest that either opinions or method were followed slavishly; nor to suggest, as Dillon does, that the playwright entertained even modest Lollard sympathies; nor does it ignore the probability that Pecock and the playwright had both been trained in the scholastic techniques which underpin Pecock's work, and that any similarities in their work are the result of this training.[23] Nevertheless, Pecock's English books provide closely contemporary rhetorical, analytical, and moral approaches to the problems of Lollardy which the playwright might then have developed for his own instructional purposes. Pecock's work, at least, provides us with insights into the playwright's technique.

If *Mankind* is viewed as belonging to the corpus of fifteenth-century work intended to recall Lollards from their errors and urge them to repent, we can more easily understand why the playwright and Pecock might use similar rhetorical tactics. Such a message, focused, in Love's case on mercy, and in Pecock's case on reasoned debate, does not conflict with the confutation of the heresy, but acknowledges its "organic" nature.[24] The intention of both Love and Pecock was to recall to orthodoxy those who had erred toward Lollardy, and in his book *The Reule of Cristen Religioun* Pecock writes

> If eny man wole aske and wite whi þis present book . . . y make in þe commoun peplis langage, herto y answere þat þis present book . . . ben so maad pricipali forto adaunte, rebuke, drive doun and conuerte þe fonnednes and þe presumpcioun of . . . hem whiche holden him silf so stifly and so singulerly, foolili and oonli to þe vce of þe bible in her modiris langage.[25]

Pecock's intention is to challenge and convert those he refers to as "yuel disposid men of þe lay partye," and instruct "oþere weel disposid cristen men of þe lay partie."[26] The *Mankind* playwright is gentler in his approach but similarly clear in the distinction he makes between wicked characters and Mankind, even though this character errs almost disastrously to the point of despair. Significantly, the play states, and then shows, that mercy is always available to those who repent, even when they believe they do not deserve it. This does not suggest uncompromising anti-Lollard polemic, but a truly

charitable Christian desire to recover the "lost sheep." The preaching of the
message of mercy and repentance is therefore crucial if it is to have the desired effect, and this is where the play creates the greatest difficulty in order
to explore the problem of how to get such a vital message across when language itself is under attack.

Mercy's opening speech, often referred to as a sermon or homily,[27] is the
focus of the dramatist's specific consideration of the process by which good
people fall into error. *Mankind* dramatizes the problems associated with
preaching, and as it does so, the language of the play engages with the fifteenth-century debate on the appropriate language to be used in the instruction of the people in Christian doctrine and theology. The rise of Lollardy,
which was characterized by an insistence on the use of the vernacular,
prompted Archbishop Arundel's Constitutions of 1409. These controlled,
among other things, who could preach, what topics could be addressed, and
what texts were to be made available.[28] *Mankind* does not challenge the restrictions imposed by the Constitutions, any more than it follows those aspects of Pecock's works which were considered heretical.

The playwright's sophisticated treatment of language in the play is consistent with the continuing debate on preaching language, which Lollardy problematized throughout the fifteenth century. The play does not overtly engage
with doctrinal matters such as transubstantiation, devotion to images, or the
priesthood of all Christians. Its references to good works (25), and the Eucha-
rist: "Ther ys non such foods" (37) are brief and in the latter instance, allu-
sive. However, its reference to worshipping in the fields, when Mankind
declares "Thys place I assyng as for my kyrke" (552) while he is still in the
field where he has been working, signals the onset of his error. Worshipping
in woods and fields was held by Lollards to be as acceptable as worshipping
in church, contrary to orthodox opinion.[29] This brief reference, coming at the
moment of Mankind's fall, suggests that the character's fall is toward heresy.
Mankind addresses the long-standing debate on preaching language in the
context of trying to prevent such a fall into erroneous opinions and conduct,
and incidentally in the context of increasing lay literacy. The debate on appropriate preaching language predated Wyclif's demands for an English
translation of the Bible and English liturgy, but took on new significance as
Wycliffites and Lollards promoted the use of the vernacular.

The play, written at a time when language was a source of the utmost cultural tension, constantly reminds the audience that it is about language. In a
climate of challenge to the status of Latin, and those who were literate in it,
by Lollard demands for a vernacular Bible and liturgy, and at a time when
lay literacy continued to increase, the play addresses most insistently the effects of preaching language, particularly aureate/latinate vocabulary, on auditors, but distinguishes clearly between evil auditors and those who recognize
the virtue of such language but nevertheless fall into error. The playwright's

concern is not necessarily, then, the generalized one it is often taken to be, and while the play offers a dramatization of the fall of a representative of humanity—Mankind himself—there are aspects of the characterization which suggest that he may be understood in more specific terms which are themselves related to the controversy surrounding language.

To see *Mankind* simply as an anti-Lollard play is to ignore the precise way the playwright distinguishes between scoffers and troublemakers of the kind who had frequently been condemned in sermon manuals which predated the rise of Lollardy, and those who, like Lollards, erred in their opinions and conduct. The scoffers and troublemakers are treated as malicious in their attitude to Mercy's preaching, and the language in which he preaches. The play does not suggest that such people are likely to respond to the redemptive message of a sermon like Mercy's; rather, it demonstrates the process by which initially virtuous people may fall into error, what its consequences are, and most importantly, shows how that error may be forgiven.

The play addresses the problem of Lollardy so as to expose the organic origins of the heretics. They were not initially outsiders, but part of the orthodox community who, in the view of that community, erred in their religious or doctrinal opinions.[30] The play carefully distinguishes between wickedness and error as it differentiates between those disrupters of sermons and mockers of preachers who could unequivocally be regarded as vicious and those hitherto good and devout persons who erred. An initial error is then shown by the playwright to lead, not to complex theological heresies, but to reductively vicious association with low forms of wickedness until it terminates in despair. The playwright does not permit heresy more than the briefest mention: it is accorded no intellectual status, but leads only to common criminality and degradation.

The detailed distinctions between viciousness and error arise from the orientation of characters toward the aureate linguistic style Mercy adopts when preaching or addressing his critics. As Myscheff and the Worldlings parody and mock his speech they become representative of those people who challenged and mocked preachers.[31] Medieval preaching manuals frequently contain complaints about such people. The author of the fourteenth-century Longleat sermons complains that "summe comyn for malice and enuye to pynchyn at the prechoris wordis."[32] In the play the disruptive characters are shown to be merely an irritation to Mercy, and to Mankind, who, before his fall, reveres Mercy's words. The difference in attitudes between Myscheff and the Worldlings, and Mankind is the precise difference between those who are thoroughly vicious and those who fall into error.

As the play sets up the distinctions between viciousness and error it addresses other problems associated with preaching. It problematizes preaching by questioning which form of language should be used in order to be effective in protecting souls from the dangers of temptation, sin, and error. The play shows clearly that preaching is ineffective in some circumstances and considers the extent to which there may be deficiencies in preaching language. These deficiencies raise questions about how preachers should instruct listeners, and, significantly, how listeners should use that instruction to avoid falling into error.

The language in which preachers addressed their salvific message to their listeners had long been a matter of concern. The Fourth Lateran Council in 1215 had first acknowledged the problems caused by the Church's exclusive use of Latin. But the problem was not confined to the illiterate laity. John Mirk, among others, wrote sermons in the vernacular in order to assist the less literate clergy, who were a problem recognized in England by, among others, John Pecham, Archbishop of Canterbury in his decree of 1281 *Ignorancia sacerdotum,* and, closer to Mirk's time, by archbishop John Thoresby's Injunctions of 1357.[33]

However, David D'Avray and others have pointed out that the laity, who were once assumed to have been too uneducated to appreciate Latin and latinate diction in sermons, were growing in sophistication and expectation throughout the fourteenth and fifteenth centuries.[34] The increasing sophistication of audiences elicits earlier complaints in preaching manuals, such as Thomas of Chobham's early thirteenth-century objection that some individuals placed more importance on decoration than on the message itself. He complained: "there are those . . . who are pleased by nothing unless it sounds sweet."[35] Pierre de Baume, writing sometime after 1322, complained that

> in the old days sermons were such as profit the people. But nowadays they have rhymes and curious comparisons and philosophical subtleties are mixed with them; so many sermons do no good, they only please the hearers as oratory.[36]

The problem caused by increasing popular sophistication was noted by William of Ockham, who in 1337–38 noted that laymen and old women would tackle trained theologians on questions of free will and contingency.[37] John Mirk responded to the problem of lay challenges, especially to less well-trained preachers, in his *Festial,* a collection of homilies composed before 1415, where he explains that he is writing one of them to assist his fellow priests

> For hyt ys oft ysene þat lewde men þe wheche buþe of mony wordys and proude in hor wit, woll aske prestes dyuerse questyons of þynges þat towchen to seruyce of holy chyrche . . . forto put hom to aschame, wherfor I haue tytuld here dyuerse poyntys whech þat byn nedfull to yche prest to know.[38]

The willingness of the laity to challenge their priests on doctrinal matters clearly caused problems for the less educated clergy, and illuminates both the intellectual sophistication of some auditors, and the value placed on the authoritative language of the Church.

Through the entertaining reproduction of the conventional complaint concerning troublesome sermongoers, *Mankind* explores the effect of preaching language on different kinds of auditors. The troublemakers have no respect for Mercy's aureate style or the message of his sermon, but Mankind values his teaching and, before his fall, is capable of reading, writing, and speaking in the latinate register which distinguishes Mercy's sermon style. However, even though Latin and latinate diction had the authority of tradition and virtue derived from association with Scripture, and Mercy uses a variety of linguistic registers,[39] none of these seems especially effective in countering his critics or providing Mankind with protection from error.

Nevertheless, the play emphatically reminds spectators that erring people like Mankind may obtain mercy and return to the orthodox Church. The action charts the virtuous resistance, downfall, and recuperation of Mankind, who may be interpreted in three ways. At the most basic level he may be taken to represent any devout lay person who has received enough education to understand and write a little biblical Latin and who succumbs to the deceits of the devil. He may, alternatively, be regarded as the familiar figure of a lay person turned Lollard. Mankind is not only *"peccator, laycus, agricola, cristianus"* but is also shown to be *litteratus*[40] in his ability to read and write in Latin. He may, however, be interpreted allegorically as representing a priest, since the corn he sows is the conventional allegory for the word of God. Mankind's virtuous work of sowing corn is then itself an allusion to preaching, which he rejects when the work becomes disrupted and difficult. Mankind's words are especially significant here. He complains, "Alasse, my corn ys lost! Here ys a foull werke" (547). In this context "lost" is glossed by the editor as "ruined," but later in the play the present tense of the verb is glossed as "be deprived of." Both interpretations may be applied to the earlier line and provide comments on Lollardy. Demonic intervention is to blame for the ruining of the corn—Titivillus, the devil associated with "idle" language has told the audience he will mix the corn with the pernicious weeds "drawke" and "durnell" (537). In the first interpretation, Mankind rejects the difficulty of preaching the word of God, but the word has itself become contaminated and thus unproductive. In the second interpretation Mankind cannot preach the productive word of God *because* it has become contaminated. In the particular contexts of the later fifteenth century the contamination of the vernacular language by Lollardy, and the heretical questioning of the efficacy of Latin could not fail to raise uncertainty about the appropriate linguistic style to be used for a sermon, and the power of language to convey the salvific message.

The interpretation of Mankind as a priest is by far the most problematic, especially in the light of his fall into sin, but it is by no means impossible,

given the recorded instances of churchmen who erred in their opinions. A
supporter of Pecock, who abjured his error, was made a monk at Abingdon,[41]
and the Lollard hunter Philip Repingdon (or Repton) had, himself, been a
Wycliffite when he was at Oxford. In the context of *Mankind*'s distinction
between wickedness and error, Repingdon is particularly significant. He and
other Wycliffites at Oxford were tried for heresy, and their opinions defined
separately as those which were heretical, and those which were erroneous.
Repingdon abjured and went on to high office, eventually becoming bishop
of Lincoln.[42] Thus the notion that the erring faithful could repent and obtain
mercy was exemplified in reality.

As Pecock constructed his response to the errors of Lollardy in his books,
he commented on the fleeting effect of preaching by asserting that books
were needed to reinforce sermons, and make their message more available
and therefore more lasting.[43] In order to get his message across to those potentially, or already in error, he chose the language favored by the Lollards,
and thus contributed to the debate on the use of the vernacular. In his books,
he promoted the dissemination of knowledge and Christian morality through
the medium of the vernacular, and his activities, carried on very much in
public and in a climate made anxious by Lollardy, ended in his trial for heresy. Showing awareness of the danger, however, Pecock declared that his intention was in no way heretical, asserting that not only the meaning but the
intention of his words should be considered. He declared in *The Donet:*

> it is not myn entent forto holde, defende, or fauoure, in þis book, or in enye oþire
> bi me writun . . . in latyn or in þe comoun peplis langage, enye erroure or heresie.
> . . . Fferþirmor siþen an errour or heresye is not þe ynke writen, neiþir þe voice
> spokun, but it is þe meenyng or þe vndirstondyng of þe writer or speker signified
> by þilk ynke writen or bi þilk voice spokun . . . forto knowe what myn vndirstond-
> ing and meenyng is . . . in wordis of my writingis, englische and latyn, certis, oon
> ful goode weie is forto attende to þe circumstauncis in þe processis whiche y make
> þere bifore and aftir, and whiche y make in oþire placis of my writingis.[44]

The precision of Pecock's assertions reveals his anxiety to defend himself,
and perhaps the use of the vernacular, from the taint of heresy, by insisting
that the intention of the writer or speaker, and the wider contexts of his writings, should be carefully considered. The *Mankind* playwright is similarly
concerned with the contexts in which language is used, and throughout the
play shows how the effect of language is altered according to the contexts in
which it is used.

For all his insistence on making knowledge of Christian morality available
to the laity in the vernacular, Pecock nevertheless supports the use of Latin
with this argument:

> þe bible in latyn in many of his parties passiþ þe capacite and þe power of ful many
> grete clerkis and of grete and kunnyng doctouris. Schulen þei þerfore caste aside þe

bible, and not rede and studie in eny oþir parti þerof? God forbede ȝhe. . . þouȝ þo grete clerkis i clerist and liȝtist maner vndirstonde not derk processis of the bible in latyn, ȝit þei ben in sum maner sweteli fed and edified bi redyng þerin.[45]

Pecock extends the idea that difficulty is no bar to effectiveness when he asserts that it can be profitable that some books are too difficult for the laity to read with ease,

> fforwhi þerbi summe and many lay men mowe be tamyd and repressid and chastisid fro pride and fro presumpcioun; And þei mowe þerbi leerne þat clerkis schulen be to hem necessari forto teche hem þerin, euen, as þei holden now clerkis necessari to hem forto preche to hem in pulpit maner.[46]

Difficulty is regarded here as a useful antidote to the kind of pride and presumption which made life difficult for Mirk's brethren. Such an opinion also justifies the use of a latinate preaching vocabulary.

Pecock is writing about writing, and about its relation to preaching, but his remarks concerning the effect of language even when this is imperfectly understood seem to be echoed in drama which represents the "creation" of preachers. A concern with effect is reflected in fifteenth- and sixteenth-century religious drama. Special note has to be taken of the very late date of the manuscripts of the Chester cycle of biblical plays, since an interest in the effect of language would have had a different cultural context for a late sixteenth-century Protestant audience than for a fifteenth-century Catholic one; nevertheless, the editors of the Chester cycle have postulated the existence of earlier forms of the cycle which included versions of play 7, the *Shepherds*.[47] This play emphasizes the beneficial effects of biblical Latin much as Pecock constructs them in *The Folewer,* when he observes that though parts of the Latin Bible are too difficult even for clerks they nevertheless benefit from reading it.

In the Chester play the shepherds try to recreate the Latin words of the Angel's song announcing the birth of Christ. After some comically parodic attempts they reconstruct the words accurately and benefit from them without translating them into English. The third shepherd remarks: "hee sange 'bonae voluntatis'; | that is a cropp that passeth all other,"[48] and Trowle the boy adds "hee sange alsoe of a 'Deo'; | me thought that heled my harte" (VII: 428–29). The conventional use of shepherds as metaphors for preachers in medieval literature is perhaps most familiar from Chaucer's *General Prologue* to the *Canterbury Tales,*[49] and Langland's *Piers Plowman.*[50] Spectators may not readily have made the connection between shepherds and preachers in *Shepherds'* plays from other cycles, but the connection is made explicit in the Chester play after the nativity, when the second shepherd declares: "Unkynd will I never in noe case bee, | but preach all that I can and knowe, | as Gabryell taught by his grace mee" (VII: 653–55), and the third shepherd follows this saying: "I will gange and goe abowt nowe | to preach this thinge in every place" (VII: 658–59). The audience is thus assured that latinate diction in sermons for the laity, like the Latin which has been unintelligible to the Shepherds, is nevertheless language which has a beneficial effect.

In Pecock's judgement, it was not simply the effect of a deed or speech which is important, but the intention for which the deed is done, or the speech used, and this is to be judged by reason—the deed or speech should fulfil the end it might be expected to fulfill.[51] Another *Shepherds'* play, the Towneley *Second Shepherds'*, makes no connection between shepherds and priests, but illuminates the question of intention as it includes language which may be interpreted as idle according to Pecock's definition because it cannot be seen to fulfill the purpose the speaker intends. The play illustrates the problem with Latin when the first shepherd prays: "Ressurex a mortruus! . . . Judas carnas dominus!"[52] Although the shepherd's intention may be devout, "Judas carnas" signifies the opposite of the shepherd's apparent Christian intention. The liturgical references are so corrupt and have such negative Christian significations that they cannot have a salvific effect. John Mirk acknowledged the spiritual deficiency of misunderstood and incorrectly spoken Latin when he told his parishioners

> hit ys moch more spedful & meritabull to you to say your "Pater Noster" yn Englysche þen yn suche Lateyn, as ȝe doþ. For when ȝe spekyth yn Englysche, þen ȝe knowen and vndrystondyn wele what ȝe sayn.[53]

The *Second Shepherds'* playwright also seems to support the use of the vernacular as the medium of prayer, and challenges the absolute merit of Latin by showing how it may be misused and given negative signification. The shepherd's attempt to replicate liturgical Latin results in his replication only of the sound, not the sense, of the language. However, this little vignette of the morning prayer suggests the extent to which the Latin that would have been part of the church-going experience for most of the audience retained its status as the language of authority, belief, and protection from evil in the minds of lay people, even when they did not understand either the form or the meaning.

Critical analysis of *Mankind* has often focused on the latinate language used by Mercy. Mark Eccles, editor of the Early English Text Society's edition of the play, remarks that "The speeches of Mercy are tedious,"[54] while Lawrence Clopper decides that Mercy must be a Dominican, and remarks that "the central portion of the play . . . can attack the pomposity and absurdities of the Dominican preaching style."[55] Mercy has been identified by other critics as a Benedictine, and a Franciscan, based on his preaching activity, and internal evidence in the form of mocking remarks by other characters.

Upon such identifications critics construct their interpretations of the audience addressed by the play. Criticism of Mercy's preaching style by modern critics ignores the evidence of the sermon manuals which suggest that medieval lay congregations valued an ornate style. When this is taken into account, it is possible to see Mercy as a secular preacher without disturbing the modern tendency to posit a relatively high-status lay audience, although, given the emphasis placed on the preaching of mercy, in the context of heresy and error, a clerical audience may be more appropriate. However, while *Mankind* confronts the audience with frequent references to preaching, the playwright is as precise as Pecock in the way he contextualizes the use of language. He moves away from simple consideration of preaching style, to consider how the salvific function of preaching language depends upon the effect it has, how effect is controlled by a speaker's intention, by the circumstances in which the language is used, and by a hearer's participation. As part of this contextualization, he compares preaching language to other forms.

Mercy's extravagantly latinate language might suggest that he is member of a mendicant preaching order,[56] but could also indicate a secular priest. A literate lay audience for the play would represent metadramatically a preacher's audience; what we would then see in Mercy's exaggerated diction is the representation of a preacher's attempt to please and impress an audience who were sophisticated enough to demand the fashionable, ornate style. Mercy seems unable to manage the divided sermon structure which would be consistent with a preaching friar,[57] but he is able to use ornate diction as he addresses the audience saying, for example:

> O souerence, I beseche yow yowr condycyons to rectyfye
> Ande wyth humylite and reuerence to haue a remocyon
> To þis blyssyde prynce þat owr nature doth gloryfye,
> Þat ȝe may be partycypable of hys retribucyon.

$$(13-16)$$

Not only the aureation, but particularly the constant rhyming on latinate terms, although consistent with versification in drama, replicates a fault condemned in preaching manuals such as Pierre de Baume's, and it is immediately picked out for mockery.

Myscheff enters repeating some of Mercy's language and rhyming with it, parodying the style. Mercy ends saying "I besech yow hertyly, haue þis premedytacyon" (44), Myscheff interrupts:

> I beseche yow hertyly, leue yowr calcacyon.
> Leue yowr chaffe, leue yowr corn, leue yowr dalyacyon.
> Yowr wytt ys lytyll, yowr hede ys mekyll, ȝe are full of predycacyon.

$$(45-47)$$

The words on which he rhymes are reductively associated with, or pun on, the activities of preaching friars, but may equally mock the attempts of a secular preacher to imitate their style, especially in the light of his insulting assertions in the last line.[58]

The initial dialogues in the play reflect challenges, other than plain insults, directed at preachers by lay people, which were commented on by the authors of sermon manuals. Myscheff asks for "clarification" saying "ser, I prey þis questyon to claryfye" (48). His "question" sounds like nonsense, and is ignored by Mercy. Later, the Worldling Nowadays asks Mercy to translate into Latin saying:

> I prey yow hertyly worschyppuh clerke
> To haue þis Englysch mad in Laten:
>
> "I haue etun a dyschfull of curdys,
> Ande I haue schetun yowr mowth full of turdys".
>
> (129–33)

Dillon reads this as part of the ridicule of Mercy's "clericall manere" by comic characters.[59] More significantly, Myscheff's parody shows latinate language being used viciously to challenge its legitimate use. The parodic invitation to translate scatological vernacular vocabulary into Latin would remind a literate audience that Latin vocabulary easily accommodates such verbal filth. Some sixty years later than the play, Sir Thomas More defended Henry VIII from Martin Luther's scurrilously abusive declaration: *"ius mihi erit pro meo rege, maiestatem anglicam luto et stercore conspergere"* [it will be my right, on behalf of my king [Christ], to spatter his English majesty with mud and shit].[60] More wrote back to Luther in Latin equally well suited to Nowadays' scatological challenge:

> *Licebit alijs pro maiestate anglica, lutum et stercus omne, quod uestra putredo damnabilis egessit, in uestrae paternitatis os stercoreum, et stercorum omnium, uere sterquileneum regere* [others will be allowed, on behalf of his English majesty, to throw back into your paternity's filthy mouth, truly the privy of all filth, all the mud and shit which your damnable rottenness has poured out].[61]

Seen in the light of this "flyting," Nowadays' scatological challenge is a reminder that Latin was not only the language of devotion and authority, but could be just as filthy and obscene as the vernacular. Taken together with Myscheff's use of latinate word forms to parody Mercy's preaching, Nowadays's challenge to Mercy represents a challenge to simplistic or unsophisticated devotion to and preference for Latin and latinate forms in preaching. The way these characters use Latin and latinate forms, which are clearly different in intention and effect from preaching language, challenges the status of Latin as the language of authority, because it can be seen to be open to manipulation by low and vicious characters.

H. Leith Spencer suggests that "audiences apparently sought . . . impressive, not ridiculous delivery"[62] from preachers, but Mercy's diction not only provokes mockery from other characters, but also perhaps from the audience, if they recognize a mismatch between his style (homiletic) and his diction (latinate). However, it is possible that the audience began by approving Mercy's ornate style. Myscheff's parody then has four possible effects. Firstly, the audience may have laughed at the parody; secondly, if they have approved the style, that approval is challenged by hearing it parodied. Thirdly, the parody challenges the idea that latinate form is all that matters; and fourthly, it introduces the idea that a distinction needs to be made according to the speaker's intention.

Mankind himself seems to be one of those literate people who values an ornate preaching style, and he uses similar aureation in his own opening speech when he remarks:

> Euery man for hys degre I trust xall be partycypatt,
> Yf we wyll mortyfye owr carnall condycyon
> Ande owr voluntarye dysyres, þat euer be pervercyonatt,
> To renunce þem and yelde ws wnder Godys provycyon.
>
> (190–93)

Mankind seeks out Mercy and asks for his aid in avoiding the temptations of the devil, and Mercy responds in simple vernacular terms saying: "Cryst sende yow goode comforte! ȝe be welcum, my frende" (217). He goes on to instruct Mankind in a mixture of linguistic registers using latinate terms, exemplum, proverb, and homely metaphor when he tells Mankind life is "but a chery tyme" (235). His ability to alter his rhetorical tone is illustrated in this speech, but *before* he makes it Mankind tells him, "O, yowr louely wordys to my soull are swetere þen hony" (225). In this context the remark does not simply suggest Mankind's reverence for this preacher, but also hints at an undiscriminating acceptance of what he has not yet heard. If merely hearing Mercy's preaching or advice were shown to be sufficient to help Mankind avoid temptation, his attitude would not seem so rash, but the audience discovers that although Mankind is also able to write and quote biblical Latin such as "Memento, homo, quod cinis es et in cinerem reuerteris" (321),[63] and "Nec in hasta nec in gladio saluat Dominus" (397),[64] in the end neither Mercy's teaching, nor Mankind's own learning protect him from temptation.

An appropriation of Latin by apparently nonclerical characters such as

Mankind is thematic in the play. New Guise mocks Mercy for being "full of Englysch Latyn" (124), and deflates his ability to use latinate terms when he says

> "Pravo te" quod þe bocher onto me
> When I stale a leg a motun
> ȝe are a stronge cunnyng clerke.
>
> (126–28)

While this would be humorously insulting to Mercy as a learned friar, it is equally amusing and deflating, and perhaps adds a touch of pathos, if he is a secular preacher, since it suggests that anyone, even a butcher, can manage the odd bit of Latin. John Watkins suggests this speech makes Latin sound absurd "in the mouths of butchers, tradesmen and artisans."[65] However, Melissa Furrow suggests that "Modern ideas of what it means to learn a language . . . are not of much use in recognising the importance of pragmatic aural and oral ability in Latin in England in the late Middle Ages."[66] The play returns to this theme of the presence of Latin in medieval society at other points, where it draws attention to the constant use of Latin, in the forms of biblical quotations, tags, and legal terminology, for all sorts of reasons, and by all kinds of people.[67] Latin is also massively perverted by Titivillus, the devil traditionally associated with the misuse of language. As he enters he declares, "Ego sum dominancium dominus and my name ys Titivillus" (475). His appropriation of Christ's title "lord of lords" reiterates the difference between the legitimate and illegitimate use of Latin, demonstrating that it can be misappropriated, but that this then serves as a reminder of the legitimate signification of the Latin phrase. The exclusivity of Latin is thus constantly challenged but equally constantly contextualized in the play, its forms and effectiveness in one context illuminating those in another. While the butcher's curse is plainly ineffective invective, the summoning of a parodic court mimics the effectiveness of Latin in juridical contexts, and both instances reflect on the effectiveness of Mercy's preaching language. The play thus presents a series of challenges to the status of Latin, and so develops the idea that intentions and circumstances define each use and effect.

While latinate preaching language is entertainingly ridiculed in *Mankind,* much of the entertainment is provided by scatological language. The entertaining sinfulness of this language may have appealed to illiterate and literate medieval spectators alike as it offers a carnivalesque license within the ludic context to transgress codes of linguistic propriety.[68] More importantly, it provides a startling antithesis to Latin and latinate forms, and continues the play's interrogation of the effects, intentions, and contexts of language. The Worldlings mock Mankind in vernacular scatological terms, this is not, however, effective in distracting him from virtue. The play reveals that the trickery of the devil is more dangerous than the open mockery of the world as Titivillus, the medieval devil associated with the misuse of language, corrupts Mankind. But he does not do so through language, and he does not openly mock or insult Mankind as the Worldlings do; he puts Mankind out of patience by making his work difficult. Once Mankind has become impatient, his language reflects his corruption.

Mankind is not distracted from his virtuous intention to plant corn by the scatological mockery of the Worldlings. Nor is he tempted by their scatological Christmas song, which is aimed at seducing the audience into sinning. As long as Mankind remembers Mercy's teaching he is safe. Mercy tells him, "Thynke on my doctryne; yt xall be yowr defence" (258), and Mankind acknowledges later that he recalls Mercy's advice when he says, "My fadyr Mercy advysyde me to be of a goode chere / Ande agayn my enmys manly for to fyght" (403–4), but when Titivillus's trick puts him out of patience, Mankind falls from virtue.

This seems to have nothing to do with language, except that Mercy's teaching appears to fail as Mankind forgets it in his impatience, problematizing its effect. If we look back to Pecock's theories of language, he described as idle—that is, lacking virtue or sinful—any word or deed that does not have the effect it is intended to have. This is not, however, the only possible interpretation of the effect of Mercy's preaching, since Pecock also declared,

> if y laboure þoruȝ vj daies togidere forto turne a wickid man from his wickidnesse, and þouȝ y may not brynge it about, ȝit my labour is ful vertuose and meritori.[69]

So, according to Pecock, the intention of the speaker defines the merit of the words, even if their effect does not last. In the play, while Mankind shares Mercy's latinate diction he remains virtuous, but when, in his impatience at not being able to work the soil, he forgets Mercy's teaching, he slips into sin. This, of course, puts responsibility on the hearer as much as the preacher, showing that it is not enough to applaud, or even replicate a preacher's style, the individual must maintain faith and moral rectitude, and not just in the face of the world, but more importantly in the face of the devil's trickery. As instruction against succumbing to the errors of Lollardy, the example of Mankind suggests the difficulty of remaining virtuous, and goes on to show the depths of vice into which the sinner falls as a consequence of his initial error, ending in the mortal sin of despair. The error itself is represented as the result of demonic intervention, but that error is then shown to open the erring person to further mortal sins. Significantly, just before Mankind's despairing suicide attempt Mercy re-enters.

Pecock asserted that differing circumstances should be understood to govern the interpretation of language, and while he was concerned with defending his own work from charges of heresy, the *Mankind* playwright constantly demonstrates how interpretations change according to changed contexts. Mercy's reappearance after Mankind's corruption provides such a change; grief-stricken, Mercy enters announcing:

> Wyth wepynge terys be nyȝte and be day I wyll goo and neuer sesse.
> Xall I not fynde hym? Yes, I hope. Now Gode be my proteccyon!
> My predylecte son, where be ye? Mankynde, vbi es?
>
> (769–71)

In response, Myscheff and the Worldlings again offer the audience the entertainment of mockery and scatological language, but the contexts have changed. Nought provides apparently gratuitous scatological information telling Nowadays:

> I am doynge of my nedyngys; be ware how ȝe schott!
> Fy, fy, fy! I haue fowll arayde my fote.
> Be wyse for schotynge wyth yowr takyllys, for Gode wott
>   My fote ys fowly ouerschett.
>
> (783–86)

Given the play's preoccupation with language, this speech can be seen to reflect on the Worldlings' own language and conduct. As Nought fouls his own foot, and warns his companions against doing likewise, his scatological language refers the audience back to earlier instances in the play where the Worldlings used similar language, and it redefines the effects of the tempters' mocking language, which are now degrading to them, rather than to the virtue of Mercy, Mankind, or the audience. While the tempters' intentions may be the same, the effects are altered by the representation of Mercy's grief, and by the accidents, including the subsequent near-hanging of New Guise, which befall the Worldlings. These accidents redirect the laughter of the audience at the evil characters, and illustrate the limitations of wickedness in the presence of Mercy.

   Throughout the play, the *Mankind* playwright carefully delineates language not simply according to form and vocabulary, but according to the intention of the speaker, the circumstances in which language is used, the effect upon the hearer and significantly, the hearer's active responsibility. Furthermore, echoing Pecock's approach to confuting Lollardy, Mercy insists everything is to be judged by reason—particularly the folly of the Worldlings. But he tells the audience:

> The goode new gyse nowadays I wyll not dysalow.
>   I dyscomende þe vycysouse gyse; I prey haue me excusyde,
> I nede not to speke of yt, yowr reson wyll tell it yow.
> Take þat ys to be takyn and leue þat ys to be refusyde.
>
> (182–85)

He is specific in not dismissing what is new, simply because of its novelty, but only what is new and pertaining to vice. As John Watkins has noted, "By explicitly associating the triad of vices—Nought, Nowadays, and New Guise—with novelty [*Mankind*] insists . . . that changing historical conditions have occasioned new and deadlier temptations."[70] The deadliest, from an orthodox point of view, was Lollardy.

The emphasis in Love's *Mirrour* and in Pecock's books was to confute Lollard errors through instruction and reason. The Norwich heresy trials between 1428 and 1431 had already offered Lollards the option of recanting and used various kinds of punishment, reserving the ultimate penalty of death at the stake for relapsed heretics.[71] The *Mankind* playwright does not offer explicit exegetical instruction, like Love, or debate, like Pecock, nor does he threaten, but sets out to remind a perceptive and sophisticated audience right from the start of the play that the reason and purpose of Christ's death on the Cross was to provide redemption and mercy for sinners. The audience is then offered dramatized examples of various levels of error and sin, before the message of the availability of God's mercy is restated. Mercy tells the contrite Mankind that judgment is God's prerogative but significantly declares that "Trowthe may not so cruelly procede in hys streyt argument / But þat Mercy schall rewle þe mater wythowte contrauersye" (841–42). However, the delivery of this message, following Mankind's fall and repentance, no longer takes the form of a sermon, but becomes a dialogue between Mercy and Mankind.

While it is hardly relevant to claim that Pecock's works provided a direct source for any playwright, in the case of *Mankind* issues of linguistic form, effect, intention, and changing contexts, seem to follow Pecock's theories closely. Marianne Briscoe has suggested that a "sources and analogues approach places too much emphasis on single sermon texts,"[72] and I agree with her reservations. There is, nevertheless, an interesting but contingent similarity between Pecock's theories and the representation of preaching and its relationship to other forms and uses of language in *Mankind*. Any apparent similarity may be explained as the result of Pecock and the *Mankind* playwright having shared the educational background that was common to literate men in fifteenth-century England. Nevertheless, as contemporary sources show, Pecock's works were widely disseminated and studied in the universities, even while they were controversial. Furthermore, knowledge of them could only have been increased by the spectacle of Pecock's public humiliation if Gascoigne is not overstating the case when he relates that: "[Pecock's] books were burned before him in the presence of the bishops, clerics, and many people"[73] and that

in the presence of twenty thousand people, [Pecock] was led in wearing episcopal vestments. At the feet of the archbishop of Canterbury and the bishops of London and Rochester, Oxford doctors of theology, and the bishop of Durham, he abjured his writings.[74]

The influence of Pecock's vernacular works on the playwright is therefore worthy of consideration. However, because issues of linguistic form, effect, and intention are present in other contemporary instructional plays, the *Mankind* playwright, may have been participating in the debate on language which predated, and was enhanced by, Lollardy. In countering Lollardy from different perspectives, Pecock and the playwright may incidentally have used similar tactics. Pecock's intervention in this debate included his defence of the vernacular from complete contamination by the Lollard heresy as he distinguishes between the heretical and the orthodox use of "þe comoun peplis langage." His caution came in the wake of Arundel's *Constitutions* and would have been necessary because of the controversial nature of some of his opinions. It is unlikely on the grounds of the play's content that the *Mankind* playwright would have felt the same anxiety; nevertheless, a similarly rigorous definition of the use of language contributes to his defense of those forms of language which the Lollard heresy problematized. So, although Pecock's linguistic theory, set out in books such as *The Donet* and *The Folower,* and the treatment of language in *Mankind* show striking similarities, in the cultural climate of the mid to late fifteenth century this may indicate no more than the degree to which the challenges posed to both Latin and the vernacular by the Lollard heresy, and Arundel's measures to suppress it, prompted similarly discriminating responses.

As *Mankind* offers an entertaining assessment of virtuous and sinful language, it also contributes to long-standing debates on the status of the vernacular, but resolves the tension between this and latinate vocabulary by emphasizing effect, intention, context, and responsibility. These supralinguistic concerns are shown to be more significant than the simple form of the language used, which is open to abuse and misappropriation. As the play engages in the debate on language it also engages in the even longer-standing debate on appropriate preaching styles. The examination of preaching language at this time inevitably touches on the plight of poorly educated secular priests and the demands of increasingly literate audiences. Their delight in ornamentation for its own sake is challenged by Mankind's declared delight in what he calls Mercy's "wordys . . . swetere þen hony" (225) and "mellyfluos doctryne" (312), which he then forgets in his impatience.

The play suggests that it is not easy to preach the vital message of mercy when language has been so problematized by Lollardy and the measures taken to counter it: when Latin is scorned and emptied of its authority, when the vernacular is contaminated by its association with heresy—how can preaching be effective? The answer the play puts forward seems to be that the responsibility does not lie wholly with the preacher. The signifying power of language is shown to be defined by the contexts in which it is used, in conjunction with traditional values ascribed to particular kinds of language. Recognizably "idle" language is still to be avoided for its association with sin and vice, while the virtue of language is shown in *Mankind* to inhere in its use rather than simply in its form.

Notes

1. Kathleen Ashley, "Titivillus and the Battle of Words in 'Mankind,'" *Annuale Medievale* 16 (1975): 128–50, here cited from 136.

2. Joerg O. Fichte, "The Representation of Sin as Verbal Action in the Moral Interludes," *Anglia* 103 (1985): 26–47 on 45–46. Fichte links idle speech to physical idleness.

3. Mark Eccles. ed., *The Macro Plays,* EETS 262 (London: Oxford University Press, 1969), *Mankind,* 1, 147.

4. Paula Neuss, "Active and Idle Language: Dramatic Images in 'Mankind'" in Neville Denny, ed., *Medieval Drama,* Stratford-upon-Avon Studies 16 (London: Edward Arnold, 1973), 41–67, here cited from 49.

5. Theodore Erbe, ed., *Mirk's Festial: A Collection of Homilies by Johannes Mirkus,* EETS ES 97 (London: Kegan Paul, Trench, Trübner, 1905), Sermon 22, 96. My emphasis.

6. Arthur Brandeis, ed., *Jacob's Well,* part 1, EETS OS 115 (London: Kegan Paul, Trench, Trübner, 1900), 148.

7. Venetia Nelson, ed., *A Myrour to Lewde Men and Wymmen,* Middle English Texts 14 (Heidelberg: Carl Winter Universitätsverlag, 1981), 212.

8. Reginald Pecock, *The Folower to the Donet,* ed. Elsie Vaughan Hitchcock, EETS OS 164 (London: Oxford University Press, 1924), 119.

My thanks to Dr. Mishtooni Bose for her help with Pecock, and to all Wessex Medieval Centre colleagues with whom I have discussed this paper.

9. Janette Dillon, "*Mankind* and the Politics of 'Englysch Laten'," *Medievalia et Humanistica,* NS 20 (1993), 41–64, here cited from 47. See also Janette Dillon, *Language and Stage in Medieval and Renaissance England* (Cambridge: Cambridge University Press, 1998).

10. Ibid., 51.

11. Ashley, "Titivillus and the Battle of Words in 'Mankind'," 130.

12. Michael G. Sargent, ed., *The Mirrour of the Blessed Lyf of Jesus Christ Oure Lord,* Garland Medieval Texts 18 (New York: Garland, 1992), lii. All translations are mine.

13. Ibid., liii.

14. Ibid., 14.

15. Eccles, *The Macro Plays, The Castle of Perseverance,* ll. 3229–597.

16. Ibid., xxxviii.

17. *multa scripta Pecock probaverunt in praesencia ipsius Pecock episcopi esse erronea, et ipsa scripta, per eum si essent defensata, esse haeretica.* [many of bishop Pecock's writings were proved in his presence to be in error, and those writings, if

they were defended by him, to be heresy] Thomas Gascoigne, *Loci et Libro Veritatum,* ed., James E. Thorold Rogers (Oxford: Clarendon Press, 1881), 212.

18. Many Lollards were, however, literate in Latin, and the "syntactically demanding prose used by Pecock and the Lollards" is commented on in Jocelyn Wogan-Browne, Nicholas Watson, Andrew Taylor and Ruth Evans, eds., *The Idea of the Vernacular,* Exeter Medieval Texts and Studies (Exeter: University of Exeter Press, 1999), 15. This suggests a grasp of Latin sentence structure continuing, or inherited, as Anne Hudson notes that "The Lollard heresy was in origin learned, indeed academic." See Anne Hudson, "Laicus litteratus: the paradox of lollardy" in Peter Biller and Anne Hudson, eds. *Heresy and Literacy, 1000–1530* (Cambridge: Cambridge University Press, 1994), 222–36, here cited from 228.

19. *Magna causa movebant clericos et dominos temporales multum contra eum, sc. quod scripsit altas materias, i.e. profundas, in Anglicis* [a great cause moved the clergy and many temporal lords against him, which was that he wrote high and profound matters in English]. Gascoigne, *Loci et Libro Veritatum,* 214.

20. Anne Hudson, *Lollards and their Books* (London: Hambledon Press, 1985), 159.

21. Reginald Pecock, *The Donet,* ed., Elsie Vaughan Hitchcock, EETS OS 156 (London: Oxford University Press, 1921), xxv.

22. John A. F. Thomson proposes that 'the rarity of surviving manuscripts suggests that this was an exaggeration'. See John A. F. Thomson, *The Later Lollards 1414–1520* (Oxford: Oxford University Press, 1965), 29.

23. Paula Neuss suggests that the play shows evidence of the author's clerical, and therefore scholastic, training when she notes "*Mankind* rather resembles the 'modern' or 'university' sermon. In this kind of sermon, the preacher did not expound a text, but took a single theme and explored it from various angles, elaborating as he went along, and introducing other topics all in the same way connected with the main theme." Neuss, "Active and Idle Language," 44. Edwin Craun notes that "it is Augustinian sign theory which informs pastoral discourse," and points out the "Augustinian emphasis on ethical internationality." See Edwin Craun, *Lies, Slander and Obscenity in Medieval English Literature* (Cambridge: Cambridge University Press, 1998), 28, 42. Jody Enders also notes the situation with reference to continental drama when she writes of a "medieval educational system whose influence was far more pervasive and homogeneous than it was once thought to be." Jody Enders, *Rhetoric and the Origins of Medieval Drama* (Ithaca and London: Cornell University Press, 1992), 163.

24. I borrow this term from Antonio Gramsci. It is a helpful way of appreciating the extent to which heretics were originally part of the orthodox community. Their changed opinions placed them outside that community. See Quintin Hoare and Geoffrey Nowell Smith, eds., *Selections from the Prison Notebooks of Antonio Gramsci* (London: Lawrence and Wishart, 1971), 6–7. Gascoigne notes that Reginald Pecock had received the support of other bishops before he abjured his errors. Gascoigne, *Loci et Libro Veritatum,* 215. For a brief summary of the situation in the fourteenth and fifteenth centuries see, e.g., John A. F. Thomson, *The Transformation of Medieval England* (London: Longman, 1983), ch. 40, and A. J. Pollard, *Late Medieval England 1399–1509* (London: Longman, 2000), 212–13.

25. Reginald Pecock, *The Reule of Cristen Religioun,* ed. William Cabell Greet, EETS OS 171 (London: Oxford University Press, 1927), 17.

26. Ibid., 19.

27. Ashley, "Titivillus and the Battle of Words in 'Mankind'", 131; Fichte, "The Representation of Sin as Verbal Action," 38; Neuss, "Active and Idle Language," 43; Dillon, "*Mankind* and the Politics of 'Englysch Laten'" 50–52.

28. Anne Hudson, *Lollards and their Books* (London: Hambledon, 1985), 146–47. See also Nicholas Watson, "Censorship and Cultural Change in Late-Medieval England: Vernacular Theology, the Oxford Translation Debate, and Arundel's Constitutions of 1409," *Speculum* 70 (1995), 822–64; and Wogan-Browne, Watson, Taylor and Evans, eds., *The Idea of the Vernacular,* 343–45.

29. Eccles, ed., *The Macro Plays, Mankind,* note to text. See also Antony Gash, "Carnival against Lent: The Ambivalence of Medieval Drama," in David Aers, ed., *Medieval Literature: Criticism, Ideology and History* (Brighton: Harvester, 1986), 94–95.

30. Gascoigne is specific in noting that Pecock *revocavit conclusiones suas erroneas et haereticas* [recanted his erroneous and heretical opinions], Gascoigne, *Loci et Libro Veritatum,* 216.

31. H. Leith Spencer describes Myscheff as "a dramatic incarnation of the preacher's bugbear . . . the disputatious layman." H. Leith Spencer, *English Preaching in the Late Middle Ages* (Oxford: Clarendon, 1993), 115.

32. Anne Hudson and H. L. Spencer, "Old Author, New Work: The Sermons of MS Longleat 4" *Medium Ævum,* 53 (1984): 220–38, here cited from 223.

33. These were published in the vernacular, Vincent Gillespie, "Vernacular Books of Religion," in Jeremy Griffiths and Derek Pearsall, eds., *Book Production and Publishing in Britain 1357–1475*(Cambridge: Cambridge University Press, 1989), 318. Pecham's *Ignorancia* was englished in the fifteenth century by a priest whose intention was to distribute forth to symple curates, curales or vpplandysche . . . hou thei shal declare vnto theire parrishens the matieres conteyned in the seid constitucioun." Phyllis Hodgson, "*Ignorancia Sacerdotum:* A Fifteenth-Century Discourse on the Lambeth Constitutions," *The Review of English Studies* 24, 93 (January 1948): 1–11, here cited from 2.

34. David D'Avray, *The Preaching of the Friars* (Oxford: Clarendon Press, 1985), 6.

35. *Tales sunt . . . quibus nihil placet nisi dulcem habeat sonum.* Thomas de Chobham, *Summa de Arte Praedicandi, Corpus Christianorum* 82 (Turnhout: Brepols, 1988), 300.

36. *olim fiebant sermones unde populus proficiebat. Sed hodie fiunt rithmi et curiositatum concordantie, et immiscentur philosophice subtiliates, ita quod in multis sermonibus non est aliqua utilitas, sed solum oratoria complacentia auditorum.* MS Bâle, Univ. Libr. B.V.6., fol 46vb: *Predicans evangelium regni.* Quoted in Beryl Smalley, *English Friars and Antiquity in the Early Fourteenth Century* (Oxford: Basil Blackwell, 1960), 44. Smalley also notes that Thomas Walys allowed colors of rhetoric for clerical audiences so long as these did not sicken the audience by being overdone (101).

37. *Et ita omnia de necessitate eveniunt et nihil poenitus contingentur, sicut quam-*

plures infideles et antiqui haeretici docerunt, et adhuc occulti haeretici et laici et vet-
ulae tenent, saepe per argumenta sua etiam litteratos viros et in sacris litteris peritos
concertantes. [as many pagans and ancient heretics taught, everything happens of necessity and nothing contingently, and still secret heretics, and laymen, and old women
often, through their arguments, catch out learned men who are skilled in debating
scripture]. "Tractatus contra Benedictum," iii, ed. H. S. Offler, *Guillelmi de Ockham
Opera Politica* 3 (Manchester, 1956) quoted in Smalley cited above, 29. This may,
however, have been a commonplace exaggeration of the situation, since the image of
the old rustic, woman, or layperson, challenging clerics occurs in other similar texts.
See, for example, Watson, "Censorship and Cultural Change in Late-Medieval England," 843. Nevertheless the evidence suggests the sophistication of the laity was
perceived to be a problem.

38. Theodore Erbe, ed., *Mirk's Festial,* Sermon 29, 124.

39. Dillon, "*Mankind* and the Politics of 'Englysch Laten'" 52–53.

40. Anne Hudson refers to the specific case of Walter Brut who described himself
in these terms but defended himself in Latin against charges of heresy. See Anne Hudson, "Laicus litteratus: the paradox of Lollardy" in Peter Biller and Anne Hudson,
eds., *Heresy and Literacy, 1000–1530* (Cambridge: Cambridge University Press,
1994), 222–36, here cited from 222.

41. Gascoigne, *Loci et Libro Veritatum,* 215. See also Reginald Pecock, *The Re-
pressor of Overmuch Blaming of the Clergy,* ed., Churchill Babington, vol. 1, Rolls
Series 19 (London: Longmans, Green, Longmans and Roberts, 1860), xviii; and J.
Fines, "Bishop Reginald Pecock and the Lollards," *Studies in Sussex Church History,*
(1981), 57–75, here cited from 63.

42. Gordon Leff, *Heresy in the Later Middle Ages* (Manchester: Manchester University Press, 1967), 568–69. Gascoigne, *Loci et Libro Veritatum,* 29.

43. Pecock declared: "prechyng to þe peple . . . schal neuer take his parfite effect,
neiþer in ȝeuyng to þe peple sufficient and stable doctryne neiþer in prentyng into hem
abiding decucioun, wiþoute þat þe peple haue at hem silf in writing which þei mowe
ofte rede or heere oft rad þe substancial poyntis and trouþis whiche ben to hem to be
prechid bi mouþe." *The Reule of Cristen Religioun,* 20.

44. Pecock, *The Donet,* 3–4.

45. Reginald Pecock, *The Folower,* 7.

46. Ibid., 8.

47. R. M. Lumiansky and David Mills, eds., *The Chester Mystery Cycle: Essays
and Documents* (Chapel Hill: University of North Carolina Press, 1983), 34.

48. Ibid., Play 7, *Shepherds,* ll. 426–27.

49. In *The General Prologue,* the narrator speaks of good and bad parsons saying
"if a preest be foul, on whom we truste, | No wonder is a lewed man to ruste; | And
shame it is, if a prest take keep, | A shitten shepherde and a clene sheep." Larry D.
Benson, ed., *The Riverside Chaucer,* 3d ed., (Oxford: Oxford University Press, 1987),
The General prologue, ll. 501–4.

50. In the C-text of *Piers Plowman,* Langland criticises bishops in terms of negligent shepherds:

> The cause of al this caytiftee cometh of many bischopes
> That soffreth suche sottes and oþere synnes regne.

The tarre is vntydy þat to þe schep by longeth;
. . . .
Thy shep ben ner al shabbede, the wolf shyt þe wolle.
Sub moli pastore lupus lanam cacat, et grex
In—custoditus dilaceratur eo.

(Passus IX, ll. 262–66)

The imagery of tar as salve for sheep is also found at the opening of the Chester play, ll. 33–34. William Langland, *Piers Plowman: The C-Text,* ed. Derek Pearsall (Exeter: University of Exeter Press, 1994).

51. See above, 2.

52. Martin Stevens and A. C. Cawley, eds, *The Towneley Plays* EETS SS 13 (Oxford: Oxford University Press, 1994), Play 13, *Second Shepherds'* l. 350. Play 12, *The First Shepherds' Play* has an evening prayer in corrupt Latin which is less problematic since the corrupt form of the language would not be easily perceived in performance (ll. 422–24).

53. Theodore Erbe, *Mirk's Festial,* 282.

54. Mark Eccles, ed., *The Macro Plays,* xlv.

55. Lawrence M. Clopper, "*Mankind* and its audience," *Comparative Drama,* vol. 8 (1974–75): 347–55, here cited from 352.

56. H. Leith Spencer remarks on "3 elaborate, probably monastic sermons . . . [which] display not only profuse preaching jargon but a number of loan-words . . . yet they certainly do not dominate these . . . sermons like the aureation favoured by Mercy." H. Leith Spencer, *English Preaching in the Late Middle Ages,* 119.

57. See also Marianne G. Briscoe, "Preaching and Medieval English Drama" in Marianne G. Briscoe and John C. Coldeway, eds. *Contexts for Early English Drama* (Bloomington and Indianapolis: Indiana University Press, 1989), 150–72, here cited from 159.

58. "Calcacyon" is glossed as "trampling" and "dalycyon" as "chattering" in the edition, but Kathleen Ashley adds "threshing" to "trampling," pointing out the significance of criticizing the "threshing" of doctrine in Mercy's sermon. Ashley, "Titivillus and the Battle of Words in *Mankind,*" 132. Janette Dillon suggests "dalyacyon" may also mean "solemn utterance," and refers to Lee Patterson's observation that it could also pun on "dilatio." Dillon, "*Mankind* and the Politics of 'Englysch Laten,'" 51, n. 44.

59. Ibid., 42.

60. John M. Headley, ed., *The Complete Works of St. Thomas More,* vol 5, *Responsio ad Lutherum,* (New Haven: Yale University Press, 1969), 311.

61. Ibid.

62. Spencer, *English Preaching,* 107.

63. Robertus Weber, ed., *Biblia Sacra iuxta vulgatam versionem* (Stuttgart: Deutsche Bibelgesellschaft, 1969), Job 34.

64. Ibid., 1 Samuel 17:47.

65. John Watkins, "The Allegorical Theatre: Moralities, Interludes, and Protestant Drama," in David Wallace, ed., *The Cambridge History of Medieval English Literature* (Cambridge: Cambridge University Press, 1999), 767–92, here cited from 772.

66. Melissa Furrow, "Unscholarly Latinity and Margery Kempe," in M. J. Toswell and E. M. Tyler, eds., *Studies in English Literature and Language* (London: Routledge, 1996), 240–51, here cited from 240.

67. Among many instances, see for example Nought's question: "estis vos pecuniatus?" and Nowadays' reply: "Ita vere, magister" (471; 473), and also New Guise's reference to Myscheff knowing his "neke-verse" (619).

68. For a discussion of the use of scatological language in *Mankind*, see Lynn Forest-Hill, *Transgressive Language in Medieval English Drama* (Aldershot: Ashgate, 2000), chap. 4.

69. Pecock, *The Folower*, 120.

70. Watkins, "The Allegorical Theatre: Moralities, Interludes, and Protestant Drama," 771.

71. Norman P. Tanner, ed., *Heresy Trials in the Diocese of Norwich 1428–31*, Camden Society, 4th Series, vol. 20 (London: Royal Historical Society, 1977), 22–23.

72. Briscoe, "Preaching and Medieval English Drama," 155.

73. *Libros suos ante seipsum comburi in praesencia episcoporum et in praesencia cleri et magni populi*, Gascoigne, *Loci et Libro Veritatum*, 215.

74. *in praesencia xx^ti milia hominum, inductus in habitu episcopali, ad pedes archiepiscopi Cantuariensis . . . et episcopi Londoniensis . . . Roffiensis, doctoris in Theologia Oxoniae, et episcopi Dunelmensis, abjuravit ibi scripti sua.* Ibid., 216.

The Theatrical Rhetoric of *Edward III*

LESLIE THOMSON

CRITICISM and analysis of *Edward III* has focused primarily on whether
or not Shakespeare's presence can be discerned in it.[1] Far less attention has
been given to the play's theatrical elements, although they would have been
especially effective in its original context. This is because *Edward III* is a
play that not only explores and dramatizes the power of rhetoric, but in doing
so also systematically manipulates the audience into experiencing and responding to the effects of its persuasive strategies. If they worked, a contemporary spectator's experience of the play in performance would have been
comforting, reassuring, even inspiring.[2] The focus here, therefore, is on the
cumulative and mutually reinforcing structural patterns—of language, actions, and especially of sounds—that constitute the play's persuasive techniques. This is not to claim that the play is a coherent whole; to our eyes and
ears at least it is an uneven work, perhaps as a consequence of revision and/
or collaboration. But it is nevertheless a viable performance-text which, I
suggest, would have been successful theater four hundred years ago because
of both its subject matter and its theatrical strategies and devices. Although
the play is unlikely to have challenged spectators' expectations, the relatively
mild pro-English propaganda is, as it were, theatrically enabled and confirmed by various complementary techniques of audience manipulation
woven through the play from start to finish. To my mind the most pervasive
and theatrically effective of these are: an emphasis on the act and language
of persuasion; the control of character exits; business related to weapons and
kneeling; and references to or the use of sounds, especially of battle. Each
element is, of course, integrated with the others in the play's structure; but
by isolating them in turn one can demonstrate how and why they work effectively together to create the rhetorical whole. The significance of this internal
coherence would be diminished, however, without the external context, especially when the focus of the work was the not too distant past of a country and
an audience for which history and xenophobic nationalism were inseparable,
powerful forces.

The Raigne of Edward the Third seems to have been relatively popular in
the period just after it was written—there were two editions within three years
(SR, 1595; Q1, 1596; Q2, 1599)[3]—and the reasons for its subsequent disap-

pearance from the stage are probably related to its negative treatment of the Scots.[4] The play's initial success was likely due at least in part to the euphoric mood of the years immediately after the defeat of the Spanish Armada; an audience saw King Edward and his son defeating France, a past threat to England's power analogous to Spain in the present. English history is important not only as a context but also, of course, in the play itself; indeed, generically *Edward III* is almost purely "history" (however altered). It is comedy only insofar as it moves "upward" to a happy ending, and certainly not tragedy— quite remarkably, there is not a single onstage death, even of a minor figure, in the course of the action. As other critics have noted, this is history drawn on and manipulated to dramatize a message about kingship, honor, and success—in fact, it is a morality tale (with *psychomachia*) in which the hero reforms and is rewarded. In showing first King Edward's triumph over himself, then England's over France, the play would have satisfied the expectations of spectators who well knew that Edward had defeated John and that the Black Prince was not killed in the battle. Indeed, although the play has been described as having two distinct parts—King Edward and the Countess, then King Edward and King John—in fact it has a single, overarching focus: the developing King/Prince, father/son relationship, begun in the first scene, continued even in the Countess scenes, then picked up again in earnest when the battle with France begins.

For the purposes of this study of the play's effectiveness onstage, the question of who and how many wrote it is immaterial (although plural authorship seems probable). The quarto is a play-text that was, as the title page says, "sundrie times plaied about the Citie of London." This ambiguous phrasing raises questions about venue, only to leave them unanswered.[5] As Georgio Melchiori notes, the play requires simply a minimal upper level (for the Countess in her castle in act 1)—no trap, no discovery space, no large props (bed, tomb, banquet table).[6] If the title-page vagueness means that the play was performed in more than one place, the basic requirements make good, practical sense; and if when the play-text was set down the venue was unknown, the authors made the best of it. Indeed, as written, *Edward III* would have been playable and persuasive in virtually any space having an upper platform and a rear wall with doors. Further, if the quarto was printed from an authorial manuscript, as Fred Lapides concludes and Melchiori concurs,[7] then it provides evidence of what mattered to the authors; certainly, as this study will show, the intricate use of repetition indicates a coordinated thematic purpose. In fact, those responsible for the play-text as we have seen it seem to have been possessed of considerable sophistication in the art of playmaking and to have known what modern readers often forget: that in a theater the words, actions, and sounds working together are the tools of persuasion aimed explicitly at an audience.[8]

Language

The rhetorical aspect of dramatic dialogue with which I am concerned here is not the use of language to debate crucial thematic issues (although that is a central purpose), but rather the characters' use of words about the uses of words—part of the play's overall exploration and dramatization of the power of rhetoric and the rhetoric of power. Repeatedly the characters are concerned with persuasion; this, in turn, creates an emphasis on the business of verbal manipulation even as it affects an audience's response. Indeed, the "action" consists largely of a series of verbal jousts. The play begins by firmly establishing the essential point that Edward III is king not only of England but also of France. In their initial exchange, Edward and Artois set out the justness of the cause that will be the focus of the rest of the action. More particularly, Artois addresses any cynical doubts about his motives in terms to which the play will repeatedly return: "But heaven I call to record of my vows: / It is not hate nor any private wrong, / But love unto my country and the right / Provokes my tongue thus lavish in report" (1.1.32–35).[9] Believing him, Edward specifically praises "the fiery vigour of [Artois'] words" (44).

By contrast, when the Countess of Salisbury first mentions the Scots, she refers to her fear of being conquered by them and "wooed with broad untuned oaths" (1.2.8); this, and mention of how they "bray" and "babble" (13, 17), undermine the Scots even before they appear or speak. King David's first speech (18–37) is a series of rhetorical iterations of defiance which are immediately and comically subverted when the Scots unceremoniously flee the approaching English. The Countess calls attention to their empty vows in mocking their departure. Soon after, the play's focus on the languages of persuasion becomes particularly explicit when she asks King Edward, "What might I speak to make my sovereign stay?" and he responds in an aside: "What needs a tongue to such a speaking eye, / That more persuades than winning oratory?" (1.2.138–40).

The King's wooing of the Countess in act 2, during which so many of the play's concerns are highlighted, gives special attention to how and why words are persuasive. Edward's besotted ruminations suggest that the Countess's way of speaking is what has captivated him: "For who could speak like her?"; "To hear war beautified by her discourse"; "Wisdom is foolishness but in her tongue" (2.1.33, 39, 40). The poetry-writing scene with Lodowick is a set-piece, a verbal emblem of the manipulative potential and danger of language. Indeed, Edward's idea that "so much moving hath a poet's pen" and of how "the strains of poets' wit" have the power to "[b]eguile and ravish soft and human minds" (73, 78–79), together with Lodowick's deliberate sabotage of the King's plan, are metadramatic reminders of a playwright's power over an audience.[10] Edward's obsessed determination escalates from enlisting Lodowick to write poetry, to wooing the Countess directly, to urging her to woo herself on his behalf:

> Then take thyself a little way aside,
> And *tell thyself* a king doth dote on thee;
> *Say* that within thy power doth lie
> To make him happy and that *thou hast sworn*
> To give him all the joy within thy power
> Do this, and *tell me* when I shall be happy.
>
> (212–17; my emphases)[11]

As the Countess later points out (2.1.250–75), Edward's purpose is, of course, to persuade her to break her marriage vows. But the concern with the breaking or keeping of vows is much broader, echoing through the play and helping to determine an audience's evaluation of the characters.[12] The King's exchange with the Countess's father, which follows her defiant departure in this scene, brings the matter to the surface. When Warwick innocently asks how he can help, the King reminds him, with a flourish of self-righteous rhetoric that is ironic only to an audience, of the proper relationship between vows and deeds:

> . . . O thou world, great nurse of flattery,
> Why dost thou tip men's tongues with golden words,
> And peise their deeds with weight of heavy lead,
> That fair performance cannot follow promise?
>
> (302–5)[13]

Warwick's soliloquy at the end of this segment effectively uses repetition to emphasize how he will try to persuade his daughter to break her "vow made by the name of God": "I'll say she must forget her husband Salisbury"; "I'll say an oath can easily be broken"; but also, "I'll say it is my duty to persuade, / But not her honesty to give consent" (2.1.357, 60, 66–67). At the end of his verbal attack on his daughter, Warwick clearly acknowledges his equivocation and heightens an audience's awareness of what he is doing: "Thus have I, in his majesty's behalf, / Apparelled sin in virtuous sentences" (2.1.410–11). Not surprisingly, when the Countess refuses her father responds, "Why, now thou speakst as I would have thee speak, / And mark how I unsay my words again" (2.1.431–32). In the final confrontation between the Countess and King, when she threatens suicide to keep her marriage vow unless he will "swear to leave [his] most unholy suit" (2.2.182), Edward is brought to reformation, expressed in apposite terms:

> Even by that power I swear, that gives me now
> The power to be ashamed of myself,

I never mean to part my lips again
In any words that tends to such a suit.

(2.2.188–91)

This vow ends the first movement of the play; but its larger rhetorical purpose is to initiate the rest of the action by persuading the audience that Edward is once more worthy of admiration. And from this point he is indeed portrayed as an honorable English king who keeps his word and performs what he promises.

The concern with oath-keeping does not disappear from the play, however; rather, in the latter half the honor of the French is called into question in similar terms and circumstances. The most notable of these is when Prince Charles's guarantee of Salisbury's safe passage is countermanded by King John, who says, "Thou and thy word lie both in my command. / What canst thou promise that I cannot break?" to which Charles responds, "What, am I not a soldier in my word?" (4.5.80–81, 92). When Charles adds that King Edward would not have broken a promise made by his son, King John relents, significantly enhancing the contrast between the two made by the broader theatrical rhetoric.

In the context of the play's concern with language, it is not merely incidental that the defeat of the French is caused partly by their misunderstanding of a prophecy. Edward's triumph over John is, not surprisingly, confirmed with words about vows when the former mocks his prisoner: "So, John of France, I see you keep your word: / You promised to be sooner with ourself / Than we did think for, and 'tis so indeed" (5.1.199–201). As repeatedly happens through the play—whether in the contestatory exchanges between characters, or in the elaborated speeches describing battles, or in the persuasion of one character by another—the devices of rhetoric are both apparent and effective. The winners use words better than the losers, and any audience can hear it.

Exits

Character exits are among the most basic elements of a play, but they can also be used as a subtle but effective means of confirming or qualifying a character's control and power at any point in the action.[14] As such, exits can be a significant aspect of a play's visual rhetoric, helping to persuade an audience to accept its message. Those responsible for *Edward III* seem to have known and capitalized on this structural device—the essence of which is repetition—to demonstrate and emphasize the key steps in the process toward the English triumph. Interestingly, the first exit is led by Prince Edward, speaking a vow of readiness to die (which he will keep), and initiating a forward movement his father will soon counter.

> Within this school of honour I shall learn
> Either to sacrifice my foes to death,
> Or in a rightful quarrel spend my breath.
> Then cheerfully forward, each a several way;
> In great affairs 'tis naught to use delay.
>
> (1.1.165–69)

King Edward maintains this momentum until the Countess, at the end of a long persuasion urging him to "stay," says "More gracious than my terms can, let thee be: / Entreat thyself to stay a while with me," which, in an aside, he does. The ironic contrast between the end of the previous scene and this one is made clear when he signals the exit: "Come on, my lords, here will I host tonight" (2.1.160–61, 166). When finally the King has made his adulterous desires plain to the Countess, she assumes that he is testing to see "[w]hether she will hear a wanton's tale or no"; taking control, she says as she departs, "From that, not from my liege, I turn away" (2.1.275, 277).[15] It is worth noting that not only does each of these three exits contribute to the audience's sense of the characters who make them, but also that each is explicitly put in the context of language: the Prince's vow, the Countess urging the King to persuade himself, and her refusal to listen to his suggestion that she break her marriage vow.

Conventionally, it is the figure in charge who initiates exits and therefore ends scenes, so when this does not happen it is worth considering why. After the Countess's rejection of his suit, King Edward attempts to enlist her father by reminding him of his "oath" of service. His departing words sum it up:

> Command her, woo her, win her any ways
> To be my mistress and my secret love.
> I will not stand to hear thee make reply:
> Thy oath break hers, or let thy sovereign die.
>
> (2.1.344–47)

Warwick remains on stage (speaking the soliloquy discussed earlier), then the Countess enters to hear her father, as he says, "in his majesty's behalf, / [Apparel] sin in virtuous sentences" (2.1.410–11). She, of course, rejects this second "wooing" as she has rejected the first, earning her father's praise. The long scene finally ends with first Warwick signalling his exit, then his daughter cueing her own. That the Countess has maintained control in the face of both the King's and her father's extended arguments is given a particularly theatrical emphasis when for the second time she departs of her own accord.

A later sequence in 2.2 might have been specifically designed to have the exits illustrate and confirm King Edward's misuse of his authority in service of his private desires rather than his public responsibilities. As he waits to hear the outcome of Warwick's persuasion of his daughter, the arrival of

Prince Edward reminds the King of his military duties. Seemingly reformed, he calls to his son, "Come, boy, forward, advance! / Let's with our colours sweet the air of France." But at that moment, Lodowick enters with news of the Countess's arrival; to his son King Edward says, "Go, leave me, Ned, and revel with thy friends"; to Lodowick, "Go, fetch the countess hither in thy hand"; and when Lodowick brings her, he is told to "go" (2.2.99–100, 106, 109, 116). The end of the King's infatuation with the Countess is signalled when, at the conclusion of the scene, he returns to directing exits in preparation for battle (2.2.139–59). His restored control over himself and his world is confirmed in a later scene-ending, forward moving couplet: "That orderly disposed and set in ray, / Let us to horse, and God grant us the day" (3.3.227–28).

The play's shift of focus to Prince Edward includes a series of exits which effectively demonstrate his ability to exercise power. In 4.4 three heralds enter in succession, first from King John, then from Prince Charles, then from Prince Philip, each offering Prince Edward a reason to surrender. It is surely not accidental that these emissaries offer three temptations, which Edward refuses in Christlike fashion. Furthermore, the importance of words is underscored when he sends each of the heralds away with instructions about what he should "tell" the man who sent him (4.4.81–86, 95–100, 110–22). The self-control of the Prince in dispatching what are essentially three "wooers" is an important element in the portrayal of him as a force for good in his own right.

Weapons and Kneeling

Two often-related pieces of business add to the visual dimension of the play's persuasive movement towards the chivalric triumph of England's King and Prince.[16] The use of various weapons and the action of kneeling are both altogether typical kinds of action in the plays of the period, on which these playwrights have capitalized with considerable nuance. The play begins with an act of kingly power when Edward makes Artois Earl of Richmond, which, although there are no stage directions, was presumably accompanied by some ceremony of bestowal and submission. Then almost immediately a sword is drawn by King Edward or Lorraine (depending on how the stage direction is interpreted[17]) and if Lorraine draws first, then Edward does so in response, either way demonstrating his readiness to fight for England's rights—before he is distracted by the Countess. When the two meet, the Countess kneels to the King ("In duty lower than the ground I kneel," 1.2.107), but he immediately raises her, beginning his demeaning infatuation. Edward himself acknowledges his unkingly subservience in apposite terms. "She is as imperator over me, and I to her / Am as a kneeling vassal . . ." (2.2.40–41).

This unnatural reversal is brought to an end only when the Countess finally takes control of the stage and of Edward—"I'll part a little from thee"; "Stir not, lascivious king, to hinder me"—as she produces her explicitly symbolic "wedding knives."[18] Furthermore, it seems she kneels again here, since when Edward has been brought to see reason by her threat of suicide to preserve her marriage vows, he twice tells her to "arise" (192, 196).

The first confrontation between King Edward and King John, in 3.3 at the center of the play, is a battle of words, not swords, and given this play's concern with language, I suggest that the reasons are thematic rather than dictated by stage limitations or an outmoded dramatic emphasis on speech over action. Furthermore, as is the case in the play overall, the Prince gradually takes over the exchange here, using the language of the popular *words/swords* dichotomy to assert what he will later do:

> Look not for cross invectives at our hands,
> Or railing execrations of despite:
> Let creeping serpents hid in hollow banks
> Sting with their tongues; we have remorseless swords
> And they shall plead for us and our affairs.
>
> (3.3.97–101)[19]

An audience would doubtless have participated vicariously in the chivalric ceremony in which King Edward has armor, helmet, lance, and shield ritualistically bestowed on his son. When the victorious Prince soon reappears with his now *"shivered lance"* and the body of Bohemia, he *"Kneels and kisses his father's hand"* (3.4.1–2, 76). He remains on his knees until his bloodied sword is brought in for the King to knight him with it saying, "Arise, Prince Edward, trusty knight at arms. / This day thou has confounded me with joy, / And proved thyself fit heir unto a king" (104–6). Significantly, King Edward's "arise" to the prince here verbally and visually echoes the two confrontations between the King and Countess, which it implicitly counters. Also noteworthy is that the King does not appear for more than fifty lines between 4.2.79 and 5.1—an unusual aspect of the play which seems inexplicable, at least in dramatic terms, unless viewed in the context of the building up of the Prince.

During the central portion of the play many other swords would be seen as the battle continues, but as is usually the case with hand-held props, unless the action is sufficiently unusual or important, no mention is made in stage directions or dialogue. Similarly, when the six citizens, *"in their shirts, barefoot, with halters about their necks"* plead with King Edward for mercy, their kneeling would be a given, even had Edward not made it a condition of their submission (4.2.77). Although in his initial rejection of the citizens' pleas Edward calls for "drums' alarum" and "threat'ning swords" (5.1.9–10), it is significant that Phillipa's intervention brings the King to assert that "we / As well can master our affections / As conquer other by the dint of sword" (5.1.50–52)—an explicit reminder of his internal and external victories charted in the play. Then comes a final combination of kneeling and sword when, in another royal act of peace and triumph, the King knights Copeland (94).

"Sheathe up your swords" King Edward commands his followers when, as dramatic convention dictated, he closes the play. But the more important and longer, penultimate speech is spoken by Prince Edward; it is he who encapsulates the metadramatic significance of the theatrical persuasion the audience has heard and seen. He imagines a future—the audience's present—in which "many princes more" will repeat his triumphs, only wishing that his heroic deeds "were now redoubled twentyfold,"

> So that hereafter ages, when they read
> The painful traffic of my tender youth,
> Might thereby be inflamed with such resolve
> As not the territories of France alone,
> But likewise Spain, Turkey, and what countries else
> That justly would provoke fair England's ire,
> Might at their presence tremble and retire.
>
>   (5.1.229–35)

Sounds

Unlike other history plays of the same period (from the late 1580s to the early 1590s), *Edward III* has no extended dumb shows, little pageantry, and no onstage battles. Indeed, as already demonstrated here, the play is mostly talk, much of it overtly rhetorical. But it is not completely without elements typical of history plays—it uses sounds. In fact, sounds are central to the play both structurally and thematically; they help to create and confirm its message or meaning. The quarto includes thirteen stage directions for a sound, and nine occasions when either one of these sounds is referred to or a character calls for or mentions a sound in what amounts to a cue, since such sounds are virtually certain to have been performed and heard. In addition, several times characters describe events or make analogies in terms of sounds, thereby emphasizing their significance. The thematic import and persuasive effect of all these are cumulative.

Just into the play is the direction *"Sound a horn,"* which an obviously in-charge King Edward immediately recognizes as "A messenger," and sends Audley to get him (1.1.50.1–51). By the end of the first scene, the King is enthusiastically preparing for war. When he tells Prince Edward it is time to leave his books and become a soldier, the Prince replies, "As cheerful sound-

ing to my youthful spleen / This tumult is of war's increasing broils, / As, at
the coronation of a king, / The joyful clamours of the people are, / When *Ave,*
Caesar! they pronounce aloud" (1.1.160–64). These words not only convey
the Prince's inexperience in the realities of war but also anticipate sounds to
come. At the start of 2.2, Derby enters from France and *"At another door,*
Audley with a Drum"—that is, a drummer—but the drum is silent because
the King is by now intent on conquering the Countess rather than Scotland
or France. Soon after, clearly acknowledging a conventional signal, Derby
says, "The Trumpets sound, the king is now abroad" (2.2.21). Ironically, this
flourish for his kingly entrance initiates the segment in which Edward's *psy-*
chomachia—the inner battle between love and war, man and monarch,
Countess and Prince—reaches its full intensity. Later in the scene, just as the
King is asking Lodowick when he will receive an answer from the Countess
to his illicit suit, he is interrupted by the sounds of war. His annoyed response
warrants full quotation.

> What drum is that that thunders forth this march,
> To start the tender Cupid in my bosom?
> Poor sheepskin, how it brawls with him that beateth it!
> Go, break the thund'ring parchment-bottom out,
> And I will teach it to conduct sweet lines
> Unto the bosom of a heavenly nymph;
> For I will use it as my writing paper,
> And so reduce him from a scolding drum
> To be the herald and dear counsel-bearer
> Betwixt a goddess and a mighty king.
> Go, bid the drummer learn to touch the lute,
> Or hang him in the braces of his drum,
> For now we think it an uncivil thing
> To trouble heaven with such harsh resounds.
> Away

(2.2.46–60)

When Lodowick has exited, Edward continues, soliloquizing in the conventional language of the Petrarchan lover, until he asks, "How now?" (72).
As Melchiori suggests, this question is probably the King's response to hearing the drum again. Certainly Lodowick immediately enters with the news
that "the drum that stroke the lusty march / Stands with Prince Edward, your
thrice valiant son" (73–74). King Edward, guiltily seeing his son as a reminder of the Queen and his own adulterous intentions, says he will "master"
himself and calls to the Prince. Just then, however, Lodowick announces the
Countess's arrival, causing Edward to dismiss the Prince and admit the
Countess. Her entrance initiates their final verbal skirmish, in which she triumphs—and, with the end of the Countess episode, the action turns to battle
with France.

Drums are heard again in 3.1, when King John announces the arrival of the King of Bohemia with Danes, and a Polonian captain and soldiers: "But soft, I hear the music of their drums, / By which I guess that their approach is near" (39). As soon as these forces exit, leaving the King and Prince Philip alone, the use of offstage sounds combines with onstage dialogue and business to suggest reasons for their eventual defeat. King John's complacency and overconfidence are conveyed to an audience when he has "bread and wine" brought on for himself and the Prince to enjoy while the sounds of war echo through the theater. *"The battle heard afar off," "Shot," "Retreat"* (3.1.116.1, 122.1, 131.1): these are the stage directions for sounds which, in counterpoint with the dialogue, create dramatic irony. The literal and metaphoric distance of the King and Prince from the battle is conveyed in their ignorant, over optimistic commentary. The most striking example occurs when the Prince exclaims, "O father, how this echoing cannon shot, / Like sweet harmony, digests my cates!", to which the King responds, "Now, boy, thou hearest what thund'ring terror 'tis / To buckle for a kingdom's sovereignty" (3.1.123–26). Here and through their exchange, the dialogue works in tandem with the sound effects to make an audience aware that the French King and Prince merely talk while others act. The scene ends with the reality, expressed by a despairing French citizen—"Away, away! Methinks I hear their drums. / Ah, wretched France, I greatly fear thy fall: / Thy glory shaketh like a tottering wall" (3.2.74–76). These words cue the sounds bridging the citizen's exit and the entrance of King Edward with his troops to begin the next scene.

The *"Alarum"* heard at the start of 3.4 signals that the real battle has begun. It accompanies the wordless action of Prince Edward pursuing the French on- and offstage, confirming both the Prince's abilities as a soldier and the vincibility of the French. Readers of the play register only the stage direction for a sound, so it has little impact. But a theater audience hears the alarum, which probably continues through the exchange between King John and Lorraine that acknowledges their defeat. Next is the *"Sound retreat"* (3.4.17.1) ordered by King Edward so his forces can rest. This brief respite is interrupted by the news that Prince Edward is in danger, to which the King responds that his son must save himself. The condemnation of the King by Derby, Audley and Artois is interrupted by Edward's "But soft, methinks I hear / The dismal charge of trumpets' loud retreat" (3.4.70–71), followed by the entrance of the Prince *"in triumph, bearing in his hand his shivered lance, and the King of Bohemia borne before, wrapped in the colours"* (73.1–2). Although there is no explicit direction for sound here, the signal for "loud retreat" was almost certainly heard. In addition, while we have little evidence of what *"in triumph"* meant, it probably referred to shouts of victory at least, and possibly also to a trumpet fanfare. Once more, then, sound accompanies an important turning point in the play—here the shift of focus from the King to the Prince. This moment can also be seen as the culmination of a sequence which has demonstrated the moral value attached to being willing to risk one's life for honor in love or war—as the Countess and Prince have done, but King John and Prince Phillip have not.

From the middle of act 3 to the middle of act 4 there is a fairly long stretch of action with neither stage directions nor dialogue cues for sound. Furthermore, before the next sound is heard, King John repeatedly mentions the ominous silence—"the world is hushed and still"; "Silence attends some wonder"; Where or from whom proceeds this silence?", "now the under earth is as a grave, / Dark, deadly, silent, and uncomfortable" (4.5.3, 6, 8, 17–18). He then exclaims, "Hark, what a deadly outcry to I hear?" having, with the audience, heard *"A clamour of ravens"* (4.5.18.1). Coming after a lengthy offstage silence in a play-long sequence of sounds, this "clamour" would be especially raucous and jarring. The segment ends with King John trying to put on a brave face; he commands Philip, "Away, and comfort up my soldiers, / And sound the trumpets, and at once dispatch / This little business of a silly fraud" (4.5.53–55).

The next scene contains the play's most extended battle sequence—although by the standards of other contemporary histories it is meager, relying as it does almost completely on sound and evocative dialogue. An *"Alarum"* accompanies the entrance of Artois and Prince Edward, another is signalled when King John comes on, and the sounds of battle probably continue through the scene. At the same time, the disarray of the French is lamented by Prince Charles in terms which might also be responding to actual sounds: "Our drums strike nothing but discouragement, / Our trumpets sound dishonour and retire" (4.6.30–31). Moreover, the description of events in such terms is evidence of a metadramatic self-consciousness about the rhetorical function of the sounds in the play.

The entrance of victors and vanquished starts the next scene as a *"Retreat sounded"* punctuates the Prince's mocking, "Now John in France, and lately John of France" (4.7.01–1). Following more irony-laden gloating from Prince Edward comes the direction *"Sound trumpets, enter Audley"* (4.7.17.1). The sounding of trumpets at the entrance of the nonroyal, wounded Audley is unusual, and the dialogue gives no clue to its significance here. But perhaps this use of sound is a way of confirming Audley's temporary role as a kind of substitute father to the Prince during the King's extended absence from the stage from 4.3 to 5.1.[20] Certainly, in both his words (especially in 4.4) and his actions through this segment, Audley articulates and embodies ideas which need to be conveyed to both the Prince and the audience. Acceptance of death and unwavering service are spelled out and demonstrated by Audley, then practiced by both father and son in subsequent scenes. In helping to guide audience understanding and response, here and through the play, Audley is one element in the play's theatrical rhetoric.

When King Edward reappears, he is in the act of assuring Queen Phillipa that Copeland will be punished for disobeying her orders. They are interrupted by the six citizens of Calais pleading for mercy, to whom the King replies, "Mine ears are stopped against your bootless cries. / Sound drums' alarum, draw threat'ning swords!" (5.1.9–10). There is no stage direction for sound or action, and probably there would have been none since the citizens' continued pleas, and especially Phillipa's intervention on their behalf (another of the play's verbal persuasions), bring Edward around to the view that "a peaceful quietness brings most delight" (56).

The final direction for sound is *"After a flourish sounded within, enter a Herald"* (5.1.175.1); he announces that, contrary to earlier report (and as most in the audience would already have known) Prince Edward has triumphed over France. At this news the proud King and father proclaims "Sound trumpets, welcome in Plantagenet!" (186); despite the absence of a confirming stage direction, there can be little doubt that now he is obeyed. Indeed, probably all the stops were pulled out for the entrance of the triumphant Prince with King John and his son prisoners, the climax of the action.

The cumulative effect of the principal verbal, visual and aural devices employed through the play and discussed here is to celebrate the dynastic line which had originated with Edward III and was to end with Elizabeth I. Sounds, and actions such as kneeling, using a sword, and exiting are mostly lost on a reader, making it too easy to underestimate or even forget their effect on an audience. But in *Edward III* it is just these elements which infuse the dialogue with meaning and would have prompted Elizabethan spectators to agree that all was well in their England. In the theater, the audience would have been given an experience of what this history play is both about and demonstrates: the successful use of the power to persuade.

Notes

1. An unsurprising but also representative example of this interpretive approach is J. J. M. Tobin's introduction to the play in the second edition of the *Riverside Shakespeare* (pp. 1732–34); see also E. Pearlman, *"Edward III in Henry V,"* *Criticism* 37 (1995): 519–36.

2. This view of the play can be contrasted with that of Larry S. Champion ("'Answere to this perillous time': Ideological Ambivalence in *The Raigne of King Edward III* and the English Chronical Plays," *English Studies* 1988: 117–29). After summarizing the prevailing critical interpretation of the play as Tudor propaganda which an audience would have accepted, he argues: "The essential flaw in such an approach is that it assumes not only a universal perspective but also an audience basically sympathetic to the monarchy and its policies and prompt to respond communally and patriotically" (118–19). He goes on to develop his view that this kind of theatrical propaganda was an attempt to control the politically restive in the audience. Conse-

quently he sees the play as metadramatically ironic to the point of being potentially subversive, a view with which it will be apparent I do not agree.

3. A summary of the available information about the quarto's registration and publication together with a discussion of its probable date of composition can be found in Georgio Melchiori's introduction to his edition of the play (Cambridge: Cambridge University Press, 1988), pp. 3–9.

4. See Georgio Melchiori, *Shakespeare's Garter Plays: "Edward III" to "Merry Wives of Windsor,"* (Newark: University of Delaware Press), 1994, 117–18, and the introduction to his edition, pp. 12–13.

5. Richard Proudfoot notes, "it is unclear whether 'about' should be construed as within or without the city." See: *The Reign of King Edward The Third* (1596) and Shakespeare," *Proceedings of the British Academy* 71 [1985], 162.

6. Melchiori, Introduction, 9.

7. See Melchiori's Textual Analysis (173), in which he cites Fred Lapides's old-spelling edition.

8. See Richard Proudfoot's British Academy lecture for a discussion of the stageworthiness (pp. 162–63) of the text and its "high degree of shapeliness and coherence" (166).

9. All quotations are from Melchiori's Cambridge edition.

10. Melchiori believes that this scene sets out views about the poet's art expressed elsewhere by Shakespeare (Introduction, 39).

11. *Power(s)* occurs twenty-three times in the play; *say(s)* thirty-six times.

12. Melchiori, 39; Champion, 121–23.

13. This is not in the source; see Melchiori's note to 2.1.302–8, which suggests a deliberate change in the characterization of Edward here. In this play, *word(s)* occurs twenty-eight times, *promise(ed)* six, *oath* sixteen, *vow(s)* five, *swear* eleven, *sworn* seven times and *tongue* is heard on thirteen occasions.

14. See my "Shakespeare and the Art of Making an Exit," *University of Toronto Quarterly* 69 (2000): 540–59.

15. In his summary of the sources for this scene Melchiori notes that this exit is only in Froissart (191–92); its origins in one of the sources does not, of course, diminish its dramatic effect.

16. See Melchiori's extended discussion of the chivalric elements of the play, especially the "ceremonial occasions" (41), which of course include swords and kneeling, although he doesn't consider them specifically.

17. See Melchiori's note to 1.1.107.

18. This business is not in the play's sources and this is the only stage direction in plays of the period specifying wedding knives (see the entry for *knife* in *A Dictionary of Stage Directions in English Drama, 1580–1642,* Alan C. Dessen and Leslie Thomson [Cambridge: Cambridge University Press, 1999].)

19. The *words/swords* pun also occurs at 3.1.189, 3.3.193–94, 4.4.128–29.

20. When the King is organizing the attack, he specifically "temper[s]" the Prince's "lusty spirit" with Audley's "gravity" (3.3.220–26).

Filling Fare: The Appetite for Current Issues and Traditional Forms in the Repertory of the Chamberlain's Men

ROSLYN L. KNUTSON

In January 1599, England had armies deployed in the Low Countries and Ireland. Of these campaigns, the Irish war was the higher priority, and commanders of garrisons at Ostend and Flushing as well as in the field received orders to supply 2,000 men from their seasoned troops for service with the earl of Essex in Ireland. But increasingly into the spring there were also reports of new and massive military preparations by an old enemy to the south. The news arrived from many sources: merchant-mariners, escapees from Spanish prisons and galleys, fishermen in the English Channel, agents of the Crown abroad, and foreigners in port cities from Brest to Brill. A particularly credible piece of intelligence arrived in May from Thomas Hawkins, who sent word by way of letters smuggled out of Lisbon Castle that the Adelantado (Don Martin de Padilla) was "mackinge Reddye" a great fleet in Seville, with 24,000 soldiers and 500,000 of "biskets," to join twelve new galleons "called the 12 Aposteles" in the Groyne: "his Cuminge ys ffor IngLande."[1] On 29 July, the earl of Bath advised the Crown that he was readying ground forces along the southern coast for an invasion. On the 31st, a Captain Bredgate communicated to Lord Cobham that Philip III planned to lead the Spanish forces himself and that the king had "Cutt ofe two of his nobell-men*es* head*es* because they did counsell him not to attempt this Enterpryse."[2] On 1 August, John Chamberlain wrote to Dudley Carleton at Ostend that "the alarme [of war] . . . begins to ringe in our eares . . . as shrill as in your besieged towne: . . . we are all here in a hurle as though the ennemie were at our doores."[3]

Londoners expected their city to be a target. John Stow described a great mustering of foot soldiers and cavalry at Mile End and St. James Field, and he reported also that on 5 August, by order of Queen Elizabeth,

the chains were drawne orethwart the streetes and lanes of the City, and lanthorns with lights, of candles (eight in the pound) hanged out at euery mans doore, there to burne al the night, and so from night to night, vpon paine of death, and great watches kept in the streetes, which hanging out of lights so continued, some four-teene nights or longer.[4]

On 8 August, Secretary Cecil heard from Sir Thomas Leighton at Guernsey that the Spaniards were already at Brest, delaying their assault only because of the weather. On the nineth, Chamberlain wrote again to Carleton that the earl of Cumberland intended to construct a bridge of "lighters, boates, west-ern barges, cables and anchors" defended by "1500 musketters" (81). Cham-berlain recognized the defensive tactic as "an apish imitation to that of Antwerp," and he noted further that the earl had to abandon this plan in favor of sinking boats in the channel because the Thames had a different "bredth and billow then the river of Antwerp" (81). On 11 August, the mayor of Lyme Regis reported that one Richard Bedford, an experienced mariner, had just arrived with a tale of being chased by two ships "about the fforLand nere Brase."[5] Bedford altered his course, taking refuge in the midst of seven ships that he supposed to be English, but when he came "verie nere them," he saw that they were disguised by their ancients and flags to be so mistaken. Now "vehementlie suspectinge them to be Spanyard*es*," Bedford fled, noting omi-nously that the ancient of one of the ships was "bloodie."

Within days, however, the threat of imminent attack evaporated. Some said that the Spanish fleet was stymied by an outbreak of plague; others, that it was gathered as a defensive maneuver only; still others, that its destination was Ireland, not Plymouth or London. By 23 August, the Council had dis-solved the muster. Chamberlain described the demobilization in a letter to Carleton dated the twenty-third: "the Hartfordshire men were sent home first and so by degrees one after another, yet they all receved pay more or lesse, some for fowre, some five dayes, and some for a whole weeke" (83). He added, though, that many remain fearful—especially those who did not un-derstand what was going on in the first place: "The vulgar sort cannot be perswaded but that there was some great misterie in the assembling of these forces, and because they cannot finde the reason of yt, make many wilde conjectures" (83).

Also through the months of January to August 1599, players in the com-pany of the Lord Chamberlain's men were making an important commercial decision. While politicians assessed the intelligence on Spanish maneuvers and military men fortified the coastline and ports of London, the Lord Cham-berlain's men were plotting a strategy for marketing their repertory of plays at a new location. Just after Christmas of the previous December (1598), Richard and Cuthbert Burbage had commissioned workmen to dismantle the structure known as the Theater in Shoreditch and to reconstruct it into a fairer building to be known as the Globe, in Maid Lane, Southwark. By August of 1599 at the latest, the Chamberlain's men opened at their new playhouse with a repertory that they had planned and prepared presumably to minimize their expenses and maximize their profits.

In this business venture, the players had an ally in the Elizabethan repertory system, principles of which may be inferred from the data entered by Philip Henslowe in his book of accounts for the Rose playhouse, from 1592 to 1603. This system enabled them to manage their current stock and acquisitions to financial advantage. To lower costs for the first few months after their move, the Chamberlain's men could have extended the stage runs of plays that had been new the year before, plays such as *2 Henry IV, Every Man In his Humor,* and *Much Ado About Nothing.* These offerings were inexpensive to continue in production because they did not require a further outlay of cash for the text, properties, and costumes. They were also easy on the players' time because they did not require rehearsals (which time could therefore be applied to the preparation of new plays). Furthermore, one or another of these plays could be scheduled to enhance the debut of a new part of a serial (*2 Henry IV,* to go with the new *Henry V*) or an apparent sequel (*Every Man In his Humor,* to go with the new *Every Man Out of his Humor*). Although the Chamberlain's men would have continued some offerings anyway, as a normal part of their operations, the move gave them an additional reason to do so, for last year's plays would have been new to playgoers who had frequented playhouses on the south bank but who had not attended the ones in Shoreditch as regularly.

However, in 1599–1600 (as in every year) the Chamberlain's men probably looked to their new plays for the greatest profits. These offerings were, of course, the most expensive to stage in terms of overhead and rehearsal time, but they stood to bring in the best receipts for the company, when the novelty of the offering attracted large crowds. It used to be that scholars, judging quality by literary standards, pointed to the plays of Shakespeare and Jonson as the most profitable commodities in the Chamberlain's repertory; these same scholars might dismiss other offerings in the repertory as "filler, plays which spoke their brief piece upon the platform and departed within a few months."[6] I would argue, though, that the economics of the repertory system was such that none of the companies could afford the luxury of new plays that were merely "filler." The Chamberlain's men, and the other commercial theatrical companies as well, expected each new play to generate revenue beyond production costs early in the run. The data in Henslowe's business diary indicate that literary quality was just one factor among many in the market value of a play. Genre, story materials, and connections with already popular offerings as sequels or spin-offs were also factors.

In two of the new plays in the 1599 repertory of the Chamberlain's men, there is evidence of additional factors: specifically, the presentation of current issues; and, the use of the time-tested formulas of characterization and moral instruction evident in medieval English literature and drama. One of

these plays—"Cloth Breeches and Velvet Hose"—is now lost.[7] It was entered
in the Stationers' Register by James Roberts on 27 May 1600 ("Entred for
his copye vnder the hand*es* of the wardens. A morall of Clothe breches &
veluet hose, as yt is acted by my lord Chamberlens servant*es.* provided that
he is not to putt it in prynte Without further & better Aucthority").[8] Apparently, the play was never printed; therefore, what I will suggest about its subject matter and form is necessarily conjectural. However, I am confident that
the title identifies the source of the play as Robert Greene's *A Quip for an
Upstart Courtier,* which was published in 1592 with the subtitle, "A Quaint
Dispute Between Velvet-Breeches and Cloth-Breeches." A second play—*A
Larum for London*—was entered in the Stationers' Register on 29 May 1600
("Entred for his copie vnder the hand*es* of the wardens. The Allarum to london. provided that yt be not printed w*i*thout further Aucthoritie").[9] A quarto
appeared in 1602 with an advertisement of the company owners on the title
page: "A Larvm For London, or The Siedge of Antwerpe . . . As it hath been
playde by the right Honorable the Lord Charberlaine his Seruants" (Greg,
no. 192).

The play lists in Henslowe's book of accounts suggest that companies at
the Rose also staged plays with topical subject matter and with long-familiar
characterizations and moral emphasis. However, most of the texts, like that
of "Cloth Breeches and Velvet Hose," are lost. Thus I can do no more than
guess at the audience appeal of plays acquired by the Admiral's men such as
"Strange News out of Poland" (1599–1600), "The Siege of Dunkirk"
(1602–1603), "Fount of New Fashions" (1598–99), and the two parts of
"The London Florentine" (1602–1603). I assume that the apparent use of
international politics in the former two, and trendy couture in the latter three,
contributed to their success. Likewise, I attribute a measure of the success of
the first of two parts of "Seven Days of the Week" (3 June 1595–31 December 1596), which played over nineteen months in twenty-two performances
for average receipt of 37s. to Henslowe, to the apparent use of a medieval
calendrical structure. However for a few of the lost plays, the titles seem to
link folk materials and moral concerns explicitly to economic, social, and
political questions: for example, "Tis No Deceit to Deceive the Deceiver"
(Admiral's men, 1598–99), "Joan as Good as My Lady" (Admiral's men,
1598–99), "Wooing of Death" (Admiral's men, 1599–1600), "The Blind
Eats Many a Fly" (Worcester's men, 1602–1603), and "Medicine for a Curst
Wife" (Worcester's men, 1602–1603). This combination of subjects and formulas suggests that the companies at the Rose, like the Chamberlain's men,
recognized the commercial potential of dramatizing topical issues in medieval structures.

The dramatist of "Cloth Breeches and Velvet Hose" had only to modernize
the subject matter in his source text to capitalize on the strategy of presenting
current issues in traditional genres; Greene had himself supplied the medieval

formulas. The entire work, *Quip for an Upstart Courtier,* is a series of dream visions, the last of which provides the story to go with the subtitle "A Quaint Dispute Between Velvet-Breeches and Cloth-Breeches." In this dream, the narrator sees "an uncouth headlesse thinge" strut arrogantly toward him from a nearby hill.[10] The monstrosity—all "legges and hose"—is a pair of Velvet Breeches "whose panes, being made of the cheefest Neapolitane stuffe, was drawne out with the best Spanish satine, and marvellous curiously over whipt with gold twist, intersemed with knots of pearle; the nether-stocke was of the purest Granado silck" (397). The outfit is completed with rapier and "dagger gilt, *point pendante*" (397). Before the dreamer can react to this bizarre sight, a second monster marches soberly toward him. This figure is "a plaine paire of Cloth-Breeches, without either welte or garde, straight to the thigh, of white kersie, without a slop, the nether-stocke of the same, sewed too above the knee, and only seamed with a little country blewe" (398). It is weaponed with "a good sower bat with a pike in the ende" (398). Immediately Velvet Breeches challenges Cloth Breeches for presuming to intrude, and Cloth Breeches counters that he has the prior right due to his lineage among the yeomanry. An argument ensues, in which each puts forward his claim to be the "most auncient and most worthy" (400). The dreamer, turned magistrate, impanels a jury to decide the case. He asks passersby to be jurymen, and he allows the pairs of breeches to disqualify those whose judgment they distrust. Greene used the serial presentation of potential jurors to achieve two ends: he drew distinctions between the moral postures of Cloth Breeches and Velvet Breeches; and he turned the parade of passersby into an estates satire, in which he indicted "the Disorders in all Estates and Trades" (393).[11]

I assume that the dramatist of "Cloth Breeches and Velvet Hose" retained the dream structure of his source, for he had contemporary precedents for staged dreams in such plays as *The Old Wives Tale,* the *Shrew* plays, and *A Midsummer Night's Dream.* Given that the play registered at Stationers' Hall on 27 May 1600 was called "A morall of Clothe breches & veluet hose," I assume further that the dramatist characterized Cloth Breeches and Velvet Breeches in moral terms. The identification of one headless monstrosity with virtue and the other with vice is implicit in the costumes of the two, and in Greene's text the characters repeatedly manifest their moral identities.[12] Cloth Breeches charges Velvet Breeches with social abuses, cataloguing the sins of "vaine-glory, self-love, sodomie, and strange poisonings, wherewith [he] has infected this glorious Island" (399). Velvet Breeches brags about his favored status and thus reveals his exploitation of a corrupt socio-political system:

> I can presse into the presence, when thou, poore soule, shalt, with cap and knee, beg leave of the porter to enter; and I sit and dine with the nobility, when thou art faine to wait for the reversion of the almes-basket. I am admitted boldly to tell my

tale, when thou are fain to sue, by means of supplication, and that, and thou too, so little regarded, that most commonly it never comes to the prince's hand, but dies inprisoned in som obscure pocket. (398–99)

The jurymen, of course, find for Cloth Breeches. In rendering judgment, they affirm the virtue of Cloth Breeches, declaring him to be "a patron of the poore; a true subject; a good house-keeper, and generally as honest as he is antient" (421). They decry the immorality of Velvet Breeches, whom they proclaim to be "begot of pride, nursed up by self-love" (421).

By choosing Greene's narrative, the dramatist had elements of estates satire set up for him in the parade of potential jurors, who represent the shortcomings of various occupations as well as the destructive effects of the attempt to rise above one's class. One target is the tradesman who has gotten rich because of the fashion for velvet breeches and now fancies himself a gentleman. Such is the tailor, who was once content to be "Goodman Tailor" but now styles himself "Marchant or Gentleman-Marchant-Taylor" (404). Another is the professional whose very work is corruption. Such is the broker, who is not only a loan shark but a fence, and the pairs of breeches agree that he should "be shuffled out amongst the knaves, for a discarded carde" (405). There are the age-old complaints about tanners who quick-cure skins, butchers who dress old meat in fresh blood, vintners who cut good wine with sack or water, and milliners who feed an appetite for frivolous accessories. The collier shamelessly confesses his cheating, and the shoemaker takes a bit of ribbing for being in a craft where all are by nature "such good-fellowes and spendthriftes" (412). The mockery of the dramatist and the stage is as familiar as the distrust of trades. Cloth Breeches chides the poet for squandering his income on food and wenches, the wanton result of which recreations is that "his plough goes and his inkhorne be cleere"; but for all that, he declares the poet "no man's foe but his owne" (420). Cloth Breeches also objects to the player, whom he considers "too full of self liking and self love" (421). He is personally offended that players are too ready to bring a "plaine countrey fellow" like himself into their plays to be laughed at "as clownes and fooles" (421).

In finding for Cloth Breeches, the jury declares for the values of old-fashioned native populists:

Cloth-Breeches is by many hundred years more antient, ever since Brute, an inhabitant in this Iland, one that hath beene *in diebus illis* a companion to kings, an equall with the nobility, [and] a frend to gentlemen and yeomen. (421)

Velvet Breeches, in contrast, is "an upstart, come out of Italy, . . . and brought into this countrey by his companion Newfanglenesse" (421). Extravagant clothing and moral corruption are linked here in the way that dramatists of moral plays link changes of clothing with the mankind figure's fall from grace, illustrated by *Mankynd* and the refashioning of Mankind's jacket by the vice characters New Guise, Nought, and Nowadays. The jury further declares Velvet Breeches to be "a raiser of rents, and an enimie in the commonwealth" (421). Greene therefore reinforced the link already established between social privilege and immorality by adding exploitative land practices and treason to Velvet Breeches's charge.

The text of "Cloth Breeches and Velvet Hose" may be lost, but it is easy to imagine why the Chamberlain's men acquired it for their opening season at the Globe in 1599–1600. From the point of view of staging, the headless figures made for sensational theater. The velvet breeches and fancy hose were a nice contrast with the plain cloth breeches with blue piping. The debate between the two was enlivened by the serial appearances of tradesmen and professionals. But some measure of the dramatic appeal would have been in the dramatist's skill in using the formulas of the dream vision, moral characterization, and estates satire from his source to convey the social, political, and economic concerns of his audience. With a successful presentation of current issues in long-familiar but still-popular literary and dramatic formulas, the Chamberlain's men had an excellent chance of generating receipts well beyond their investment in the text and the cost of the unique costumes for the star parts. It might once have been assumed that such a play, by its very presence in the hands of printers in May 1600, had lost its commercial value to the company, but the opposite might be true. As Peter Blayney argues, the Chamberlain's men apparently meant to release a number of plays in May but for reasons now unknown waited until August to release more. What enhances the commercial stature of "Cloth Breeches and Velvet Hose" in the playhouse, even though it was never printed (the stationers' choice, not the company's), is that plays of obvious value such as *As You Like It, Henry V, Every Man In his Humour,* and *Much Ado About Nothing* were in the August batch.[13]

The text of *A Larum for London* was eventually printed after its registration in May 1600, and its appeal for audiences and readers is immediately evident in the focus of the narrative on the atrocities of war. The dramatist based his play on the siege of Antwerp in 1575–76 by a coalition of armies headed by the Spanish. In the opening sequence, Sancto Danila (Sancho d'Avila), the leader of a band of mutinous Spaniards, prepares to make an assault upon the town. The governor of Antwerp quibbles with foreign allies, counseled duplicitously by the traitor, Cornelius Van End. The governor fails to enlist the aid of Stump, a one-legged soldier, who rages through the town berating citizens for their ingratitude toward "lam'd, diseas'd, or any way distrest" veterans.[14] The Spanish coalition has just one tough fight (against the allies of Antwerp); then the massacre begins. At his own initiative, Stump assembles a company of rabble soldiers, and he intervenes to save a few lives. However, the Spanish are too powerful, and Danila claims the town. At the end of the play, in a surprise show of battlefield ethics, Danila prevents the Spanish troops from desecrating Stump's corpse.

By the choice of this war narrative, the dramatist of *A Larum for London* tapped into the fear among Londoners of a Spanish invasion, as illustrated by documents in the Elizabethan state papers in 1599, plus the correspondence of John Chamberlain and the *Annals* of John Stow (narrated in the opening of this essay). Moreover, stories of victimized merchants and mariners fed the anxiety felt by many Englishmen for their physical safety. With a depressing frequency, London churchgoers were solicited for contributions to help victims of attacks by Spaniards on the high seas and along the coast of England. In the mid-1590s, Thomas Harridance, clerk of St. Botolph Aldgate, recorded a number of these collections in a set of books that he kept in addition to the register proper, and they now provide a gloss on these troubles. For example, on 9 February 1595 there was a collection at St. Botolph Aldgate for John Leasing "who . . . had greate losses at sea in a ship named the Roebuck of Sr Ihon Burrowes, and is at this tyme deteyned prisoner with the spanyard*es*."[15] On 15 June in the same year, Thomas Finch, a merchant from Feversham, was authorized to seek donations "for that he had susteyned sundrie greate Loss*es* of shipps good*es* & Marchandyse*es* stayd w*i*thin the Realme of spayne as also Cast away vpon the high seas by oc*c*ation of Tempest & fowle weather to the value of *1660* pownd*es* sterling to the vttere Impoverishing & vndoing of him his poore wyfe and six smale children" (GHL, ms. 9234/5).

With the story of the fall of Antwerp, the dramatist also played on the belief that a Spanish presence in the Netherlands contributed to a general lawlessness along the north coast of Europe and thus increased the danger to commercial trade. There was ample evidence in the activities of pirates who operated with impunity out of renegade ports such as Dunkirk. Richard Clarke, a mariner, "receyved greate hurte*es* & hinderances by the Dunkerkers at sea and otherwayes in her Ma*j*estie*es* service to the greate hinderance of him his poore wyfe and thre smale children" (GHL, ms. 9234/5 [15 June 1595]). Richard Vaughan, who was master as well as part owner of a ship called the *Grace of God,* had a harrowing experience. Intercepted as he came from France, "laden with wynes & other Marchandize to the value of three Thowsand pownd*es* & vpward*es*," he was "sett vpon by pyratt*es* at sea belonging to Donnkerke who Robed and spoyled the said Richard Vaughan and all the Rest of his company of ship and good*es* & did take the said Ric*hard* with eyght more of his said company as prisoners & Captyve*es* of the w*hich* doth three Remayne as *y*et for there Ransome" (GHL, ms. 9234/5 [18 January 1595/96]).[16] Even insignificant men were victimized, as was the case of Robert Otes, a fisherman, who was robbed at sea by "the donnkerkers" (GHL, ms. 9234/35 [22 December 1594]); and John Barker, who "was detayned prisoner at Dunkerke" (GHL, ms. 92343/6 [22 August 1596]). In

1599, Anthony Atkinson of Hull complained to Sir John Stanhope that ships were being terrorized by pirates from Dunkirk, who "chase all [the] poore fishermen a shore, and those they take are stripped naked." [17] Atkinson added that the pirates "take out of sundry shipps such masters as they thinke good and forceth them to be ther pilots alongst these northeren Coasts."

To tell his story, the dramatist of *A Larum for London* chose theatrical motifs derived from medieval English literature and drama; in so doing, he intensified the political rhetoric. The play is an exemplum, with the figure of Time in the role of preacher. In the illustrative narrative, the dramatist extrapolated certain features from traditional characterizations evident in the moral play and Corpus Christi cycles.[18] He used various characteristics of the Vice to enhance the villainy of the Spanish commanders and their collaborators.[19] He seems to have drawn on the Herod plays to emphasize the cruelty of the Spanish soldiers and the distress of the citizens of Antwerp. In the figures of Sancto Danila and Stump, the dramatist of *A Larum for London* turned to more contemporary stage models, but these characterizations too have medieval analogues.

The figure of Time is both prologue and epilogue, and it sets the moral orientation of the play. Like an Old Testament prophet, or contemporary doomsday preacher, Time delivers the sermon that the narrative will illustrate. In the prologue, Time claims to have *"searcht the worlds corrupt enormities"* and to have been drawn to *"this faire concourse heere met together,"* that is, the audience at the playhouse (ll. 4, 12). Recognizing that the length of the play offers spectators the *"calme leasure to beholde their faultes"* (l. 13), Time urges them to attend to the sight of the city's punishment and, if their *"hearts be not of Adamant"* (l. 20), to learn from the example of Antwerp to mend their degenerate ways. In the epilogue, Time reiterates the lesson, casting the historical event in terms of biblical parallels such as Sodom or Jerusalem. Playgoers must heed the warning, or London too may become a town like Antwerp,

> *Whose bleeding fortune, whose lamenting cryes,*
> *Whose streetes besmear'd with bloud, whose blubred eyes,*
> *Whose totter'd walls, whose building's ouerthrowne,*
> *Whose riches lost, and pouerty made knowne:*
> *May be a meane all Cittyes to affright,*
> *How they in sinne and pleasure take delight.*
>
> (ll. 1673–78)

Within the play, additional voices sound the theme. Antwerp's allies, for example, grieve that the citizens have disregarded the example of "many bleeding instances" of cities blessed with wealth but cursed by vanity (l. 661). An old blind father, Tiresias-like, has prophesied the fall of the city.

Having set this moral frame, the dramatist differentiated the Spanish commanders according to strategies associated with the Vice. He began the narrative by staging a pair of elaborate deceptions through which the Spanish lull
the citizens of Antwerp into a false sense of security. Sancto Danila is responsible for the first ruse. He orders his soldiers to hide behind the castle walls
so that the scouts from Antwerp will not notice a military build-up. Then he
orders the artillery gunner to fire shots that appear to be merely a display of
fire power, a kind of saber-rattling, but that are in fact the opening volley in
the attack on the town. Meanwhile, the duke of Alva is cut off from the bulk
of the Spanish forces. As a means to rejoin Danila, Alva spreads the rumor
that he is dead, and he uses the stratagem of a funeral march to pass through
the defenses of the town.

The cortege of Alva is an effective stage device, comparable in theatrics to
ruses by the Vice in moral plays. It is also an opportunity for the dramatist to
vent anti-Spanish sentiments. Danila is onstage with a couple of whimpering
burghers when a signet sounds and two men enter *"with mourning penons"*
(s. d., l. 260). A drum sounds the approach of the funeral processions, and a
horse covered in black enters, carrying the body of Alva. Soldiers follow,
"trayling their Pykes" (s. d., ll. 262–63). As the march continues across the
stage, commoners from the town hurl insults at the hearse. One gleefully
imagines that the devils will enjoy an "olde trymphing in hell" at the arrival
of Alva's soul (l. 280), and he calls Alva "worse then the Spanish inquisition" (l. 283). Another avers that "if euer man would haue eaten vp the Cani-
balles, twas he" (ll. 284–85). Still a third jokes nervously that the hatred of
the people will "curse him out of's graue" (l. 288). And indeed, when the
stage is cleared, Alva rises from the hearse to answer their insults with a
boast:

> Well, I am dead, but *Aluas* spirit (ere long)
> Shall haunt your ghostes, and with a fatall troope,
> Come in the dreadfull night about your walles,
> Grimme death did nere affright the fearfull martiall,
> As I will fright these Bouzing Begians.

> (ll. 311–15)

In this image of a revenge that outlives the grave, the dramatist played upon
the same fears that Shakespeare exploited in the image of Caesar's spirit
"With Ate by his side come hot from hell" in *Julius Caesar,* another politically charged offering in the repertory of the Chamberlain's men in the opening season of the Globe (1599–1600). But there was a difference in historical
immediacy. In *A Larum for London,* the dogs of war were Spanish, and in
1599 they were thought to be barking at England's vulnerable southern
belly.[20]

Cornelius Van End is another character whose villainy and stage behavior carry the mark of the Vice. Van End is supposedly an adviser to Champaigne (Champagny), the governor of Antwerp, but he is instead a Policy or Ambidexter. He meets in secret conference with Danila, exchanging information on a gathering of the governor and burghers for the promise of a share of the Spaniards' "spoyle and honour" in the upcoming siege (l. 36). He advises the governor in a meeting of the potential allies of Antwerp. As each nobleman offers help, Van End whispers to the governor to refuse: "In silence be it my Lord, you need the*m* not" (l. 376). He exploits the governor's cowardice by suggesting that the Spaniards will become even more belligerent if the allies' offers of help are accepted, and he appeals to his greed and selfishness by impugning the allies' motives: "Friends and defence, are less esteem'd then pelfe" (l. 417). Furthermore, the dramatist of *A Larum for London* gave this traitor certain linguistic trademarks of the Vice. Van End counsels the governor in asides. He warns Danila in a coded message, or spy-speak, that Antwerp is preparing to defend itself:

> Tell him from me, the Flies begin to swarme;
> The Sunne growes hot, the heards do shake their hornes,
> The Shepheards bring great flockes home to the folde;
> Say, if the Butcher slaughter not in time,
> The beastes will surfet and the Soldiers pyne . . .
>
> (ll. 488–92)

Excited by the slaughter to come, Van End gloats in soliloquy that the day of battle to come will be "dismall to the towne" but a "holly-day" for him and the Spaniards (ll. 499, 496).

The dramatist of *A Larum for London* found ways to present the massacre of the people of Antwerp in the Corpus Christi cycles. The "Herod" plays provided an antecedent for the bloodlust of Alva, who orders the citizens to be rounded up and chained "together in the Market place, / By hundreds and two hundreds" (ll. 830–31). He exults that none will be spared: "neither widdow, matron, nor young maide, / Gray-bearded Fathers, nor the babe that suckes" (ll. 833–34). The dramatist supplied mercenaries who are worthy of Herod's soldiers in cruelty and arrogantly vulgar speech, and he supplied victims who inspire a pathos analogous to that of the bereft mothers and slaughtered infants in Corpus Christi "Herod" plays. In one horrific episode (scene 10), two children, Lenchy and Martin, try to escape from the invaders, who have already killed some of their friends ("Little *Maria,* and *Hans Vanderbrooke*" [l. 1112]). Hearing a great noise, the girl, Lenchy, embraces her brother to hide him from the approaching soldiers, who run on stage shouting in demotic Spanish: "Kill, kill, kill. / . . . Fuora villiaco, fa, fa, fa, fa" (ll. 1127, 1134). To the plea of Martin to spare his sister, one soldier says "Cut the Bastards throates" (l. 1138). Lenchy hangs on a soldier, crying "Haue you the heart to kill a prettie Girle?" (l. 1142). But the soldiers laugh and curse: "Zwounds, dash out their braines" (l. 1146). When Harmon, the blind father, and his wife enter, seeking their children, the soldiers answer with more insults: "Out you Brabant bitch, thinke you with whining / To preserue your whelpes?" (l. 1158–59); "Cut all their throates" (l. 1162). They then stab the father, mother, and children.

Unlike this piteous family, many of the victims of the massacre are sinners. Even so, the dramatist used incidents from sacred narrative to generate compassion for them, even as he criticized their immoral behavior. For example, in the first of the episodes of plunder (scene 6), the governor's wife is attacked by two soldiers who strip her in view of the audience in a search for jewels. Imitating the soldiers at the crucifixion, they cast lots for "who shall haue her" (l. 750). Stump will intervene before the soldiers rape her, but first he judges her:

> Heere is she, that would not haue been seene
> with a moath vpon her, for a thousand pound;
> That spent as much on Munkeys, Dogs and Parrets,
> As would haue kept ten Soldiers all the yeere.
> Zblood I haue seene her, where I haue past by her
> In the streetes, to stop her nose with her sweete gloues,
> For feare my smell should haue infected her. . . .
>
> (ll. 756–62)

Despite her unworthiness, Stump rescues her because he believes that she has suffered enough abuse.

The two main characters in the play, Sancto Danila and Stump, are more apparently kin to types of protagonists in Elizabethan than medieval drama. Danila is a Marlovian conqueror, with a streak of the post-Marlovian villain. Like Tamburlaine and the duke of Guise, Danila relishes conquest. He scorns the puny civilians of the town: "When once the Alarum soundes (like silly mice) / they'll hyde them in the creuice of their walles" (ll. 58–59). But there is an eroticism in Danila's attitude toward power that is evident in post-Marlovian revengers such as Aaron in *Titus Andronicus,* Eleazor in *Lust's Dominion,* and Pope Alexander VI in *The Devil's Charter.* To Danila, Antwerp is a woman, the "flower of *Europe,*" and he is "rauisht with the sight of her" (ll. 75, 76). Being a woman, she "must be Courted" (l. 78), and he chooses the Petrarchan blazon for that wooing:

> . . . from her nostrils comes
> A breath, as sweete as the Arabian spice.
> Her garments are imbrodered with pure golde;

> And euery part so rich and sumptuous,
> As Indias not to be compar'd to her. . . .

(ll. 78–82)

Yet the Antwerp of his fantasy is not a shy virgin. "Amorous as the wanton ayre" (l. 75), she resists only to enhance her pleasure; she "inuites" the assault upon "her sportfull bed" (ll. 83–84). When he has breached the city walls, Danila becomes a caricature of the conqueror. He orders an old citizen to hand over his daughter or feel "the sharpe point of [his] Semiter" (l. 949). Under torture, the citizen confesses that his daughter is in a nunnery. Danila claims her nonetheless, saying that his victory would be as incomplete without her "as a banquet without companie" (l. 1053). But he does not keep her long. When it appears that she might be rescued, he casually pulls out a pistol and shoots her.

Stump is a Flemish soldier who roams the streets of Antwerp befriended in his bitterness only by the evidence of his service to the state, that is, his crippled leg ("my olde rotten stump and I" [l. 746]). At the time that *A Larum for London* was written, there were other instances of veterans on stage. Rafe, in *The Shoemaker's Holiday,* was a contemporary, as was Musco in disguise as a beggar-soldier in *Every Man In his Humor.* Stump is a crusty version of this figure. He ridicules the burghers for denying the danger of the Spaniards and asks scornfully if they will persist "Vntill the verie instant, you doe feele / Their naked swoords glide through your weasond-pipes?" (ll. 574–75). When the governor of Antwerp pleads with him to take up arms against the invaders, Stump berates the citizens for their lack of charity. He complains that they pay a cobbler his wages, or a laborer to clean out their kennels, but let a disabled soldier "Appeale for succour" then look at him as if they "knew him not" (ll. 613–14). The governor continues to plead, and Stump offers mockingly to provide a "groates-worth" of service for the charity he has received: "a groate I had, / And so much as a groate amounts vnto you, / My swoord shall pay ye in exchange of blowes" (ll. 624–26).

The issue of the disabled veteran was a sensitive one in England at the time. The daybooks of Thomas Harridance at St. Botolph Aldgate are full of collections for men who had sustained injuries in her majesty's service; many sought contributions toward an alms room. Henry Ro was injured more severely than Stump; according to Harridance's entry, Ro was a "sowldier who went vpon ij stilte*s* havinge bene maymed in her ma*jesties* Warrs" (26 October 1589).[21] In the churchwardens' accounts of St. Helen Bishopsgate, there are frequent entries of quarterly donations for "maymed soldiers."[22] No doubt these entries are representative of institutionalized donations throughout London parishes in the 1590s for maimed soldiers and mariners from the Spanish, Dutch, and Irish wars. Men who could secure a passport for collections had a safety net, as did those who—as grocers, haberdashers, skinners, or freemen of another of the guilds—were provided with rooms, stipends, or occasional hand-outs from their company. But the presence of maimed veterans on the London stage—perhaps especially in 1599 when a great mustering was taking place—was an uncomfortable reminder of the cost of protecting the nation.

For most of the play, Stump operates alone, alternately harassing victims like the governor's wife and defending them from further torture at the hands of the invaders. Toward the end, however, he comes upon a troop of Walloons who are about to flee, and he rallies them to follow him: "Let's doe something yet worthy the talking of" (l. 1454). He and a captain exit to the battlefield and reenter wounded and dying. In a rather fine speech, Stump confesses to bloody deeds in the service of the state and forgives Antwerp its ingratitude. Danila's soldiers, Myrmidon-like, want to drag the bodies of Stump and the captain behind horses from town to town as an example to the vanquished, but Danila refuses.[23] He recognizes their valor with an epitaph:

> Their pride was honourable, deseruing loue
> Rather then hate; . . .
> There neuer liued two more Heroycke spirits;
> That for their Country haue deseru'd as much,
> To be renouned; as euer *Curtious* was,
> Or Romaine *Decius,* or the two valliant *Cocles;*
> They for their country could but loose their liues,
> These haue in equall seruice done as much.
>
> (ll. 1644–45, 1649–54)

Although Danila and Stump are kin to types of military figures onstage in playhouses around London in 1599, their characters have a medieval spin. Both have the wicked wit of a Vice. Before the attack on the town, Danila surveys the weaponry of his troops. He disdains the small arms of falchions, harquebuses, and culverins as "crackers" (l. 170) and "fire-worke" (186); and he calls on the artillery gunner to entertain the carelessly feasting citizens with the music of cannon fire. When two burghers complain that he should have parleyed with them instead of firing, he calls the cannon shot "a bolde Embassador" and laughs, "did we not send our poast / Euen now vnto you? / And wrapt our Packet in a ball of lead?" (ll. 252–54). As he waits for the burgher's daughter to be fetched from the nunnery, he entertains himself with the torture of an English factor, who is strappadoed in view of the audience. When he is sure the man has no more gold, Danila releases him with a jest that conflates a biblical and classical sacrifice: "harke (peeld sheepe) / Goe hide thee in some bush, till waxing houres / Giue thee another fleece to cloath thee with" (ll. 1016–18).[24]

Stump is witty also. When he rescues the burgher's wife from Van End, he stones the traitor and jeers, "Heere, weare this waightie Iewell in thy hat" (l. 1328). Stump then turns the stones into the coin of death: "Giue these two vnto *Charon* for your passing. / And with this last, present grim *Belzebub*" (ll. 1333–34). Frequently, his wit is the vulgar railing of a satyr. When he is berating the citizens for not having armed themselves in anticipation of the Spanish invasion, he scoffs, "doe you thinke with belching puffes, that flye / From your full paunches, you can blow them backe?" (ll. 576–77). When he discovers a fat burgher whom the Spanish soldiers have strung up by the thumbs (scene 14), he cuts the man down, all the while cursing him as "the Tallow-cake, the Rammish Fat, / That would not giue a penny to a Soldier" (ll. 1513–14). Stump scorns the man for his girth, which he equates with avarice. He calls him a "dung-hill of . . . carryon flesh / . . . [not] fit for any thing but to feed wormes" (ll. 1524–27). When the man offers a reward, Stump insults him again and sends him away: "Guts, trouble me no more" (l. 1541). The burgher lumbers off, and Stump marks him as an emblem of Antwerp's diseased parts:

> How like *Leuiathan,* his clumsie limbes
> Walke not but tumble, that sad common wealth,
> Nourceth such Droanes to sucke her honny vp,
> In time of need shall finde as small supply,
> As he hat been to *Antwerpes* wretchednes. . . .
>
> (ll. 1546–50)

By emphasizing moral outrage, the dramatist associated Stump's abusive language with the instructive, admonitory voices of teachers and preachers in medieval drama.[25]

Danila, in a parallel role, is the scourge of God. The siege is framed by speeches in which he sees himself as a necessary corrosive. The citizens have been "remisse and negligent" (l. 47). They have chosen "soft effeminate silkes" and "dalliance" over vigilance (ll. 47–49); they are therefore "fat for slaughter, fit for spoile" (l. 50). Surveying the sacked town, the "streetes . . . thwackt with slaughtered carkasses" (l. 1617), Danila expresses compassion for the townspeople—briefly. Then he remembers his mission:

> . . . they were wanton and lasciuious,
> Too much addicted to their priuate lust:
> And that concludes their Martirdoome was iust
>
> (ll. 1623–25)

Like the satyr, the scourge was both an Elizabethan and medieval character. Tamburlaine saw himself in this role, and Old Testament prophets saw invading armies as the purgative instruments of God's justice.

Without playhouse records similar to those left by Philip Henslowe for seasons of performances at the Rose, theater historians cannot now know which plays in the repertory of the Chamberlain's men were profitable commodities and which were not. There were "fillers" every season, but contrary to the former disdain of scholars for plays without much apparent poetic excellence, the fillers were not the new plays, whoever the dramatist; they were the plays being continued from the previous season, which could be performed again and again without cost. New plays were always valuable commodities; they were expected to create new playgoers and to attract habitual playgoers to the company's playhouse on a given afternoon. There is every reason to believe, from a commercial point of view, that "Cloth Breeches and Velvet Hose" and *A Larum for London* fulfilled these expectations for the Chamberlain's men and that they did so in a year when the company had much at risk financially. Both were showy pieces, filling the stage with action and visual attractions. Both exploited playgoers' sensitivity to current social, political, and economic issues. Both used characterizations and the rhetoric of morality that had been popular with playgoers for generations. The dramatist of *A Larum for London* had an additional stratagem to please audiences. He advertised the name of the company's playhouse and its painted heavens in the opening lines of the prologue:

> *Round through the compasse of this earthly ball*
> *The massie substance hanging in the skie. . . .*

(ll. 1–2)

About a year later, another dramatist with the Chamberlain's men thought these features of the playhouse were still a draw, and he alluded to them in *Hamlet.*[26]

Notes

The Public Record Office (PRO) houses the Elizabethan State Papers, Domestic Series (S.P.); the Guildhall Library (GHL) houses parish records. In transcriptions, I have removed superfluous punctuation and expanded scribal contractions in italics. A much earlier version of this essay was submitted to a seminar led by James Shapiro at the annual meeting of the Shakespeare Association of America in 1991. Also I wish to thank Wayne Narey for a close and appreciative reading.

    1. PRO, S.P. 12/270/104. "Groyne" was a popular name for the port of La Coruña on the northwest tip of the Spanish peninsula.

    2. PRO, S.P. 12/271/140.

    3. Norman E. McClure (ed.), *The Letters of John Chamberlain,* 2 vols. (1939; rpt. Westport, CT: Greenwood, 1979), I, 78. All quotations from Chamberlain's letters are taken from this edition; subsequent citations are given in the text.

    4. STC 23336, p. 1304.

5. PRO, S.P. 12/272/30; subsequent citations from the mayor's letter are taken from this document.

6. Bernard Beckerman, *Shakespeare at the Globe, 1599–1609* (New York: Collier-Macmillan, 1962), 16. I take this quotation somewhat out of context and thereby do Beckerman an injustice. His work on the Globe repertory is the best kind of revisionist theater history, demonstrating beyond doubt that the Chamberlain's men would have been foolish not to have used the repertory system as it is illustrated for us in Henslowe's diary. But he does unfortunately underrate some of the company's offerings and thus provide just the phrase I want to convey a dismissive attitude formerly common among scholars. Furthermore, his definition of unsuccessful plays confuses the issue of profit with the length of a stage run. The Admiral's men established their business at the Rose in 1594–1596 by giving thirty of thirty-eight new plays that lasted six months or less and that covered twelve performances or fewer. This fact suggests to me that plays became profitable to the company much earlier in the run than has been supposed. I infer from the data in Henslowe's business records that a company would have considered a new play well worth the investment if it ran for eight to twelve performances over four to six months.

7. I indicate the titles of lost plays with quotations marks; the titles of surviving plays are in italics.

8. "Cloth Breeches and Velvet Hose" was listed separately on the fly leaf of the register (Register C) under the heading "my lord chamberlens mens Plaies Entred" (W. W. Greg, ed., *A Bibliography of the English Printed Drama to the Restoration,* 4 vols. [London: Bibliographic Society, 1939] I:15; see also Greg II, "Lost Plays" # 22). The use of the present tense in the register entry ("is acted") is my authority for assigning the play to the repertory in 1599–1600. Greg is my source for information and wording in entries in the Stationers' Register and on the title pages of quartos.

9. *A Larum for London* was listed on the fly leaf of Register C along with "Cloth Breeches and Velvet Hose," and I assume a contemporaneous stage run (fall 1599 to spring 1600).

10. *Harleian Miscellany,* V (London, 1809), 397; subsequent citations are given in the text.

11. I rely here on the discussion of estates satire in *Chaucer and Medieval Estates Satire* by Jill Mann (Cambridge: Cambridge University Press, 1973), 3–10. Working from the definition of estates literature by Ruth Mohl (*The Three Estates in Medieval and Renaissance Literature,* 1933), Mann considers "any literary treatments of social classes which allow or encourage a generalised application" of Mohl's criteria to qualify as estates satire (3). She summarizes Mohl's criteria as follows: "an enumeration of the 'estates' or social and occupational classes, whose aim seems to be completeness[;] . . . a lament over the shortcomings of the estates[;] . . . the philosophy of the divine ordination of the three principal estates, the dependence of the state on all three, and the necessity of being content with one's station[;] . . . [and] an attempt to find remedies, religious or political, for the defects of estates" (3).

12. The dramatist of "Cloth Breeches and Velvet Hose" would have found additional evidence of the moral orientation of his source in the dedication to Thomas Burnabie, in which Greene declared that he had "shadowed the abuses that pride had bred in England: how it had infected the Court with aspiring envie, the Citie with

griping covetousnesse, and the Countrye with contempte and disdaine" (393–94). Further, in the address to gentlemen-readers, Greene explained that his target was not Velvet Breeches's "weede, but the vice; not the apparell when 'tis worthily worn, but the unworthie person that weares it" (394).

13. Peter W. M. Blayney, "The Publication of Playbooks," *A New History of Early English Drama,* eds. John D. Cox and David Scott Kastan (New York: Columbia University Press, 1997), 383–422, esp. 387. *As You Like It* was not printed at this time, as far as is known. I point out elsewhere that a peculiarity of the plays printed in this second of Blayney's "peak periods" of publication in 1600–1601 is the advertisement on the title page of the name of the patron, which is tantamount to advertising the name of the company (*Playing Companies and Commerce in Shakespeare's Time* [Cambridge: Cambridge University Press, 2001], 69).

14. W. W. Greg (ed.), Malone Society Reprint (London, 1913), l. 612; subsequent citations are given in the text. I have expanded a scribal abbreviation in italics.

15. GHL, ms. 9234/5 (daybooks for 1594–96 and 1598–1600); subsequent citations from the daybooks are given in the text.

16. Vaughan apparently settled in St. Botolph, for a son was born there to a man by that name on 16 August; his presence would have served as a reminder of the dangers of going to sea (GHL, ms. 9234/6). A Dutch sailor, Nicholas Peterson, who was "late of a ship called the hope of fflushing in sealand," was buried in the parish on 17 September 1596; his fate reminded parishioners of another hazard, not necessarily for mariners only: "he was a bursten man . . . being sick of a surfett taken by drinking of new drinke" (GHL, ms. 9234/6).

17. PRO, S.P. 12/270/109; a subsequent citation is given in the text. That the problem of pirates out of Dunkirk and other coastal cities in the Spanish Netherlands persisted into the early 1600s, and that it was a good theatrical subject, is evident in the title of one of the new plays that the Admiral's men began to buy from Charles Massey in March 1603: "the sedge of doncerke wth alleyn the pyrate." Though it has sometimes been mistaken as part of the title, the phrase "with Alleyn the pirate" must surely indicate that the company star, recently out of retirement, was taking the lead role as a villainous defender of the brigands' haven.

18. John Wasson offers a word of caution in the automatic assumption that the kinds of plays most fully represented by extant texts—i.e., the moral interlude and Corpus Christi plays—were the only or even primary source of influence on Elizabethan dramatists. He cites the miracle play, *Life of St. Meriasek,* as an instance of such features as the "raging tyrant" and "threatened mass murder of 3140 innocent children" ("The Morality Play: Ancestor of Elizabethan Drama?" in *The Drama in the Middle Ages: Comparative and Critical Essays,* eds. Clifford Davidson, C. J. Gianakaris, and John H. Stroupe [New York: AMS Press, 1982]): 316–27, especially 322.

19. The association of Spaniards with deceit and treachery is a common theme in the pamphlet literature of the time. In *A Discourse of the Vsage of the English Fugitiues, by the Spaniard,* for example, a man who claimed to be a pensioner of Philip II wrote to warn disaffected Englishmen from making his mistake: "my indeuor is to let you knowe what hell, torment, and vexation it is to liue heere, among this vnquiet, trouble-some, & traiterous crew" (STC 15562, sig. E^v). His method was to enumerate the treacheries of Spaniards against their allies and to expose their exploitation of

religion for personal and political gain. He began with a story of English soldiers who helped Spain win in the Low Countries but who were driven to foraging the country-side for sustenance after they were released from service without being paid. Caught by Spanish soldiers, the English troops were massacred. One of their captains who was being held for ransom was abandoned to the enemy, even though his blind father (a Fleming) petitioned the Spanish duke for help: "the Duke badde take awaie the olde dronken foole: the griefe whereof strake the old man so to the heart, that he went home and dyed within six dayes, and his sonne for lacke of his raunsome was shortly after hanged at *Perges*" (sig. C). The author conceded that Spanish priests in England "speak so deuoutly, looke so smoothly, and write with such counterfeited grauitie and holines, that it is hard for any man to eschue their deadly baits" (sig. E), but he warned that their intent was not for the advancement of religion but "to ouerthrow vs all at last" (sig. D).

20. Alva evokes another Globe play of political villainy by complaining that "the dogs bark at me, a plague vpon them all, / I thinke they doe not hate the Deuill so" (ll. 306–7). For a text of Shakespeare's plays, I use *The Riverside Shakespeare,* ed. G. Blakemore Evans (Boston: Houghton Mifflin, 1974).

21. GHL, ms. 9234/2. A sample of other disabled veterans with passports is as follows. Richard Wybird was a soldier who served in Flanders for over two years "and there was grievivslye wownded and maymed namely at sutfine Legar" (26 October 1598 [GHL, ms. 9234/2]); in April of 1590, Wybird collected for an alms room. William Browne was a gunner who had "in her ma*jesties* service agaynst the span-yards in the barke of ffeversham and in that service was shott thorowgh his bodye and grievously wownded in sondrie places and by meanes of the same maymed for ever" (10 January 1590 [GHL, ms. 9234/2]). The wounds were in fact fatal; some six years later, when his widow collected at the parish for Browne's orphans, Harridance noted in the entry of that collection that Browne had served "in the late warre*es* in fflaunders . . . at the winning of steuwike skonce in frieseland [and] was there slayne" (22 August 1596 [GHL, ms. 9234/6]). John Williams was "a poore and maymed sowldier who in Respect of his former service in the Low Countries and Lose of his Legg and Right arme was graunted the R[oom] of one of her [the queen's] Almes men in the cathedrall church of worcester" (26 January 1590 [GHL, ms. 9234/2]). John Bennet was "a sayler beinge A devnshere man Who had both his legg*es* shott off in a ship withe Dr martin fforbusher his cossen at sea in the princes service" (31 January 1590 [GHL, ms. 9234/2]). John Davis was a mariner "who Lost the vse of his Legg*es* and was maymed in a ship of the Queenes Ma*jesties* named the Nonperilla agaynst the spainyard*es*"; military service was apparently a Davis family tradition, for Harridance recorded further that "this Ihon Davis was of Yonghall in Ireland who had his ffather also cruelly Mvrdered and slayne in her Ma*je*sties service in Ireland" (24 September 1592 [GHL, ms. 9234/2]). Barnabie Danbers, mariner, "lost both his legg*es* in her Ma*jesties* service" (9 June 1594 [GHL, ms. 9234/4]).

22. GHL, ms. 6836. Typical entries in the records of St. Helen Bishopsgate are a payment in October 1596 of 6s. 6d. for "one quarters releife for maymed soldiers dewe at maychaellmas last past," a three-quarters payment of 32s. 6d in 1598–99 for "maymed soldiers," and a payment of 43s. 4d. in 1600–1604. The parish of St. George Botolph contributed 19s. 6d. in 1602 for a three-quarter payment of tax for maimed soldiers (GHL, ms. 951/1).

23. Ann L. Mackenzie queries whether this act is a corrective to previous villainy by Danila. She concludes that it, as well as the Duke of Alva's sparing of Egmont's life, was merely a token gesture, making the two Spaniards only "marginally less villainous" ("A Study in Dramatic Contrasts: The Siege of Antwerp in *A Larum for London* and *El Saco de Amberes*," *Bulletin of Hispanic Studies* 59 [1982]: 283–300, esp. 295 and 296).

24. The dramatist perhaps intentionally developed a nationalistic level of propaganda with the factor and another character in the play, the English governor. During the council meeting with the governor of Antwerp just prior to the sack of the city, the English governor points out wisely that the Spaniards have given every indication of a desire to destroy Antwerp totally. The treatment of the English factor illustrates the psychopathology of the Spaniards. After surviving Danila's strappado, the unfortunate man is captured by the duke of Alva, who hoists him again. No sooner is he released (Alva lets the factor go because he has no more gold) than he is caught by Verdugo, another Spanish thug, who is not so merciful. Thwarted by the factor's empty pockets, Verdugo orders, "Hang him out-right" (l. 1285). In a play with many powerful stage moments, the cavalier manner in which an English factor was tortured and murdered must have carried a special terror for audiences at the Globe.

25. In this same time frame, the Admiral's men are playing the two-part play on the life of Sir John Oldcastle, the prologue of part one of which specifically and pointedly denies celebrating a "pampered glutton" (Peter Corbin and Douglas Sedge, eds., *The Oldcastle Controversy* [Manchester and New York: Manchester University Press, 1991], l. 6). This reference is of course to Sir John Falstaff, the "old lad of the castle" (I.ii.41–42) in Shakespeare's *1 Henry IV*. The Chamberlain's men themselves performed a play at their patron's London house that John Chamberlain's called "Oldcastle." The player who took the role of Falstaff (perhaps in both parts of the *Henry IV* plays) was presumably available for the part of the burgher in *A Larum*. If we knew more about patterns of casting, exploitation of thematic ironies, and intertextual gestures across roles and repertorial lines, the significance of such coincidences could be pursued further.

26. I refer to Hamlet's complaint to Rosencrantz and Gildernstern in which he refers to "this brave o'erhanging firmament, this majestical roof fretted with golden fire" (II.ii.300–301).

Dramatic Authorship and Publication in Early Modern England

DOUGLAS A. BROOKS

No name was available for the authors of these unattributable Rose plays until 1940, when Virginia Woolf realized that they were all written by Anon and that Anon could be described. He was the leading playwright in London from the establishment of the permanent theatre in 1576 until the emergence of printed plays which carried their author's names. . . . Anon was created by the audience. He was writing their language for them, reflecting their idiom, giving them plots which they gathered to see.

—Scott McMillin, *The Elizabethan Theatre &
The Book of Sir Thomas More*

THE subject of this essay is the authorial predicament of dramatic texts written, circulated, performed, and published in England between the early years of the sixteenth century and the closing of the public theaters in 1642. For the sake of my analysis, I divide this period into four artificial, but nevertheless meaningful phases of activity. The first phase covers roughly the first half century of printed drama, from 1511 to the incorporation of the Stationers' Company in 1557. The latter date marks an important development in the history of the London Book trade when, as Marcy North has noted, "booksellers, printers, and binders received royal authorization for their status as members of a complex urban industry."[1] Because the newly enhanced status of the book trade can be expected to have had an impact on the authorial status of printed texts, I look next at plays published in the two decades between the incorporation of the Stationers' Company and the opening of the first public theater in 1576. For the third phase, I consider the authorship of dramatic texts written and published from 1576 to 1642, the sixty-six years of theatrical activity that constitute the first era of the professional stage in London. Finally, since drama written before the closing of the theaters in 1642 continued to be printed afterward, I look briefly at the authorial status of plays published between 1642 and the first decade or so following the Restoration.

In her important study of the authorship of early modern printed nondramatic texts, North demonstrates "the continued usefulness of anonymity and name suppression," and she brings to light "some of the possibilities for the manipulation of these conventions within the printed book trade of the sixteenth and early seventeenth centuries."[2] My analysis of extant play texts and other early modern sources of evidence about the authorial status of playwrights, on the other hand, indicates that drama constituted something of a special case in the period, and that dramatic authorship behaved differently. In what follows, I suggest that beginning in the seventeenth century, two notions of dramatic authorship were readily available for appropriation: author-centered for playwrights who courted publication; anonymous for company-oriented playwrights who mainly channeled their talents into entertaining theater audiences. As the long reign of what Michel Foucault famously termed the "author function" began to consolidate its power in the first half of the seventeenth century, the former notion was destined to win the day, and I have offered an account of that complex victory elsewhere.[3] My primary concern in this essay is with the story of the losers, the story of those playwrights who toiled away without credit in the first era of an emergent English theater industry. Furthermore, I argue here that early modern drama coheres rather poorly with two widely held critical beliefs about authorship in the period. The first of these beliefs, that the emergence of the author figure was linked to transgression can be traced back to Foucault. According to a second bit of critical received wisdom, articulated initially by Elizabeth Eisenstein, the invention of the printing press gave birth to the modern author figure. Neither of these two scholarly narratives is particularly well suited to describing the authorship of early modern plays, partly because, as I hope to make clear, the theater as a site of textual production, was largely incompatible with various strategies of individualization that accompanied notions of the modern author into being.

Arguing that the history of the word *anonymous* "supports Foucault's contention that the author has a particular point of emergence as a cultural fiction," Jeffrey A. Masten observes:

> *Anonymous* does not take on its recognizably modern sense in English ("bearing no author's name; of unknown or unavowed authorship") until the late seventeenth century; earlier, around 1600, the word signifies "a person whose name is not given, or is unknown," but does not connect persons with texts. Beginning around 1676, however, anonymous begins to signal the author-ization of a text, the importance of someone, anyone, speaking.[4]

What interests me most about Masten's observation is the rather odd way he links the initial use of anonymous in 1676 "to signal the author-ization of a text" with "the importance of someone, anyone, speaking." To be fair, Masten is simultaneously alluding to a line written by Samuel Beckett—"'What does it matter who is speaking,' someone said, 'what does it matter who is speaking'"—that he quotes at the outset of his essay and to Foucault's essay, "What is an Author"[5] which also begins with the same Beckett quote. Nevertheless, in the specific case of dramatic authorship, it is precisely the fact that someone, anyone is speaking, that plays are primarily concerned with speech, which makes their "author-ization" so complex. In the particular case of English history, we can find some evidence of a conceptual strain or conflict between drama's generic status as a text in which people speak and its "author-ization" as far back as Bede's eighth-century treatise, *De arte metrica.* Asserting that "[t]here are three types of poem," Bede proceeds to categorize them as either "active or imitative," "narrative," or "common or mixed," and defines the first category as follows: "In the dramatic or active type the characters *(personae)* are presented speaking without any intervention by the poet, as is the case with tragedies and fables."[6] For Bede, what distinguishes drama as a genre from other types of writing is the presence of characters speaking and the absence of an author. This definition of dramatic poetry, probably the first to be penned in England, represents an early staging of the relation between actor and author,[7] and in his version of a critical scenario that can be traced back to Plato's *Republic,* the author gets cast in a relatively minor role as the character who does not intervene. More recent critics have concurred. Distinguishing between nondramatic and dramatic forms of writing, G. E. Bentley, for example, characterizes the latter in the following way: "In the world of theater . . . the impact of the author's creation is in good part determined by the playwright's cooperation with his colleagues in presentation. . . . The production of plays, in whatever era, is always a cooperative art."[8]

When religious drama in England came to prominence in the later Middle Ages, the necessarily cooperative nature of its production must have been obvious to all involved. Men from a wide range of professions came together to bring plays to performance, and, as Bentley notes, "[t]he plays they performed are nearly all anonymous."[9] Although Foucault's assertion that "the name seems always to be present, marking off the edges of the text"[10] fails to hold true for the authorship of medieval plays, we might expect to witness a major change in the situation as we move forward to consider drama written in early modern England—an era which, for most historians, began sometime between the importation of the first printing press from the Continent by William Caxton in 1476 and the Accession of Henry VII to the throne nine years later. First inspired by Jacob Burckhardt's time-tested statement that in the Renaissance "man became a spiritual *individual,* and recognized himself as such,"[11] then emboldened by polemical manifestoes on authorship from Roland Barthes, Jacques Derrida, and Foucault, numerous recent scholars have located the birth of the author in the early modern period.

Surely, as North observes, "[a] reverence for certain names, those of the Latin *auctores* for instance, existed long before the sixteenth century."[12] In the particular case of Chaucer, as Kevin Pask has recently argued, the poet's earlier transformation into a major vernacular author figure was enhanced by printers/publishers not long after the arrival of the first presses in England.[13] Initially, however, there was no comparable interest in the careers of English playwrights. As Peter W. M. Blayney observes, "[b]efore Elizabeth came to the throne in 1558, the drama had made virtually no impact on the English book trade."[14] And although Shakespeare would emerge from the largely collaborative conditions of the London playhouse to become the icon of individualized authorial production, much of the evidence of dramatic authorship in the period does not wholly support recent efforts to theorize the birth of the modern author figure.

Perhaps the most influential of these theories, that the emergence of the author figure was predominantly a juridical affair, rests on Foucault's oft-quoted claim that, "[t]ext, books, and discourses really began to have authors . . . to the extent that authors became subject to punishment, that is, to the extent that discourses could be transgressive."[15] It would be difficult to overestimate the impact of this statement, but the evidence is far less persuasive. Some seventy-five years after Caxton ushered the country into the age of mechanical reproduction, the first legislation to fret over the transgressive potential of drama in England was passed by the Privy Council under Edward VI. This 1551 bill, a royal proclamation seeking to expand existing acts against "Beggars and Vagabonds," included the following proviso—almost as an afterthought: "Nor that any common players, or other persons, upon like paines, do play thenglish tong, any manner Enterlude, Play or matter, without they have special licence to shew for the same, in writing under his majesties signe, or signed by vi. Of his highness privie counsaill."[16] Thus, the originary legislative attempt to license plays, like Bede's definition of drama, privileged the speaker and the spoken, even specifying a prohibition against the use of "thenglish tong." Two years later, within months of Mary I's accession, an edict "Prohibiting Religious Controversy, Unlicensed Plays, and Printing,"[17] brought the stage and the page within close legal proximity of each other. Aspiring to the "reformation of busy meddlers in matters of religion, and for redress of preachers, printers, and players,"[18] the law sought to enjoin the "playing of interludes and printing of false fond books, ballads, rhymes, and other lewd treatises in the English tongue."[19] A new monarch had come to power, and the country had been plunged back into Catholicism, but anxiety over English and indifference to authorship remained constant. Neither of these early legislative endeavors to monitor plays and players recognized the existence of playwrights. Two subsequent juridical efforts, a Special Commission of 24 December 1581, which established an official post for reviewing the content of plays prior to performance,[20] and a 22 June 1600

Privy Council order, which sought to redress "bothe the greatest abuses of the plaies and plaienge houses," and threatened "[c]ommittinge to prison the owners of Plaiehouses and players as shall disobey & resist these orders,"[21] similarly failed to acknowledge that plays had authors. More than anything else, this half century of legislative activity indicates that although dramatic "discourses could be transgressive"—to borrow Foucault's words—in the eyes of those officials who struggled to regulate them, none of these "discourses really began to have authors."

Arguably, the first drama in early modern England to benefit from the individualizing authorial potential of transgression was *Sejanus, his Fall,* a play attributed—in print—to Jonson two years after being performed. As Richard Dutton observes, "*Sejanus* would seem to be the first occasion on which any dramatist was made to answer *by the government* for his text—that is, treating a play-text as if it were a printed book. . . . Indeed, the possibility that the examination followed the *publication* of the play in 1605 rather than its 1603 *performance* should not lightly be discounted."[22] As I have argued elsewhere, Jonson was one of the first playwrights to embrace publication, largely because he was seeking an alternative market for plays that were received poorly in the theater.[23] *Sejanus,* which treats the complex political career of Aelius Sejanus in the court of Tiberius, was the dramatist's inaugural theatrical failure, and it was only performed once. Two years later, Jonson recalled the audience's response to the play in the published text's dedication, writing that it "suffered no less violence from our people here than the subject of it did from the rage of the people of Rome." In the play's preface, the first of such extant paratexts to be written by a dramatic author, Jonson informed prospective readers that, "this Booke, in all numbers, is not the same with that which was acted on the publike Stage, wherein a second Pen had good share" (¶3). Taken together, the dedication and the preface imply that the "second Pen" was to blame for the play's disastrous outing in the theater. In this light, Jonson's decision to litter each page of the published text with marginal citations of classical sources—in order, as he puts it, "to shew my integrity in the Story"—begins to make sense.[24] Jonson was desperate to demarcate the page from the stage. The printing house offered him an opportunity to erase the play's shared, communal origins in the theater and to transform it into an individualized, authorial scholarly work. If, as Dutton intimates, the authorities singled out Jonson after the play was published, then it seems likely that they were able to do so only because Jonson had already worked so hard to single himself out. In other words, Jonson may have been the first playwright "made to answer *by the government* for his text" because he taught the government which questions to ask. What the case of *Sejanus* makes clear is that in the specific context of early modern English drama, Foucault may have put the cart before the horse.

According to another critical narrative that has gained considerable currency since the advent of the computer age, the invention of the printing press gave birth to the modern author figure. Perhaps the earliest proponent of this position was Elizabeth Eisenstein, and her magisterial study, *The Printing Press as an Agent of Change,* stimulated tremendous scholarly interest in what came to be known as "print culture." Convinced—despite the title of her book—that the single most important attribute of the press was its power "to preserve and pass on what was known,[25] Eisenstein argued that this new technology generated a radically new desire: "the wish to see one's work in print (fixed forever with one's name in card files and anthologies)."[26] Suddenly, there was a new game in town, thanks to Gutenberg, and Eisenstein called it the "game of books and authors."[27] The introduction of printing to England, as noted earlier, did bolster Chaucer's reputation as an author, but he could not have dreamed of seeing his "work in print." Ancient and classical writers also reaped the authorial benefits of the press, but they too were dead. Contemporary writers, especially playwrights, were much less successful. Their lack of experience with and mistrust of print compelled them to develop a "language of justification and disavowal" in which, as Wendy Wall observes, they "rethought manuscript authority and printed literary wares through a wealth of tropes, forms, and textual apparatuses."[28] More often than not, such rethinking was expressed in terms of violation because the writers claimed a given text had been published *against* their wishes. In the context of early modern drama, the most notorious example of an authorial disavowal appears in a preface to the second edition of *Gorboduc* (1570), England's first vernacular tragedy. True to form, however, the play's two authors did not write the preface, and their names were not included on the play's title page. Instead, the text's printer, John Daye, took it upon himself to inform readers that the play was "never intended by the authors thereof to be published."[29] Similarly, there is no evidence that Shakespeare, who clearly won the "game of books and authors," ever submitted any of his plays for publication, and less than half of them, the 1623 Folio asserts, appeared as "diverse stolne, and surreptitious copies" (TLN 23) before his death. Indeed, as Samuel Johnson long ago noted, "[n]o other author gave up his works to fortune and time with so little care."[30]

If in fact authors of drama did wish to see their plays—along with their names—"fixed forever," as Eisenstein contends, many of them were forced to sit on the sidelines for nearly a century. The title page of the first two extant printed dramatic texts written in English, *1 & 2 Fulgens and Lucrece* (1512–1516?) indicates that they were "Compyled by mayster Henry Medwall. Late chapelayne to the ryght reverent father in god Johan Norton cardynall."[31] The attribution conjures up an image of the good chaplain busily compiling bits and pieces of classical source materials for the sake of patching together the script of "a godely interlude" that would breathe new life into the exploits of a Roman senator and his daughter. While this image of the author at work cannot be easily reconciled with that of the creative genius promoted by the "compilers" of Shakespeare's plays more than one hundred years later, Master Henry Medwall actually fared better in print than most of his successors. Twenty-seven different dramatic texts—many of which identify themselves as "interludes"—were preserved and passed on during the nearly half-century that separates the publication of *Fulgens and Lucrece* from the incorporation of the London Stationers' Company in 1557.[32] Nineteen of these texts (70 percent) were published anonymously—in the post-1676 meaning of the word. The authorial status of the other eight texts is provided below:

TABLE 1

Year	Title	Title-Page Attribution
1530	1 Nature	complyld by mayster Henry Medwall
1533	The Play of the Weather	made by John Heywood
1534	The Play of Love	made by John Heywood
1534	2 Nature	compyld by mayster Henry Medwall
1544	The Four P's	Made by John Heewood
1548	The Chief Promises of God	Compyled by Johan Bale
1548	The Temptation of Christ	Compyled by Johan Bale
1548	The Three Laws	Compyled by Johan Bale

As the information in Table 1 indicates, the names of only three playwrights (linked to 30 percent of extant dramas) were "fixed forever" by the press during this period, and only one of them, John Heywood or Heewood, was credited with the more authorial activity of making his plays. Print condemned the other two, Master Medwall and John Bale, to spend eternity embalmed as compilers.

Some tentative support for Eisenstein's claim, however, can be glimpsed after the incorporation of the Stationers' Company in 1557 when, as North observes, the London book trade "developed into a lively English enterprise characterized by the increased organization and regulation of industry members, the proliferation of book producers assuming various roles in the production process, the scrambling for new and marketable texts, and the development of publication conventions unique to print."[33] During the two decades between incorporation and the opening of the first public theater in 1576, printed drama seems to have come into its own. While only twenty-seven extant dramas were published in the previous half century, forty different extant dramas appeared in print over the next nineteen years. Remarkably, only thirteen (33%) of these texts were published anonymously. The authorial status of the other twenty-seven texts is provided below

TABLE 2

Year	Title	Title-Page Attribution
1576	Troad	The Sixt Tragedie of the most grave and prudent author Lucius, Anneus, Seneca
1560	Thyestes	The Seconde Tragedie of Seneca
1561	Hercules Furens	The first Tragedie of Lucius Anneus Seneca
1563	Oedipus	out of Seneca
1565	The Tragedie of Gorboduc	whereof three Actes were wrytten by Thomas Nortone, and the two laste by Thomas Sackvyle
1566	Agamemnon	The Eyght Tragedie of Seneca
1566	The Cruel Debtor	by Wager
1566	Medea	The seventh Tragedie of Seneca
1566	Octavia	The ninth Tragedie of Lucius Anneus Seneca
1567	The Interlude of Vice	by John Pikeryng
1568	Like Will to Like	Made by Vlpian Fulwel
1569	Patient Grissil	Compiled by John Phillip
1569	The Longer thou Livest . . .	Newly compiled by W. Wager
1569	The Disobedient Child	Compiled by Thomas Ingelend
1569	Cambises	By Thomas Preston
1570	Enough is as Good as a Feast	Compiled by W. Wager
1571	Damon and Pithias	Made by Maister Edwards
1573	Supposes	A Comedie written in the Italian Tongue by Ariosto, and Englished by George Cascoygne
1573	Jocasta	A Tragedie written in Greke by Euripides, translated and digested into Acte by George Gascoygne and Francis Kinwelmershe
1573	The Masque for Lord Montacute	Gascoignes devise of a maske
1573	Free-Will	A certayne Tragedie wrytten fyrst in Italian by F.A.B. . . . . translated into Englishe by Henry Cheeke
1574	The Interlude of Minds	Set forth by HN
1575	Appius and Virginia	By R.B
1575	The Entertainment in . . . Bristow	Devised and Published only by Thomas Churchyard

1575	Gammer Gurton's Needle	Made by Mr. S. Mr. of Art
1575	The Glass of Government	Done by George Gascoigne Esquier
1576	The Tide Tarrieth no Man	Compiled by George Wapull.

Such a high level of attribution would not be seen again until the seventeenth century. Although five of the title pages continued to rely on the word "compiled" to represent authorship, the attribution accorded the 1557 translation of *Troas*—"The Sixt Tragedie of the most grave and prudent author Lucius, Anneus, Seneca"—represents the first use of the word "author" in the history of extant printed dramatic texts. (The word "author" would not be used again on the title page of a play until the publication of Jonson's *Every Man Out of his Humour* in 1600). Indeed, with six plays linked to his name, Seneca did rather well in the first decade of Elizabeth's reign.[34] The other attribution here that merits some attention is the one featured on the title page of *Gorboduc* at the height of Seneca's published popularity. As I noted earlier, a second edition of this play appeared five years later without title-page attribution, its printer maintaining that it was "never intended by the authors thereof to be published." The first edition, however, includes a remarkably precise indication of its authorship: "whereof three Actes were wrytten by Thomas Nortone, and the two laste by Thomas Sackvyle." No other extant dramatic text published in early modern England would be so conscientiously ascribed, and it is likely that Seneca's status as an author was to blame.[35] The only other dramatist to make a comparable name for himself in the period was George Gascoigne, but the significant shift from anonymous to attributed texts, as well as the marked increase in the rate of publication, suggests that the business of writing for the stage was in transition. No doubt Seneca's powerful authorial presence helped to foster change, as did the accession of Elizabeth I, who attended a performance of *Gorboduc*. It is also conceivable that the establishment in 1557 of the Stationers' Company, an organization that controlled the London book trade, brought new rules to the game.

In spite of print's capacity "to preserve and pass on what was known," dramatic texts were treated abysmally once the era of the professional stage got underway. For the sixty-six year period that begins with the founding of The Theatre in 1576 by James Burbage and ends with the closing of the theaters in 1642 by Parliamentary decree, my analysis of the *Annals of English Drama* results in the titles of approximately 1,400 dramatic texts (plays, interludes, entertainments, and masques).[36] For the fifty-two year period beginning in 1590, Bentley puts the total number of known titles at 1,500,[37] and he speculates that, "there probably were written as many as 500 plays of which we know not even the titles."[38] William B. Long estimates that 3,000 manuscript playbooks were once in circulation at this time.[39] It should be amply clear from any one of these figures that the period witnessed an astonishing burst of creative activity—one that was rather ineptly captured and documented in print. Only 469 complete dramatic texts—written between 1576 and 1642—in 961 complete editions are extant,[40] and less than five percent of these texts survive only in manuscript.[41] Comparing the number of extant printed dramas with information provided in the *Annals* indicates that the press facilitated the survival of less than a third (32 percent) of those dramatic texts for which we have at least the titles. If we rely on Bentley's figure of 1,500 known titles, then only 30 percent of dramatic texts written in the period survived in print. Taking into consideration his speculation of an additional 500 lost titles reduces the survival rate to a dismal 22 percent. Long's estimate of 3,000 playbooks translates into a survival rate of 16 percent.

The impact of print on dramatic authorship is—tentatively—more heartening. My examination of title pages (or transcriptions of title pages) of extant printed dramatic texts indicates that 367 (82 percent) of them are attributed in full or abbreviated form to one or more authors, and that slightly less than 20 percent were published anonymously. These figures might be cause for celebration in the Eisenstein camp, but juxtaposing them with the authorship of known titles listed in the *Annals* is somewhat sobering. While the variety of dramatic texts and performance sites covered by the *Annals* precludes it from being the perfect source for determining shifts in the status of dramatic authorship, the following comparison of attribution levels for the six full decades of the London professional stage is suggestive:

TABLE 3

	1580–89	1590–99	1600–09	1610–19	1620–29	1630–39
No. of Titles:	100	260	300	220	230	260
% Attributed:	58	54	75	74	81	89

As the figures in Table 3 indicate, roughly half of all known titles written and/or performed in the first two decades of the professional theater are anonymous. After 1600 the authorship of known titles begins to correspond with that of extant printed dramatic texts, and by the final decade the attribution rate of known titles actually surpasses that of extant printed drama. Singling out this period as the "most vigorous decade for publication of plays," James P. Saeger and Christopher J. Fassler observe that "more than twenty-five plays were printed on average in any given year of this decade and more than ten of them were new plays."[42] And according to Blayney's analysis, 45 percent of all extant dramas were published during the years 1623–1642.[43] Clearly, the longer playhouses, printing houses, and playwrights played the game of books and authors, the better they got at it. Nevertheless, one last qualification is in order. If we juxtapose the abysmal survival rate of extant printed dramatic texts (roughly 30 percent) with the high attribution rate of those same texts (roughly 80 percent), and factor in progressively rising rates of both publication and attribution, then at least one important thing about drama in this sixty-six year period comes into view. Anonymous authorship may have been appropriate for the "cooperative art" of the theater in England, but beginning one century after the introduction of the press, it significantly increased the vulnerability of dramatic texts. Indeed, the text of a given play was much more likely to survive if it were attributed, especially, as I have argued elsewhere, if it were attributed to a single author.[44] Playing on the etymology of the word "text," from the Latin *texere,* "to weave,"[45] we can say that, what had suited the stage, did not suit the page. Eventually, as the publication of Jonson's *Sejanus* indicates, what had not suited the stage, would suit the page quite well.[46] In the specific case of printed drama, then, it seems that Eisenstein, like Foucault, put the cart before the horse. The invention of the press may have generated the desire to see one's work fixed forever, but relatively few dramatic texts survived. The attribution of a dramatic text to an author, however, significantly enhanced its chances of survival. Thus the fate of many early dramatic texts may have been decided by archivists and collectors who gathered their future treasures according to the whims of an increasingly tyrannical author function. When, in 1613, Sir Thomas Bodley famously wrote to his head librarian, Thomas James, instructing him to exclude "almanacs, plays, and proclamations" from the collection of books he was amassing, he succinctly captured the vulnerability of printed drama by grouping it with other traditionally anonymous texts. Ten years later, Bodley must have experienced a change of heart, because records kept by his librarian indicate the purchase of the 1623 Shakespeare Folio. A large and expensive calfskin-bound folio celebrating the work of a single author after his death was one thing, a cheap, ineptly printed quarto text patched together, perhaps, by two or three jobbing dramatists at the playhouse was quite another. William Prynne, a contemporary of Bodley's, indignantly observed that, "[s]ome Play books since I first undertook this subject, are growne from *Quarto* into *Folio,* which yet beare so good a price and sale, that I cannot with griefe relate it, they are now (e) new-printed in farre better paper than most Octavo or Quarto *Bibles,* which hardly finde vent as they."[47] Such responses to the materiality of texts in the first age of mechanical reproduction make an important point: much of what we know about early modern dramatic authorship has been shaped by changing notions of authorship itself, inasmuch as those notions have largely determined the survival of dramatic texts. One glimmer of hope just beyond this hermeneutic circle would appear to be evidence of authorship and publication in the period gathered by the Stationers' Company. Two reasons for optimism present themselves. First, because the institution was dedicated to the publishing industry, it should have been aware of evolving consumer attitudes toward print. Second, with the exception of a five year gap from 22 July 1571 to 17 July 1576, handwritten Company records have been remarkably well preserved—in spite of the fact that no one began to edit and publish them until the end of the nineteenth century. For these reasons, I want to shift our attention from the evidence of dramatic authorship that can be gathered from title pages of extant printed dramas, to that which comes to us from Stationers' Company records.

The official incorporation of the London Stationers' Company on 4 May 1557, the day its charter was approved, represents a major watershed in the history of textual production.[48] Bringing together booksellers, stationers, printers, binders, and other producers, the company rapidly became the locus of the book trade in early modern England. Moreover, as Robin Myers and Michael Harris note, "the Company was from the first engaged with issues of control," and its main tasks included "overseeing apprenticeship, limiting the number of master printers, and restricting the production and sale of the printed materials registered in its Entry Books."[49] The basic rules for governing the licensing of books had already been established in 1538 by Henry VIII, though, as Blayney observes, "Henry's main concern had been with imported books, so he had elected himself sole licenser for importation."[50] Motivated by fear of a nascent public sphere, subsequent monarchs and their councils sporadically attempted to check the dissemination of printed texts, but in the second half of the sixteenth century the Stationers' Company emerged as England's primary institution for monitoring and regulating publication.[51] In this sense, 1557 marks the point at which the grounds of the two critical paradigms we have been examining, the juridical and the material, essentially converged. In fact, as D. F. McKenzie observes, the incorporation of the Company had been set in motion a decade earlier by a proclamation of 8 July 1546 which decreed "that every book should bear the author's and the printer's name, and exact date of printing, and that the printer should present a copy to the mayor of his town, before he began general distribution."[52] Beyond marveling at these mayors' good fortune, it seems reasonable to presuppose that the Stationers' Company helped to nurse the modern author figure from fragile infancy to robust adolescence.

Obviously, in the long run the company failed to adhere to its embryonic mandate that every book should bear its author's name, or there would be no extant anonymous texts from the period. But one of the things the company did begin to do with some regularity in 1557 is maintain record books which have come down to us more or less complete as Registers A, B, C, D, E, F, and G. As McKenzie playfully notes, referring to the events of that year, "in one sense the Company had literally turned over a new leaf when it received its Charter: it made several new books for its records."[53] Within these new books, a designated clerk recorded all manner of legal, financial, and— even—moral concerns touching the production, publication, sale, and circulation of printed texts ranging from one-page broadsheets to oversized folio Bibles. For our limited purposes here, however, the most important things these clerks recorded were entries indicating that a given stationer (printer/publisher—these categories of activity were not clearly distinct yet) was the acknowledged owner of the text or texts he intended to print/publish.[54] To identify these entries as a protoform of copyright only confuses the issue, and even the modern notion of licensing—though many entries include a form of the word—isn't quite right.[55] Rather an entry in the Stationers' Register simply meant that John (or occasionally Jane) Doe had voluntarily approached the company about printing/publishing a text, then paid a fee for being recognized as that text's owner. The existence of such an entry could be used at a later date to prevent another stationer from printing/publishing the same text. As Blayney puts it, "[a]n entry was an insurance policy."[56]

The first Stationers' Register entry solely concerned with the publication of a dramatic text appears in October/November of 1557, and reads as follows:

> To henry Sutton to prynte an enterlude upon the history of Iacobe and Esawe out of the xxvij chapeter of the fyrste boke of moyses Called genyses and for his lycense he geveth to the howse   iiij····d.[57]

The basic form of this entry, which would be replicated in nearly all future entries, reflects the nature of the company's concerns. The name of the stationer, Henry Sutton, appears first, some identification of the text to be published appears second, and the amount of the fee Sutton was required to pay appears last. In many entries, the second section, which was often quite fluid, could record—in the case of drama—details about a text's genre ("a comedie called . . ."), its performance ("plaied before her maiestie by the Children of Paules"), and its authorship. There is no reason, however, to believe that the clerks who maintained the registers often troubled themselves about whether or not a stationer was misrepresenting the text's origins. Thus, an entry of 2 May 1608 entitles one "mr Pavyer" to profit from the dissemination of "A booke Called a yorkshire Tragedy written by Wylliam Shakespere," though few Shakespeare scholars today believe he wrote the play.

The clerk who wrote the entry for the dramatic text we began with did not include the name of the writer who compiled the "enterlude upon the history of Iacobe and Esawe" from the Bible. That he carefully copied the drama's source and the name of the source's alleged author does not reflect a concern with authorship, but rather an effort merely to record the title of the work under which it was to be published. The title page of the second edition—the first is not extant—reads: "A newe merry and wittie Comedie or Enterlude, newly imprinted, treating upon the Historie of Iacob and Esau, taken out of the xxvij. Chap. Of the first booke of Moses." And while the name of the merry wit responsible for this "Comedie or Enterlude" does not appear, the remainder of the title page is dedicated to listing "The partes and names of the Players who are to be Hebrews and so should be apparailed with attire."

What was good for the early modern publishing industry may not have been good for authorship, and an examination of register entries for dramatic texts suggests that in the game of books and authors stationers started out cheering for their team. For the period between the incorporation of the Stationers' Company in 1557 and the opening of the first public theater two decades later, there are forty-one separate entries concerned with dramatic publication. Thirty-three (81 percent) of these entries are anonymous in the sense that they make no reference to the authorship of the text or texts that are to be published. Of the eight entries that do record the name of an author, four of them belong to Seneca, whose name appears each time as part of the play's title. A February 1566 entry for *Agamemnon,* for example, entitles Thomas Colwell to print "a boke intituled the eighte Tragide of Senyca." Only four (10 percent) of the entries mention the names of living authors. Correlating this information with evidence from extant dramatic texts published in the same period is complicated by two facts: some register entries entitled a stationer to publish more than one text; and, as I noted earlier, the company's records are missing for the years 1571–76. Moreover, despite the company's efforts to monitor the London book trade, roughly one-third of all books published in the period found their way to the bookshop without being entered into the Register.[58] Still, if we recall that forty different extant dramas appeared in print during the same period, and that only thirteen (33 percent) of these texts were published anonymously, we are left with a rather marked disparity between our two sources of data. In the two decades prior to the opening of the first public theater, printers/publishers of drama favored authorship, the organization that sought to regulate them was largely indifferent to it. The only thing the two groups could really agree on was Seneca. If, as Marshal McLuhan asserts, "the oral tradition in Western literature is transmitted by the Senecan vogue, and was gradually obliterated by the printed page,"[59] then we seem to be listening here to that author's swan song. An analysis of Stationers' Register entries concerning dramatic publications in the six full decades of the professional stage follows:

TABLE 4

Year	Total Entries	Anonymous Entries	Attributed Entries
1580–89	9	5 (57%)	4 43%) (3 classical)
1590–99	63	57 (91%)	6 (9%) (1 classical)
1600–09	120	107 (89%)	13 (11%) (0 classical)
1610–19	57	44 (77%)	13 (23%) (0 classical)
1620–29	43	28 (65%)	15 (35%) (0 classical)
1630–39	153	62 (41%)	91 (59%) (1 classical)

One thing should be immediately obvious from a glance at Table 4: beginning in 1590, publishers of dramatic texts significantly augmented the workload of clerks who maintained the Register, especially during the third and sixth decades, when 273 separate entries were written. And although the total number of entries (445) is remarkably close to the total number of extant printed dramas (450) written in the same period, it would be a mistake to draw a connection between these two figures, as several of the entries refer either to more than one text or to later editions of texts previously entered. Far more compelling, however, is what the information in Table 4 indicates about the Company's attitude toward dramatic authorship. In the first decade, when classical authors dominate, roughly half of the entries record the name of an author—though the number of entries is too small to be significant. During the second decade, when the public theaters became increasingly popular and company playwrights began to churn out plays, publishers quickly responded by attempting to create a market for printed drama. Less than ten percent of the entries that document this surge in activity acknowledge authorship. Remarkably, the number of entries written during the next decade doubles, but concern with authorship remains nearly unchanged. Of the authors' names that get recorded in the thirteen attributed entries, only the following three appear more than once: Jonson (four); Shakespeare (three); George Chapman (two). Jonson's struggle to transform himself through publication from a playwright into an author seems to have been chronicled by the company's clerks, because only Seneca appeared as frequently.

One reason for the Company's lack of interest in dramatic authors during these two decades can perhaps be gleaned from records Philip Henslowe kept during eighteen years (1592–1609) of his involvement with the Rose Theatre—the playhouse where, according to Woolf, the leading playwright known as Anon worked. When we consult *Henslowe's Diary,* which Bentley calls "far and away the most detailed record of authorship that has come down to us,"[60] we find the titles of 282 different plays, only forty of which are extant.[61] In fact, for 170 of these plays, Henslowe's records are our only source of information. Of the 282 plays mentioned by Henslowe, two-thirds of them, as Bentley notes, "are the work of more than one man."[62] It would be misleading to draw a direct correlation between Henslowe's records and those kept by the Stationers' Company, because some of these plays did not get published till several years after they were written, and most did not survive the perilous journey from playhouse to printing house. Nevertheless, the high level of multiple authorship documented by Henslowe indicates that playwriting in this period, like the theater itself, was largely a "cooperative art"—an art which may not have been easily rendered in the limited authorial dialect spoken by London Stationers.[63] Indeed, not one of the nineteen attributed entries written in the period 1590–1609 ascribes a dramatic text to more than one author, and only two of the twenty-eight attributed entries written in the next twenty years credit Francis Beaumont and John Fletcher with the joint authorship of a play.

Returning to the information in Table 4, we find that in the next two decades (1610–29) the number of attributed entries remains nearly constant (thirteen and fifteen respectively), but the total number of entries falls by a half and almost two-thirds, respectively. Only during the last full decade of the professional stage, when the publication of dramatic texts soars, does the number of attributed entries (ninety-one) surpass the number of anonymous entries (sixty-two). This abrupt increase in the recording of authors' names by the Stationer's Company suggests that a century and a half after England entered the age of print, the authorship of dramatic texts had become a factor in the regulation of their publication. And the newly heightened status of the dramatic author would be enhanced during the next two decades, despite the fact that the closing of the theaters in 1642 forced professional playwrights into an eighteen-year retirement. For the period beginning in 1640 and ending with the accession of Charles II in 1660, there are 128 entries concerned with dramatic publication. Ninety-four of these entries (74 percent) record details of a given text's authorship, and many of them do so with considerable care. Moreover, several of the thirty-four anonymous entries pertain to plays or collections of plays that had already been entered repeatedly, so it may have been unnecessary to include attribution. During these two decades, the phrase, "written by," is employed with great frequency, and one entry of 23 November 1650 records that a play titled "the distracted State" was "written in the yeere 1641 by John Tatham." I am tempted to think the clerk who penned this entry was using the play's year of authorship to comment on the playwright's prescience. Another entry of 27 September 1658 records that "a booke called The Shephards Paradice" was "written by a Person of Honour." In a A true, perfect, and Exact Catalogue, published three years later, a printer/publisher named Francis Kirkman informed readers "that if you please to repair to my Shop, I shall furnish you with all the Plays ever yet printed. I have 700 several Plays, and most of them several times over." He concluded his sales pitch by assuring them that the plays he had for sale were "written by worthy Authors" (A2r).

As the first great era of the professional theater in early modern England came to an end, dramatic authors began to achieve something like recognition from the institution that helped to regulate printers/publishers' efforts to translate plays from the stage to the page. As with all translations, something would get irrevocably lost, something would be gained. Once the "cooperative art" of the theater had been utterly displaced by the disorder of civil war, authorship became integral to the regulation of published dramatic texts, and even the largely shared activity of writing for the stage would get captured in print. Thus, Humphrey Mosley, who published the first collection of plays dedicated to collaborative authorship—the 1647 Beaumont and Fletcher Folio—begins his preface to that volume with an analogy to the theater, only to remind his readers that the theater no longer exists:

> As after th' *Epilogue* there comes some one
> To tell *Spectators* what shall next be shown;
> So here, am I; but though I've toyld and vext,
> Cannot devise what to present ye next;
> For, since ye saw no *Playes* this Cloudy weather
> Here we have brought Ye our whole Stock together
>
> (G2r)

Mosley hopes that readers' memories of the good ol' days of the London stage will ensure the success of this large, expensive, and risky publishing venture, but he doesn't leave the book's fate to nostalgia alone. As Julie Stone Peters observes, "[t]o justify the cost of his folio, Mosley must protest (as he does a little too insistently, again and again), that his stagewriters are 'poets,' 'authors,' the creators of 'Dramaticall Workes,' not mere makers of plays."[64] In short, Mosley decides to locate his enterprise within an emergent practice of promoting dramatic authorship for which there were only a few precedents. Reaching beyond what he called "the loathed stage," Jonson had begun working with printers like Walter Burre and William Stansby in the first decade of the seventeenth century to transform himself from a playwright into an author. Initially, as we saw, this transformation entailed the eradication of "a second Pen" and the introduction of scholarly annotations. Eventually, such efforts at authorial self-fashioning culminated in the 1616 publication of the *Workes of Beniamin Jonson,* the first folio collection of contemporary plays printed in English history. Bentley best captures the import of this watershed event when he remarks of Jonson's *Workes,* "probably no other publication before the Restoration did so much to raise the contemporary existence of the generally belittled form of plays."[65] Jonson was frequently ridiculed in his day for making the semantic transition from play to work, but future playwrights like Beaumont and Fletcher and their publishers would enjoy the benefits. The playwright who benefited the most, however, was Shakespeare. Having died in 1616, the year Jonson became the first English playwright to publish his own canon, Shakespeare would be resurrected seven years later. Like many playwrights who wrote for the professional stage during the first two decades of its existence, Shakespeare had had an early run-in with "Anonymos." The printed title pages of the following "Shakespeare" plays provided no indication of authorship: *Titus Andronicus, The First Part of the Contention betwixt the two famous Houses of York and Lancaster, The True Tragedy of Richard Duke of York, Romeo and Juliet, Richard III, 1 Henry IV,* and *Henry V.* But in 1623, Shakespeare's named authorship would be fixed for all time by the Folio collection that presented us with thirty-seven plays "Published according to the True Originall Copies."

But there's another author of drama whose story I want to end with, one who wrote many more plays than Jonson, Shakespeare, and Beaumont and Fletcher combined. Indeed, as Scott McMillin observes, "he was the leading playwright in London from the establishment of the permanent theatre in 1576 until the emergence of printed plays which carried their author's names." Because he lacked what Joseph Loewenstein, referring to Jonson, calls a "bibliographic ego,"[66] he was much more comfortable in the world of the playhouse than that of the printing house. Consequently, few of his plays have survived. McMillin, who has studied one of his unpublished manuscript plays carefully, reports that he "was created by the audience," and that he devoted himself to "writing their language for them, reflecting their idiom, giving them plots which they gathered to see." But as early modern drama embarked on its slow migration from the theater to the archive, his popularity waned. When Parliament padlocked the theaters in 1642, he nearly disappeared. Two hundred years after the advent of print, and one hundred years after he entered the profession of playwriting, his name, oddly enough, began "to signal the author-ization of a text."

Notes

I'm very grateful to James L. Harner for reading an early draft of this essay and making a number of helpful suggestions.

1. Marcy North, "Ignoto in the Age of Print: The Manipulation of Anonymity in Early Modern England," *Studies in Philology* 91 (1994): 390–416; here cited from 390.

2. North, "Ignoto," 391.

3. See my *From Playhouse to Printing House: Drama and Authorship in Early Modern England,* (Cambridge: Cambridge University Press, 2000).

4. Jeffrey A. Masten, "Beaumont and/or Fletcher: Collaboration and the Interpretation of Renaissance Drama," in *The Construction of Authorship: Textual Appropriation in Law and Literature,* eds. Martha Woodmansee and Peter Jaszi (Durham, NC: Duke University Press, 1994), 361–82; here cited from p. 361.

5. Michel Foucault, "What is an Author?" trans. Catherine Porter in *The Foucault Reader,* ed. Paul Rabinow (New York: Pantheon Books, 1984), 101–20.

6. Quoted in A. J. Minnis, *Medieval Theory of Authorship: Scholastic Literary Attitudes in the Later Middle Ages,* Second Edition (Philadelphia: University of Pennsylvania Press, 1988), 57.

7. For an important recent discussion of the evolving relationship between actor and author, see Julie Stone Peters, *Dramatic Impressions: Theatre and Print, Text and Performance in Europe 1480–1880* (Oxford: Oxford University Press, 2000).

8. G. E. Bentley, *The Profession of Dramatist and Player in Shakespeare's Time, 1590–1642* (Princeton: Princeton University Press, 1986), 8.

9. Bentley, *Profession,* 3.

10. Foucault, "What," 107.

11. Jacob Burckhardt, *The Civilization of the Renaissance in Italy,* trans. S. G. C. Middlemore (New York: Penguin Books, 1990), 98 (original italics).

12. North, "Ignoto," 392.

13. See Kevin Pask, *The Emergence of the English Author: Scripting the Life of the Poet in Early Modern England* (Cambridge: Cambridge University Press, 1996), especially pp. 14–18.

14. Peter W. M. Blayney, "The Publication of Playbooks," in *A New History of Early English Drama,* eds. John D. Cox and David Scott Kastan (New York: Columbia University Press, 1997), 383–422.

15. Foucault, "What," 103.

16. Quoted in Richard Dutton, *Mastering the Revels: The Regulation and Censorship of English Renaissance Drama* (Iowa City: University of Iowa Press, 1991), 19. Dutton identifies this proclamation as "the first definite attempt to institute a formal system of licensing of materials to be performed, which implicitly also meant censorship" (19).

17. Proclamation 390. "Offering Freedom of Conscience; Prohibiting Religious Controversy, Unlicensed Plays, and Printing," *Tudor Royal Proclamations Vol. II. The Later Tudors (1553–1587),* eds. Paul L. Hughes and James F. Larkin (New Haven: Yale University Press, 1969), 5.

18. Hughes and Larkin, *Tudor,* 5.

19. Hughes and Larkin, *Tudor,* 6.

20. Included as Appendix D ("Documents of Control) in E. K. Chambers, *The Elizabethan Stage Vol. IV* (Oxford: Clarendon Press, 1923), 286.

21. Included as Appendix D in Chambers, *Elizabethan,* 330, 331.

22. Dutton, *Mastering,* 164 (original italics).

23. Brooks, *From,* 40–53. See also Zachary Lesser's excellent essay, "Walter Burre's Knight of the Burning Pestle," *ELR* 34 (1999): 335–61.

24. On Jonson's use of scholarly annotations, see Evelyn Tribble, "Genius on the Rack: Authorities and the Margins in Ben Jonson's Glossed Works," *Exemplaria IV* (1992): 317–63.

25. Elizabeth Eisenstein, *Print Culture and Enlightenment Thought: The Sixth Hanes Lecture Presented by the Hanes Foundation for the Study of the Origin and Development of the Book,* (Chapel Hill, NC: Hanes Foundation, 1986), 6. The most recent critique of Eisenstein's notion of the fixity of print is offered in Adrian Johns' study, *The Nature of the Book: Print and Knowledge in the Making* (Chicago: University of Chicago Press, 1998), especially pp. 28–40.

26. *The Printing Press as an Agent of Change: Communications and Cultural Transformations in Early Modern Europe Volumes I and II* (Cambridge: Cambridge University Press, 1979), 121.

27. Eisenstein, *Printing,* 121.

28. Wendy Wall, *The Imprint of Gender: Authorship and Publication in the English Renaissance.* (Ithaca: Cornell University Press, 1993), 21. On "disavowing authorial

prefaces," see Gerard Genette, *Paratexts: Thresholds of Interpretation,* trans. Jane E. Lewin (Cambridge: Cambridge University Press, 1997), 280–84.

29. For a fuller discussion of *Gorboduc's* authorship and publication history, see Brooks, *From,* 23–43. On Daye's preface, see Wall, *Imprint,* 182–84.

30. *Samuel Johnson on Shakespeare,* ed. H. R. Woudhuysen (London: Penguin Books, 1989), 114.

31. Transcribed in Greg, *Bibliography,* I, 81.

32. All figures in this section are based on my analysis of transcriptions of extant title pages included in Greg, *Bibliography,* 81–103. For an excellent recent discussion of drama and publication in the first half of the sixteenth century, see Greg Walker, *The Politics of Performance in Early Renaissance Drama* (Cambridge: Cambridge University Press, 1998), 6–50.

33. North, "Ignoto," 390.

34. On Seneca's popularity in this period, see E. M. Spearing, *The Elizabethan Translations of Seneca's Tragedies* (Cambridge: W. Hefer & Sons LTD, 1912). The best recent study of English Senecanism is Gordon Braden, *Renaissance Tragedy and the Senecan Tradition: Anger's Privilege* (New Haven: Yale University Press, 1985).

35. Norton and Sackville's play constituted England's first effort to produce its own tragic tradition, and as John Gassner observes, "[e]arly Tudor tragedy followed classical models . . . In *Gorboduc,* the five-act dramatic form, the choruses, and the reports of off-stage action by a Nuntius, or Messenger, as well as the general theme of revenge, are Senecan features." *Medieval and Tudor Drama* (New York: Applause Theatre Book Publishers, 1987), 403.

36. *Annals of English Drama,* Third Edition, ed. Alfred Harbage, S. Schoenbaum, and Sylvia Wagonheim (London: Routledge, 1989).

37. Bentley, *Profession,* 199.

38. Bentley, *Profession,* 16.

39. William B. Long, "'Precious Few': English Manuscript Playbooks," in *A Companion to Shakespeare,* ed. David Scott Kastan (Oxford: Blackwell Publishers Inc., 1999), 414–33; here cited from 414.

40. James P. Saeger and Christopher J. Fassler, "The London Professional Theater, 1576–1642: A Catalogue and Analysis of the Extant Printed Plays," *Research Opportunities in Renaissance Drama* 34 (1995): 63–109; here cited from 67. This number refers only to plays performed on the London stage. If we include masques, entertainments, closet dramas, and university plays, the number of extant dramatic texts rises to 560. See Blayney, "Publication," 384.

41. For two recent essays on dramatic manuscripts, see Long, "'Precious,'" in *A Companion to Shakespeare,* Kastan, 414–33; and Paul Werstine, "Plays in Manuscript," in *New History of Early English Drama,* Cox and Kastan, 481–98.

42. Saeger and Fassler, "London," 67.

43. Blayney, "Publication," 384.

44. See Brooks, *From,* 140–88.

45. The term's etymology, as McKenzie observes, refers "not to any specific material as such, but to its woven state, the web or texture of the materials." *Bibliography and the Sociology of Texts* (London: The British Library, 1985), 5.

46. In fact, *Sejanus* did well after it was put into print by George Eld sometime

after August of 1605. References to *Sejanus* recorded in Jonson's lifetime indicate that the play was very highly regarded, and it received considerable praise from many of his contemporaries such as R. Goodwin, Lucius Carey, James Howell, John Taylor, and Owen Felltham, all of whom contributed commendatory verses to the printed edition. In the seventeenth century, dramatists frequently paid Jonson the compliment of borrowing from the play, and during the Restoration period, Dryden praised him for choosing to relate, rather than represent, the death of Sejanus.

47. For two excellent recent studies of early modern attitudes toward printed drama, see Heidi Brayman Hackel, "'Rowme' of its Own: Printed Drama in Early Libraries," in *A New History of Early English Drama,* eds. Cox and Kastan, 113–32; and "The 'Great Variety' of Readers and Early Modern Reading Practices," in *A Companion to Shakespeare,* ed. David Scott Kastan (Oxford: Blackwell Publishers Inc., 1999), 139–57.

48. For details of the company's charter, see Cyprian Blagden, *The Stationers' Company: A History, 1403–1959* (Stanford: Stanford University Press, 1960), 37–38.

49. *The Stationers' Company and the Book Trade 1550–1990,* eds. Robin Myers and Michael Harris (New Castle: Oak Knoll Press, 1997), vii.

50. Blayney, "William Cecil and the Stationers," in Myers and Harris, *Stationers,* 11–34; here cited from 11.

51. For an excellent recent study that examines the Company's role in regulating publication, see Cyndia Susan Clegg, *Press Censorship in Elizabethan England* (Cambridge: Cambridge University Press, 1997).

52. D. F. McKenzie, "Stationers' Company Liber A: An Apologia," in Myers and Harris, *Stationers',* 35–59; here cited from 39.

53. McKenzie, "Stationers," 42.

54. For a lucid discussion of the distinctions between printers and publishers in the period, see Blayney, "Publication," 389–92.

55. For a lucid discussion of the distinctions between "authority," "licensing," and "entrance" in the period, see Blayney, "Publication," 396–405.

56. Blayney, "Publication," 404.

57. The only previous entry concerns the publication of two interludes along with four treatises. My analysis in this section is based on Greg's transcriptions of drama-related Stationers' Register Entries included in *Bibliography,* vol. I, pp. 1–78.

58. Blayney, "Publication," 400.

59. *The Gutenberg Galaxy* (Toronto: University of Toronto Press, 1962), 28.

60. Bentley, *Profession,* 199.

61. Bentley, *Profession,* 15.

62. Bentley, *Profession,* 199.

63. For astute recent studies of collaborative dramatic authorship, see Masten, "Playwriting: Authorship and Collaboration," in *A New History of Early English Drama,* eds. Cox and Kastan, 357–82; and *Textual Intercourse: Collaboration, Authorship, and Sexualities in Renaissance Drama* (Cambridge: Cambridge University Press, 1997).

64. Peters, *Dramatic,* 273.

65. Bentley, *Profession,* 55–56.

66. Loewenstein, "The Script in the Marketplace" *Representations* 12 (1985): 101–14: here cited from 101.

Printing Conventions and
the Early Modern Play

PAUL J. VOSS

MOST books printed in early modern England followed recognizable trade conventions; these conventions, in turn, helped to direct the reading experience and to control possible meanings. Discrete printed plays, not including masques, court entertainments, civic pageants, or collections of plays, are no exception. A survey of printed plays, in fact, displays both the power of printing conventions to shape reading habits and the adaptability of the printing press to reflect changes in those very practices. In other words, printing conventions actually helped create, define, and transform the *literary* status of the early modern printed play.[1] Although the fit between printing activity and audience response is never neat or fixed for all times, printed texts bear witness to concerted trade practices and likely audience response.

Considering plays as printed documents with somewhat predictable conventions, regardless of relative dramatic unity or textual quality, affords an interesting perspective on possible audience reception and the function of the printed play in a burgeoning literary culture.[2] Although literary scholars continue to cite the 1616 publication of Ben Jonson's *Workes* as the defining moment for printed plays, the evidence suggests rather a complex and admittedly curious negotiation among printers, publishers, and authors years prior.[3] Three significant developments, all perhaps unrelated, register the transition from the ephemeral to the literary well before 1616. To appreciate fully this evolution, one must consider the importance of both bibliographical and linguistic evidence—both the subtle printing conventions and the more conspicuous paratextual matter. By examining such evidence, I hope to show that early in the reign of Elizabeth I, printed quarto plays were promoted initially as aids to staging a drama and later as records of performance.[4] By the end of the sixteenth century, as both the performed and printed play became far more common, it seems likely that plays started to be *read* as literature. Finally, during the reign of James I, printed plays started to be *treated* as literature.

II

Printed plays should not be regarded as a microcosm of the early modern printing universe. Peter Blayney analyzes the printing of plays between the years 1583 and 1642 and concludes, in fact, that "printed plays never accounted for a very significant fraction of the trade in English books."[5] Moreover, early modern readers hardly considered printed plays as artifacts worth preserving: purchasers rarely saved the quarto play as a discrete publication and quarto plays survive in relatively few copies. T. A. Birrell calls the individual Renaissance play a "vulnerable, throwaway quarto . . . an ephemeral pamphlet or chapbook."[6] But while not prized as a valuable possession like many other books, the printed play, most likely, enjoyed a diverse readership and large sales.[7] The nearly six hundred different plays printed in England before 1642 testify to their popularity among certain groups of people. On this basis alone, printed plays stand as important bibliographical documents.

This fluid status of the printed play—popular yet not well respected or highly treasured—mirrors the standing of plays as evolving literary forms. During this period, printed plays changed from *texts* largely designed to assist individuals staging a given play to *works* meant to be read and enjoyed as literature. Although the untidiness of the evidence precludes absolute conclusions about all printed plays and visible exceptions urge caution in arriving at definitive assessments, the development of the printed play as a form can be charted with some reliability from 1560–1640. The marks on the paper and the words on the page tell a story and provide evidence of consistent practices. Interpretive bibliography allows us to retell those stories about printing habits observed four centuries ago. Our task remains to present persuasive accounts of those habits, even if the evidence appears haphazard and fragmentary.

Material bibliographers prefer to cite actual trade conventions as evidence of readership and reception. Jerome McGann, for example, considers any text "as a laced network of linguistic and bibliographic codes."[8] McGann argues for the importance of considering "such matters as ink, typeface, paper, and various other phenomena which are crucial to the understanding of textuality."[9] The "bibliographic codes," as McGann refers to them, serve an important function in the history of the printed play.[10] While few precise details concerning specific reading practices or target audience survive, paper size and print type stand as two possible indications of readership. Some generalizations about paper size and type can be summarized briefly. Most printers, prior to 1616 (and well into the eighteenth century), set individual plays in quarto.[11] Short quartos were a common format for ephemeral publications (including plays) and pamphlets. Early modern printers and publishers often used the octavo and smaller formats for godly books (including devotional literature) and the larger, more expensive folios for substantial works of history, religion, and law. Octavos could be placed in the pocket and taken on any destination; folios commanded respect when placed upon a bookshelf. Quarto size for the short play suggests a "pamphlet-like" publication—relatively inexpensive and disposable.

Bibliographers also consider type as one possible indication of intended audience. Prior to 1590, printed plays and other nondramatic pieces of literature were commonly set in black letter, a more "native type" (although imported) introduced into England with the printing press. After 1590, however, roman became the preferred type for printed plays. Printers continued to use black letter for a variety of texts, including horn books, jest books, ballads, news quartos, and other printed matter marketed toward the semiliterate and lower classes; at the same time most official government documents and law statutes continued to be printed in black-letter until the mid-eighteenth century. According to Mark Bland, the 1590 publication of Sidney's *Arcadia* in roman established a new trend for all pieces of literature—dramatic and nondramatic—with speed and "surprising precision."[12] As a result, roman became associated, more or less, with middle-class literature. Printed plays fell into that category. For example, seven plays printed in 1590 survive; all were set in black-letter. Eighteen extant plays were printed in 1591; seventeen were set in roman. After 1590 (and the publication of both Sidney's *Arcadia* and its companion text, Spenser's first three books of *The Faerie Queene*), the vast majority of printed plays were set in roman. In fact, no new play printed after 1605 was set in black-letter.[13] The conflicting impulses of quarto size (that is, portability and disposability) and roman type (that is, literary production and permanence) perhaps bear witness to the evolution of printed plays from something more or less utilitarian into something more self-consciously literary—from a playtext to be used into dramatic literature to be read.

While significant, bibliographical codes cannot tell the entire story of this evolution. Other clues need consideration as well. While paper size and print remain important, the conspicuous lack of prefatory matter stands as perhaps the most unusual feature of the early modern printed play. Most English books printed in the sixteenth and seventeenth centuries, including short news pamphlets and other ad hoc publications, contain prefatory matter of some sort. In fact, scholars now believe that prefaces, epistles, and dedications serve an essential role for understanding the function and reception of printed books. New Historicists, especially, emphasize the so-called "mediating" presence of prefatory material. Thomas Berger, for example, asserts that the preliminary matter to Shakespeare's First Folio (1623) "authorizes and legitimizes the volume."[14] Arthur Marotti likewise argues that "we should pay special attention to the 'front matter' of early printed books, since such features as frontispieces, title pages, dedications, epistles, and commendatory verse historically mediated texts in revealing ways."[15] Gérard Genette famously calls such material "paratexts" and carefully investigates the function of paratextual matter. According to Genette, paratexts—defined as those liminal devices such as prefaces, forewords, and blurbs—actually form part of the history of any given text and must receive scholarly attention.[16]

Yet the Elizabethan printed play, quite apart from prevailing book-trade conventions of the period, contains little front matter of any kind. Scholars usually mention this only in passing. Blayney, for instance, briefly notes that the majority of printed plays have no "preliminary matter."[17] For Elizabethan drama, in fact, the majority is overwhelming.[18] Of the 133 public-theater plays printed between 1576 and 1602 (ninety-four first editions and thirty-nine reprinted editions), fewer than ten have front matter of any kind. Very few printers, publishers, or authors felt compelled to add any preliminary matter to printed plays. Prefaces, dedications, and other blurbs remain conspicuously absent. In sum, Elizabethan printed plays largely conform to conventions of quarto size, of roman type, and of no prefatory material.

The Elizabethan printed plays of Shakespeare provide a convenient example. Despite the varied printers (at least ten different printers were involved) and the span of nearly ten years (1594–1603), Shakespeare's twenty-six printed plays (thirteen first editions and thirteen reprints) are remarkably conventional in most respects.[19] Beginning with *Titus Adronicus* in 1594, all of Shakespeare's Elizabethan plays were printed in quarto and set in roman without any prefatory matter. Genre distinctions can provide an illuminating contrast. Shakespeare's nondramatic works, like most other nondramatic texts from the period, also followed trade conventions. For nondramatic works, this meant including a dedication and/or epistle of some type. Both *Venus and Adonis* (Shakespeare's best-selling work) and *The Rape of Lucrece* (1594) have dedications to "the Right Honorable Henry Wriothesley, Earl of Southampton, and Baron of Tichfield." The *Sonnets* (1609) contain the famously puzzling epigraph beginning "TO. THE. ONLIE. BEGETTER. OF. THESE. INSVING. SONNETS. Mr. W. H."[20] In Elizabethan England, poetry already enjoyed the status as a literary production worthy of dedication; plays were still in the process of earning that status.[21]

If the existence of prefatory material is important for audience reception and possible mediation, as seems to be the case in nondramatic literature and other books of all types, absence of such material should likewise be considered informative, even crucial, for understanding the printed play. The lack of front matter in printed plays produces two primary effects. First, the absence of prefatory matter places a greater burden on the title page to advertise and promote the play; second, the paucity of conventional mediating factors renders the experience of reading the printed play more immediate and direct—more dramatic—than that of most other printed books. Not surprisingly printers, publishers, and dramatists reacted to these realities in concerted fashions.

With or without accompanying prefatory materials, title pages serve a variety of important (and obvious) functions to any printed book. In addition to providing an imprint with the printer's name and device, wholesale and/or retail shop location, city, and date of printing, title pages also attempt to attract potential buyers. In books without front matter, title pages stand as the only place for the publisher to "sell" the book.[22] These standardized title pages act, in effect, as self-contained advertisements and the printing press allowed the mass-produced, identical title page to evolve into prominence.[23] To this end, printers and publishers of plays produced extra copies of the title page (with blank versos) and attached them to poles, doors, carts, and other fixtures around the city, creating an unsophisticated, but effective, network of advertising.[24]

In addition to placing a premium on the title page, lack of front matter may have actually influenced the way Elizabethan readers experienced printed drama. Obviously, printed plays carried significant internal frameworks of mediation (that is, stage directions, dramatis personae, act/scene divisions, and prologues/epilogues), but relatively few plays have preliminary interruptions or explanations from printers, publishers, or playwrights attempting to mediate the reading experience before it begins. The reader of the Elizabethan play, as a result, enjoyed more freedom in creating the dramatic experience—the "meaning" of the play—than the reader of an English Bible, a printed sermon, a news report, or just about any other type of printed book containing front matter.

The evidence may suggest, however, that early Elizabethan printed plays were not *primarily* intended to be read. The lack of prefatory matter and the relatively few attempts to direct the reading experience would then make sense. In this scenario, individuals used the printed plays, rather, to stage plays themselves or to imagine what such staging would look like. While the two activities of staging and reading could clearly overlap, the printed play during this period becomes more a "do-it-yourself" form of entertainment and less a piece of literature to be read and thoughtfully digested. A number of early Elizabethan interludes printed before the first public theater opened in 1576, in fact, support such a notion. Numerous plays printed in the 1560s and 1570s provide remedial instructions on the title page for staging the play. Many of the plays conspicuously provide lists of characters for doubling and tripling of roles while proclaiming the numbers of actors required to stage the play. The title page to the interlude *Lusty Juventus* (Greg 41; ca. 1560) states that "foure may play it easily, taking such partes as they thinke best: so that any one take of those partes that be not in place at once." Likewise *The Interlude of Vice* (Greg 48; 1567) breaks up the parts among six actors needed to stage the play. *Cambises* (Greg 56; ca. 1570) also provides a clear diagram for the "division of the partes." Some plays even provide instruction about costuming. Both *Impatient Poverty* (Greg 30; 1560) and *Jack Juggler* (Greg 35; 1562) include crude woodcut illustrations of the characters, perhaps to help with wardrobe. The title page to *Jacob and Esau* (Greg 51; 1568) provides specific costuming directions: "The partes and names of the Players who are to be consydered to be Hebrews and should be apparailed with attire." All of these early Elizabethan plays, and many more, include conspicuous paratextual material important for staging plays.

The printed interludes often recognized this function, providing a working text while allowing for flexibility and adaptation. The title page to *Damon and Pithias* (Greg 58; 1571) registers this adaptability. The title page promotes the entertainment as "newely imprinted, as the same was shewed before the Queenes Majestie . . . except the Prologue that is somewhat altered for the proper use of them that hereafter shall have occasion to play it, either in Private, or open Audience." This blurb suggests, in other words, that while an accurate record of court performance remained important, so too did the afterlife of the production in both staging and reading. While we would certainly like to know more about "them," the "occasion," and the "Private or open Audience" mentioned on the title page, it seems clear that the printed play possessed a certain utility for those who wanted to stage a play or wanted to imagine what the staging would look like.

This is especially true before 1576 and the construction of the first English public theater built by James Burbage. After the opening of The Theater, very few plays continued to include staging information on the title page. While sheer coincidence may explain this phenomenon, another explanation seems more likely. If someone wanted to see how a printed play looked in performance, that option now existed; readers of a given play now had a living model of dramatic representation. Printers and publisher perhaps recognized this and stopped including staging material now deemed superfluous or redundant.[25] This repeated emphasis upon *staging* a play in the 1560s and 1570s would give way to a primary emphasis on *reading* a play as the century drew to a close. If one considers both bibliographical and linguistic codes—especially the paratextual matter included by the publishers—the printed play, in a few short years, would become essentially a reading experience. As publishers no longer included directions for staging plays, the reading experience began to emerge as primary.

As the reading experience evolved, printed plays also competed with another related activity. Consider, for example, the differences between attending a performance at the theater and reading a printed play at home. The staged play, as numerous well-documented studies attest, received considerable censure from a variety of sources in late-Elizabethan England.[26] But the printed play, despite its high-profile and similar subject matter, received relatively few attacks. Alexandra Halasz notes that "the danger of plays was un-

derstood in terms of their eventness and their platform was seen as
susceptible to control [and], it was also possible to understand the paper stage
as participating in a manageable, relatively innocuous circulation."[27] Ramie
Targoff, while not discussing printed plays per se, makes a similar point: "For
the ecclesiastics of the English church, as for the antitheatricalists, the individual's participation in a public performance produced internal changes that
were unlikely to occur in the private domestic sphere."[28] Critics of the theater
primarily feared the public nature of the event, although widely underestimat-
ing the power of literature to produce change within a reader. The individual
reading the play in the domestic sphere would not be exposed to the potentially pernicious aspects of playgoing. The printed play isolates the reader
from the unsavory elements of the theater; as a result, the printed play could
be seen as an ally of and not an enemy to opponents of the theater.

The printed play read as literature differs, quite obviously, from attending
a performance of the same play at a theater. Halasz believes that "print publication presents the play in purified, rarified form," offering "the liveliness of
participation and the detachment of judgement and contemplation."[29] Bibliographical codes, once again, play a significant role in this audience reception.
Printing plays in roman type—a more plain and austere type, less likely too
distract the reader than black-letter, and a print type more conducive to detachment and contemplation—allowed "a new diversity of presentation."[30]
Small quarto size made the plays easily portable; roman type allowed for
reflection. Additionally, the conspicuous lack of front matter also supports
the notion of contemplation and intimacy. Moreover, many of the less important or less sophisticated features of a stage play, scenes included for primarily visual benefit or physical comedy, could simply be removed from the
printed version of the play, allowing the reader even greater freedom to concentrate on words over spectacle.[31]

A preface written by Richard Jones to his 1590 edition of Marlowe's *Tamburlaine,* one of the few Elizabethan prefaces, implies precisely this advantage
of the printed play: "I have purposely omitted and left out some fond and
frivolous gestures, digressing and, in my poor opinion, far unmeet for the
matter, which I thought might seem more tedious unto the wise than any way
else to be regarded."[32] The "fond and frivolous gestures" Jones alludes to
can only be surmised, but obviously he considered a reading audience more
intelligent and more sophisticated than the theatergoer, and he fashioned a
printed play to suit that audience. Jones also considered some aspects of the
stage play location-specific and not transferable to print.[33] Jones, in effect,
attempts to transform the play from public, popular drama into a more private, contemplative piece of literature: the preface actually begins a continual
but haphazard process of that transformation. In time, such explanatory prefaces would not be needed and would be replaced by dedications, epistles, and
other established conventions, signaling, in effect, this change of status.

Printed plays could remove the distractions and digressions of the theater, suggesting that these newly conceived plays were to be read. Moreover, the transition from public theater to private library makes the printed play similar to the printed sermon: public events copied inexpensively for the individual reader to ponder repeatedly at leisure. Neither the printed play nor the printed sermon—short, flimsy quartos sold unbound (like most books), unable, in fact, to stand alone on a bookshelf—would be treated with delicate hands. Both would be read and reread, eventually falling apart from use and abuse; quarto plays, as a result, are much rarer than folio collections. Yet the printed sermon frequently carried front matter—especially the epistle dedicatory, a preface from the author, and/or marginal glosses—to help the reader appreciate the sermon further, to aid in understanding, and to control possible responses.

In 1590, the printed play becomes, for Jones, a literary publication quite unlike the scores of interludes printed during the previous three decades. Although few other Elizabethan printers or publishers promoted plays in this fashion, Jacobean printed plays were treated, in effect, like other literary documents.[34] *Tamburlaine* was among the first play accorded a preface and signaled an imminent shift in presentation. The change in Jacobean printing conventions registers this new literary status.

III

Scholars have long considered Ben Jonson's *Workes* (1616) a seminal literary publication. Often seen as a foundational text, the impressive folio conferred a new stature onto the printed play. Indeed, it stands as a remarkable publishing venture. It would be a mistake, however, to see this event as the only or even the primary catalyst in the evolution of printed plays. The transition from *plays* to *works,* from the trivial and nonliterary into the serious and artistic, actually took place in the various plays written by a variety of authors in the decades prior to 1616. This change from play to work, obviously, did not occur in a single, isolated instance but over a period of years. The quarto play, gradually presented as literature, made folio publication of plays more or less predictable and not the iconoclastic event it so often seems. The Jonson folio, in other words, reflected (in large paper) a trend already established for printed plays. The publication did not necessarily inaugurate the change in perception; the folio presentation actually confirmed it. Jonson, to be sure, helped alter the presentation of quarto plays, but the foundation for such an assessment occurred years prior. Early in the reign of James I, printers, publishers, and dramatists began including a variety of prefatory materials to quarto plays with increasing frequency, already suggesting a different attitude toward the printed play.

Zachary Lesser shows how one publisher, Walter Burre, attempted to create a literary text from a failed play script.[35] In his impressive examination of *The Knight of the Burning Pestle*, Lesser cites bibliographical and linguistic evidence—continuous printing and Latin tags—to challenge the notion that drama become literature only after 1616: "Burre's plays tell us that even earlier [than 1616] there was a market for plays targeted at select buyers, and that in fact such plays more easily found a market in print than on stage."[36] Lesser examines in detail one local instance of this evolutionary process; he demonstrates how publishers began to signal a new type of literary production geared toward a specific target audience well before 1616. With the flexibility of the printing press, publishers could (and did) target certain audiences with specific printed materials.

Examining the printed Jacobean plays of Shakespeare offers a convenient, although not fully proportional, point of departure to support this argument. Expanding the discussion to include other dramatists, printers, and publishers provides an equally rich, but admittedly less tidy, body of evidence. While the broadly sketched conventions outlined above obtain in most instances, notable exceptions exist. Once again, in many of the cases, the exception proves the rule. While few Elizabethan plays contain front matter, Jacobean plays more frequently include dedications, epistles, and prefaces. Consider, for example, that the eight first edition plays of Shakespeare printed in Jacobean England (in addition to the twenty-four reprints) were printed in quarto and set in roman, but two of the plays (25 percent) have prefaces.

Both prefaces, not surprisingly, comment upon the printing, publishing, and advertising of plays in the early seventeenth century. The first preface, the now-famous "A Never Writer to an Ever Reader. News", appeared in one issue of *Troilus and Cressida* in 1609. The preface, added by Henry Walley, hardly squares with the evidence accumulated from the various title-page advertisements extolling frequent, public performances of those plays. Walley begins, "Eternall reader, you have heere a new play, never stal'd with the Stage, never clapper-clawd with the palmes of the vulgar" (*2). Walley repeats this sentiment later, praising the play "for not being sullied, with the smoaky breath of the multitude" (*2V). Walley also markets the play with a "warning" to all potential purchasers of Shakespeare: "And beleeve this, that when hee is gone, and his commedies out of sale, you will scramble for them, and set up a new English Inquisition. Take this for a warning" (*2v). Walley's prophetic comments aside, the hyperbole of the preface attempts to promote the play as something more than merely a stage play—an artifact of a different type and valuable in its own right.

The second preface, added by the publisher Thomas Walkley and entitled "The Stationer to the Reader," appeared in the 1622 edition of *Othello*. Walkley, called a "fascinating rogue" by E. A. J. Honigmann,[37] published a variety of books between 1618 and 1641, frequently adding prefaces, including introductory remarks to a couple of plays in the Beaumont and Fletcher canon. Walkley's preface to *Othello* actually notes the oddity of printing any book (and in this case a play) without prefatory matter: "To set forth a booke without an Epistle, were like to the old English proverbe, A blew coat without a badge."[38] As the publisher, Walkley recognized the singularity of printed plays in failing to include front matter, believing, against trade convention, that some ornament must also adorn the printed version of the play. As a piece of literature, Walkley implies, the play *deserves* an epistle as ornament; that the play ultimately received an epistle confirms his belief. Walkley was not, of course, the first to utter such sentiments; he reflects, however, a change in perception. Prefaces, epistles, dedications, and other types of front matter associated with patronage and serious literature became far more common in Jacobean plays. Consider that nearly 50 percent of the ninety-four extant first edition plays printed between 1603 and 1616 contain front matter of some type (the figure for Elizabethan plays, it should be recalled, was less than 10 percent) and one gets the impression that printers, publishers, and authors treated quarto plays differently after, say, 1603. Why? Jacobean dramatists themselves may provide some answers.

Thomas Heywood, among the first and most prolific writers of prefaces and epistles to printed plays, also believed his printed plays deserved some ornament. Heywood, in his preface to *The Golden Age* (Greg 294; 1611), articulates an early statement of what was to become a common attitude regarding the printing of plays: "This play comming accidentally to the Presse, and at length having notice thereof, I was loath (finding it my owne) to see it thrust naked into the world, to abide the fury of all weathers, without either Title for acknowledgement, of the formality of an Epistle for ornament. Therefore rather to keepe custome, then any necessity, I have fixt these few lines in the front on my Booke."[39] Conventional posturing aside, Heywood's preface, as he admits, stands not as necessity but as ornament. His stance, however, begs the question: Why give ornament to something considered trivial and nonliterary? Because, Heywood might respond, *my* plays are not trivial or nonliterary. The preface, like Walkley's later epistle, suggests a changing attitude towards plays, and he considers them printed matter of literary value and worthy of adornment.[40] Part of this change can be attributed to the very conception of printed plays. Some plays, it seems, were written for the stage; others were refashioned and printed for the library. Others still served both functions.

Ben Jonson, in a preface to his tragedy *Sejanus,* notes that the printed version of the play differs from the previously seen stage version of the same play and hence becomes a new artifact—an artifact primarily for reading. Jonson informs the reader, ostensibly, to protect the reputation of another anonymous author: "I would inform you, that this Booke, in all the nu[m]-bers, is not the same with that which was acted on the publike Stage, wherein a second Pen had good share: in place of which I have chosen, to put weaker (and no doubt less pleasing) of mine own, then to defraud so happy a *Genius* of his right."[41] Jonson employs the trope of false modesty, an infrequent posture for the quarrelsome playwright, while advertising the new version of his play. This printed play exists not as a record of some past performance, a guide to stage the play, or a puff for future performances. Jonson also included printed marginalia in *Sejanus*—something rare in printed plays but rather common in various other books. According to William Slights, "[n]early every kind of book was provided with marginalia at some time in the period."[42] Printed plays, as Slights notes, stand as a primary exception to this convention.[43]

Joseph Loewenstein argues that "Ben Jonson's are among the first dedicated texts of *printed* drama in the history of the English theater."[44] Dedications appeared, the evidence shows, before Jonson. George Chapman, in fact, stands as a more likely pioneer in this regard. A number of Chapman's early plays contain dedications, including *The Conspiracie and Tragedie of Charles Duke of Byron* (Greg 274/75; 1608), *The Widowes Teares* (Greg 301; 1612), and *The Revenge of Bussy D'Ambois* (Greg 307; 1613).[45] Jonson obviously plays an important role in the transformation of printed plays, and after the publication of his *Workes* in 1616, dedications in printed plays became more common. James Shirley, for example, frequently included dedications in his printed plays, and a number of Caroline dramatists followed suit.[46]

The anonymous playwright J.C. prefaced his play *A Pleasant Comedie, Called the Two Merry Milke-Maids* in 1620 with a slightly different sentiment than Jonson. The playwright assumes the usual pose of the reluctant author unwillingly publishing his play only after unauthorized copies started to circulate. Although sometimes confused with the so-called "stigma of print," this highly conventional stance ends with an advertisement for the play itself:[47] "[The play] was made more for the Eye, then the Eare; lesse for the Hand, then eyther: and had not false Copies travail'd abroad (even to surbating) this had kept in; for so farre the Author was from seeking fame in the publishing . . . Some good words here you shall finde for your Money, else it keepes not touch with the Title."[48] The preface sends a dual, even conflicting, message: "Made more for the eye" could mean either spectacle (that is, intended for the stage) or reading (that is, intended for the study). Unwittingly, the preface captures the essence of transition.

The playwright John Marston makes a somewhat similar point years earlier in his preface to *The Malcontent* (Greg 203; 1604). Marston, stung by criticism of his dramatic inventions, defends his plays as entertainments, not as factual histories. He worries, however, about the actual publication of his play: "I would faine leave the paper; only one thing afflicts mee, to thinke that Scenes invented, meerly to be spoken, should be inforcively published to be read, & that the least hurt I can receive, is to do my selfe the wrong"

(A3v). For Marston, the events of the play—the speaking words—take priority over the written expression of the same matter. Marston struggles with the changing status of plays as he employs the language of coercion to describe the publication of printed drama.

Marston strikes the same chord two years later in the preface to *The Wonder of Women or the Tragedy of Sophonisba* (Greg 231; 1606). Once again, Marston pleads for understanding and entreats his reader "not to taxe me, for the fashion of the Entrances and Musique of this Tragedy, for know it is printed onely as it was presented by youths, & after the fashion of the private stage."[49] Marston, unlike Jonson and others, did not happily embrace the possibilities, including the relative permanence, print offers. The burdens of authorship and the demands of the readers, Marston seems to imply, create unreasonable notions of exactness for printed plays. Yet the very existence of the preface, coupled with Marston's defensive posture, suggests a concerted attention directed toward plays as literature and not merely spectacle or entertainment.

The mercurial Heywood presents yet a third perspective on printed plays. Heywood privileges the staged play over the printed version and only reluctantly consents (as if he had the consent to give) to the printing. At first glance, this objection appears rather conventional, as many authors assumed such a posture. Heywood's complaint differs in an important manner, however. Heywood objects to the dual profiting in both the performance and printing of plays: "For though some have used a double sale of their labours, first to the Stage, and after to the presse, For my owne part I heere proclaime my selfe ever faithfull in the first, and never guiltie of the last."[50] Heywood finds fault with those who promote both the staged and printed versions of their plays; his allegiance remains, at least in 1608, firmly with the theater. This obvious irony apparently escaped the author of the printed preface.

John Webster also critiques both theater patrons and potential readers in his preface to *The White Devil* (Greg 306; 1612). Rowdy and boisterous behavior of playgoers generated more than a few complaints in Tudor and Stuart England; booksellers also complained about browsing and purchasing habits of customers. Webster's invective compares both activities: "I have noted, most of the people that come to the Play-house, resemble those ignorant asses (who visiting Stationers shoppes their use is not to inquire for good bookes, but new bookes) I present it [this play] to the general view."[51] For Webster, neither the patron of the theater nor the stationer possessed the sophistication required to appreciate his play. In sum, Jacobean dramatists, in contrast to their Elizabethan counterparts, offer a complex body of evidence to investigate. In all cases, the significance lies in the conversation itself: for some individuals, plays were finally worthy of such discussion.

Certain economic factors of the printed play also merit attention. The amount of disposable income for the "average, literate Elizabethan" (if such a person existed) factors into any consideration of these interrelated issues. Andrew Gurr estimates that "over the years between the 1560s, when the first purpose-built playhouses were established, and 1642, when all playhouses were closed, well over fifty million visits were made to playhouses."[52] Yet, as Gurr admits, relatively few traces of such prolific activity exists. In comparison, given an estimated press run of eight hundred, the 371 new quarto plays written for professional public performance listed by Peter Blayney would yield only 296,800 printed plays. Obviously the number of reprinted plays would increase those figures. Even if doubled or tripled, the number of printed plays represents only a small fraction of the fifty million customers offered by Gurr. The number of spectators dwarfed the number of readers; in this sense, the printed play indeed seems insignificant. Yet this distinction between attendance and reading raises another related issue.

Like other forms of entertainment, plays cost a certain amount of money to attend. On any given afternoon, the consumer needed to decide whether to patronize a play, a bear-baiting show, a dice game, or to purchase a printed play. One preface acknowledges how reading plays may actually keep individuals away from games of dice: "You shall finde this published Comedy, good to keepe you in an afternoone from dice, at home in your chambers."[53] Likewise, the printed play competed against other forms of reading material. The numerous broadsides, the ubiquitous news quarto, collections of poems, the prose romance, and scores of other books also courted potential buyers. No individual consumer could afford all pleasures and literate patrons exercised discretion when buying books. Yet in the zero-sum world of disposable income, the printed play also competed against the staged play: Money spent for one activity could not be spent on another. Loewenstein concurs, stating that "the printshop and the theater were, in many ways, competitors."[54] So while the successful stage play could increase exposure and demand for printed drama, the printed play, in effect, competes against its staged progenitor for both monetary and aesthetic appreciation.

Although printed plays never accounted for much of the book trade, they obviously deserve careful attention for a number of reasons. Printed plays bear witness to many issues that interest literary historians and bibliographers. The evolution of the printed play—never tidy, never consistent—sheds light on publishing patterns, trade conventions, reading habits, and authorial status. Although this broad survey does not fully account for local readings, the exceptional, or the curious, it does attempt to explain the surviving evidence in more than general terms. Bibliography reminds us that material conditions play an essential role in the production of printed books. Close attention to prefaces and epistles provide additional evidence about dissemination and reception of these texts. Taken together, the complex story of printed plays—from trivial to literary—may come more clearly into focus.

Notes

A shortened version of this paper was presented in a seminar at the annual Shakespeare Association of America Conference directed by Alexandra Halasz on 8 April 2000. I would like to thank Thomas L. Berger and George Walton Williams for their thoughtful comments on earlier drafts of the essay.

1. All scholars of English printed drama benefit from the work of W. W. Greg, *A Bibliography of the English Printed Drama to the Restoration,* 4 vols (London: Bibliographical Society, 1939–1959). I provide the Greg number for each play cited in the essay.

2. For a comprehensive analysis of the "good" versus "bad" quarto controversy, see Laurie E. Maguire, *Shakespearean Suspect Texts: The "Bad" Quartos and Their Contexts"* (Cambridge: Cambridge University Press, 1996). See also, Random Cloud [Randall McLeod], "The Marriage of Good and Bad Quartos," *Shakespeare Quarterly* 33 (1982): 421–31.

3. See, for example, Timothy Murray, *Theatrical Legitimation* (New York: Oxford University Press, 1987) and *Ben Jonson's 1616 Folio,* eds. Jennifer Brady and W. H. Herendeen (Newark: University of Delaware Press, 1991).

4. These two uses, theatrical text and reading text, are not, of course, mutually exclusive.

5. Peter W. M. Blayney, "The Publication of Playbooks," *A New History of Early English Drama,* ed. John D. Cox and David Scott Kastan (New York: Columbia University Press, 1997), 385.

6. T. A. Birrell, "The Influence of Seventeenth-Century Publishers on the Presentation of English Literature," in *Historical and Editorial Studies in Medieval and Early Modern English,* ed. Mary-Jo Arn and Hanneke Wirtjes (Groningen: Wolters-Noordhoff, 1985), 166.

7. See, for example, Heidi Brayman Hackel, "'Rowme' of Its Own: Printed Drama in Early Libraries," in *A New History of Early English Drama,* ed. John D. Cox and David Scott Kastan (New York: Columbia University Press, 1997), 113–30. Hackel shows how some collectors, like Sir Thomas Bodley, objected to the proliferation of printed plays, while other collectors, like Sir John Harrington, Ralph Seldon, and Edward Dering, purchased plays in considerable quantities.

8. Jerome J. McGann, *The Textual Condition* (Princeton: Princeton University Press, 1991), 13.

9. McGann, *Textual Condition,* 13.

10. McGann's work remains valuable and thought-provoking. I quibble, however, with his term "bibliographic codes." A more accurate term, it seems, would be "bibliographical codes." The distinction, though minor, is similar in kind to the difference between "historic" and "historical."

11. Some Elizabethan plays were printed in octavo, including all editions of Marlowe's *Tamburlaine* and *The Massacre at Paris.*

12. Mark Bland, "The Appearance of the Text in Early Modern England," *Text* 11 (1998): 104. Blayney also notes the importance of type and concludes that "the preference for roman type suggests that the publishers of the plays were aiming more at the middle class than the working class" (415). For a discussion of "black letter liter-

acy," see Keith Thomas, "The Meaning of Literacy in Early Modern England," in *The Written Word: Literacy in Transition,* ed. Gerd Baumann (Oxford: Clarendon Press, 1986), 97–131. For a highly informative account of roman type, see W. Craig Ferguson, *Pica Roman Type in Elizabethan England* (Aldershot: Scolar, 1989). See also C. C. Mish, "Black Letter as a Social Discriminant in the Seventeenth Century," *PMLA* 68 (1953): 627–30.

13. Bland, "Appearance," 106.

14. Thomas L. Berger, "The New Historicism and the Editing of English Renaissance Texts," *New Ways of Looking at Old Texts,* ed. W. Speed Hill (Binghamton: MRTS, 1993), 196.

15. Arthur F. Marotti, *Manuscript, Print, and the English Renaissance Lyric* (Ithaca: Cornell University Press, 1995), 223.

16. Gérard Genette, *Paratexts: Thresholds of Interpretation,* trans. Jane E. Lewin (Cambridge: Cambridge University Press, 1997). Paratextual matter indeed plays a crucial role in many sixteenth-century books. For an analysis of poetic paratexts from Elizabethan Bibles, see Paul J. Voss, "'Created Good and Faire': The Fictive Imagination and Sacred Texts in Elizabethan England," *Literature and Theology* (June 2000): 125–44.

17. Blayney, "Playbooks," 406.

18. Between 1583–1602, Greg lists 117 works (Blayney lists ninety-six public plays) and only four contained a preface. Between 1603–1622, Greg lists 192 works (Blayney 115); twenty-three plays contain prefaces (not counting the 1616 folio of Jonson). Between 1623 and 1642, Greg lists 251 works (Blayney 160); eleven plays have prefaces.

19. According to the *STC,* the following people printed quarto plays written by Shakespeare: Allde, Bradock, Creede, Danter, Eld, Harper, Jaggard, Mathewes, Norton, Okes, Parsons, Purfoot, Roberts, Short, Simmes, Stafford, Stansby, White, Windet, and Young.

20. For a discussion of the epigraph, see Donald W. Foster, "Master W. H., R. I. P.," *PMLA* 102 (January 1987): 42–54. Some scholars now believe that the 1609 publication of the *Sonnets* represents an authorized publication. See, for example, A. Kent Hieatt, Charles W. Hieatt, and Anne Lake Prescott, "When Did Shakespeare Write Sonnets 1609?" *Studies in Philology* 88 (1991): 69–109.

21. Franklin B. Williams, "Commendatory Verses: The Rise of the Art of Puffing," *Studies in Bibliography* 19 (1966): 1–14, singles out Shakespeare and Sidney as two conspicuous exceptions to the vogue of puffery: "With the curious exception of Sidney and Shakespeare, all the chief poets (including Spenser and Milton) wrote puffs" (6). Williams adds that "no work of Shakespeare's published in his lifetime contains a commendatory as its bush" (14).

22. In an important forthcoming essay, Alan B. Farmer and Zachary Lesser, "Vile Arts: The Marketing of English Printed Drama, 1512–1660," *Research Opportunities in Renaissance Drama,* investigate how publishers signaled potential audience through title pages (they examine 1109 different titles pages from printed plays). According to Farmer and Lesser, publishers used theater name (as opposed to theater company) to distinguish a play. See also, James P. Saeger and Christopher J. Fassler, "The London Professional Theater, 1576–1642: A Catalogue and Analysis of the Ex-

tant Printed Plays," *Research Opportunities in Renaissance Drama* 34 (1995): 63–109.

23. Thomas L. Berger, "Looking for Shakespeare in Caroline England," *Viator* 27 (1996): 323–59, analyzes dozens of title pages of the printed quartos of Shakespeare's plays. While Berger's observation concerning the relative stability of the Elizabethan, Jacobean, Caroline title pages is correct, part of his conclusion, "Shakespeare in Caroline England is a special kind of Shakespeare, surely not the universal genius we have made him out to be" (355), appears more fragile. The consistency between Elizabethan and Caroline title pages could have a number of reasons; Shakespeare's ostensible lack of fashion and/or his relative irrelevance to a mid-seventeenth-century audience is only one of them.

24. Ronald B. McKerrow, *An Introduction to Bibliography for Literary Students* (New Castle: Oak Knoll, 1994), states "It seems clear that title-pages were actually posted up as advertisements" (909) and cites a number of sixteenth and seventeenth-century allusions to the practice (n. 2). For an analysis of title pages, the proliferation of advertisements, and the efforts of printers/publishers to attract readers in the sixteenth century, see Paul J. Voss, "Books for Sale: Advertising and Patronage in Late Elizabethan England," *Sixteenth Century Journal* 29 (Fall 1998): 733–56.

25. The difference is quite pronounced. Prior to 1576, a majority of printed interludes included some information helpful for individual performance. After 1576, few do so. *The Conflict of Conscience* (Greg 78; 1581) includes "the Actors names, devided into six partes, most convenient for such as be disposed, either to shew this Comedie in private houses, or otherwise." The most notable exception, curiously, is *Mucedorus* (Greg 151) first printed in 1598. The single most popular play of the period (with thirteen printed editions prior to 1640), *Mucedorus* includes characters so grouped that "eight persons may easily play it" (A1v).

26. Numerous books and articles explore the various reactions against theater and play-going. See, for example, Jonas Barish, *The Antitheatrical Prejudice* (Berkeley: University of California Press, 1981).

27. Alexandra Halasz, *The Marketplace of Print: Pamphlets and the Public Sphere in Early Modern England* (Cambridge: Cambridge University Press, 1997), 184.

28. Ramie Targoff, "The Performance of Prayer: Sincerity and Theatricality in Early Modern England," *Representations* 60 (Fall 1997): 60.

29. Halasz, *Marketplace,* 185.

30. Bland, "Appearance," 126.

31. Birrell, although not addressing the issue per se, would disagree. He states that "the quarto play was read for its story, not for its poetry" (166) and "Printed verse drama in the seventeenth century was presented, and received, as light fiction, not as poetry" (167). Birrell does not explain, however, why some printers would include act and scene divisions (elements of drama) or continuous printing (elements of verse) or even observe the distinction between poetry and prose if such matters were wholly incidental.

32. Christopher Marlowe, *Tamburlaine* (Greg 94; 1590), A2. Jones wrote two other early prefaces, including "The Printer to the Reader" prefacing George Whetstone's *Promos and Cassandra* (Greg 73; 1578). Jones ends the epistle by declaring "for my owne part, I wil not faile to procure such bookes, as may profit thee with delight"

(A3v). In his preface to the no longer extant entertainment called *The Princely Pleasures* (Greg 90; 1576), Jones claims that high demand for the "sundry pleasaunt and Poeticall inventions" encouraged him to print the text: "All which have been sundrie tymes demaunded for, aswell at my handes, as also of other Printers, for that in deede, all studious and well disposed yong Gentlemen and others, were desyrous to be partakers of those pleasures by a profitable publication."

33. Fifty years later, Richard Brome, *The Antipodes* (Greg 586; 1640) briefly makes an intriguing claim for additions to his printed play: "Courteous Reader, You shal find in this Booke more then was presented upon the Stage, and left out of the Presentation, for superfluous length (as some of the Players pretended) [.] I thought it good al should be inserted according to the allowed Original" (L4v).

34. In the preface to his play *The Unfortunate Mother* (Greg 581; 1640), Thomas Nabbes makes a rather unusual claim in his dedication to the "right Worshipfull Richard Braithwaite Esquire": "I have (though boldly being a stranger) elected you, to countenance a piece, that (undeservedly I hope) hath beene denied the credit which it might have gain'd from the Stage" (A2). Nabbes appears to claim that the play was never performed and it went straight to print. This may suggest that the acting company turned down the play.

35. Zachary Lesser, "Walter Burre's *The Knight of the Burning Pestle*," *English Literary Renaissance* 29 (Winter 1999): 22–43.

36. Lesser, "Walter Burre," 38.

37. E. A. J. Honigmann, *The Texts of Othello and Shakespearian Revision* (New York: Longman, 1996), 21.

38. *Othello* (Greg 379; 1622), A2. Walkley added prefaces to a number of his other books as well, including a short preface to Beaumont and Fletcher's *A King and No King* (Greg 360; 1619) and *Philaster* (Greg 363; 1622). He did not, however, add prefaces to other plays printed about this time, including the first impression of *Phylaster* (STC 1681; 1620), *The Tragedy of Thierry King of France* (Greg 368; 1621), or a later edition of *A King and No King* (Greg 360; 1625).

39. Thomas Heywood, *The Golden Age* (Greg 294; 1611), A2.

40. Heywood makes this same point years later in a preface to Marlowe's *The Famous Tragedy of the Rich Jew of Malta* (Greg 475; 1633). In the preface, Heywood takes credit for the recently added prologues and epilogues and states "so now being newly brought to Presse, I was loath it should be published without the ornament of an Epistle" (A3). Heywood then dedicates the play to "Mr. Thomas Hammon, of Grayes Inne."

41. Ben Jonson, *Sejanus* (Greg 216, 1605), *2.

42. William W. E. Slights, "The Edifying Margins of Renaissance English Books," *Renaissance Quarterly* 42 (1989): 685.

43. Slights also states: "As for *Sejanus,* no one has satisfactorily explained why Jonson would include a painstaking account of his Latin sources in the 1605 quarto edition of the tragedy and then without explanation turn around and drop all that material from the 1616 folio edition of his *Workes*" (687). Perhaps Jonson felt the quarto play needed gravity of presentation; the folio play already secured such respect.

44. Joseph Loewenstein, "The Script in the Marketplace," *Representations* 12 (Fall 1985): 101–14, 109.

45. John Fletcher's play *The Faithfull Shepheardesse* (Greg 287; 1610?) contains a most unusual three-person verse dedication. For the dedication, Fletcher wrote poems to Sir Walter Aston, Sir William Scipwith, and Sir Robert Townesend.

46. For a discussion of four Caroline dramatists and the emergence of the "profession," see Ira Clark, *Professional Playwrights: Massinger, Ford, Shirley, and Brome* (Lexington: Kentucky University Press, 1992).

47. J. W. Saunders, "The Stigma of Print," *Essays in Criticism* 1 (1951): 139–64, first postulated this often-cited theory. Steven W. May, "Tudor Aristocrats and the Mythical 'Stigma of Print'" *Renaissance Papers* 10 (1980): 11–18, provides a persuasive counter argument. For a recent reevaluation of the "stigma of print" theory, see Jean R. Brink, "Manuscript Culture Revisited," *Sidney Journal* 17 (Spring 1999): 19–30.

48. J.C., *A Pleasant Comedie, Called the Two Merry Milke-Maids* (Greg 364; 1620), A2.

49. Sig., A2.

50. Thomas Heywood, *The Rape of Lucrece* (Greg 273; 1608), A2.

51. John Webster, *The White Devil* (Greg 306; 1612), A2. Many authors complained about the fashion of book-browsing in Elizabethan England. For a look at the emphasis upon "new" titles, see H. S. Bennett, *English Books and Readers 1558–1603* (Cambridge: Cambridge University Press, 1965), esp. 267–69.

52. Andrew Gurr, *Playgoing in Shakespeare's London* (Cambridge: Cambridge University Press, 1987), 4.

53. Thomas Middleton and Thomas Dekker, *The Roaring Girl* (Greg 298; 1611), A3.

54. Loewenstein, "The Script in the Marketplace," 105.

The Crone in English Renaissance Drama

JEANNE ADDISON ROBERTS

THE word *crone* conjures up for many moderns images of ugly old age, deformity, decay, nefarious witchcraft, and ultimately of death. Old women more than old men function as grim reminders of the grave and are therefore to be defeated, ridiculed, or simply ignored. However, the connotations of the word crone may be ambiguous. The *Oxford English Dictionary* supports the negative associations, speculatively relating the word to the early Modern Dutch for "old ewe," and suggesting a connection with the northern French word for "carcass" or "carrion." The examples given illustrate the view that the usual definition of a crone is "a withered old woman." But one unillustrated possibility listed does suggest that crone might be an obsolete form of "crown," and this opens up a region of possibility that might be worth exploring by modern feminists who want to liberate the crone from her accumulated repulsive images and elevate her to a position of wisdom and power.[1]

Although Renaissance drama (I focus on the period from 1566 to 1625) strongly supports the negative view, there are a few examples of powerful crones who contribute positively to the establishment of justice and order in their worlds. I define the crone broadly as a mature woman not characterized primarily as virgin, wife, sex object, or potential mother. My category thus includes some women who are younger than the conventionally characterized crone but who still occupy marginal positions not encompassed by the sexually classifiable niches of virgin and wife/whore. In Renaissance drama the crone is usually invisible, unnecessary, or threatening. She is perhaps most notable for her absence, but where she appears she is likely to be trivialized, sexualized, or demonized.

Trivialized crones are usually stupid or naive, but harmless figures of fun; they may also be moving but helpless victims, sometimes mad or nearly mad. Sexualization takes the form of representing the crone as a salacious nurse or bawd who appears in innumerable incarnations. Demonized crones are perceived as witches and harbingers of death, nearly always repulsive and threatening. Curiously, this subspecies, usually malign, sometimes, though not often, includes benign figures of special powers. The following discussion will center on three categories of crone and their subspecies, but I will first touch briefly on some roots of traditional literary attitudes toward old women.

There is considerable evidence that since earliest patriarchal societies women have been valued chiefly for their sexual and reproductive potential, and once this has faded, the woman ceases to be of major value, although she may be a threat. The earliest western literature already represents attitudes that remain prevalent in later literature. Old women are absent from Hesiod, and even Homer's Penelope and Helen, dignified as they are by inclusion in the poem, are important only in relation to the men around them, a relation no longer primarily sexual. Odysseus's old nurse Eurykleia who survives his return, and identifies him by his scar, seems in something of the same category as his aged dog who lives only long enough to recognize his master.[2] In Hesiod and Homer the crone, because she is omitted or trivialized, is negligible; but myths and folk tales preserve traces of powerful prepatriarchal goddesses who inspired awe as well as fear of her imagined powers.

Indeed, although both Hesiod and Homer reflect the beliefs of their times, both also preserve glimpses of a more ancient prehistoric time which seems to have imagined women without linking them narrowly to their sexual relationship to men. Hesiod speaks of a pre-Olympian Titan named Hecate, who later shared rule with Zeus and who specialized in war, athletics, and hunting.[3] Very early this goddess is referred to as Triple and is called by many names, all incorporating but not isolating her roles as Creator, Preserver, and Destroyer and as ruler of heaven, earth, and the underworld.[4]

Vicenzo Cartari, describing the antique gods in 1587, preserves in his engraving the image of the Triple Goddess as Diana, Luna, and Perserpina.[5] He suggests this goddess's power in Diana's wings, arrows, and tamed lions; her affinity for animals in the lions, dog, and serpents; her linkage to the phases of the moon in Luna's headdress; and her mystery in the shrouded figure of Perserpina. There is no overt depiction of the crone. She is not a separable aspect of the goddess. Later patriarchal cultures both trivialized and demonized Hecate by turning her into the queen of witches. One of Hecate's names was, in fact, Trivia because she was goddess of crossroads, places like that in *Oedipus the King* where three roads (tri-via) meet. The trivialization of her name signals an increasing marginalization of her powers and of the whole concept of the Triple Goddess. However traces of her memory are preserved in Homer's goddesses, each of whom might qualify as a crone by definition—the virginal but multifaceted Athene, the maternal Demeter, and especially the mysterious Perserpina, whom Odysseus repeatedly names as the ruler of the underworld. Other goddesses like Aphrodite, Hera, and Artemis may blur, but they also preserve attributes of the earlier goddess, inspiring both fear and awe.

In the later, better documented world of Greek tragedy, however, an astonishing phenomenon occurs. Women who may be classified as crones— Clytemnestra, Medea, Agave, Helen, and even Phaedra—move to center stage. Indeed their centrality seems inverse to the actual position of women in Greek society. These stage characters seem to suggest, rather than real experience, the power of the repressed—the subconscious male perception of the dangers of female vengefulness, irrationality, and lust. By contrast, Greek comedy, which explores social rather than individual problems, has very few important women characters of any age. *Lysistrata* is, of course, an exception, but it focuses so relentlessly on sex that older women are consigned to an angry but hardly threatening chorus. Menander sets up the patterns generally followed in Roman comedy. His women's roles in general are trivial and peripheral. Though virgins may be the subject of negotiation, they have very few lines. Greek literature as a whole, then, developed models of the absent crone (Hesiod, Homer, and Menander), the demonic crone (Clytemnestra, Medea, Agave), the vindictive crone of supernatural powers (Medea), and the crone as loyal wife or passive victim (Penelope, Hecuba, and Alcestis). Phaedra's pandering nurse and the still possibly erotic Helen and Phaedra are early examples of the sexualized crone.

Roman comedy continued the Greek tradition of male actors and further developed conventionalized characters with few roles for "females." The courtesan becomes a stock instrument of plot. The older women are wives (often desexualized and shrewish but powerless) and nurses (sexualized by their relationship to marriageable daughters). According to Georges Minois, Roman society had proportionately more old people than Greek society, the majority of them men.[6] This fact may be reflected in Roman Comedy's portrayal of the *senex,* the odious old man who regularly blocked the union of young lovers. There was no equivalent stock character named for the old woman. (If there had been, it would have been *anus,* the Latin word for old woman—can this unfortunate pun be wholly fortuitous?) Mother and shrewish wife *(matrona)* did sometimes appear; the nurse *(nutrex)* became a conventionalized character; and *anus* did sometimes have a minor servant role.

George E. Duckworth reports that in the comedy of Plautus and Terence seventy-five women speak, but they are all relatively minor—maids, courtesans, wives, virgins, and, only incidentally, a procuress.[7] According to Kathleen M. Lea, even in later Italian popular comedy, when female actors were introduced, the early dramatic convention was to conceal the woman. She was the object rather than the subject of the action. Some companies continued to have no actresses, and the maximum number, when they did appear, was three. These were featured, often in doubled roles, as wives, nurses, procuresses, and midwives, but rarely as central figures.[8] The absent or trivialized crone had become institutionalized.

There seems to have been a rather surprising female majority among the aging elite of Renaissance Italy. This was apparently a new development. Minois records that from antiquity to the fifteenth-century women died earlier than men, but that sixteeth-century aristocracy reversed this situation. He suggests that this fact may help to account for the hatred of old women shown by Renaissance artists and men of letters (he mentions Flemish and German painters, Ronsard, DuBellay, and Erasmus).[9] Such women were likely by their survival, to make apt Theseus's complaint in *A Midsummer Night's Dream* (1595–96), about the step dame or the dowager "Long withering out a young man's revenue" (1.1.6).

Although Minois acknowledges that the spirit of Renaissance rebirth celebrated youth, he also contends that a gap existed between the way people talked of old age, especially female old age, with contempt and bitterness, and society's actual behavior. He concludes that "if a dislike for old women existed, it was mainly a literary device."[10] Perhaps so, but it is impossible to discount the evidence of the hundreds of old women burned as witches during this enlightened era. The literary hostility toward the crone, which is a recurrent feature of English Renaissance drama, must have had some basis in reality. It cannot be attributed simply to resentment of the aging Elizabeth since it occurred as well on the continent where such powerful rulers as Queen Isabella and Catherine de Medici may also have bred resentment.

The rediscovery of classical texts may have provided historical models of powerful and frightening older women. Even though Greek tragedy was still largely unknown to British playwrights, such models of menacing crones as the Fates, the Furies, Medea, Phaedra, and Erichtho were widely available in Seneca, Ovid, and Lucan, who both knew Greek literature and were known to the English. Other operative forces are unclear, but may include in England the closing of the convents that had sheltered older women and provided them with an unthreatening social niche.[11]

In Renaissance English drama, crones continue to be absent or trivialized as they have been in earlier periods, but sexualizing and demonizing become much more prevalent than they have been since the days of Greek tragedy. In both tragedy and comedy old women, when they have power, are typically, at least superficially, frightening and disturbing of patriarchal order. The following discussion is meant to be suggestive rather than exhaustive. I have ranged freely over the drama of the period from 1566 to 1625 without attempting to classify examples generically or to demonstrate historical development, although these topics might be profitably pursued. I have not attempted either to examine authorial biases although these obviously exist. I have proceeded rather on the assumption that dramatic portrayals—all but one by men—reflect pervasive and persistent attitudes of the period, which are rooted in the Western tradition. Interestingly, in the one known play by a woman, Elizabeth Cary's *The Tragedy of Mariam, Fair Queen of Jewry,* never presumably staged, but published in 1613, the portraits of the two crones, Alexandra and Doris, seem especially bitter. Both women are powerless and vindictive. Doris, Mariam's predecessor as wife of Herod, understandably, pronounces vituperative curses on Miriam and her children

(4.8.616–24), but Mariam's mother, Alexandra, also heartlessly repudiates her own daughter, declaring that death is too good for her (5.1.41–44).[12]

The scarcity of crones does not, as it might have done earlier, simply reflect demographic reality, but is probably more often the result of the perpetuation of long-standing conventions. Of course the unwelcome survival of real older women may also have contributed to their denigration when they do appear in drama. Even Elizabeth herself may have received diminished adulation as she grew older, and her death in 1603 may well have unleashed a backlash.[13]

Trivializing, sexualizing, and demonizing—both malign and benign—are then part of a long tradition. As a reflection of the domination of male authors and actors it may constitute an expression of conscious and unconscious fears, prejudices, and superstitions of a patriarchal society. In such societies, where women are valued for their sexual relationship to men and their powers of propagation, men are likely to ignore the crone as unnecessary, to regret her as a social burden, to be repelled by their imagination of her voracious and unproductive lust, to fear her as a reminder of death, and also perhaps to retain some archaic memory of her mysterious wisdom and power—a memory possibly reinforced by or even originated in a recollection of some seemingly all-powerful female figure who was their first attendant and love object. An examination of specific cases will illustrate the dramatic incarnations of the crone.[14]

In *The Old Law* (1618) by Middleton, Rowley, and perhaps Massinger,[15] the noble Cleanthes argues that old age is "the holy place of life, chapel of ease / For all men's wearied miseries" (3.2.279–80). However, his is a lone voice protesting a "grave and necessary" new law that is intended to "cut off [those] fruitless to the republic" and "finish what nature lingered at" (1.1.56, 121–22). The law mandates eliminating those beyond the age of bearing arms or children, that is, men at eighty and women at sixty. (The discrepancy between the fatal ages for men and for women, not present in the source, reveals openly the sexism as well as ageism of the legislators.) Gnotho, the chief misogynist of the play, defends the law joyfully because it will enable him to dispose of his old wife and take a new one ("a piece of old beef will serve to breakfast, yet a man would be glad of a chicken to supper") (3.1.355–56). Women are, after all, *"only necessary to the propagation of posterity"* (1.1.167–68), and when they are old, they become witches, practitioners of dangerous medicine, or bawds ("schoolmistresses of sweet sin"—his ambivalence toward sin if not toward old women is patent). Cleanthes, it emerges, is in fact literally concerned with idyllic old age for *men*—for him old women are virtually invisible; and the views of Cleanthes and Gnotho in regard to the old women are largely supported throughout English Renaissance drama and in much of later literature.

It is no doubt churlish to complain that Berger and Bradford's extremely useful *Index of Characters* contains no entry for old woman but includes them under the heading *senex*. This categorization suggests both the realities of the drama and a pervasive bias of criticism. The *senex* listing, not surprisingly weighted toward men, omits such notable crones as Gammer Gurton, Madge Mumblecrust, Mistress Horseleech, Mother Mortage, Mother Sawyer, and Madame Decoy,[16] among others, although bawds and witches are amply recorded elsewhere. As in the drama, crones of any type are rarely featured in criticism. The scarcity of mothers in Shakespeare has been frequently remarked,[17] and, although he has a few notable older women, they are often ignored. This pattern pervades the drama of the period. Neither Christopher Marlowe nor Ben Jonson, for example, is notable for sustained or subtle depictions of older women. The bias is perpetuated in criticism.

The *senex* is a recurring and classifiable character type because, attractive or not (and he usually is not), he is a focus of power, and, at least in theory, the central object of filial piety. In fact, old men, though much more plentiful than old women, may not fare better in Tudor-Stuart drama. In Thomas May's *The Old Couple* (1636),[18] for example, the marriage contemplated between Lady Covet, who is eighty, and Sir Argent Scrape, who is ninety-five, is condemned by the other characters as profane and unnatural—designed to propagate not the race but merely their gold. Both parties are objects of contempt and derision—she is on crutches and eventually both are in chairs. Euphues speaks for society when he says,

> I cannot tell whether such strange
> Unsatiable desires in these old folks
> That are half earth already, should be thought
> More impious, or more ridiculous.

(3.1027–30)

The real target of the satire is their avarice, especially inconvenient in the old. Both parties are tricked out of their money. The marriage is aborted. Still, only she is referred to as "old rottenesse" (3.980), and the notions of an old female miser is so uncommon as to appear a contradiction in terms. When she is actively interested in erotic liaison, the old woman is likely to be represented satirically as of interest only as a source of income. The folly of the aged woman's vanity is also satirized because it seems oblivious to the realities of wrinkles and sagging bodies.

Crones barely surface in Elizabethan drama as developed human types. When they are not merely trivialized, their attributes are fragmented into nurse, bawd, widow, and witch—all figures of some power as threats to the male. Nurses, bawds, and widows are reduced to manageable proportions by sexualization, and witches are dealt with by demonization. All three strategies normally consign crones to positions which men can ultimately explain and control.

The drama of the period expresses encounters between culture—the center of human interaction defined by and for males—and the various forms of the wild—peripheral areas with which culture must necessarily deal.[19] In theory women in patriarchal society are domesticated into culture in roles under male domination—thus the virgin is possessed and disposed of by her father, and culture hopes for the secure transference of this property from father to husband. Wife and mother ideally have clearly defined subordinate roles. Each assigned female stage is subject to rebellion or violation, but the guidelines are clear. By contrast the crone is an anomalous figure, disquieting because she does not fit neatly into the cultural picture. Anomalous figures call for classification and incorporation. The widow in drama, if she is rich, is dangerously free of male control and needs to be remarried. If poor, she exists, like other unattached old women, on the suspect fringes of culture and is liable to be expelled and castigated as a witch. In a few rare cases the crone is venerated as a wise woman.

Nurses, not necessarily defined by age but usually family retainers of long standing, constitute a large category of disturbing women. They are usually nurses of women and serve as female confidantes—necessary to the drama, but suspect as possible messengers between the tamed world of culture and the dreaded wild of uncontrolled female sexuality. It is an easy step from nurse to bawd. But although threatening, nurses and bawds can be dealt with by law and authority. The witch is an acknowledged outlaw. Even the rare wise older woman, whom culture tries to assimilate, frequently has little real power. When she succeeds, her victories take on an aura of the miraculous.

As depicted in drama, very few crones have the privilege of choosing their own destiny. Mother Sawyer in the Rowley/Ford/Dekker *The Witch of Edmonton* (1621), initially a harmless old woman, is widely vilified as a witch. She says,

> Why should the envious world
> Throw all their scandalous malice upon me?
> 'Cause I am poor, deformed and ignorant,
> And like a bow buckled and bent together
> By some more strong in mischiefs than myself,
> Must I for that be made a common sink
> For all the filth and rubbish of men's tongues . . . ?
>
> (2.1.1–7)

Cursed and reviled as a witch, she very easily slips into becoming one. In George Chapman's *The Widow's Tears* (1605), Arsace, the notorious bawd, is described as "a virtuous dame, sometimes of worthy fame, now like a decayed merchant turned broker, and retails refuse commodities for unthrifty gallants" (1.3.141–44). The clichés about the crone become self-fulfilling prophecies.

Trivialized crones in comedy are usually naive or stupid objects of rather gentle humor. Gammer Gurton is typical. Although she may be gullible and suspicious, with a disproportionate regard for the "fayre long strayght [needle], that was [her] only treasure" (1.4.5), she is harmless. However, she and Dame Chat are butts of the humor, especially in their farcical fight in act 3. Gammer Gurton accuses Dame Chat of stealing her needle and calls her "bawdie bitch," "callet" [scold], "slut . . . kut [?] . . . rakes [obs. term of abuse] . . . [and] jakes." Chat retaliates with "drab," "olde witch," "skald [scold] . . . bald . . . rotten . . {and} glotten [clotted]" before knocking her opponent to the floor (3.3.1–49). A fight between two mature women without much reason similarly launches the plot of Henry Porter's *The Two Angry Women of Abingdon* (1588).[20] The conflict again revolves around trivia. Unlike male duels or battles, female fights are funny because nothing serious is at stake and the spectator can indulge a sense of superiority at the pettiness and ineptitude of the struggle. By contrast the happy collusion between Mistress Page and Mistress Ford in Shakespeare's *The Merry Wives of Windsor* (1598) offers a refreshing exception.

Stupid or trivialized crones are so plentiful, so predictable, and such one-dimensional objects of humor that there is little point to elaborating the type in detail. Examples appear early and survive late. Mistress Quickly in Shakespeare's *Henry IV I and II* (1596–97, 1598), easily duped and given to malapropisms, is a good example. Even the eloquent and persuasive Duchess of York, who succeeds in saving her son's life in the memorable scene near the end of Shakespeare's *Richard II* (1595) is deprived of weighty status by the new King's dismissive comment on admitting her to his chamber:

> Our scene is alt'red from a serious thing,
> And now chang'd to "The Beggar and the King."
>
> (5.3.79–80)

As the period fades, William D'Avenant produces a particularly unattractive example of the type in the rich widow of the subplot of *Love and Honour* (1634).[21] Her would-be husband rejoices that she will be cheap to woo because she is "very deafe" and need not be courted with music, and she has "no teeth fit for a dry banquet" and so does not need to be feasted (2.3.43–45). Her wooer adds that she is past dancing "unless with crutches in an antimasque." She herself says " 'tis more than 58 years since [she] has hams to trudge" and that she is more taken with the grave than the pleasures of the marriage bed. She is nonetheless persuaded to a loveless marriage. She is then ridiculed by her new spouse, who says that lying with her was worse than being "lock'd in [a] surgeon's box" (4.2.113). He wishes that she "would be so courteous as now to dy" and leave open her chest and money bags (4.2.59–61). Widows are particularly plentiful in the drama of the period. Berger and Bradford list ninety of them; and though they are somewhat varied, they are most often reduced to objects of marital greed. Their power ceases with their marriage.

One other species of relatively minor but often memorable crone is the articulate, frequently mad woman, who for all her skill in language, is a helpless victim. Although she may be strikingly depicted, she is trivialized by her impotence and by her pitiable loss of rationality. The archetype is Isabella in *The Spanish Tragedy* (1587). Although her madness is overshadowed by the more grandiloquent and efficacious madness of Hieronimo, Isabella's mad scene (3.8) contains her poignant imagination of her son enthroned in heaven.

Her version of revenge—to attack the arbour where her son was hanged, making it "fruitless for ever," and similarly to curse her own womb and stab "the helpless breast that gave Horatio such" (4.2)—is typical of the limited possibilities in these plays for effective female vengeance. In Webster's *The White Devil* (1612) Cornelia's mad grief at the death of one son at the hand of the other is equally ineffectual, but haunting in its linguistic reminiscences of Ophelia and in Cornelia's grimly beautiful song, "Call for the robin redbreast and the wren" (5.4.95ff.).

Shakespeare has several examples of this type, not only the mad victims but also the helplessly resigned like the widowed Duchess of Gloucester in *Richard II,* who, unable to move John of Gaunt by her eloquence to avenge her husband, departs with the echoing words,

> Desolate, desolate will I hence and die:
> The last leave of thee takes my weeping eye.
>
> (1.2.73–74)

Queen Elizabeth and the Duchess of York in *Richard III* and Constance in *King John* might be considered in this subgroup, and even the formidable Lady Macbeth dwindles into a helpless and perhaps suicidal madwoman. One of the most moving examples of all is Katherine of Aragon in *Henry VIII* (1613), dethroned after twenty years through no fault of her own. Although she is wonderfully eloquent in her own defense, she has after she has been divorced no recourse except death. She imagines, accurately, that

> Like the lily
> That once was mistress of the field, and flourish'd
> I'll hang my head and perish.
>
> (3.1.151–53

She has a vision of eternal happiness, but her final wish reveals the narrowness of her earthly choices. It evokes an image of the death in life that has become her only destiny. She says to her women,

>   . . . strew me over
> With maiden flowers, that all the world may know
> I was a chaste wife to my grave. Embalm me
> Then lay me forth. Although unqueen'd yet like
> A queen, and daughter to a king, inter me.
>
>   (4.2.168–72)

The women in this category—the mad and the impotent—are not trivial except as they are powerless. Their poignance lies in their recognition and despair.

Sexualized crones, usually nurses and/or bawds, are similarly ubiquitous and predictable instruments of exposition and plot. Berger and Bradford list fifty-seven nurses and sixty-two bawds (some of these are men). Sexualizing these crones confines them to severely limited roles, both menacing and containable. Cultural constructs, they retain elements of the female wild. As such, they can cause trouble, but they can also be eliminated or ignored because their livelihood depends on their connection with culture. The nurses may be as individualized as Juliet's nurse in Shakespeare's *Romeo and Juliet* (1595) or mere ciphers, but all tend to be pragmatists who accommodate to circumstances even if their actions countenance such Renaissance taboos as adultery, fornication, miscegenation, infanticide, murder, or incest. The nurse in Shakespeare's *Titus Andronicus* (1592?) seems disturbed at her mistress's liaison with Aaron the Moor only after the ocular proof of it emerges in the form of a "babe as loathsome as a toad," "dismal, black, and sorrowful," and she seems content to have the child christened with a dagger's point. (4.2.66–70) Juliet's nurse finds no problem with urging her mistress to a bigamous marriage with the County Paris (3.5.213–25). Balia in George Gascoigne's *Supposes* (1566) arranges for her unwed mistress to pass "many pleasant nightes together" with her supposed servant Dulippo (1.1.20–22). Nutriche in John Marston's *Antonio's Revenge* (1600) eggs on her mistress, Maria, who is about to marry her husband's murderer, assuring Maria from her own experience of four husbands that "variety of husbands [makes] perfect wives" (3.2.1–15). And Putana in John Ford's *'Tis Pity She's a Whore* (1632) advises her mistress Annabella to choose as her husband "a plain-sufficient, naked man" (1.2.92–93), concluding after Annabella has revealed her incestuous preference for her brother, "if a young wench feel the fit upon her, let her take anybody, father or brother, all is one" (2.1.44–45).

Nurses may be mistrusted by women as well as men. Juliet finally rejects her nurse. And Dido in Christopher Marlowe's *Dido Queen of Carthage* (1594)[22] turns violently on her (apparently eighty year old but still amorous) nurse when the boy Ascanius disappears. She speaks of her as a "cursed hagge" with "withered veins and dry sinews," and a "false dissembling wretch" "traytoresse to kind, and cursed Sorceresse" (5.1.212–24). The Old

Lady, friend of Anne Boleyn in Shakespeare's *Henry VIII,* serves the typical functions of a nurse in an intriguingly ambiguous way. In the face of Anne's protestations to the contrary, the Old Lady pragmatically advises that she herself would venture maidenhead to become Queen and suspects that Anne's denial of this possibility is spiced with hypocrisy (2.3.24–26). The Old Lady turns out to be right, and, though she seems at the moment to be advocating adultery, her advice merely serves to point up the moral murkiness of Henry's political situation. Anne's actions cannot be totally sanctioned because of the living presence of the sympathetic Katherine of Aragon, but Anne cannot be wrong because she is the mother of Elizabeth. The Old Lady highlights the dilemma and lives to preside grumpily over the disappointing arrival of a daughter.

Nurses thus threaten the borders of culture at every turn. Technically within cultural bounds as household servants, they nonetheless have power to subvert patriarchal law through their pragmatic accommodations. Their association with fertility makes them doubly hazardous, connecting them with other families, especially at the crucial moment of birth, and regularly facilitating female regression to the wild.[23]

Bawds, by their profession, similarly enable transgression of cultural restrictions on women. Useful as they are to males, their names—Mistress Faugh, Maquerelle, Putana, Madonna Fingerlock, Mistress Horseleech, Madame Decoy, Mother Mortgage, and Mistress Overdone[24]—attest to their disreputable status. Though not exactly demonized, bawds, like nurses, are peripheral figures who inspire both fear and contempt. These necessary but treacherous crones are described in terms that convey revulsion as well as condescension. Mary Faugh in John Marston's *The Dutch Courtesan* (1604) is characterized as a "rotten, rough-bellied bawd" and a "blue-tooth'd patroness of natural wickedness" (1.2.4–5). Such types are even more likely to be toothless—a condition that suggests repulsive age and dissipation, but also perhaps betokens their ultimate impotence.

The most interesting category of crones in the drama of the period is that of the malign and benign demonics. Witches are the most prominent subspecies. Berger and Bradford list twenty-five plays in which they appear. There seems to be a particular pleasure in enumerating their grisly practices, most of them still familiar diabolical clichés. Ben Jonson's Hagges in *The Masque of Queens* (1609) report such exploits as gathering wolves' hairs and mad dogs' foam, stealing skulls from charnel houses, and killing infants for their fat. His witches also collect hemlock, henbane, adders-tongue, and nightshade. And they ride a great buck-goat. These hags have awesomely Jonsonian classical roots, and they retain also echoes of archaic Hecate worship. Their Dame enters looking more like a prehistoric goddess than a traditional witch. She is "naked arm'd bare-footed, her frock tuck'd, her hayre knotted and folded with vipers; In her hand a Torch made of a dead-Man's arme, lighted;

girded with a snake" (286). The Dame's invocation, like Medea's in Ovid, calls upon Hecate, the "three-formed Starre" of triple Name and claims, like Prospero, the ability to stir up the sea and turn day to night (294–96).

And yet ultimately Jonson's witches are powerless. They complain that all their charms "do nothing winne," and they exist only to be routed by the sound of music signaling the appearance of Heroic Virtue and the panoply of Queens who are the stars of the show. Other witches are enjoyed for their sinister machinations, but there always seems an element of mock-seriousness about them, as if they are playing on the fantasies of the fevered imagination but only within limits. Dispas in John Lyly's *Endymion* (1588)[25] boasts

> I can darken the Sun by my skill, and remove
> the moon out of her course; I can restore youth
> to the aged and make hills without bottoms.
>
> (1.4.20–22)

She is depicted as an old woman who has "fifty years practiced that detested wickedness of witchcraft." But, in spite of her successful spells, she cannot rule hearts. Cynthia warns her:

> Breathe out thou mayst words, gather thou mayest herbs, find out thou mayest stones agreeable to thine art, yet of no force to appal my heart, in which courage is so rooted, and constant persuasion of the mercy of the gods, so grounded, that all thy witchcraft I esteem as weak as the world doth thy case wretched. (5.3.21–32)

Mother Sawyer's pathetic witcheries are punished by death in *The Witch of Edmonton* (by William Rowley, Thomas Dekker, John Ford, et al., 1621). Although the vitality of Middleton's mischievous crones in *The Witch* (before 1627) makes them seem almost celebratory, they too are controlled. We hear that Hecate will live a total of six-score years, but she knows that she will die at midnight after three years. They may have grisly ingredients, but her very invocations seem more playful than frightening:

> Titty, Tiffin
> Keep it stiff in
> Firedrake, Puckey
> Make it lucky
> Liard Robin
> You must bob in.
>
> (5.2.62–67)

And such spectacular special effects as her flight on the Great Cat are good theater but inconsequential to plot. She can cause Antonio's impotence with his wife but not with his whore, and she cannot "disjoin wedlock" (1.2.172).

Obviously some threat to culture, she is fairly easily overcome. She is also degraded by her incestuous relationship with her loutish son, Firestone.

Perhaps the most devastating description of a witch is that of Erictho in Marston's *The Wonder of Women, or Sophonisba* (1606). She is summoned from the deepest hell to help Syphax win the love of Sophonisba. He tells us

> Dreadful Erictho lives, whose dismal brow
> Contemns all roofs or civil coverture.
> Forsaken graves and tombs, the ghosts forced out
> She joys to inhabit.
> A loathsome yellow leanness spreads her face,
> Unknown to a clear heaven. But if dark winds
> Or thick black clouds drive back the blinded stars
> When her deep magic makes forced heaven quake
> And thunder spite of Jove, Erictho then
> From naked graves stalks out, heaves proud her head
> With long, unkempt hair loaden, and strives to snatch
> The night's quick sulpher. Then she bursts up tombs,
> From half-rot cerecloths then she scrapes dry gums
> For her black rites. But when she finds a corse
> New graved whose entrails yet not turn
> To slimy filth, with greedy havoc then
> She makes fierce spoil and swells with wicked triumph
> To bury her lean knuckles in his eyes.
> Then doth she gnaw the pale and o'ergrown nails
> From his dry hand. But if she find some life
> Yet lurking close, she bites his gelid lips,
> And sticking her black tongue in his dry throat,
> She breathes dire murmurs which enforce him bear
> Her baneful secrets to the spirits of horror.

(4.1.98–122)

One could hardly ask for a more arresting series of frissons. But Erictho hardly lives up to her advance billing. Instead of helping Syphax she tricks him into bed herself in the guise of Sophonisba, enforcing his silence while the consummation is in progress. Afterward she merely laughs at him as he rages at the "rotten scum of hell" who has aroused his "abhorred heat." She retorts that his "proud heat well wasted" has made her limbs grow young after three score years of lustfulness. She concludes however, that though witches "can make enraged Neptune toss / His huge curled locks without one breath of wind" and "make heaven slide from Atlas' shoulder," it is not "within the grasp of heaven or hell / To enforce love" (5.1.1–20). Erictho has enacted a male nightmare by appropriating his valuable sperm, but in the end her actions are hardly more than a practical joke.

In *Gorboduc or Ferrex and Porrex* (1562), by Thomas Sackville and

Thomas Norton, the three Furies from Hell with their serpent, whip, and burning firebrand accurately foreshadow but do not precipitate the destruction of the family and kingdom. God himself is the only hope for restoring peace. Even in *Macbeth* (1606), where the witches are rather more serious, they do not *cause* Macbeth's actions. They objectify his ideas and mislead him with prophecies, but he is responsible for his own actions. The witches finally become instruments of the establishment as they sponsor the masque of English kings, alarming Macbeth but reassuring the audience about the future. The crone as witch inhabits the drama to frighten—these old women are up to no good, but ultimately the text reduces them to their proper subordinate status.

There can be no doubt that the crone in all her forms in Renaissance drama is a reminder of disintegration and death—of physical decay, of crooked and deformed bodies, of rotten and toothless mouths, of the corruption of cultural mores, of the enervating effects for men of the loss to women of seminal fluid, of the reality of a hell with special connections to women, and of the pervasive conjunction of womb and tomb, reinforced by the persistent linking of women to the earth. There may even be some archaic memory of the Triple Goddess as Creator, Preserver, and Destroyer. The three widowed queens who interrupt the nuptials of Theseus and Hippolyta in Shakespeare's and John Fletcher's *The Two Noble Kinsmen* (1624) are witnesses to the stench and mortal loathsomeness of the foul fields where their rotting husbands lie unburied and prey to scavenger ravens, kites, and crows (1.1.41–47). Of the three Fates, Atropos, clipper of the thread of life, is typically depicted as an old woman. And old women traditionally prepared bodies for burial and acted as mourners. If the crone so relentlessly calls up the specter of death, small wonder that she should be erased from consciousness, denigrated, and demonized. It also seems logical that in her more virulent forms she is confronted but ritually defeated, acculturated, or forgotten. The treatment of the crone in this drama constitutes in effect a denial of death and disorder.

This prevailing pattern is modified in a few rare cases where the crone seems to be linked not with hell but at least tangentially with heaven. Her function may still be death-defying, but it takes the form of uttering and performing acts that affirm providential order. Her imagined shapes may be rooted in memories of the Triple Goddess as Preserver, or in echoes of Virgil's Cumaean Sybil. She may evoke visions of the Virgin Mary as human intercessor between earth and heaven—a role made manifest in representations of her miraculous assumption, a favorite subject of Renaissance artists, although interestingly such paintings regularly show her surprisingly rejuvenated. Typically they show the Virgin, surrounded by assisting angels, ascending into heaven, but they also suggest her inspiration and offer hope to those below. Mary's mother, St. Anne, also functions in art as an aged but ageless woman of miraculous fertility. Like her daughter she seems divinely rejuvenated. It is also possible that this image of a benign crone reflects the aura of an aging but still powerful reigning queen. (The Q1 Epilogue of the anonymous *Mucedorus* [1590], shows Comedy and Envy joining together to pray that the Queen may live to be three times as old as Nestor [1.18,p.126]).

Sometimes the crone as superwoman is very close to the margins of the crone as witch. Queen Margaret, transformed from the active schemer and brutal fighter of Shakespeare's *Henry VI* plays (1589–91?), hovers like a venomous harpy on the edges of the court in *Richard III,* but powerless as she is, her curses prove to be precisely carried out. Their accuracy supports her claim to status as a prophetess, and she says rather paradoxically of her devastating curses,

> I will not think but they ascend the sky,
> And there awake God's gentle-sleeping peace.
>
> (1.3.286–87)

The fulfillment of her curses builds for the audience a sense of divine justice that mitigates the play's violence. Buckingham's last repentant words recall her warning about Richard:

> Thus Margaret's curse fall heavy on my neck;
> "When he," quoth she, "shall split thy heart with sorrow,
> Remember Margaret was a prophetess."
>
> (5.1.25–27)

Other crones who voice the truth are likewise curiously passive. The six-hundred-year-old Sybilla in Lyly's *Sapho and Phao* (1584)[26] first appears impressively seated in her cave assuring Phao, who has come to her for advice, that "though you behold wrinkles and furrows in my tawny face, yet may you happily find wisdome and counsell in my white haires." But she does nothing, and her "advice" turns out to be at best a disappointing tissue of cliches, and at worst a mouthing of male misreadings of female desires. She confides in Phao:

> I tell the a straung thing, womenne strive,
> because they would be overcome: force they call
> it, but such a welcome force they account it,
> that continually they study to be enforced.
>
> (92–95)

At the play's end, having helped Phao not at all, she can only warn him that other things hang over his head that she cannot reveal to him. Mother Bombie in Lyly's play of that name (1589) is much more developed. She is "an old cunning woman who can tell fortunes, expound dreams, tell of things that be lost, and divine of accidents to come. She is called the good woman who yet never did hurt" (3.1.31–35). Mother Bombie is an accurate prophet who speaks the truth, but Lyly has given her very little to do. Violet Jeffrey argues that she is "entirely unessential and could well have been left out without any loss;" but G. K. Hunter persuasively defends her as a prophetess giving an important "dimension of mystery and misunderstanding" to the play. Harriette Andreadis goes further, saying, "In her seeming omniscience, she is rather like a figure of some benign supernature observing with detachment as the natural order rights itself." "She acts as a promise of order at the height of confusion" and thus seems a providential agent (60–62).

Interesting twists on the theme of the old wise woman occur in John Fletcher's *Woman Pleas'd* (1620) where the female hero, Belvidere, disguises herself as a deformed old and ugly hag, who, though old and "of a crooked carcasse" has a "voice . . . like the harmony of Angels" (4.2.21–28). She watches over her lover, Silvio, and coaches him in the correct answer to the riddle of what a woman wants. Like Sybilia's advice, the answer is revealingly misogynistic—what women want is "their will," but when they have it they abuse it and know not how to use it (5.1.126–42). In her deformed shape Belvidere elicits her lover's promise that he will marry her. She becomes then the butt of many jokes: her teeth are scarce come yet; she has a large nose and a knotty back and a "fine little eye like an elephant's." The benign crone becomes a ludicrous love object. The tables are only turned when she magically changes back to the youthful Belvidere, erasing the Hag. The woman Silvio has called "Mother" is successfully transformed to wife. This process, reminiscent of Chaucer's *The Wife of Bath's Tale,* is a recurring theme of folklore. It seems psychologically apt, and once again the specter of decay is miraculously banished.

The crone in Thomas Heywood's *The Wise Woman of Hogsdon* (1604)[28] is similarly ambiguous. Although billed as a wise woman, she is clearly a charlatan who does palmistry with the help of a secret closet for eavesdropping. She also runs a brothel and delivers bastards, disposing of them benignly (pp. 305–6). Chartley, a young rake engaged to two women, both conveniently named Luce, calls the old woman "the witch, the Beldame, Hagge of Hogsdon," and "Inchantresse, Sorceresse, Shee-devill, Madam *Hecate,* Lady *Proserpine,*" and an "Old Dromedary," thereby arousing the wise woman's wrath and vengeful spirit. Another visitor tells her that though she looks like the devil's dam, except for the fact that her "teeth stand like hedge-stakes" in her head, he would kiss her (pp. 290–97). Villified in stereotypical terms, and apparently discredited, the wise woman, instead of conforming to type springs a series of surprises. She manipulates a complicated plot to a satisfying ending in a way that reveals her to be truly wise. She does work "magic" in pairing off appropriate couples and ensuring a just and happy ending. Even Chartley comes to find love in his heart for "mother midnight" (352). This uncommon benign crone triumphs delightfully over all the clichés of popular expectation.

As always, Shakespeare is of particular interest in his uses of and deviations from the norms. Four examples of invented or elaborated old women are especially striking as subtly developed variations on conventional patterns. The Abbess, who serves as the *dea ex machina* in *The Comedy of Errors* (1592–94), the autumnally wise and reverend Countess of Rossillion in *All's Well that Ends Well* (1602–1603), the formidable Volumnia of *Coriolanus* (1607–1608), and the "magical" Paulina of *The Winter's Tale* (1610–11) are neither trivialized nor sexualized, and what "demonic" powers they possess are healing or at least stabilizing.

Emilia, the Abbess who presides over the resolution of *The Comedy of Errors* is a Shakespearean invention. She resides in a Christian priory, but like Thaisa of *Pericles* (1607–1608), who also found religious refuge in Ephesus, she may share the ambience of the great temple of Diana that once graced that city. Intriguingly Ephesus is also identified in tradition as the site of the last years of the Virgin Mary.[29] Emilia as Abbess/Mother combines chastity and fertility in her image of a nun giving birth to sons after thirty-three years of labor (5.1.401). She is strong-minded but strictly an instrument of patriarchy—protecting the males, reproving the independent-minded wife, and emerging from confinement to the priory only to rejoin her miraculously recovered spouse. A supporter of Providential order, she defeats death and chaos by reasserting cultural ties.

Volumnia, greatly developed by Shakespeare from Plutarch, similarly shores up a disintegrating patriarchal culture. Having shaped her son into the ideal Roman fighting machine, she is forced to sacrifice him to the common good. In her final appearance on returning to Rome after consigning her son to certain death among the volscians, she assumes an ironic goddess-like status, having personally survived as Creator, Preserver, and Destroyer.[30] She denies death only by accepting it, and she ends as one of Shakespeare's darkest tragic figures, the childless mother of Rome. Unlike other old women, she has been given the privilege of choice and permitted to live with the consequences.

By contrast the Countess of Rossillion, another Shakespearean invention not in his source, becomes part of a curious female coalition mounted against her son. The women's goal is benign—the integration of the recalcitrant Bertram into society, but their methods are highly unorthodox. Unlike the Abbess and Volumnia, the Countess is relatively passive, but by ruling her own domain and by siding with Helena, her ward, against Bertram, her son, she becomes a rare example of a matriarchal crone. She combats sterility in favor of fertility and thus denies death. She also seems a precursor of Shakespeare's greatest crone, the much more active Paulina of *The Winter's Tale*, again an invention of Shakespeare.

The Abbess, Volumnia, and the Countess derive much of their importance from being the mothers of sons, but Paulina stands alone as a wise woman who can rule a king in her own right. If she has children, we never see them, and she is husbandless for most of her career. She embodies two benign dimensions of the Goddess—her appearance with the newborn Perdita images her as maternal Creator, and her sixteen-year sequestering of the supposed-dead Hermione establishes her as Preserver. She calls herself an "old turtle," but, through her stunningly theatrical presentation of "magical" resurrection and reunion, she seems more like a reincarnated Ceres bringing the world from a bitter winter's tale to a springtime celebration of the return of fertility. Whether Leontes's hasty arrangement of her remarriage is a welcome part of the celebration or a political defeat for the powerful crone is a matter of individual decision.

Perhaps the most extraordinary of all Elizabethan crones is Delphia, the title character of Fletcher's *The Prophetess* (1622), probably revised by Philip Massinger in 1629. She has predicted that Diocles will be Emperor of Rome after he has killed a mighty boar, and although he believes her to be a "holy Druid" (1.3.95) and a "rare soothsayer" inspired with "prophetic fire" (1.3.129-32), she is also the object of the usual calumnies. Diocles's nephew Maximilian distrusts "old wives' dreams." He is tired of feeding "her old chaps" while "she sits farting at us, / And blowing out her prophecies at both ends!" Old women, he claims, "will lie monstrously" and like the devil are malicious, proud, covetous, revengeful, and lecherous. It is "to veil over these villainies [that] they would prophesy" (1.3.82–115). He changes his tune when Delphia paralyzes his arm to prevent his shooting an arrow at her, and it quickly becomes clear, as Delphia has maintained, that her "sure prediction" can no more fail than the day or night does" (1.2.20–21).

Delphia is a female Prospero. Like him she can bedim the noontide sun, and she has other powers equal to "the gods and nature's wonders." She borrows winged dragons from Ceres and calls on the music of the spheres to attend her so that she and her niece Drusilla can hang over Diocles's tribunal and observe his actions (2.1.64–72). The two do indeed enter "in a Throne drawn by Dragons" (2.3.SD). Delphia points out that at the spectacle the eye of heaven has hidden behind clouds and

> . . . the pale moon
> Pluck'd in her silver horns, trembling for fear
> That my strong spells should force her from her sphere
> Such is the power of art.
>
> (2.3.4–7)

Diocles shows some resistance to Delphia's plan to marry him to her niece, but with the aid of thunder and lightning, and special rites to Hecate, Delphia manages to keep him in line. When captured by Geta, who imagines her a "traiterous quean" who keeps twenty devils (3.2.93), she presents him with Lucifera, a She-devil so bewitching that she leaves Geta feeling "burnt to ashes" and endowed with a glass-house in his codpiece. He resolves to abdicate the pleasures of authority to seek another trade (3.2.118–24). At the play's end Maximinian reappears as a rebel, subdued only by Delphia's sound and light show complete with thunder and lightning, earthquake, and a hand with a bolt that appears in the heavens threatening "vengeance on ungrateful wretches" (5.4.112SD). Delphia concludes with the promise to provide her new nephew-in-law, now Emperor, with the "room and glory" he aspires to (5.4.146–57). Although she lacks the psychological subtlety and mythical resonance of Paulina, Delphia has powers and special effects that exceed even Prospero's. She is so accurate in predicting the future and so successful in controlling resistance to her plans that she almost removes the suspense from the plot. She secures an emperor, albeit a reluctant one, as spouse for her niece; she dominates both Persians and Romans; and she prevents a civil war, all with a fine sense of theater. And her spectacular celestial navigation lends her, like the Virgin, an aura of divinity.

The play was licensed by Sir Henry Herbert on 14 May 1622, and Bertha Hensman suggests that the activities of the jester, Geta, as dispenser of fantastic monopolies, may have topical reference to to Sir Francis Bacon's trial for bribery in 1621. The play was so popular at its performance in the summer of 1629 that Herbert chose it as his benefit play for that year, recording a profit of £6 7s.[31] The appeal of a powerful peacemaker and preventer of civil war may have been strong at that historical moment, following Parliament's passage of *The Petition of Right* in 1628, and in the year of Charles I's dismissal of Parliament. The special effects must also have been dazzling. But the genesis and centrality of the female wizard is more difficult to explain. Fletcher seems to have picked up a reference in his source to a Druidess who predicted that Diocletian would become emperor, but he expanded and developed her role into the force that unifies the historical and romantic threads of his plot.[32] Whatever her origins, Delphia becomes the unparalleled example of the awe-inspiring and death-defying crone. In the history of Renaissance drama John Fletcher, as her creator, deserves a special niche—not too far from Shakespeare—for his presentation of the possibility that the later years of the human life cycle might be as interesting for women as for men.

But his is a voice crying in the wilderness. The exceptions to the representations of the crone as harbinger of death are so rare as to prove the rule. For a reader of Renaissance drama who considers crones seriously, it is very difficult to avoid sharing the conviction that they are mad, wicked, simpleminded, passive, suicidal, negligible, or nonexistent. In each case, because of their seemingly ineradicable associations with death, they must be repressed, ridiculed into insignificance, or assimilated uneasily into culture. The denial of death is a major stimulus to creativity, but it need not always lead down the same paths.[33] The contemplation of Volumnia, the Countess of Rossillion, Paulina, and Delphia might provide hints of ways that the crone could be extricated from the dead end of defeat, decay, and dissolution.

Notes

All references to William Shakespeare are to *The Riverside Shakespeare* ed. G. Blakemore Evans, et al. (Boston: Houghton Mifflin, 1997). Seven of the plays discussed are included in *Drama of the English Renaissance,* ed. Russell A. Fraser and Norman Rabkin, 2 vols. (London: Macmillan, 1967), and I have used this text for reference to these plays (*Gammer Gurton's Needle, Supposes, The Spanish Tragedy, Mucedorus, The Widow's Tears, The White Devil,* and *'Tis Pity She's a Whore*). All references to Marston are to the World Classics *John Marston: "The Malcontent" and Other Plays,* ed. Keith Sturgess (Oxford: Oxford University Press, 1997). References to Jonson are to *Ben Jonson,* ed. C. H. Herford, Percy, and Evelyn Simpson, 11 vols. (Oxford: Clarendon, 1925–52). References to Dekker are to *The Dramatic Works of Thomas Dekker,* ed. Fredson Bowers, 4 vols. (Cambridge: Cambridge University Press, 1955). References to Francis Beaumont and John Fletcher are to *The Dramatic Works in the Beaumont and Fletcher Canon,* ed. Fredson Bowers et al., 10 vols. (Cambridge: Cambridge University Press, 1953–82). References to *The Witch* and *The Witch of Edmonton* are to *Three Jacobean Witchcraft Plays,* ed. Peter Corbin and Douglas Sedge (Manchester: Manchester University Press, 1986.)

1. See especially Barbara G. Walker, *The Crone: Woman of Age, Wisdom, and Power* (San Francisco: Harper and Row, 1985).

2. *The Odyssey of Homer,* trans. Richard Lattimore (New York: Harper and Row, 1975), 292.

3. *The Homeric Hymns and Homerica,* trans. Hugh G. Evelyn-White (London: Heinemann, 1914), 109–13.

4. For background and discussion of the Great Goddess, see: Robert Graves, *The White Goddess: A Historical Grammar of Poetic Myth* (New York: Farrar Straus, and Giroux, 1966); Erich Neumann, *The Great Mother: An Analysis of the Archetype,* trans. Ralph Manheim (Princeton: Princeton University Press, 1974); and Anne Baring and Jules Cashford, *The Myth of the Goddess: Evolution of an Image* (London: Arkana, 1991).

5. *Le imagini de i dei de gli antichi* (Venice, 1587), 78. I am grateful to Dr. H. Diane Russell, Curator of Old Master Prints at the National Gallery of Art, who generously shared with me her broad knowledge of Renaissance art. The catalogue of her Gallery show, *Eva/Ave: Women in Renaissance and Baroque Prints* (New York: The Feminist Press, 1990), is an invaluable resource and contains an extended and beautifully illustrated discussion of some of the topics discussed here.

6. Georges Minois, *History of Old Age from Antiquity to the Renaissance,* trans. Sarah Hansbury Tenison (Chicago: University of Chicago Press, 1989), 79.

7. George E. Duckworth, *The Nature of Roman Comedy: A Study in Popular Entertainment* (Princeton: Princeton University Press, 1952), 253.

8. Kathleen M. Lea, *Italian Popular Comedy: A Study in the Commedia dell'Arte 1560–1620*, 2 vols. (Oxford: Clarendon, 1963), I: 112–20.

9. Minois, *History of Old Age*, 292–93, 254–56.

10. Ibid., 301.

11. The closing of the convents and monasteries in England was confirmed by Henry VIII in the passing of the Act of Supremacy, 1536–38. *Dictionary of National Biography*, 9: 540.

12. Elizabeth Cary, *The Tragedy of Mariam, Fair Queen of Jewry*, ed. Barry Weller and Margaret W. Ferguson (Berkeley: University of California Press, 1994). For an extended discussion of Cary's relationship with her mother see Meredith Skura, "The Reproduction of Mothering in *The Tragedy of Mariam, Fair Queen of Jewry:* A Defense of Biographical Criticism," *Tulsa Studies in Women's Literature* 16 (1997): 27–56.

13. Leah S. Marcus discusses both the ambiguity of feelings toward Elizabeth and the increasing gap between the image and the physical reality in *Puzzling Shakespeare* (Berkeley: University of California Press, 1988), 103–4.

14. I am grateful to Professor Alan Dessen, who graciously shared his encyclopedic knowledge of English Renaissance drama and greatly assisted my search for crones.

15. *The Old Law*, ed. Catherine M. Shaw (New York: Garland, 1982). Dates for plays are usually those given in the listed collections or recorded in *An Index of Characters in English Printed Drama to the Restoration* by Thomas L. Berger and William C. Bradford, Jr. (Englewood, Colo.: Microcard Editions, 1975).

16. Respectively: "Gammer Gurton's Needle" (1575) by William Stevenson and "Ralph Roister Doister" (1566) by Nicholas Udall in *English Drama: An Anthology 900–1642*, ed. Winfield Parks and Richmond Croom Beatty (New York: Norton, 1935); "The Honest Whore, Part 1" (1605) by Thomas Dekker, "The Staple of News" (1626) by Ben Jonson; "The Witch of Edmonton" (1621) by William Rowley, Thomas Dekker, and John Ford, et al.; "The Lady of Pleasure" (1635) by James Shirley, ed. Ronald Huebert (Manchester: Manchester University Press, 1986).

17. See for example Coppelia Kahn, "The Absent Mother in 'King Lear'" in *Rewriting the Renaissance: Discourses of Sexual Differences in Early Modern Europe*, ed. Margaret W. Ferguson et al. (Chicago: University of Chicago Press, 1986), 31–49. Bruno Bettelheim notes a similar pattern in fairy tales—the absence of a living "good" mother. He says "the typical fairy-tale splitting of the mother into a good (usually dead) mother and an evil stepmother . . . permits anger at this bad 'stepmother' without endangering the goodwill of the true mother." *The Uses of Enchantment: The Meaning and Importance of Fairy Tales* (New York: Knopf, 1976), 69.

18. Thomas May, *The Old Couple*, ed. Sister M. Simplicia Fitzgibbons (Washington, D.C.: Catholic University of America Press, 1943).

19. See Jeanne Addison Roberts, *The Shakespearean Wild: Geography, Genus, and Gender* (Lincoln: University Nebraska Press, 1991) for further discussion of this idea.

20. Henry Porter, *The Two Angry Women of Abingdon*, in *Representative English Comedies*, ed. Charles M. Gayley, 4 vols. (New York: Macmillan, 1916).

21. William D'Avenant, *Love and Honour*, ed. James W. Tupper (Boston: D.C. Heath, 1909).

22. Christopher Marlowe with Thomas Nashe, *Dido Queen of Carthage,* in *The Complete Works of Christopher Marlowe,* ed. Fredson Bowers, 2 vols. (Cambridge: Cambridge University Press, 1981).

23. See Jeanne Roberts, "Shakespeare's Maimed Birth Rites" in *True Rites and Maimed Rites: Ritual and Anti-Ritual in Shakespeare and His Age,* ed. Linda Woodbridge and Edward Berry (Urbana: University of Illinois Press, 1992).

24. Respectively: *The Dutch Courtesan, The Malcontent, 'Tis Pity She's a Whore, The Honest Whore Part 1, The Honest Whore Part 2, The Lady of Pleasure, The Staple of News,* and *Measure for Measure.*

25. John Lyly, *Endymion,* in *The Complete Works of John Lyly,* ed. R. Warwick Bond, 2 vols. (Oxford: Clarendon, 1902).

26. See note 25.

27. John Lyly, *Mother Bombie,* ed. Harriette Andreadis (Salzburg: Salzburg University Press, 1975).

28. Thomas Heywood, *The Wise Woman of Hogsdon,* ed. Michael H. Leonard (New York: Garland, 1980).

29. Geoffrey Ashe, *The Virgin* (London: Routledge & Kegan Paul, 1976), 185.

30. For a sustained discussion of Volumnia as an aspect of the Great Goddess, see Peggy Munoz Simonds, "*Coriolanus* and the Myth of Juno and Mars," *Mosaic* 18, 2 (spring 1985): 33–50.

31. Bertha Hensman, *The Shares of Fletcher, Field, and Massinger in Twelve Plays of the Beaumont and Fletcher Canon,* 2 vols. (Salzburg: University of Salzburg Press, 1974), 2: 296.

32. Ibid., 2: 298–306, for a discussion of sources.

33. See Ernest Becker, *The Denial of Death* (New York: Macmillan, 1973).

Prostitution in Late Elizabethan London: The Case of Mary Newborough

GUSTAV UNGERER

Intoduction

WALLACE Shugg, about two decades ago, deplored the lack of an extensive study of prostitution in Elizabethan and Jacobean London. In the meantime, our knowledge of the sex trade in Tudor London has dramatically improved thanks to the pioneering work of Ian W. Archer and Paul Griffiths. Their investigations, however, are not as comprehensive as the researches undertaken by Ruth Mazo Karras for medieval England. Despite this reservation, chapter 6 in Archer's study is a milestone.[1] Archer deserves credit for ushering in a new departure in the exploration of Elizabethan prostitution. He has made a clean break with the old method pursued by literary critics and historians of crime who were prompted to recover the experienced realities of the underworld from characters represented in imaginative literature. He is the first to have begun the systematic recovery of Elizabethan prostitution in London from archival sources, mainly from the Bridewell Court Books, providing authentic information on its organization and structure (henceforth BCB).[2] Scholars are bound to benefit from his findings, but they will deplore that he has fashioned his analysis out of material limited to the 1570s, to the unsuccessful "crack-down" on prostitution unleashed by the metropolitan authorities and the governors of Bridewell. Feminists will find fault with his disinterest in the fate of the individual prostitute; they are likely to take him to task for treating a prostitute as an anonymous statistical entity.

Paul Griffiths, in his turn, has deepened our insight into the dynamic and structure of London prostitution in the 1570s, but has not extended his archival researches into the last decade of the sixteenth century and the first of the seventeenth (BCB, vols. 4 and 5).[3] One of his study's main objectives is to warn against the difference between historically authentic prostitution and the contemporary narratives accommodated to the didactic agendas of rogue literature, repentance pamphlets, and fictionalized criminal biography. The method of lumping together the historical experience of the 1570s with the

The contents of this article have been arranged thus:

Introduction
Marriage to a Highwayman
The Establishment of Eleanor Dethick, alias Mrs. Windsor, and of David
    English, Minister of St. Katherine's Christchurch
Mary Newborough's Italian Patrons in Mrs. Windsor's Establishment: Tomas
    Marini and Paolo Gondola
Mary Newborough in Mrs. Miller's Establishment and a Historic Coach Ride
Apparel Proclaims the Prostitute in the Playhouse: The Fashioning of
    Elizabeth Reignoldes
Price Structure and Contraceptives
A Support Network Among Prostitutes and Katherine Arden's Pregnancy
Agnes Wilkinson's Establishment and Lord Cobham's Sons Sir William and
    George Brooke as Patrons of Barbara Allen and Alice Woodstock, alias
    Partridge
The Dramaturgy of a Processional Spectacle: The Carting of Mary
    Newborough [1600]
Eating Disorders of a Bridewell Spinner and the Tradition of Spinning Songs
The Bridewell Scandal of 1602
    Farming out Bridewell to four Contractors
    Bridewell under the Sway of the Prostitutes
    Chastisement and Resistance of the Prostitutes
    Plots and Attempts to Escape from Bridewell
Mary Newborough's (Mock) Repentance and Release
George Handford's Song About "Mall Newberry her Repentance" (1609)
City Scandal or Court Scandal: A Topical Allusion to a Dark Lady in
    Shakespeare's Twelfth Night

literary accounts of the Restoration and the close of the seventeenth century is not commendable.

A paper of much lesser scope and weight is Carol Kazmierczak Manzione's *Sex in Tudor London,* which turns out to be a simple anthology of sexual misdemeanor. The author ignores the innovative work done by Archer and Griffiths and, with one exception, all the individual cases she presents do not go beyond the 1570s. She can at least claim to supplement Archer's and Griffith's source material insofar as the majority of her documentary evidence is taken from the Guildhall Library.[4]

In view of the vast territory still left unexplored and unmapped, I have chosen to rescue from oblivion and anonymity a group of women who have been denied their individual voices. I have ventured to unlock, empirically and paradigmatically, the reality as experienced by the following bawds and prostitutes, to wit, Eleanor Dethick, Anne Miller, Agnes Wilkinson, Mrs

Cesar, Mrs Willford, Helen Cootes, Elizabeth Stapleton, Elizabeth Reign-oldes, Alice Woodstock, Barbara Allen, Katherine Arden, Lucy Morgan, Mary Digby and others, and particularly by Mary Newborough, the wife of George Newborough, gentleman turned highwayman, in the closing years of the sixteenth and the early years of the seventeenth century. For her contemporaries Mary Newborough was a paragon of sinfulness; from our postmodern perspective she was an extraordinary woman who proved her mettle when facing the ordeal of public shaming in 1600 and who in 1602 withstood the brutality of one of the Bridewell contractors, standing up in defence of her female inmates against the inhumanity of the punitive system. I have also looked into the lives of their patrons, foreign and native, and, where necessary, I have delved into their personal careers and disordered sexual orientations. Mary Newborough's Italian patrons have opened up a neglected field of transcultural exchange and of mercantile activities between England and Italy at the close of the sixteenth century.

The recovery of Mary Newborough's story does not only mark the crossing of a temporal threshold dividing the 1570s from the 1590s, it also breaks new ground in reclaiming what has been considered to be virtually irrecoverable: the individual experience of a woman fallen to the level of prostitution; the authentic voice of a supposedly voiceless miscreant; the culinary predilections of a sophisticated mistress; and the spirited resistance of an undaunted detainee.[5] The self-fashioned voice of this remarkable woman, who took to selling her body out of economic necessity when her husband was imprisoned, emerges fairly unaltered from the BCB. Her individual voice, admittedly, is quite often absent, but the reason for its absence has partly to be sought in some powerful protectors who must have requested her examinations to be excised from the BCB.

The story of Mary Newborough is made up of the stuff which under the hands of Nashe and Dekker used to be reduced to stereotyped narratives: marriage to a gentleman turned highwayman, decline and fall into prostitution as a survival strategy, several arrests and detentions in a house of correction, attempts to escape, punishment and public shaming, repentance, conversion, and rehabilitation. Nashe and Dekker do not seem to have responded to the Newborough scandal; they left the field to a composer, George Handford, who in his unpublished *Ayres to be sunge to the Lute and Base Vyole* (1609) set to music what reads like a versified mock repentance of "Mall Newberry."

The examinations conducted by the governors of Bridewell and the depositions made by Mary Newborough's entourage, her male and female colleagues, all yield valuable information on what Archer has called one of the most highly organized sectors of criminal activity in London. They afford close-up insights into the workings of prostitution: its structure, business networks, solidarity among prostitutes and female brothel keepers, possessiveness of procurers, immunity of patrons (noblemen's sons, clergymen), patterns of clientage (wealthy foreign merchants, servants of court officials), rate of sexual consumption, floating fee and rent scale, transport by coach, playgoing, and staggering expenditure on gorgeous garments as provocative signifiers of commodified sex. They particularly throw new light on London's sexual geography as situated in the inner reaches of the city and not as exclusively consigned to the outer reaches of civic space.

Archer and Griffiths have come to question the appropriateness of relegating to the margins of society, even to the underworld, an illicit profession which boasted so many close ties with the center of power. The neglected Bridewell records of the 1590s do confirm that the concept of marginalization needs reassessing. It does not quite fit an activity that was tacitly acknowledged to be an integral part of the established order. Before 1546 when prostitution was regulated by the civic authorities, it had been confined to the margins and Liberties of the capital, but after the closure of the licensed brothels in 1546 prostitution dislocated itself from the borders. It invaded the whole territory of the city and by 1590 had situated itself at the very heart of the Elizabethan government. The records disclose that there was an upward movement from marginality to the very center. Thus in 1598 Whitehall provided the dramatic setting of an incident that threatened to convert the palace into a breeding ground of sexual incontinence. (Sir) George Brooke, the dissolute son of William Lord Cobham, abused his privileged position in turning his Whitehall office into a *chambre séparée* where to gratify his *plaisirs du corps*. The sexual geography of London can, therefore, no longer be consigned to the outer borders of the civic space, the red-light districts, the suburbs, the spaces beyond, as literary representations, among them Shakespeare's plays, make us believe.[6] The establishments run by Eleanor Dethick, Agnes Wilkinson, and Anne Miller are living proof that prostitutes plying their trade in the city were not geographically segregated, but were both individually and collectively an integral part of city life. The sexual misconduct of the four Brookes, William Lord Cobham, Henry Lord Cobham, George Brooke, and Sir William Brooke will be addressed separately. In this context, the Oldcastle/Falstaff name change in Shakespeare's *1 Henry IV* (1598) promises to assume a new perspective.

The Bridewell depository treasures material that is likely to decode another Shakespeare controversy. There is unanimous agreement that Sir Toby Belch in goading Sir Andrew Aguecheek into displaying his talents as a reveller and dancer is making an allusion to a woman whose tarnished reputation had become common gossip in London: "Wherefore are these things hid? Wherefore have these things a curtain before 'em? Are they likely to take dust, like Mistress Mall's picture?"[7] There is, however, disagreement over the identity of Mistress Mall. I will be arguing that this is a metaphorical allusion to the city scandal raised by Mary Newborough rather than to the court scandal raised by Mary Fitton.

My approach to the subject and the manner of presentation have been conditioned by the nature of the available records. An unbroken chronological survey of Mary Newborough's life, her curriculum as a prostitute, her detentions and releases from prison between 1596 and 1603 are hard to recover from the BCB given their incompleteness. I shall, therefore, first address Mary Newborough's marriage to a Somerset gentleman turned highwayman, then focus on her alignments with the establishments run by Eleanor Dethick, alias Mrs Windsor, and by Mrs Miller, and finally examine her involvement in the Bridewell scandal of 1602, her (mock) repentance and release that occurred a few months before her husband's death.

Marriage to a Highwayman

The beginnings of Mary Newborough's transgressive life is related to her husband's career as a highwayman. George Newborough, gentleman, of Berkley in Somerset, had been convicted of highway robbery (violent theft) on two Somerset "husbandmen," Nicholas and Edward Hawkyns, of Cheddar. He had thus forfeited his estate, but on 5 November 1596, Sir John Popham, the Lord Chief Justice presiding over the Court of King's Bench, signed his pardon.[8] Newborough must have been tried before a local court, either the magistrates or the judges of assize, but unfortunately few petty sessions records survive before the nineteenth century and the quarter sessions rolls start in continuous series only from 1607.[9]

George Newborough (spelling variants are Newborow, Newburgh, Newberry) was born the eldest son of Roger Newborough and Magdalen, daughter of Robert Turberville, of Bere Regis, Dorset. He inherited the manor and advowson of Berkley and, in 1579, married Jane, daughter of Richard Bodenham, esquire. He fathered a son and a daughter, Roger and Cecily. Roger married the fourteen-year-old Mary, daughter of Francis Chaldecot of East Whiteway, Isle of Purbeck, Dorset, at Steeple, on 18 April 1598, at a time when his father was still held prisoner by warrant of the King's Bench. His mother Jane was dead; she had been buried at Berkley on 11 March 1589.[10]

It follows that George Newborough must have contracted his second marriage with Mary some time between 1589, when he was about in his thirties, and 1596. A search of the parish registers of Berkley has provided no evidence of George's remarriage. The cohabitation of George and Mary was put an end to with George's apprehension and conviction of felony. It does not seem likely that it was even resumed if we bear in mind that on 14 October 1598 Sir John Popham issued a warrant for committing Mary Newborough, "the wyfe of George Newburoughe, who is a prisoner in the Kinges Bench," to Bridewell and keeping her there at his pleasure (BCB 4, fol. 42v). After her release she was again committed to Bridewell in September 1599 and remained in prison until January 1600. She was again imprisoned in July 1601 and detained until 17 January 1603 (BCB 4, fol. 348r). George died on 10 August 1603, and, on 22 September, administration of his estate in Berkley was granted to John Kevile of Crediton, Devon. The granting of the administration may mean either that George died intestate or that his will was irrecoverable or that he had simply neglected to settle his widow's estate. The grant was revoked in favor of his widow Mary on 21 November 1604. The revocation indicates that Mary had some rights, perhaps by marriage settlement, which entitled her to claim the estate.[11]

What may have been the reasons for the downfall of George Newborough who had inherited the rank of a gentleman and who ended up as a criminal in one of London's prisons? Was he simply a young gentleman seeking an easy living?[12] The most plausible explanation is that he was no longer able to keep up the social standing of a gentleman and as he felt that his status was devalued by the threat of poverty, he preferred taking to the road to facing the ungentlemanly prospect of making money by manual labor. It is very unlikely that he joined or even headed a gang. He must have been on his own, mounted on his horse, when he waylaid the two Somerset farmers, stripping them of their purses. He presumably conformed to the pattern of the "amateur lone wolf," as A. L. Beier defined the typical real-life highwayman, who used to work with an accomplice or two and whose strategy was "grab-and-run," if he was a footpad, or grab-and-ride, if he was on horseback.[13] Shakespeare fashioned the criminal conduct of Falstaff and his cronies at Gadshill out of such instances of gentry disorder.

George Newborough's attack on the two Somerset farmers was a felony, a grave crime, which carried the forfeiture of lands and goods. He was apprehended, convicted, incarcerated, reprieved, and then pardoned in November 1596, but not released from prison. His career as a highwayman was relatively short, lasting about five years, and certainly devoid of anything sensational, romantic, or heroic except for his reprieve and pardon. What saved him from forfeiting his estate was undoubtedly the birthmark of gentility and possibly Sir John Popham's sympathy with a gentleman of his own country.

There can be no denying that there was some interaction between George Newborough's criminal behavior and his wife's abandonment to prostitution. The imprisonment of her husband must have obliged Mary to eke out a living on her own, probably even to make extra money to improve her husband's accommodation and diet in prison as befitted his gentle status.[14] She obviously resorted to prostitution as a survival strategy out of economic necessity, selling her body to support herself and her husband. Her marriage to a member of the gentry stood her in good stead when she came to face the ordeals of carting, detention, and correction in Bridewell. Without an ingrained sense of class consciousness it is inconceivable that she would have dared to raise a sharp protest against Nicholas Bywater, tanner, one of the four contractors in Bridewell in 1602, for savagely beating her and some of her fellow inmates. As consort of a gentleman turned highwayman she had the clout to assume a leading position among the female detainees, building up female resistance and negotiating for humane treatment. Mary Newborough, a fallen gentlewoman, stands out as the driving force that brought into being a female esprit de corps in prison.

The Establishment of Eleanor Dethick, alias Mrs. Windsor, and David English, Minister of St. Katherine's Christchurch

Mary Newborough's career as a prostitute, as already mentioned, must have been concurrent with her husband's term of imprisonment. Her earliest infractions are likely to have occurred in 1596 when her husband was confined in Newgate or King's Bench prison. But there is no way of finding out when she first gave herself over to prostitution, for the BCB for 1596 is missing. The first entry recording her delivery to Bridewell is dated 14 October 1598 (BCB 4, fol. 42v). On that day, a Saturday, Sir John Popham, the Lord Chief Justice, committed her to Bridewell together with Margaret Dickenson, wife of John Dickenson, captain, and Mary Holcrafte, wife of John Holcrafte, servant to Sir Edward Clere, all of them to be "kept during the pleasure of the Lord Chief Justice (BCB 4, fol. 42v). Mary Newborough was facing her first cross-examination in Bridewell on Wednesday, 29 November 1598. On being "demaunded whether euer she . . . did lodge or soiourne at anye tyme in the house of one William Lacke, cooke in St. Katherines Court neare the Tower, she answered and offered to take her oth that she neuer lodged in her lyfe" in Lacke's house. Her answer, of course, does not imply that she did not know Lacke. She may simply have pretended to be indignant at being suspected of having had illicit relations with a cook.[15] The governors of Bridewell, however, must have had cogent reasons for questioning her. They were soon to find out that she was a calculating woman who did not hesitate to take substantial sums of money, when she was in desperate financial straits, even from a servant to alderman Paul Banning.

Mary Newborough's next cross-examination on record is dated 3 July 1601 (BCB 4, fol. 249v), but thanks to the persistent cross-examinations of Helen Cootes, prostitute, and of Eleanor Dethick, bawd, conducted by the governors on Saturday, 21 March 1599, we do know that Mary Newborough was plying her trade in Eleanor Dethick's establishment in 1597/98 (BCB 4, fol. 72r–v).

Eleanor (Eliner, Hellener) Dethick, mostly referred to as Mrs. Windsor, was "a notorious bawd" advanced in years (BCB 4, fol. 75r). She was running a fashionable brothel tailored to suit the tastes and demands of a national and international elite clientele. Her premises abutted onto the churchyard of St. Katherine's Christchurch in the parish of Creechurch within Aldgate and benefited from their proximity to the church.[16] A wily woman living on good terms of Christian fellowship with her neighbors, Mrs. Windsor was operating her house with the blessing and backing of David English, the minister of St. Katherine's. Parson English was, as it were, the *spiritus rector,* whose companionship lent her enterprise an aura of respectability. The "familiarity between" the two, as Helen Cootes testified to the governors, was so close that when Mrs. Windsor "would go to churche, she would send to the sayd Mr. English and cause the churchyard dore to be opened for that her house is next to the churchyard" (BCB 4, fol. 72r).

The ritual entrance into the church was apparently orchestrated by Mrs. Windsor in order to raise her social status and increase her profile among her neighbors. Her clients were respectable citizens of the upper middle class. Why should the brothel keeper not be as respected as her customers and neighbors? Parson English, in any case, connived at upgrading her prestige among the parishioners of Creechurch within Aldgate. Ignoring the traditional pew rights, he went to the length of allocating his business partner a privileged seat in St. Katherine's where pews used to be arranged according to degree.[17] This was a clear breach of status boundaries.

Clergymen making sexual advances to the women under their spiritual care is a much recorded phenomenon.[18] The depositions of more than one male and female witness recorded in the BCB do, in fact, confirm that the married minister of St. Katherine's was a *coureur de femmes.* Struggling in vain to draw a line between the holy and the carnal service, he became an *habitué* of Mrs. Windsor's bawdyhouse. Thus Mr. Wigges, one of his parishioners, certified that his minister's sexual incontinence was common gossip. Parson English, he said, "did vsually go vpp and downe in the parish to mens wyues, maydes and other women and yf he saw any of them sadd, he would saye," couching his gospel in a sexual innuendo, "what ayleth you, why are you so sadd, me thinkes you lacke some thing yf you so come to me and I will helpe you" (BCB 4, fol. 74v).[19]

The parish gossip was corroborated by Helen Cootes, one of Mary Newborough's comrades-in-arms. She gave evidence that Parson English, about Christmastime 1597, attempted to seduce Mrs. Windsor's kitchen maid, "Jane, who hath a long nose." She saw the two "go into a chamber" where the parson "sett the sayd Jane on the bedde syde." She also bore witness that parson English, overwhelmed by the motions of his flesh about 7 March 1598, took Cecily Gray, "Mris Windsors mayde" to a separate "chamber," where he "laied her on a bedd and putt the dore close to and did kysse her." Helen underscored the trustworthiness of her evidence, adding that her testimony was "very trew, for that she went into another chamber adioyning to it where she might see all ouer the chamber" (BCB 4, fol.72r). Cecily Gray, widow, mother of two children by William Gray of Berkshire, who had died at sea in 1595, was given a fair chance to defend herself before the governors. She "vtterly denied" that she had sexual intercourse with the parson (BCB 4, fol. 72v). After a three weeks' term of detention, she was discharged, on 21 April 1599, on condition that she bound herself to appear before the Lord Mayor within five days (BCB 4, fol. 79r).

There is no evidence that David English cast a lecherous eye on the prostitutes operating in Mrs. Windsor's establishment, but to believe Helen Cootes, he was on familiar terms with at least one of them. He was obviously very much in control of what was happening and of who was plying her trade in the premises. As a partner of Mrs. Windsor he seems to have had a say in recruiting the prostitutes and in supplying the patrons. Thus, "Mr. English knew," as Helen Cootes stated, "that Mary Newborough and Elizabeth Stapleton, and Ffraunces [mistaken for "Mary"] Digby did vsually lye at the sayd Mris Windsors house." Significantly, the day after Mrs. Willford, another of the prostitutes, had been released from Bridewell, he joined her company as if to welcome her back home. He drank "wyne with her and Mris Windsor and did eate bread and cheese togither" and may even have worked out the future operations of Mrs. Willford (BCB 4, fol. 72r).

Whereas the prostitutes parson English consorted with did not escape punishment, he got off scot-free. He was immune from being prosecuted by the secular authorities of Bridewell. No charge of misdemeanor was brought against the thirty-one-year-old minister of St. Katherine's despite the fact that he was undermining the efforts of both the civic and ecclesiastical authorities to regulate sexual behavior in London. His case was shelved on 17 November 1599 when the governors issued the order that "there shalbe no coppyes made out of the court booke touching Mr. English, the minister being charged by Helen Cootes" (BCB 4, fol. 123v). He no doubt pursued his career in the Anglican church. He may have been identical with the David English who was appointed Vicar of Stepney, Middlesex, in 1603, rector of Patching, Sussex, in 1606, and of Clapham, Sussex, in 1607.[20]

The immunity granted to David English convincingly demonstrates some of the reasons why the moral campaign fought by the governors of Bridewell against prostitution was doomed to failure. Their prosecution against the delinquent minister was apparently thwarted by the ecclesiastical authorities. Archer has shown that also court connections compromised the reformatory work of the governors. Many brothel keepers and prostitutes remained immune from prosecution in the 1570s by virtue of their protection from influential citizens and from courtiers.[21] In the present case, Mrs. Windsor, bereft of Parson English's protection, depended on the mercy of the Bridewell governors and municipal authorities. As she was "found to be a notorious bawd," she was scheduled to be tried at the Guildhall (BCB 4, fol.75r), but "in re-guard of her great yeares," the Lord Mayor, Sir Stephen Soame, ordered on 16 April 1599 that "she shall be spared of his punishment" (BCB 4, fol. 78r). She was not put through the cruel ordeal of public shaming in the city of London, nor through the routine of corporal punishment and hard manual work. Presumably, Sir Stephen felt pity for the old bawd whose work at the frontier of the skin must have left its branding mark.

Mrs. Windsor's punishment was commuted into a fine of £5 to be paid "towards the relief of the poor people in this hospitall." The amount of the fine allows of the conclusion that Mrs. Windsor was one of the more substan-tial parishioners of Creechurch within Algate. She was running a prosperous establishment which guaranteed an income that placed her in the upper third of London society. The fine presumably amounted to her annual tax levied by the city authorities; in which case her annual income would have to be assessed at £100.[22]

The Lord Mayor also ruled that she should "putt in suretyes to avoyd the citty of London and libetyes therof" (BCB 4, fol. 78r). Expulsion orders, however, were unenforceable in the city of London as they were in other Eu-ropean towns. Residential containment outside London was at most a tempo-rary measure which was to prove counterproductive in enhancing rather than curbing the mobility of bawds, prostitutes, and pimps. As Pompey puts it to Mistress Overdone: "Though you change your place, you need not change your trade."[23]

Admittance to the sisterhood operating under the wings of Mrs. Windsor and Parson English conferred upon its members the social standing of *demi-mondaines* and guaranteed the amenities of a good serving system. Mrs. Windsor was the linchpin of her academy. She headed a retinue of two ser-vants, Jane and Cecily Gray, and some four courtesans. She acted as purveyor of board and lodging, as supplier of sumptuous robes hired from pawnbro-kers, and kept, as did most of her colleagues, a check on the health of her practitioners. Among the courtesans who plied their trade in the Windsor/English enterprise in 1597/99 were Helen Cootes, Mrs. Willford, Elizabeth Stapleton, and Mary Newborough.[24] There was no hierarchy among them, each having her own set of clients. Mrs. Windsor and her partner saw to it that, if possible, they rented themselves out as private mistresses to one cus-tomer forming long-term liaisons.

Helen Cootes's uneven partnership with the pimp George Eden sheds fur-ther instructive light on the workings of late Elizabethan prostitution. The pimp was a cog indispensable for running the sophisticated machinery of prostitution geared to the demands of the upper class. Eden turned out to be a domineering bully who ferried his powerless partner in a citywide shuttle service as if she were a commodified piece of property.[25] Helen Cootes hap-pened to meet him, as she confessed to the governors, about March 1598 when she lay ill in bed at Mrs. Hodge's establishment in Love Lane. He gave her some "almon[d] milke," known as an emollient, and some other medicine. As soon as she was about to recover, he offered to put her "in a good place." Dazzled by the prospect of carving out a living, she "was content to go with him" (BCB 4, fol. 72r).

The pimp/prostitute partnership stripped Helen Cootes of human dignity. Eden's power consigned the powerless Helen Cootes to abject submissiveness. Once under Eden's repressive domination, she was deprived of the agency of a self-fashioning individual. An expert in London's sexual geography, Eden placed her in Mrs. Wilkinson's establishment, which was frequented by the brothers George and Sir William Brooke (BCB 4, fol. 77r). Then he moved her to the aligned settlement run by Mrs. Windsor, where she stayed in service for "three quarters of a yeare" until December 1598 (BCB 4, fol. 72v), bestowing her favors on one wealthy client. Mrs. Windsor offered her a temporary haven of security and a stable liaison. Thereafter she was facing a downgrading from private mistress to common prostitute who was paid according to the volume of the clients she served. Between December 1598 and March 1599, when she was committed to Bridewell, the callous Eden forced her to put in fleeting visits to various houses. Thus he placed her in a bawdyhouse in Eridge, a market town in Sussex. Thence he sent her back to Mrs. Windsor; and from there he shunted her to Pickthatch, a notorious red-light district. Her downward mobility eventually came to a halt in Clerkenwell, the most infamous haunt of thieves and loose women. At long last, on 21 March 1599, marshall Read committed her "to the Hospitall of Brydewell" (BCB 4, fol. 73v).

When Helen Cooltes lay at anchor in Mrs. Windsor's house, between April and December 1598, she operated as mistress to one Mr. Baker of Coleman Street Ward, who "would paye for her dyett." In the eyes of Mrs. Windsor, Mr. Baker was "a very honest gentleman" who used to give her an additional fee, "sometyme Xs and sometyme 5s" whenever he had sexual intercourse with Helen Cootes. Once he also presented her with a "silver spoone" (BCB 4, fol. 72v).

Helen Cootes's detention in Bridewell was surprisingly short. It lasted from 21 March to 28 April 1599. The sentence the governors pronounced on her and her pimp shows that they knew how to draw a line between exploiter and victim. George Eden was to be arraigned for his misdemeanors "at the next session of gaiole delivery which shalbe holden for London and Middlesex" (BCB 4, fol. 76v). Helen Cootes, like Mrs. Windsor, was spared public humiliation and corporal punishment. She was not even fined, for the governors obviously realized that the pimp had lined his pockets at the expense of his prostitute. Helen Cootes was discharged "vppon suretyes to appeare from court daye to court daye during the space of one moneth and at th'end of the sayd moneth to avoyd the Citty of London and County of Middlesex" (BCB 4 fol. 79v).

One major point remains to be highlighted. The moment Helen Cootes's ties with George Eden were severed by their confinement, the subservient prostitute recovered her voice and her dignity as a woman. She does not seem to have been a simple rate worker ticking to the irregular rhythm of ever-shifting sexual alliances. Holding her ground against the governors' close questioning, she "did also charge the sayd Eden to his face that he placed her at diuers houses which the sayd Eden could not deny" (BCB 4, fol. 77r). She had also "charged" David "English to his face . . . that he knew that Mr Robert Offley kept . . . Mris Willford" as his private mistress. The clerk of the BCB minutes, as if to make sure that he conveyed the immediacy of the situation, added the interlinear remark that Parson English was "present at her examination" (BCB 4, fol. 72r).

The charge brought by Helen Cootes against Parson English clearly aimed at unmasking him as an accomplice of Mrs. Windsor. Her accusation implied that Robert Offley was patronizing Mrs. Willford through the agency and with the approval of the minister of St. Katherine's. Robert Offley had, in fact, the perfect credentials for being admitted to the bawdyhouse as a steady customer dispensing his patronage to a private mistress. He was a solvent member of the middle class, a merchant of good standing, who, on 7 January 1592, together with the alderman Paul Banning and Andrew Banning, the first to be involved with Mary Newborough, signed the second charter of the Levant Company, which granted to fifty-three merchants, for a period of twelve years, the monopoly of English trade to Venice and Turkey.[26] He was probably the same man to whom the Lieutenant of Ordnance granted, on 30 January 1601, the office of bowstring maker in the Tower, which entitled him to a fee of 6d a day.[27] He had married, on 3 February 1589, Anne, daughter of Sir Edward Osborne, founder and first governor of the Levant Company (1592) and of Anne Hewett, at St. Dionis Backchurch, London. They had a son John Offley.[28]

Robert Offley's liaison with Mrs. Willford seems to have been of long standing, for "Mr Sympson, the Marshall, in his lyfe tyme," as Helen Cootes heard, "did take the sayd Mr Offley and Mris Willford in bedd togither" in Thames Street (BCB 4, fol. 72r). Thereafter the two sought or were offered sanctuary in the Windsor/English establishment. There is some evidence suggesting that Mrs. Windsor, though taking the money Robert Offley paid for his mistress's board and lodging, money earned by the lucrative import of currants from Venice and her dependencies, Zante and Cephalonia, did not honor their contract.[29] He was deceived into believing that Mrs. Windsor kept Mrs. Willford as his private mistress for his use only. But Cecily Gray, the brothel's maid, testified that "diuers men" used to visit the house at night and "the gentlemen would sometymes giue her money for her paynes" she took in lighting "them vpp to the" chamber of Mrs. Willford (BCB 4, fol. 72v).

On the one hand, the stories of Helen Cootes and Mrs. Willford corroborate the commonplace knowledge that the negotiations between prostitute and pimp or bawd were of a purely economic nature. The control of the prostitute's body lay in the power of either the pimp (usually a man) or the bawd (in most cases a woman). In either case the relationship entailed the commodification of the prostitute's body. On the other hand, Mrs. Willford's story reveals a hitherto forgotten organizational aspect which will be confirmed by Mary Newborough's clientage. The distinctions between the different categories of prostitutes were less clear-cut than the social historians would make us believe. Even a prostitute who rented herself out as a private mistress and resided in an expensive brothel, such as Mrs. Willford and Mary Newborough, succumbed to the economic pressures exerted by the brothel keepers. A long-term liaison, which on average lasted from three to nine months, did not preclude the kept mistress from selling her body to several patrons. These could turn up in age groups composed of colleagues or of friends and relatives. The majority were presumably voyeurs burning with desire to see the experienced hot blades among them at work.

Another salient feature of Elizabethan clientage was the large body of foreigners serviced by prostitutes. The foreign clients ranged from ambassadors and their retinues to merchants and refugee craftsmen.[30] Mrs. Windsor's establishment, immune to national prejudices, opened its doors to an international clientele that could afford to pay the expensive maintenance of her courtesans. Two of them, Elizabeth Stapleton and Mary Newborough, had hooked wealthy foreigners, the first a Huguenot craftsman and the second three Italian merchants who shared her body in turn.

Elizabeth Stapleton, as Mrs. Windsor confessed to the governors on 21 March 1599, "did lye at her house about a yeare" ago. Making a clean breast of her trade, she testified that "one Mr Tibold, an Estraunger, being a younger brother, did usually lye" at her house "with the sayd Elyzabeth Stapleton." She tolerated the couple, as she put it in self-defense, "because the sayd Elyzabeth" had told her that her patron had promised to "marry her." However, it transpires from her threadbare defense that it was rather the generous financial arrangement made by the Frenchman that had moved her to admit him to her establishment. He paid Mrs. Windsor "a marke a weeke for the dyett of the sayd Elyzabeth" (BCB 4, fol. 72v). Considering that the value of a mark was 13s 4d, this was a fair price compared to the 4s to 6s which a prostitute paid for board and lodging in the 1570s.[31]

The brief description of "Mr Tibold" as given by Mrs. Windsor furnishes the key to identifying the Frenchman as Christian Thibaud (Tibaut, Tibauts, Tybouts), the younger brother of Adrian Thibaud, both dwelling in the house of Peter van Lore, of Utrecht, jeweler and stonecutter, parishioner of St. Gabriel Fenchurch, Langbourn Ward.[32] The Dutchman was a successful artisan who was supplying the Elizabethan nobility with jewelry. By 1595 he had become an acknowledged goldsmith-banker who could afford to advance money to impecunious noblemen; in 1621 he was knighted for the financial support given to the Elector Palatine, King James's son-in-law.[33] It seems therefore logical to assume that the two Thibaud brothers were also success-ful jewelers, probably business associates of Peter van Lore. The income tax return for each of them in 1599 was assessed at £10 4s 4d, a sum which would correspond to an annual income of £100.[34] Christian Thibaud was clearly liv-ing a life of affluence which prompted him to move beyond the boundaries of his immigrant community. It is, however, doubtful that his integration and assimilation had progressed far enough for him ever to marry an English-woman and a prostitute into the bargain. The odds were stacked heavily against Elizabeth Stapleton if we bear in mind that a contemporary of hers, one Dorothy Powell, of Blandford, had been kept by a Frenchman who for-sook her after he had fathered two or three children on her body.[35]

Mary Newborough's Italian Patrons in Mrs. Windsor's Establishment: Tomas Marini and Paolo Gondola

Mary Newborough's notoriety as the consort of a gentleman turned high-wayman gave her an easy entrée into the pretentious establishment run by Eleanor Dethick, alias Mrs. Windsor, and supervised by David English, the minister of St. Katherine's Christchurch. One can take Helen Cootes's word at face value that David English gave his personal approval to Mary's resid-ing in 'Mris Windsors house" in 1597/98 (BCB 4, fol. 72r). In fact, as Mrs. Windsor confessed to the governors on 21 March 1599, Mary was residing in her house and cultivating "one Thomas Maryne, an Italian," as her patron, who used to bring the Gondola brothers along with him (BCB 4, fol. 72v).

Tomas Marini (Maryne) was in all likelihood a descendant of the Marini of Genoa who had settled in Southampton as merchants in the first half of the sixteenth century and had stayed on in England after the Italian trade fell into decline. The Marini who chose to remain in Southampton were endenizened and became men of property. Some of them moved up to London where they obtained the freedom of the city as merchants.[36] As an Anglicized Italian born in England, Tomas Marini was entitled to set up house in London. However, his eating habits, despite the process of transculturation he must have gone through, still betrayed his cultural background. The patronage he dispensed on Mary Newborough came close to converting her into an Italianate En-glishwoman at least as far as the Italian cuisine was concerned. Surprisingly, this was a point Mrs. Windsor deemed worthy of mentioning in her cross-examination. "Mary Newboroughs dyett," she told the governors, "was vsually dressed at the sayd Marynes house & and sent to her house for the sayd Mary Newborough" (BCB 4, fol. 72v).

This was, somehow, an admission of serving inferior food. Presumably, Mrs. Windsor's English ladies of pleasure had never raised a complaint about the quality of her board and lodging, but Tomas Marini must have found the cookery of Jane with the "long nose" provincial, her food unpalatable and perhaps even detrimental to the health and sexual efficiency of his mistress. After all, he paid Mrs. Windsor 10s whenever he had sexual intercourse with Mary Newborough and obviously expected an appropriate performance in return. Without proper food, in terms of Renaissance physiology, the production of blood was endangered and since blood was believed to be the carrier of the generation, blood deficiency impaired the generation of human life and reduced sexual potency.[37] The prospect of a bloodless courtesan deprived of sexual power must have been unbearable to Marini. His deep-seated anxiety over sexual potency is likely to have been the reason for the gastronomic care he thought Mary Newborough was entitled to and for opening up a private catering service shuttling her "dyett" across London between his house and Mrs. Windsor's brothel.[38]

Contrary to England, Italy had developed a high cuisine, claiming culinary leadership in Renaissance Europe. Whereas English cookery books recommended plain food to the English housewife as against foreign culinary pretension, Italian cookery books such as Giovanni de Rosselli's *Epulario, or The Italian Banquet* (1598)[39] praised varied dishes, offered fewer meat recipes, and paid more attention to vegetables, fruit, pastries, and soups.[40] The authority on the difference between the Italian and English eating habits was Giocomo Castelvetro. During his long residence in Elizabethan England, some seventeen years of humanist commitment to cross-cultural interests between Italy and England, he noticed how under the presence of Italian and French refugees the English upper class began to accommodate their cuisine to Continental taste. Castelvetro wrote for English consumption a treatise on Italian food which was sponsored by Sir John Harington of Exton and which he dedicated to Sir John's sister Lucy Harington, Countess of Bedford, from London on 12 May 1614. In this *Brieve racconto di tutte le radici, di tutte l'herbe, et di tutti i frutti, che crudi o cotti in Italia si mangiano. Cosi molti belli giovevoli segreti, non senza buon proposito per entro esso descritti tanto intorno alla salute de corpi humani quanto ad vtile degli hortolani necessari,* Castelvetro advised his English readers to eat less meat and more vegetables, herbs, salads, fruit, and instructed them how to grow and cook them.[41]

We can infer that the quality of the Italian food which was being ferried across London to delight the palate of Mary Newborough and to enhance the output of her sexual performance reflected the advanced nutritional knowledge at the close of the century. This inference is corroborated by the eating habits of Paolo Gondola whom Tomas Marini introduced to Mary Newborough. Some of Gondola's business letters, addressed to his Florentine friend and former colleague in London, Gualtieri Panciatichi, in the early 1590s, read like a culinary contest in which the hotshot Gondola was striving to outdo his friend. Thus Gondola parried his friend's boast that he had relished Florentine garden-warblers ("beccafichi") by brandishing a list of "dilichatezze" he had treated himself to in London: capons, beef ("bifo"), venison pies, figs ("fichi"), raisins, melons, pears, apples, and women ("fiche").[42]

Tomas Marini's awakening of Mary Newborough's taste for refined Italian dishes and delicacies, however, proved a blessing in disguise, for Marini's cuisine was of a totally different class and origin from the dietary regime imposed on her in Bridewell. There she was subjected to a dietary level well below that of her status as a gentlewoman. On meat days she was entitled to four ounces of meat and eight ounces of coarse bread as well as a pint of porridge and a pint of beer. On fish days, there was milk, cheese, pease pudding, and fish on the menu.[43] There were no salads, no fruit, and no dainties. As the prison food did not agree with Mary Newborough, special arrangements had to be made for her at her own expense. Thus on 14 December 1599, the governors decreed that her "mayde," Susan Adams, "shall come to her and bringe her monye or smockes or such like thinges and that she shall haue whyte breade other than the houses allowance" (BCB 4, fol. 128r). Again, on 8 August 1601, she was granted the privilege to speak with her mother and her kinswoman in the presence of a governor and to "haue the sicke dyett only of the house if she will not eate the house dyett" provided "her mother pay for the same euery weeke before hand" (BCB 4, fol 250v).[44] Fortunately, there was a dramatic change when in the spring of 1602 the four contractors were to embark on a gastronomic spree, converting Bridewell into a high-class brothel which regaled its guests with the house prostitutes and aphrodisiac dishes.

The admittance of the Gondola brothers to Mrs. Windsor's brothel is easier to be accounted for than Tomas Marini's readiness to share Mary Newborough's body with his two compatriots. Their entrance into Mary's chamber of assignation has to be explained in terms of the house policy of clientage, which, as exemplified by the case of Mrs. Willford, consisted in coupling, for commercial reasons, even a kept mistress with more than one patron. Thus Mrs. Windsor brought herself to admit to the Bridewell governors that "one Thomas and Pawle Gundelo, estrangers, did vsually come to her house with the sayd Maryne and sometyme they came alone to the sayd Mary Newborough" (BCB 4, fol. 72v). She did not disclose to the governors if the three Italians had agreed with her on some sort of rotational right to having sexual intercourse in her establishment.

As will be seen, the Ragusan Paolo Gondola (Pavle Gundulic), actually needed no guide to London bawdyhouses. He had been indulging in the city's nightlife since his coming to London about 1589, sowing his wild oats among the whores operating in the notorious red-light districts. By 1591, however, he had let off enough energy and was settling down to a more responsible way of life as a pushing merchant on the lookout for a prostitute who was suitable to his new status. Tomas Marini, the endenizened Italian who was still committed to an Italian mode of life, apparently helped Gondola to come to terms with his sexual appetite in introducing him to Mary Newborough. The Italian merchants residing in early Tudor England had always been displaying a spirit of intense corporate identity, and the small community of Mediterranean merchants left in late Elizabethan London still harbored a modicum of solidarity.[45]

Paolo Gondola had acquired the rudiments of trade and commerce in Ragusa (Dubrovnik). After his father's death in 1588, Paolo, in the interest of the future development of the family enterprise, had obviously gotten in touch with the Ragusan patrician merchant Nicolò de Gozzi (Nikola Gucetic) who had settled in London as early as 1552. Accordingly, de Gozzi's London office became Paolo's training ground for his advanced commercial and political education (ca. 1589–1592). When he felt he had gained enough experience, he severed his ties with de Gozzi and opened up a firm of his own in 1591, working together with his brothers Tomas in London, Marin in Ancona, and Anton, Givo, and Mato in Ragusa.[46]

Nicolò de Gozzi, beside the rival firm of the Florentine Filippo Corsini, was the largest importer of Continental goods as well as a substantial exporter of English merchandise. He ranked among the wealthiest London-based foreign merchant bankers and taxpayers.[47] There is no doubt that de Gozzi was professionally a highly qualified master with a practically unrivaled business experience of long standing and a Europe-wide network of agents. He was, to use a term coined by M. E. Bratchel, a paragon of the Italian bachelor uncles, though admittedly a rather late instance, who used to dedicate their careers to the survival of the family businesses in foreign countries.[48] It was not easy for young Italian expatriates in their late twenties to get on well with a man who adhered strictly to a set of rigid principles. Gualtieri Panciatichi, the son of a Florentine patrician family, of the same age as his colleague and later correspondent Paolo Gondola, could not stand the discipline of the old man and within a year quitted his service.[49] He dismissed de Gozzi, his "maggiore" or "principale," as an old fool ("un pazzo vecchio"), as a man of a very strange nature ("un huomore molto strano").[50]

Paolo Gondola represented a new type of expatriate Mediterranean merchant. Unlike his predecessors in early modern England, he strove to understand English mentality and to make contact with Englishmen and Englishwomen. It was much easier for the young Italian clerks stationed in London in the first half of the century to feel at home in their new surroundings, considering that they were from the very start integrated into the community life organized by the various Italian "nations." For Gondola and his companions there was no "Lumbardeshall," a general meeting place specially opened up for Italian expatriates, where social activities were officially mounted and channeled. Worse, there was no corporate religious observance. Church services for expatriate Catholics had always been a social occasion of high significance, giving them a sense of cultural identity.[51] The right to attend Mass was so vital a problem for Gondola that he was thinking of leaving England unless he found an opportunity. He found several.[52]

In the absence of the old corporate hospitality and of the communal life as observed by the Italian Catholics in early Tudor England, the clerks of Nicolò de Gozzi, under the leadership of the vibrant business executive Paolo Gondola, took matters into their own hands. Giuseppe Simonelli,[53] Mauro Berti,[54] Orazio Franciotti,[55] Alesandro Manelli and others used to meet every Sunday for a game of football and then would repair to what must have been the Elephant (Oliphant) on Bankside for a boisterous round of songs and presumably for some more rounds of drinks.[56] The inn, where the de Gozzi and presumably the Corsini management met in the early 1590s, became the principal focus for their frolics, games, and ritual acts of drinking. On Bankside, they released, in a spirit of male camaraderie, their pent-up energies, indulging in what was looked down on as the violent game of football.[57] Paolo Gondola, the manager of the Italian football team, unfortunately does not record whether or not they played against an English side in what would have been the first international football encounter between a disorderly English and a sophisticated Italian team performed on the playing field in either the Paris Garden Liberty or the Bishop of Winchester's Liberty. What we do know is that he was dissatisfied with the quality of the English footballs and therefore ordered a set of a dozen balls of the best quality made in Florence, presumably bladders cased in leather, and of the size used in England.[58] If Paolo Gondola and his friends were still playing games on Bankside and throwing parties in the Elephant in 1594, Shakespeare is likely to have heard of their weekend frolics.[59]

Gondola's sporting prowess and revels were an expression of his youthful energy and of his bond of friendship with his Italian colleagues. However, his romps in bawdyhouses were not so much the result of male solidarity among convivial companions as demonstrations of his self-assertive masculinity and sexual superiority. Thus, he boasted in his first letter addressed to Gualtieri Panciatichi in Florence that he had taken Alesandro Manelli to the brothel, where Manelli deported himself as a fumbler, a "choglione," that is, in John Florio's rendering, "a noddie, a foole."[60] Sexual intercourse with the prostitute Pottone[61] he was in love with did not work, though Gondola had instructed his friend many times how to go about it.[62] Gondola also dismissed Panciatichi's assertion that he had tasted "la dolcitudine inglese" in a London brothel as the idle boast of a sexual botcher.[63] Gondola's debauched activities, orchestrated to arouse the envy of his mates, came to a halt by October 1590, when sobered up by financial straits, he confessed to Panciatichi that he had given up frequenting the brothels and was now on course to make and save money.[64]

In fact, Gondola had, despite the dissipation of his resources, saved some money from his earnings. His possessions in June 1590 were assessed at £10 and for 1591 he counted on making £100, that is as much as the approximate 1598 income of Mrs. Windsor, Mary Newborough's brothel keeper.[65] He had come to England about 1589 to build up a business of his own and within two years had obviously learned from experience that without harnessing his sexual drive and cutting down his expenses incurred in frequenting the prostitutes he would never be able to carry out his professional plans. He therefore took to cultivating a more mature image of himself as a businessman of some standing and as a dashing lover yearning for a stable sexual relationship. He did, indeed, make his way as a wealthy merchant and lover.

Gondola happened to entangle himself in a romance he kept secret from his friends in London. Love like a *coup de foudre* came over a young country "gentildona di molto bona casa et adesso molto braua e denarosa" (gentlewoman of a very good and wealthy family), whom Gondola is likely to have met among his English recusant friends. The young woman was so taken with the Ragusan that on getting the wrong news that he was about to leave England, she rode, with her mother's consent but without her father's knowledge, helter-skelter to London, escorted by two servants. Thanks to the help given her by "nostra Gioanna," the hostess of the Dolphin,[66] as Gondola reminded Panciatichi, the runaway daughter sank, disheveled and dissolved in tears, into his arms and spent a day or two with him in the Dolphin.[67]

They made love in Gioanna's inn. Three weeks later the seemingly worried Gondola informed Panciatichi that "La mia signora è tornata a casa dell suo pedre" [*sic*], adding that he feared he had impregnated her. He does not seem to have had in mind to abandon her. On the contrary, he rose to the situation, generating paternal feelings and male pride. If his "signora" (mistress of his future household) was "impregnata," he vaunted, she was going to bear him a son, "haueremo un Paulo giouane," the spitting image of his father.[68] Overwhelmed by her smothering kisses ("basci") and caresses ("carezze"), Gondola sensed, probably for the first time since his coming to England, that commercial sex yielded no emotional gratification. The young daughter of a wealthy country gentleman, presumably of the Catholic faith, seems to have embodied Gondola's ideal of feminine beauty. It was her plumpness that aroused an erotic frisson. Thus the galvanized Gondola confided to Panciatichi that she looked much more beautiful, "più bella . . . di un gran pezzo," than when his friend had seen her in England, for she had put on weight and body fat and had grown a great deal, "sendo diuentata grassa e più grande e fatta."

Gondola's affair with the young country gentlewoman, his forays into what Thomas Coryate was to call "places of evacuation,"[69] and his cultivation of Mary Newborough in 1597/98 can be read as an attempt, however crude, to take root in a new country. Gondola, as mentioned, does not conform to the pattern of late medieval expatriate Italian merchants who remained unassimilated and transient. He represents a new type of Mediterranean expatriate who shed the old sojourn mentality, making a bid for professional and cultural integration. The taverns and brothels, the women and prostitutes, played as important a part in his transcultural process as did his professional relations. His course of acculturation can also be traced in his effort, however primitive it turned out to be in his early stage of apprenticeship, to break down the language barrier and acquire a smattering of English. Unlike his Florentine friend Gualtieri Panciatichi, he had no hesitations about learning English the natural and practical way, eschewing the academic way of consulting the modern language manuals. His personal access to English consisted in picking up swear words and sexual slang in the London taverns and brothels.[70] His male brand of bawdy humor and the linguistic insouciance with which he must have addressed his partners smoothed his way to professional success. His various partnerships with English and foreign merchants bear witness to his commercial efficiency and increasing integration into the London business world.[71]

By the time he was cultivating the favors of Mary Newborough, Paolo Gondola, a converted libertine and prodigal, had made a name for himself as a respected merchant stranger, even though he had failed to monopolize the Ragusan trade after Nicolò de Gozzi's death in 1595. His sexual desire obviously found fulfillment in copulating with this gentlewoman turned prostitute, whose financial expectations he satisfied with the money earned by trading in wines and raisins imported from the Levant and in costly fabrics from Italy. He may not have warmed up to her as much as he had done to the runaway daughter in the Dolphin. However, the fact that her physical wellness was being monitored by his colleague Tomas Marini suggests that their negotiations transcended the impersonal nature of commercial sex. English must have been the vehicle of communication between the three of them or rather five of them if we think of Gondola's brother and Mrs. Windsor, the bawd. Their conversation was certainly not as cultured and learned as the poetic flights of a Venetian courtesan and her worshipers. It was probably limited to Italian food, fashion, cosmetics, and sex. The better days in Mary Newborough's past as a gentlewoman may have been another topic. Their state of affairs in Mrs. Windsor's brothel was put an end to when on Saturday, 14 October 1598, Sir John Popham committed Mary Newborough to Bridewell. Gondola, unfortunately for historians, does not seem to have been summoned to appear before the Lord Chief Justice or before the governors of Bridewell.[72]

Mary Newborough in Mrs. Anne Miller's Establishment and a Historic Coach Ride

The reformatory policy pursued by the governors of Bridewell, as far as Mary Newborough was concerned, proved a failure. After the closure of Mrs. Windsor's establishment and the release of all the transgressors in April 1599—Mary was presumably the last to be discharged about the beginning of May 1599—none of the culprits turned up in the Bridewell records again with the exception of Mary Newborough. As soon as she was again at large, she fell back into the old rut. A gentlewoman with social pretensions, she threw in her lot with Mrs. Anne Miller, in whom she recognized a kindred spirit. By June 1599, she was operating in Mrs. Miller's brothel in Ch[ic]k Lane, as Elizabeth Reignoldes, one of Mrs. Miller's prostitutes, testified to the governors.

Elizabeth Reignoldes, in her examination conducted by the governors on 15 August 1599, bore witness "that about eight weekes now past Mrs Newborowgh did come to Mrs Millers house." Mary, quite in keeping with her social status, turned up with "her mayd whome she calleth Mrs Hudson," giving out that she was the wife of Mr. Hudson, a haberdasher of St. Paul's churchyard. Hudson, however, was a cover. Her real name, to believe Elizabeth Reignoldes, was Susan Adams (BCB 4, fol. 101r). Susan, as will be seen, remained faithful to Mary and in times of adversity proved an invaluable link between her imprisoned mistress and the outside world, Mary's family (her mother), and Mr. Adams's haberdashery when in 1602 the house of correction was converted into a seraglio.

As for the identity of the "gentleman," who according to Elizabeth Reignoldes, "did vsually lye . . . with the said Mrs Newborough" in Mrs. Miller's house, some of their names can be retrieved from the Bridewell records, but, strange to say, their names are not given away by Mary. Her examinations have not been preserved, they seem to have been excised from the BCB possibly under the pressure of some powerful protectors. Two of them are known by name. After Mary's renewed detention about early September 1599, one Mr. Farnham (FFarnam) and Edward Fenton sued for Mary's enlargement. The Bridewell court, sitting on 29 September, ordered them to be bound for Mary's future behavior (BCB 4, fol. 105r). Mary's discharge, however, was suspended owing to her liaison with John Abel.[73]

John Abel was a retainer of Paul Banning (Bayning), alderman of Farringdon Without, called Fleet Street Ward (1593–99).[74] Mary Newborough may have caught his eye in St. James's Park while "the shewe of the souldiours" was on.[75] On that memorable day in late August, Mary had an appointment with Katherine Arden in Paul's Wharf, presumably an inn in Paul's Wharf, the street leading from the Thames to St. Paul's Churchyard. From there the two traveled on together by coach to see the great muster in St. James's with the purpose to make it their own field day (BCB 4, fol. 128r). The general musters were military as well as social gatherings in the Elizabethan calendar. The whole manhood of a city or county, from sixteen to sixty, was liable for military service and was expected to show up.[76] Hence the muster was a welcome hunting ground for the two *femmes de péché,* looking down from their coach on the *va-et-vient* of martial exercises and scheming to set aflame the men in arms and the packs of onlookers. Their presence threatened to transform a drill ground into a space of assignation.

Whether or not Mary Newborough and John Abel made their fatal acquaintance on the occasion of one of the August musters in St. James's Park, John happened to be "lewdly entysed into" Mary Newborough's "wicked company" in the summer of 1599. Within a few weeks he "purloined" £70 from his wealthy master and as he seems to have been a highly sexed young man infatuated with Mary Newborough, he carelessly invested this illicit windfall into Mary's body and the demanding task of living up to the style of a sophisticated courtesan. The handsome amount, which would have enabled a nobleman to keep two mistresses for the space of twelve months, "was recouered by the labour of" John Crooke, recorder of London and one of the governors of Bridewell, from Mary Newborough, "a notorious woman of euill lyfe," as well as from "her maintayners," presumably Mr. Farnham and Edward Fenton, and it was eventually handed back to its owner by the recorder.[77]

Yet alderman Banning, who like Robert Offley had made a fortune investing his money in the trade of the Levant Company and who was the head of a vast household made up of many retainers, clerks, and servants, among them three black slave-maids, donated the retrieved money "as a godly and charitable beneuvolence" to Bridewell there "to be emploied by the wisedome of the masters & gouernors . . . for a continuall stocke to sett idle persons to worke for the benefitt of the common wealth & good of this hospitall" (BCB 4, fol. 120 r).[78] Thus John Abel's theft unleashed a dynamic financial process which promised to work out for the benefit of a civic institution. Money, originating from importing currants from Venice, Cephalonia, and Zante and diverted to be spent on the body of a prostitute, was eventually invested in the rehabilitation of delinquents.

The gravity of Mary Newborough's transgression accounts for the length of her detention in Bridewell. Elizabeth Reignoldes and Mrs. Miller got away with short detentions. Elizabeth was committed to Bridewell on 15 August 1599 (BCB 4, fol. 100v) and was released on 1 October (BCB 4, fol. 105v). Mrs. Miller was taken to Bridewell by Mr. Read, the marshal, on 18 August

(BCB 4, fol. 102r) and on 19 September was fined £10, twice the amount of Mrs. Windsor. She was to be discharged provided she "putt in suretyes" for her future behavior and for abiding by the order to move out of London (BCB 4, fol. 105r). Mary's detention, however, lasted five months from about early September 1599 to 31 January 1600 (BCB 4, fol. 142r). The rigors of prison life, the drudgery of penal servitude, the poor quality of prison diet, and the forced abstinence from trading her body began to tell on her. Therefore the governors who met on Friday, 14 December, allowed her maid Susan Adams to "bringe her monye or smockes or such like thinges" and granted her the privilege to "haue whyte breade other then the houses allowaunce" (BCB 4, fol. 129r). This was clearly a concession to Mary's social status.

Moreover, the governors, worried about Mary Newborough and Katherine Arden's health, ordered on December 14 that the two should share the same room in company with Mary Digby. They also ruled that Katherine Arden should be discharged provided she put "in good and sufficient securitie to this house for her good behaviour and appearaunce within three dayes warninge" (BCB 4, fol. 129r). Mary Digby was discharged on 31 December and ordered to "avoid the Citty & Libertyes therof" (BCB 4, fol. 131r–v). Mary Newborough, as mentioned, stayed on alone in her room until 31 January 1600. On the same day, Luce Morgan, another gentlewoman turned prostitute, was released (BCB 4, fol. 142r).[79] The face-to-face community of prostitutes in jail was a dangerous invitation to socialize with like-minded transgressors, a measure that was bound to thwart any attempt, subsidized by benefactors such as Paul Banning, to reclaim the criminals.

Mary Newborough and Katherine Arden's ride from St. Paul's Wharf to St. James's Park in August 1599 is the first historically documented instance of prostitutes making use of the new mode of conveyance.[80] In emulation of her social compeers, among whom keeping a private coach had come into vogue by 1590, Mary planned to go to "the shewe of the souldiours" by coach. She was expecting Katherine Arden to come to Paul's Wharf by coach, but as Katherine turned up "without coacheman" because she could obviously not afford to hire a coach, Mary, "gentlewoman lyke," as her new bawd Mrs. Miller used to say, saw to it that they reached St. James's Park by coach. In fact, the newly organized urban transport system dramatically increased the mobility of London's well-to-do citizens, among them the better sort of prostitutes. Operating from central London, the prostitutes in hired coaches could now range easily through the city and the places beyond, the suburbs, and solicit customers at any public space. Mary Newborough's appearance at St. James's Park in a four-wheeled, open-sided, roofed and upholstered but unsprung coach, in company of what was another cab-moll, must have caused quite a stir among the onlookers and the "souldiours." This shrewdly orchestrated and conspicuously choreographed encounter between soldier and prostitute gave Mary Newborough's notoriety an extra boost.[81]

Mary Newborough's presence at St. James's Park is living proof that the parks in the city's neighborhood were favorite resorts for assignation and for soliciting clients and as such they were an integral part of the sexual geography of Elizabethan London.[82] It is also worth noting that the outer reaches of civic space owing to the new fashion of urban transport were appropriated by prostitution operating from the inner reaches of the city, whereas the closure of the public stews in 1546 had worked contrariwise, prostitution moving from the borders of civic space, the suburbs, to the inner reaches. This mobility has gone unnoticed by literary critics who cling to the view that most brothels were situated in the suburbs, particularly in Southwark.

Apparel Proclaims the Prostitute in the Playhouse: the Fashioning of Elizabeth Reignoldes as a Prostitute

Not so much the coach proclaimed the gentlewoman turned prostitute at the St. James's Park muster as did her apparel. It goes without saying that Mary Newborough on her historic ride to St. James's Park made her sweeping appearance in full regalia. Her sartorial self-fashioning was, no doubt, a matter of personal style, but nonetheless it could not have escaped being conditioned by the code of her profession as laid down by the brothel keepers such as Mrs. Miller in the late 1590s or as practiced by Black Luce (Mrs. Baynam) and Gilbert East in the 1570s.[83] Thus the entrepreneurial Mrs. Miller expected Elizabeth Reignoldes to "go gentlewoman lyke," suggesting to her that she "might buy" a "gowne of iiij^{li}" from "one Mrs Stainey," who, to believe the governors, was "a notable common whore." As she was not dressed à la mode, Mrs. Miller supplied Elizabeth with the appropriate garments in which to solicit, but eventually Elizabeth bought a gown of her own which "cost xlijs" (BCB 4, fol. 100r–101r). The description of the robes borrowed from Mrs. Miller constitutes the first authentic record to shed light on the fashioning of an Elizabethan prostitute as a public persona in the late 1590s and will have to be taken for a model of what Mary Newborough's dress must have looked like which she wore at the muster of the soldiers. But before addressing this issue, it is opportune to dwell on Elizabeth Reignoldes's record as a prostitute in Mrs. Miller's establishment.

From the BCB emerges the microbiography of an enterprising young woman whom marriage to Edmond Reignoldes, an elderly saddler dwelling in the Old Bailey, the street leading to Ludgate, had doomed to keep a low profile. Prostitution, she deceived herself into believing, would open for her the door to social success. Indeed, under Mrs. Miller's self-interested tutelage, she was prodded into assuming the high profile of a prostitute dressed up in robes well above her station and frequenting the playhouse as a marketplace of sex. She was by no means an ingénue any longer when she joined Mrs. Miller's business at Easter 1599—Easter Day fell on 11 April—and stayed on with her until the beginning of July 1599. She had already been plying her trade in the establishments of Mrs. Wilkinson and of Mrs. Cesar, whose acquaintance she had made during her former detention in Bridewell. But when it came to selling her body to "any man," she refused to obey. She balked at playing the game of a professional prostitute the moment she became painfully aware of the fact that her body belonged to Mrs. Miller and her clients. Mrs. Miller had to remind her that if she did not abide by the rules of her métier, "she must leaue of her trade." Elizabeth Reignoldes was eventually ready to give it up after her renewed detention in Bridewell. After six weeks only, on 1 October 1599, she was allowed to go back home "in reguard that her husband is content to accept of her againe & to pardon her" (BCB 4, fol. 105v). However, Elizabeth's case does reek of halfhearted repentance.[84]

Mrs. Miller was running her business with the help of two maids, Jane, the chambermaid, and Katharine, the kitchenmaid, who would have eked out a meager existence without trading their bodies to the affluent clients. Among them were the "gentlemen . . . called the Tirrells," who used to "lye there all night" and, as it seems, would·have "the vse" of Elizabeth Reignoldes's "body" each in his turn (BCB 4, fol. 100v). The most openhanded of Elizabeth's clients turns out to have been John Cotton, "a gent., the Lord Chamberlines man," who whenever he "had th'vse & carnall knowledge" of her body "gaue her Xs" (BCB 4, fol. 101r). He was, besides the Tirrells as a group, the biggest single trout in Mrs. Miller's pond, whom Elizabeth caught in the spring of 1599. A page of the Royal Wardrobe, empowered to look after the Windsor Castle Gardens in 1596 with an additional annual salary of £4, he was promoted groom of her Majesty's Wardrobe in 1597. As an officer of the Royal Household, he was running, under the superintendance of the Lord Chamberlain, an office of his own in Whitehall. By 1617 he was Keeper of the Standing Wardrobe of Westminster.[85] In May 1599, he maneuvered himself into hot waters. His calls to Mrs. Miller's establishment had obviously drained his financial resources, each visit costing £1, that is, 10s for Elizabeth Reignoldes and 10s for the money-grubbing Mrs. Miller. This would seem to explain why he was driven to ask Richard West, the Teller of the Exchequer, to help him out of his financial scrape in advancing the money to pay the Queen's rent for his office in Whitehall.[86] It is therefore legitimate to speculate that Elizabeth Reignoldes in borrowed feathers and the officer of the lower echelon of the Royal Wardrobe, which used to collaborate with the Office of the Revels and the Office of the Works in staging plays and masques at court, made their encounter in one of London's playhouses while attending a performance of the Lord Chamberlain's Men.[87]

In any case, Elizabeth Reignoldes can claim to be the earliest identified woman and prostitute known by name to have frequented the theater.[88] Mrs. Miller had urged her to "dwell with her where she should liue quietly & go gentlewoman lyke." Elizabeth agreed and within a week she "went to a playe." As she was still an inexperienced playgoer, the business of marketing herself as a prostitute failed, but on returning to Mrs. Miller's house after the play was over, she met a gentleman she had already slept with in Mrs. Miller's establishment. They supped together and then she "lay with him in bedde all night" while Mrs. Miller was taking care of another customer (BCB 4, fol. 100v). Unfortunately, the BCB do not disclose how many times Elizabeth repeated her playhouse experience; yet the circumstances would seem to favor the assumption that from April to June 1599 she was the steady theater companion of John Cotton.

Elizabeth Reignoldes, moreover, happens to be the first prostitute whose examination discloses an intimate inventory of her apparel. Whereas contemporary descriptions and representations of prostitutes as given in chronicles, rogue pamphlets, and plays are actually stereotyped simplifications of reality, formulas inscribed in a text in order to evoke the gendered body of a prostitute, the actual dress rehearsal Mrs. Miller mounted in her brothel reads like a preparation for Elizabeth's coming-out in the spring of 1599. Mrs. Miller "caused" Elizabeth as soon as she set foot in her house "to putt on a crimson damask petticote of white and redd, & a great farthingale couered ouer with yellow cotton, & a wrought veluett gowne with a payre of satten sleeues cutt with a haire-brayne cutt, & arabata imbrodered with white flowers of needlework with a border of gold buttons, with a white tyer vppon her head" (BCB 4, fol. 101r).[89] No mention is made of a décolletage for displaying the breasts, nor of the use of cosmetics, nor of shoes displayed.

Thus the inventory drawn up by Elizabeth Reignoldes for the governors of Bridewell leaves no doubt that Mrs. Miller had no scruples about dressing a saddler's wife well above her station, transforming her into what Philip Stubbes used to call a puppet or rather a mummy sinning against propriety. With the help of her two maids, Mrs. Miller was putting the sartorial assemblage together, beginning, I assume, with the "great farthingale," with what was obviously a cartwheel farthingale mounted to hold out the petticoat but ultimately to extend Elizabeth's physical presence and thereby commodify her sexualized body.

Then it was the turn of the petticoat, the main garment, to be adjusted to Elizabeth's body. It was usually made of expensive material in bright colors, in the present case of "crimson damask" imported from France or Italy. The petticoat consisted of a trailing skirt and a stiff bodice reinforced with stays and it usually opened in an inverted V so as to show the ornaments of the fabric.[90] As for the gown, it used to be more elaborate than the other garments, imparting an air of dignity to its wearer. Accordingly, Elizabeth Reignoldes was rigged out with a "wrought veluett gowne." It had "a payre of satten sleeues," slashed in the latest hare-brain fashion.[91] It was the most expensive item of the equipage, for which Mrs. Miller must have paid more than Mrs. Stainey paid for hers, that is £4.[92]

The sartorial pièce de résistance of an Elizabethan gentlewoman's dress was her extravagant neckware and headgear. Elizabeth Reignoldes's was quite in tune with the prevailing fashion. She wore an "arabata imbrodered with white flowers of needlework with a border of gold buttons." In plain English, she wore a ruff, supported on a frame of wire, called a rebato, which was covered with embroidered linen.[93] Pinning the ruff to the rebato was a time-consuming business. Her headgear in the shape of "a white tyer," made perhaps by Christopher Mountjoy, heralded the end of the ritual of refashioning Elizabeth Reignoldes's identity as a high-ranking prostitute. It was a very expensive ceremony which must have lasted one or two hours and which cost Mrs. Miller a fortune.[94] It turned the sexualized space of the bawdy house into a theatrical space with the brothel keeper engendering the prostitute's transformation and the maids watching and helping the process.

What emerges from this satorial performance is the fact that brothel keepers with social pretensions had their largest investments in the wardrobe of their prostitutes.[95] This finding is corroborated by Barbara Allen, who catered to Sir William Brooke, clad in the "Gowne and apparell" given her by Agnes Wilkinson, and also by Alice Woodstock, alias Partridge, who resorted to (Sir) George Brooke's Whitehall office in "a gentlewomans Gowne left in pawne with" Agnes Wilkinson (BCB 4, fol. 8r). Hence it is no surprise that Mrs. Miller and Mrs. Wilkinson felt obliged to recover their heavy expenses in raising the rate of their fees.

Mrs. Miller's professional strategy of increasing her income by kindling Elizabeth Reignoldes's passion for sartorial display demanded Elizabeth's unconditional surrender. She did talk her into buying a gown of her own for £2 2s and made her walk the streets of London "gentlewoman lyke" in costly and lavish attire, which she thought was "fitt for the degree" of the customers, to borrow a term from Gilbert East's examination, whom she expected to be hooked and taken to her house. Thus, the gorgeous apparel was first and foremost a trap for wealthy customers to be caught in or, to put it in business terms, it was, as it were, an outgrowth of professional dress regulation shaped to increase sexual consumption and thereby the rate of gain. Elizabeth Reignoldes may not have realized that when she turned up in a London theater in Mrs. Miller's luxurious equipage, she was, in fact, transgressing the legislated dress codes. In terms of the sumptuary laws as laid down to protect the distinctions of rank and wealth, she was a saddler's wife inappropriately and inordinately dressed up. On the other hand, Mary Newborough being a gentlewoman did not break the social boundaries of gender identification when, in seductive apparel, which must have rivaled the garments of a Venetian courtesan, she rode in a coach to St. James's Park.[96]

Price Structure and Contraceptives

Before 1546, price regulation was imposed on prostitution by the civic authorities, but with the closure of the public brothels in the suburbs and the
subsequent transference of prostitution to the private space of the city, the
regulation of prices was left to the individual brothel keeper, prostitute, pimp,
and client. From then on the prices were regulated by the pressures of the
open market. Instead of a uniform price—for instance, the rent of a chamber
for a prostitute was formerly fixed at 14d a week[97]—there was a myriad of
individual prices. Each brothel keeper was free to fashion his own price list,
but for him/her it was very difficult to estimate the price with so many vari-
ables to be taken into account. As for the prostitute, each made up her own
price, which varied according to her status and her experience. The price
structure, therefore, appears to have been in a state of disorder. The disorder,
however, was only a reflection of a hierarchical system. Contrary to received
opinion, the BCB do yield some reliable information as to how the individual
prices and payments were negotiated. What emerges from the BCB and from
other records is the application of a floating scale of fees and rents. This price
scale, by the way, does not correspond to the simplified and stereotyped price
structure in the fictional world of imaginative literature, which was far removed from reality.[98]

The brothel keepers calculated their rates on a sliding scale according to
the amount of money they invested in their establishments. Thus, the more
money they invested in renting a house, the higher the prices they exacted. A
superior establishment catering to clients of high social rank was also obliged
to keep a well-stocked wardrobe for its prostitutes. Mrs. Miller and Mrs. Wilkinson are a case in point. In addition to the heavy sartorial expenses, Mrs.
Miller had also medical fees to settle. She was clever enough to take preven-
tive measures against conception and the transmission of venereal diseases.
As Elizabeth Reignoldes informed the governors, Mrs. Miller, in person,
would, after every copulation, "squirt white wines & other waters, which she
had of a surgeon, into their bodyes," that is, into their vaginas, "therby to
cleanse their bodyes for feare to be with child or other distastes" (BCB 4,
fol. 101r).[99]

We have it, then, on the authority of Elizabeth Reignoldes that Mrs. Miller
was *femme à tout faire,* clothing and feeding her prostitutes and reducing
the dangers of their nonprocreative sex. Aware, as she was, of the hazards of
prostitution, Mrs. Miller had mounted a medical service with the backing of
a barber-surgeon. She subjected, to believe Elizabeth Reignoldes, all the *filles
de joie* operating in her establishment, presumably Mary Newborough included, to vaginal baths of "white wines," and "other waters," in all likelihood vinegar and herbal potions. What Elizabeth Reignoldes may have

forgotten to mention to the governors are stewed prunes, the staple dish recommended by the venereologist William Clowes as a guard against contracting venereal disease. She made no reference either to the practice of postcoital urination as a contraceptive.[100]

The use of drugs as a contraceptive was not new, but the collaboration between brothel keeper and a barber-surgeon may have been a novelty. One would have expected Mrs. Miller to have sought the cooperation of a woman, a midwife or a wise woman, known for her use of herbal drugs to regulate fertility, but apparently she did not confide in the service of a woman presumably because a midwife was especially vulnerable to accusations of witchcraft and sorcery. On the other hand, Mrs. Miller overlooked the possibility that as an unlearned woman practitioner administering herbal drugs and alcoholic vaginal baths in a makeshift antiprocreative dispensary she was courting the danger of being accused of committing an act of witchcraft. She escaped such an accusation thanks to the apparent leniency of the Bridewell governors.[101] Mrs. Miller was apparently a kind of "herb woman" as Lysimachus chooses to call Marina's bawd in *Pericles*.[102]

The brothel keepers of elite establishments belonged to the high-income groups of London society. They enriched themselves by exacting money from their prostitutes for board and lodging; from their clients for having sexual intercourse with their prostitutes; and they required their prostitutes to deliver a percentage of their personal fees to them. Thus the weekly rent for board and lodging in the 1570s was 4s to 6s, in some individual cases 20s and 30s.[103] In the 1590s, the rent rose and was often paid by the clients. Christian Thibaud paid Mrs. Windsor 13s 4d "for the dyett" of Elizabeth Stapleton; so did Mr. Baker for Helen Cootes, Robert Offley for Mrs. Willford; but Thomas Marini preferred dressing Mary Newborough's diet in his house to paying the weekly rent to Mrs. Windsor (BCB 4, fol. 72r–v). In addition to the weekly rent paid either by the prostitutes or their clients, Mrs. Windsor got 10s from Tomas Marini whenever he had the use of Mary's body and from Mr. Baker for the body of Helen Cootes. But sometimes Mr. Baker paid only 5s and, when he was apparently short of money, with "a siluer spoone" (BCB 4 fol. 72v). Mrs. Miller was much more demanding. She charged her clients the same amount they paid to the prostitutes.

The portion of the gains delivered by the prostitutes to their keepers, in the 1570s, varied from 20, 50, to 75 percent.[104] The examination of Elizabeth Reignoldes gives us some insight into the floating scales negotiated between her and the various keepers she worked for. With Mrs. Cesar the arrangement was 20 to 25 percent; with Mrs. Wilkinson the scale was progressive: 12d "of euery 4s & 5s," 18d "of euery 6s," and 24d "of euery 10s;" with Mrs. Miller the agreement was at least 50 percent of her own fee, preferably 75 percent. Thus when John Cotton had sexual intercourse with Elizabeth Reignoldes, Mrs. Miller let Elizabeth know "that she was wont to haue as much money giuen her by the gentlemen as any of the women had for their paynes & besides to haue halfe of this money, which is vijs vjd of Xs,. Wher-vppon" Elizabeth "gaue her Vs of her Xs" she had got from John Cotton (BCB 4 fol. 101r). This corresponds to the kind of arrangement the bawd in *Pericles* expects Marina to honor "and do" her "the kindness of our profession" after having done "for clients her fitment."[105]

Clearly, in the sex trade the brothel keepers benefited most from the price structure. In the late 1570s, James Maye's wife of the Three Tonnes without Aldgate earned £100 a year, which placed her and some other colleagues who made as much in the upper third of London society.[106] In the 1590s, Mrs. Miller and Mrs. Windsor belonged to the same category to judge from their fines of £10 and £5 respectively and from Elizabeth Reignoldes's statement that Mrs. Miller "gott good store of money." She could therefore afford to open up another establishment in Beech Lane, for which she paid an annual rent of £12 or £16 (BCB 4, fol. 101r).

A prostitute's fee was the result of the negotiations between each prostitute and her client. The negotiated fee depended, first, on the client's affluence and, second, on whether he was a low-risk client, a gentleman, an office-holder, or a high-risk client such as a soldier. The fee of the low-risk clients varied from 3s to 10s. As for a high-risk client, Ann Morgan of Wells, a typical urban public whore, charged soldiers half a crown, double her standard fee.[107] The scale of fees was, of course, also determined by the prostitute's status. Long-term mistresses such as Aemilia Bassano/Lanyer or Christiane Hobson were granted £40 per annum, whereas street whores such as Elizabeth Compe, "a verie lewd queane," would be "naughtie," as she told the governors of Bridewell, "with anyone for ijd," that is obviously for a temporary favor.[108] A short-term mistress such as Thomasin Breame, in the 1570s, exceptionally commanded as much as £10 an afternoon, normally she made 10s, the same as Mary Newborough and Helen Cootes seem to have received from their patrons[109] The fee of Elizabeth Reignoldes clearly depended on the quality of the establishment she was working with. In Mrs. Cesar's house, her clients gave her 4s and 5s; in Mrs. Wilkinson's, her fee ranged from 4s, 5s, 6s to 10s; and in Mrs. Miller's from 5s to 10s (BCB 4, fol. 100r–101r). The distinctions between the individual clients were obviously not levelled by the purveyors of commercial sex.

Moreover, the value of a prostitute appears to have been regulated by her experience. The question that arises is whether Elizabethan prostitutes were considered a commodity for male consumption whose value corroded with frequent use or whether the value of their bodies increased by the weight of copulation.[110] The evidence emerging from the BCB would seem to favor the view that a prostitute with little experience was less appreciated by her clientele than a seasoned practitioner. Admittedly, virgins enjoyed a special status in brothels, but their virginal bodies did not command the highest prices.

Whereas Marie Donnolly and Thomasin Breame received £10, Mrs. Corbet sold Katherine Williams's "maidenhead to one Mr. Paul Mowdler, a merchant," most likely a merchant stranger, for £2.[111] Mrs. Wilkinson, in 1598, took advantage of the demand for sexual traffic with virgins. She sold the "maydenhead" of Mrs. Babb, her maid, and of Alice Woodstock, whom she kept for George Brooke, presumably for no more than £2 (BCB 4 fol. 100r). The certainty of being the first to penetrate a woman's body, even if it belonged to a potential prostitute, was for some men the best safeguard against contracting a venereal disease. (Sir) Horatio Palavicino is a case in point, George Brooke may have been another, and Lysimachus in *Pericles* holds the same view (The Arden Edition, 4.6.23–25).[112]

Given the social stratification of prostitutes, rivalry among them must have been rampant. Disappointingly, the BCB have not zoomed in on this issue simply because no cases turned up in an institution whose reformatory sexual policy was aimed at the prostitutes catering to the middle class. That the problem did exist is borne out by Ben Jonson. In *Bartholomew Fair* (1614), he raises the issue of clothing as a marker of professional hierarchy and as conducive to competition and envy. Punk Alive, mistaking Dame Overdo, wife of Justice Adam Overdo, for a rival, deals her some blows for undermining her existence: "A mischiefe on you, they are such as you are, that vndoe vs, and take our trade from vs, with your tuft-taffata hanches . . . The poore common whores can ha' no traffique, for the priuy rich ones; your caps and hoods of veluet, call away our customers, and lick the fat from vs" (4.5.65–71).[113]

A Support Network Among Prostitutes and Katherine Arden's Pregnancy

Before examining Mary Newborough as an agent of female resistance in Bridewell, it seems sensible to address the nature of women's alliances and networks in prostitution. Recent feminist studies have recovered from oblivion women's manifold manifestations of gender-oriented affiliations, but, strange to say, have neglected to look at women's affiliations in prostitution. This is a highly promising field of research. It requires extensive investigation well beyond the scope of my modest contribution.[114] Archer and Griffiths have addressed the issue of networking and cooperation without paying special attention to the agency of female brothel keepers and to the spirit of group solidarity manifested by bawds and prostitutes. They have come to the conclusion that there was no integrated city network, each keeper remaining fully independent. They do, however, acknowledge that the leading brothel keepers, the majority being women, were known to each other and willing to cooperate in pooling their prostitutes. Thus, Elizabeth Kirkham, while lying in the house of Gilbert East, in the later 1570s, was ferried to the house of Black Luce (Mrs. Baynam) whenever she had "great guests" to entertain.[115]

It would, indeed, have been virtually impossible to weld together the patchwork of London brothels in the 1570s and 1590s into an efficient network, but there is evidence that female keepers and prostitutes struck up affiliations, first, in the face-to-face community of Bridewell and, second, in the daily traffic of metropolitan prostitution, which went beyond the simple pooling of prostitutes and the sharing of resources and gains.[116] Thus, Elizabeth Reignoldes, while detained in Bridewell, began her networking with Mrs. Cesar who happened to be affiliated with Mrs. Wilkinson and Mrs. Miller. At the time she was working under the guidance of Mrs. Miller, Elizabeth was invited by Mrs. Wilkinson, in whose house she had been working before, to attend "the christening of one Jane, Mrs. Wilkinson's sister, who neuer had a husband; where there was Mrs. Farringdon, Mrs. Ireland, Mrs. Langley & Mrs. Jone, that lieth at Mrs. Langleys, & Elizabeth Lister," and when the christening party drew to a close, Elizabeth "was bidden by them to see Katherine Arden about Easter last, hauing no husband, & lay in childbed" (BCB 4, fol. 100r).

Elizabeth Reignoldes's testimony affords one of the very rare insights into the private lives of late Elizabethan prostitutes. What transpires from her evidence is that about 11 April 1599 Mrs. Wilkinson threw a party to celebrate the late christening of her sister. She invited three of her colleagues: Mrs. Farringdon, Mrs. Ireland, living in Whitefriars, and Mrs. Langley; and four prostitutes: her sister Jane, Elizabeth Reignoldes, Mrs. Jone, and Elizabeth Lister, to attend the party. The celebration was clearly arranged as a demonstration of female solidarity among bawds and prostitutes who were bound together by kinship and business interests. It was a festive reunion of likeminded women who had formed a support network as a strategy to overcome their social marginalization and secure their work.

The solidarity the prostitutes showed in the face of Katherine Arden's confinement commands further attention. Though Katherine was not affiliated with the prostitutes who came together to celebrate the christening of Mrs. Wilkinson's sister, they nonetheless asked Elizabeth Reignoldes to look after her. They knew that she used to lie in brothels run by male keepers and were therefore worried that she would not properly be attended to during her confinement in mid-April 1599. Moreover, the prospective mother could not count on family and neighborhood solidarity, as was the norm. All she could hope for was to rely on the help of those women who shared with her the experience of being immersed in the illicit sex business. She was facing the prospect of giving birth to her child without the attendance of a midwife "in one Pugsby's house in St Peter's Lane," Clerkenwell, a notorious red-light district outside the city walls. Elizabeth Reignoldes may have been the only female witness of the delivery.[117]

The least one can say is that marginalization had forged a nurturing culture for the benefit of prostitutes in need, particularly in "childbed." Thus Mary Newborough affords a further display of female solidarity among prostitutes. She lent support to Katherine Arden in her struggle to resume trade after her confinement. In August 1599, she took Katherine Arden, as mentioned, on a historic coach ride to St. James's Park to see the muster of the soldiers. Katherine's success at St. James's remains doubtful. In any case, she landed up in Bridewell, and at her first examination, on 10 November, she told the governors a pack of lies, making them believe that she and her husband had "come from beyond the Seas at Easter last" and that she had lain in Fetter Lane "at the house of one Mr. Boulton" (BCB 4, fol. 128r). When examined again, on 14 December, she confessed that she actually "lay in one Pugsby's house in St Peter's Lane," which branched off from St. John's Street in the direction of Cow Cross. A pimp called Randall had taken her there. She was now in bad health. Accordingly, the court ruled that she "shalbe together in one rome with Mary Newboroughe and Mary Digbye for that she soundeth [swoones] diuers tymes." The court also ordered that she was to be discharged provided she put "in good and sufficient securitie . . . for her good behavior and appearaunce within three dayes warninge" (BCB 4 fol. 129r).

Despite the admonitions of the governors, Katherine Arden acted as agent of her own ruin. She was soon back in Bridewell and, as will be seen, was to be involved in the Bridewell scandal in 1602. She became, for her contemporaries, a paragon of the rotten whore. Ben Jonson, in "Epigram 133" titled "On the Famous Voyage," describes a wherry being rowed up Fleet Ditch, associating Kate Arden with the stench of decaying meat: "The meate-boate of Beares colledge, *Paris-garden,* / Stunke not so ill; nor, when she kist, KATE ARDEN." And in "An Execration upon *Vulcan*" he maliciously magnified the power of her tinderbox (pudend), infected by a burning clap, as being so virulent that it "Kindled the fire" of the Globe Theater in June 1613.[118] Again Richard Brathwait in *Barnabae Itinerarium* (1638) stripped her of all dignity, inscribing her name in his text purely for the sake of rhyming (pp. 28–29):

> Near Horne-Alley, in a garden,
> A wench more wanton than Kate Arden
> Sojourns, one that scorns a Wast-coat,
> Wooing Clients with her basket.[119]

Kate Arden and with her Jane Fuller disprove the popular belief that prostitutes were less fertile than other women because frequent intercourse made their wombs too slippery for conception. Jane Fuller had two illegitimate children by Sir Edward Baynton's brother and after marriage became one of London's prominent bawds of the 1570s.[120] Kate Arden was not successful in climbing up the rungs of the professional ladder. She is likely to have abandoned the child she gave birth to at Easter 1599, leaving it to the care of a London parish.[121]

Agnes Wilkinson's Establishment and Lord Cobham's Sons Sir William and George Brooke as Patrons of Barbara Allen and Alice Woodstock, alias Partridge

Agnes Wilkinson was not only the dynamo of a female support network, she was also the respected manageress of a high-class establishment whose reputation penetrated the borders of the ruling class. Thus she distinguished herself as the confidential sex agent of Sir William Brooke (1565–1597) and (Sir) George Brooke (1568–1603), the two younger sons of William Lord Cobham (1527–1597). The two brothers were pursuing different careers: William was a dashing gentleman officer who, about 26 October 1597, returned from the Islands Voyage to the Azores as the battle-tested captain of the *Dreadnought;* George, handicapped by a childhood accident that had left him lame, compensated his lack of physical agility by acquiring a reputation for being a studious and learned gentleman cut out for a career as a courtier.

There was a strong brotherly bond between the two younger Brookes which, surprisingly in terms of the family affiliations, manifested itself in their admiration and emulation of the earl of Essex. William saw in Essex the lodestar of his military vocation and George the epitome of courtly and intellectual accomplishment. The bond between the two brothers is also documented in William's will and again in the mutual undertaking to harness their sexual energies through the services of Mrs. Wilkinson's establishment. Their elder brother Henry Brooke (1564–1619), in the eyes of Essex the very antithesis of what an aristocrat should aspire to be, is likely to have lived out his sexuality as a bachelor gentleman in a different establishment.[122]

Agnes Wilkinson, wife of Michael Wilkinson, dwelling in Love Lane, kept Barbara Allen at the request of Sir William Brooke for his use only. The terms of their arrangement, which remained in force for about five weeks only (November 1597 until 8 December 1597), were the same as the terms observed in Mrs. Miller's establishment. Sir William gave Barbara Allen 30s. "to haue th' use of her body" and Mrs. Wilkinson claimed half the amount. In addition to 30s., Sir William agreed to pay "fyve shillinges a weeke" for Barbara Allen's "board" and for the assurance that Barbara enjoyed the status of a kept mistress. But as we have seen with Helen Cootes and Mary Newborough, other clients frequenting Mrs. Wilkinson's house were also

entitled to occupy Barbara Allen. In order to keep the high standard of their
establishment, Mrs. Wilkinson and her husband were obliged to dress up their
prostitutes à la mode. Accordingly, Barbara Allen was fitted out with a costly
"gowne and apparell" in the latest fashion of a gentlewoman.[123]

The sexual relations between officer and prostitute were doomed to be of a
short durée. Agnes Wilkinson remembered taking Barbara Allen to Sir William's residence on 8 December 1597, two days before he "was slaine"
(BCB 4 fol. 9r). On 10 December, Sir William added a codicil to his will,
leaving his lands, leases, and Spanish prisoners taken on the Islands Voyage,
to his brother George, then betook himself to Mile End, London's training
ground, to fight a duel with Thomas Lucas who had challenged him, presumably for debt. He was mortally wounded and died regretted by his many
friends, among them "the best sort," as his cousin Percival Hart reported to
John Leveson, a deputy Lieutenant of Kent.[124]

The Bridewell examinations of Agnes Wilkinson and her prostitutes in
March 1598 also afford an insight into the disordered and subversive sexuality of George Brooke. There is no getting away from the fact that his sexual
drive knew no boundaries. He did not hesitate to convert his office in Whitehall into a place of assignation in 1598 and in 1602 he had no second
thoughts, as will be shown below, about exploiting the conversion of Bridewell into a brothel and participating in upsetting the order of a civic institution that had originally been designed to discipline unruly women and
prostitutes. Neither his traffic with prostitutes, among them Mary Newborough, nor his marriage, in 1599, to the brave Elizabeth Burgh, who bore him
a son and two daughters, prevented his sexuality from getting out of control.
In an act of incest, he seduced his wife's sister Frances, who was engaged to
Francis Coppinger, George's own nephew and ward, and left her impregnated.[125]

It fell to the inexperienced Alice Partridge to quench George Brooke's un-
appeasable sexual appetite. Alice, born into a Holborn lower-class family,
had been in service as a maidservant in the prestigious household of Lady
Margaret Hoby. On an average, a young servingwoman stayed on for a period
of four years in the same household, but Alice did not satisfy the demands of
Lady Hoby and was therefore dismissed after "halfe a yere" (BCB 4, fol.
8r). One of the best educated women of her age, who boasted an outstanding
command of modern languages, Lady Hoby must have been a difficult mistress to get on with. She was chronically suffering from bad health, causing
her husband Sir Edward Hoby anxiety as early as 1586 when she was just
nineteen years old. We have it on the authority of Simon Forman, whom she
was to consult in 1601, that she had got gout in her hands and feet and inevitably suffered from melancholy and phlegm. Under these circumstances, it is
not surprising that Alice Partridge did not qualify as a suitable maidservant,
falling short of the strict expectations of her ailing mistress in 1597.[126]

The servant status left young women in a singularly exposed position. Once expelled from their household jobs, young female domestic servants in early modern London were forced to prostitute themselves in order to survive. Alice suffered the fate of the dismissed maidservants.[127] It was her own mother who put her to service as a prostitute with Agnes Wilkinson. Mrs. Partridge, as Mrs. Wilkinson explained to the Bridewell governors, came to her establishment in person, asking to help "her daughter to a service or to helpe her to some frende" of hers (BCB 4, fol. 8r).

The moment Alice Partridge entered Mrs. Wilkinson's academy, she was put through a process of transmutation whose sole aim was to bereave her of her own identity and in its stead mould a new sexual orientation tailor-made for the commodification of her body. The first operation undertaken by Mrs. Wilkinson was a name change. As Alice told the Bridewell governors, her new mentor "willed" her "to change her name from Partridge to Alice Woodstock saieng ells it would be a descreditt vnto her" (BCB 4, fol. 8r). The term partridge, in fact, had come to denote, in Elizabethan slang, a lascivious woman. Her name would have been appropriate for a street whore, but it would not have befitted a bona-roba who was being groomed for sex work in the highest circles of Elizabethan society.[128] The second step taken by the ambitious brothel keeper in refashioning Alice Partridge's identity was to apply sartorial surgery with a view to impart on Alice the air of a courtesan. She dressed Alice up in a costly "Gowne" which a gentlewoman had "left in pawne with her" (BCB 4, fol. 8r).[129] Alice, dispossessed of her identity, was given a new lease of life that was to last about three months until the beginning of March 1598, when marshal Reade apprehended her together with Agnes Wilkinson, Barbara Allen, and two housemaids in the special hideout of the establishment in Love Lane (BCB 4, fol. 9r).

We do not know how Alice Woodstock, alias Partridge, coped with George Brooke's transgressive sexuality, but we do know that she lost her maidenhead to him in his Whitehall chamber. George Brooke had apparently no second thoughts about abusing his position and converting the palace into a potential breeding ground of sexual incontinence just as the four contractors of Bridewell in 1602 were to dishonor their contract in transmuting the former palace into a brothel. Brooke had commissioned a pander, one "Mr. Allen," to find a suitable prostitute and it was Allen who introduced Alice Woodstock to Brooke in Whitehall.

The arrangement between patron, pimp, bawd, and prostitute led to a newsworthy incident in Whitehall which gave Alice Woodstock an unpleasant insight into the dangerous waters she had been drifting. One day, as she reported to the governors of Bridewell on 4 March 1598, when Mrs. Wilkinson took her "to one Mr. Brooke at the Courte, being the Lorde Cobham his Brother, to his chamber," they were not received by George Brooke, brother of Henry Brooke, eleventh Lord Cobham since March 1597, but by his pimp

Allen. Mrs. Wilkinson then fell out with Allen over the amount of the commission he had promised her for her pains. Allen drew his dagger, threatening to stab Mrs. Wilkinson "if she would not be quiet." As she did not relent, Allen "thrust" her into the "Thames neare White Hall," presumably Whitehall Stairs, "and there had been drowned" if her husband had not rescued her (BCB 4, fol. 8r). Obviously, Michael Wilkinson must have sensed the explosive situation and had accompanied his wife as a sort of private bodyguard. The impressionable young witness must have mistaken what may have simply been a ducking for drowning her bawd.

The other Brookes, William Brooke, tenth Lord Cobham, and Henry Brooke, eleventh Lord Cobham, must have been as deeply enmeshed in prostitution as were William and George. William Lord Cobham, in McKeen's view, somehow adjusted to old age as a single man after the death of his second wife in 1592. But an adjustment without a female partner to bed down was unthinkable for the old man. He thus approached the widowed Magdalen Browne, Lady Montague, a Catholic, and then after the eccentric lady had repulsed his marriage proposal, he struck up a dubious liaison, in October 1595, with one Mrs. Broome and her husband, which E. A. J. Honigmann suspects to have been a "Sir Walter Whorehound" triangle.[130] As for Henry Brooke's sexual misbehavior, he is on record as having fathered an illegitimate son. The gossip was reported by the countess of Southampton in a letter addressed to her husband, who was then with Essex on the Irish campaign, and dated 8 July 1599. She had learned that "Sir John Falstaf" (dehistoricized code name for Henry Brooke) had "by his Mrs Dame Pintpot" (possibly a code name for a prostitute besides being an allusion to Mrs. Quickly, the hostess of the Boar's Head Tavern) been made father of a miller's thumb, "a boye thats all heade and veri litel body." A miller's thumb was a small cob fish, and as Leslie Hotson has pointed out, the joke was disguised as a sly coded wordplay on Cobham.[131]

By 1597 Henry Lord Cobham had been saddled with the Falstaff sobriquet and he was again ridiculed as "the silliest millers thombe" in *Nashes Lenten Stuffe* (written 1598, published 1599). He was the cob fish "nibbling" at Nashe's "fame" for having continued Shakespeare's Oldcastle satire in libelling Henry Lord Cobham in the lost play *The Isle of Dogs* (1597), a joint venture by Nashe and Jonson.[132] Jonson paid for his disrespect with two months' imprisonment. As soon he was set free, he resumed his attack on Lord Cobham in holding up to ridicule, as it seems to me, the family's "folly" of tracing their distinguished ancestry back to Sir John Oldcastle and the reign of William the Conqueror. Thus Cob, the water bearer in *Every Man in His Humour,* which was performed by the Lord Chamberlain's Men in September 1598, is proud of fetching his pedigree and name from the first red herring that was eaten in Adam and Eve's kitchen.

In view of the concerted campaign against the Cobham family among writers in 1596–99, there is some point in speculating that the sexual misdemeanors of the Brookes might be a possible key for decoding the mystery behind the hotly debated name changes of Oldcastle to Falstaff and Brooke to Broome. Does it make sense to read Falstaff, the "abominable misleader of youth," "the aged counsellor of youthful sin," and the sexualized lowlife of the Boar's Head Tavern with its threat to the moral well-being of the nation, in short the representation of the obverse of a healthy court and state, as a caveat against the Brookes? If it does, it would explain why members of the Brooke family, most likely William Lord Cobham, who was appointed Lord Chamberlain on 8 August 1596, intervened and saw to it that Shakespeare changed the name of his ancestor Sir John Oldcastle in *1 Henry IV,* and why, after his death, his son Henry Lord Cobham saw fit to have the name of Brooke altered in *The Merry Wives of Windsor.*[133]

The Dramaturgy of a Processional Spectacle: The Carting of Mary Newborough [1600]

In an undated letter addressed to his brother Bassingborne, Philip Gawdy reported that Mary Newborough and Mary Digby had "bene carted three dayes together" through the streets of the city of London. A highly ambitious young follower of the earl of Essex given to gathering court news and hot gossip, Gawdy does not seem to have cared to find out the reasons that led the city authorities to mete out the severest possible punishment to the two molls. But he released some valuable information that Lord Chief Justice Popham, the highest common-law judge in England, and Mary Newborough "can not agree by any meanes, but for ought that I perceyue, Mall Neuberry goes by the worst since." Sir John Popham had, in fact, again committed May Newborough to Newgate prison.[134]

Gawdy also falls short of giving his brother a detailed chronicle of the misfortunes that befell the two Marys during those three mortifying days they were being exhibited to the crowds, exposed to the biting mockery of the newsmongers, and left at the mercy of those aggressive spectators who supported the enforcing of moral standards in their town. It is, however, possible to make up for Gawdy's imperfect account in reconstructing the paradigm of a civic spectacle that has surprisingly remained understudied. What follows is a provisional attempt to recover the humiliations the two women must have gone through, humiliations cast in accordance with an age-old scenario and meticulously revised and improved by the civic authorities of the 1590s with a view to letting the Londoners participate in the shaming of unbound female sexuality. Carting, as will be shown, had some affinities with other processional rituals ordered by the magistrates for violations of sexual or gender norms.

Carting was not a gender-specific punishment as was, for instance, *dena-satio* as inflicted on prostitutes in medieval Nuremberg and Augsburg.[135] It was inflicted on both Englishmen and women throughout the sixteenth century irrespective of their social status. Thus Roger Gill, saddler, and John Inman, with his wife, were carted to the pillory in Cornhill in 1523 for acting as bawds to priests.[136] About 1540, when John Stow was still in his youth, the priest of St. Michael in Cornhill was carted "through the high street and the markets of the city" for having attempted to seduce the wife of the draper John Atwood instead of playing out "a game at tables," that is backgammon, "for a pint of ale" that he had begun with Atwood, who was, however, called away on business.[137] Another clergyman, parson Chekyn of St. Nicholas in Old Fish Street, suffered the indignity of carting in 1553 for offering the sexual services of his wife.[138] John Hollynbryg, gentleman, of St. Giles in the Fields, pleaded guilty in 1575 to keeping a common brothel, for which offense he was sentenced to be carted from Newgate to St. Giles.[139] The practice was still very much in use in the last decade of Queen Elizabeth's reign. Francis Curatory and his wife Mary, who were running a common brothel, were sentenced, on 31 December 1602, to be carted to Pickthatch and then to be whipped at Bridewell.[140]

Isaac Herbert Jeayes, the editor of Philip Gawdy's correspondence, put the undated letter to December 1600. His dating, however, does not fit in with the chronology of Mary Newborough's career as a prostitute. Her carting must have taken place some time after 31 January 1600, when she was released from Bridewell, and 13 June [1600], when Gawdy in another letter informed his brother Bassingborne in Norfolk that Mrs. Fowler had become "as infamous allmost as Mall Neubery."[141] Gawdy was comparing another notorious case of bawdry, which erupted in 1600, to Mary Newborough's case. The comparison, however, is rather lame, for Gawdy, a distant relative of the Fowlers, was obviously biased against Mary Newborough, qualifying her as a criminal. In doing so, he turned a blind eye to the fact that Richard Fowler had been committed to the Tower in August 1599 on suspicion of plotting against the queen. During Fowler's imprisonment, his wife, to put it in terms of Gawdy's one-sided perspective, "parted from her husband, being a most honest gentleman, and lyued at her owne pleasure, and consorted her selfe with euery companyon." She was therefore sentenced, "to be carted to Bridewell and there whipt, her mignon captaine Heines," as John Chamberlain committed to paper for the delectation of Dudley Carleton, "to stand on the pillorie and imprisoned."[142] Captain William Haynes was hanged in Smithfield in April 1602 for killing his fellow prisoner in the Fleet and "Fayre" Mrs. Fowler was to be "apprehended and committed for coyning of forrain gold" in July 1612.[143] Counterfeiting money carried the death penalty.

Carting was a processional spectacle, a liminal mode of cultural performance, that lasted several hours. But for Mary Newborough and her companion

Mary Digby the length of the shaming ritual was exceptional, exceeding the norm laid down for public exposure. The two miscreants, as Philip Gawdy noted, were carted on three consecutive days. Gawdy does not disclose if the diagram of the marshalling provided alternative routes for the cortège, but even if the procession should have stuck to one and the same route, there is no denying that after three days' carting Mary Newborough's sexual misdemeanors had dramatically been brought home to all and sundry. In the eyes of the London populace she was branded as the bête noire of the Bridewell birds. As regards the length of the punishment, there is only one parallel case known to me. The "lusty chantry priest" of the parish church of St. Michael in Cornhill, who about 1540 ingratiated himself with John Atwood's wife over "a game at tables," was carted "through the high street and markets of the city" on three market days.[144]

The processional route mapped out by the civic authorities for carting sexual offenders through the city coincided in its central section with the traditional route laid out for royal entries and civic ceremonies such as the annual Lord Mayor's show. The stations or stopping places of the route can be gathered from the sentences of Prudence Crispe, alias Drewrye, alias Wingfield, and of Elizabeth Holland, whose cartings Mary Newborough is bound to have witnessed. Prudence Crispe, sentenced to be carted on 1 January, and Elizabeth Holland, on 23 November 1597, were "put into a carte at Newgate" and from there were taken to Smithfield. The next station where their processions came to a halt was at their lodgings and then they wound their way along the heart of the city across Cornhill and Cheapside. From there they proceeded to Bridewell, "there to be whipped, and finally back to Newgate." Both were detained in prison until they paid their fines of £40 each and "put in sewerties" for their "good behaviour." Thereafter they were released from Newgate and were free to resume their old trade.[145]

We can take it for certain that Mary Newborough and Mary Digby were sentenced to be carted along the same processional route as marshaled for Prudence Crispe and Elizabeth Holland. The major alterations in the dramaturgy of Mary Newborough's carting were, as mentioned, the repetition of the ordeal on three days and, second, given her status as a gentlewoman, the likely cancellation of the goaring ritual at Bridewell in the presence of the governors and aldermen. Thus we cannot go wrong in believing that the route laid out for the two Marys obliged them to negotiate the most congested places and landmarks of the city. Smithfield, the first station, was London's permanent horse and cattle market. A triangular open space measuring five or six acres, it accommodated a throng of dealers, shoppers, and loiterers who, alerted by the disharmonic performance of the mock musicians, must have swarmed around the cart, possibly a two-wheeled cart, stared at the papers on the victims' heads, whereon was written their offenses, and listened to the proclamation of their wrongdoing.

The next station, one of the main fixtures of the punitive spectacle, was the visit to the rooms of the convicted prostitute; in Mary Newborough's case either her mother's house or the establishment run by her last keeper. This stop left no doubt about the strategy of correction pursued by the civic authorities. Mary Newborough was sentenced to be humiliated not only before the whole city, but also before her relatives, her neighbors, and her associates. The carting reached its climax when the noisy procession paraded along the east-west thoroughfare with its landmarks in Cornhill and Cheapside: the Standard and Conduit or Tunne in Cornhill, the Great Conduit, the Standard, the Cross, and the Little Conduit at St. Paul's Gate in Cheapside. At every single station, Mary Newborough must have gone through the pains of facing the hostile response of the wealthy citizens and the discriminating comments of the water carriers placed at the standards, the principal sources of the city's water supply.[146]

Rough music was a routine accompaniment of carting. Thus for the cortège of Elizabeth Holland, in November 1597, basins were ordered "to be runge before her" from start to finish. Francis and Mary Curatory faced no better in early January 1603. There was no reason for sparing Mary Newborough the noisy music performance with its double function. On the one hand, it had a practical side to it, announcing the arrival of the carting and drawing the crowds; on the other, the tinkling of barbers' basins, or the clatter and ringing of pipes, pots, and pans at the head of Roger Gill's carting (1523), was a charivari-like evocation of the struggle between order and disorder that was being enacted on the platform of the cart. It was a reminder that the aim of the shaming ritual was, despite all appearances to the contrary, the reformation of the culprit.[147]

An incident threatened to upset the timetable and the marshaling of the procession. We have it on Philip Gawdy's authority that one of the two Marys "had lyke to haue bene killd with a blowe of a stone vppon her forehede."[148] Instead of disclosing which of the two Marys it was had a narrow shave, Gawdy fell to interlarding his account with a bawdy afterthought that is inappropriate and in poor taste. Without a flicker of sympathy he observes "that stones not being sett in their right places maye as well offende as please." Pelting the carted victims with rotten eggs, vegetables, and filth was part of the officially sanctioned dynamic of carting. Roger Gill, John Inman and his wife, in 1523, were carted to the pillory in Cornhill there to be pelted.[149] Adulterers, however, according to Alesandro Magno, a young patrician merchant of Venice on a visit to London in August and September 1562, were to be carted through the city and rotten eggs and stones to be thrown at them.[150]

Mary Newborough was not the sort of public figure to condescend to act the gendered part of the submissive woman or penitent offender. An undaunted, self-assertive, class-conscious gentlewoman, who was to brave the brutality of one of the Bridewell undertakers in defending herself with a pair of scissors, she is likely to have assumed a defiant posture of self-defense, parrying with sangfroid the jeers and catcalls of the populace lining the streets and markets. Just as she was to turn her hand to converting Bridewell into a brothel in 1602, she may as well have seized the opportunity to convert the bare boards of her cart into a mobile stage and the streets and markets into a city-wide open-air theater. If so, throwing stones can be seen as the interactive response of hostile community action. Whatever the reasons for pelting her cart with stones, Mary Newborough was not broken in by the ritual of humiliation. On the contrary, she seems to have slipped into the unscripted part of a spoilsport, subverting the spectacle fashioned to celebrate the defeat of the flesh in much the same way as in 1603 she was to slip into the part of a repentant magdalen, deceiving the prison parson and some of the governors, simply because she made up her mind to put an end to her detention in Bridewell. Her carting demonstrates that by 1600 Mary Newborough had become an ill-famed London celebrity protected by some patrons, but prosecuted by the civic authorities in the name of law and order.

Eating Disorders of a Bridewell Spinner and the Tradition of Spinning Songs

The next thing we hear of Mary Newborough after her carting is that the governors of Bridewell, sitting on 3 July 1601, sentenced her to have "a blew gowne putt on . . . in open court and ordered" her "to be set to spinning." They had given her a fair hearing, but must have resented the defiant answers they were given and been taken aback by her calculated waywardness and recalcitrant attitude. They were called in to investigate whether she had bought five parcel-gilt spoons from "Elizabeth Overburye, alias Robinson, wydowe," which Richard Layton is likely to have induced Elizabeth to steal from Justice Butler or from another master. Mary Newborough condescended to acknowledge that she "doth knowe Richard Layton, who lay sometymes at Sir John Peters, and that he is now in the Low Cuntryes, as she thincketh." She also confirmed that she knew Elizabeth Overbury "when she dwelt with Mr. Justice Butler and also with others." But as for the spoons, she answered that "it may be she bought" them "and payd xxxixs . . . when she lay in the Strond, and it may be that she did not buy any such of" Elizabeth Overbury, "and otherwyse she will not aunswer" (BCB 4, fol. 249v).

Elizabeth Overbury, "a notable whore," was, as it were, an ambulant visitor to Bridewell, listed as "a vagrant" and processed in the BCB as "exad, po & dd," that is, examined, punished, and delivered (released). The first entry, dated June 1599, has it that she was "dwelling neare" Holborn Bridge "with one Mrs. Reynoldes, widdow," from whom she got "no wages, only meate and drinke for her service" obviously as a maid and prostitute. The governors' suspicion that she had been committing thefts in order to eke out a living was well-founded. In May 1603, she was, in fact, to land up in Newgate prison before the Lord Chief Justice committed her to Bridewell. She proved more cooperative and communicative than Mary Newborough and was accordingly released on 18 July 1601. As for Richard Layton, he may have been one of the numerous Bridewell detainees who used to be conscripted for Her Majesty's service in the Low Countries against the Spaniards.[151]

The governors were most worried by the rumors that influential patrons of Mary Newborough were scheming to get her out of Bridewell in order to circumvent the accusation of having acquired stolen goods or even having been privy to the theft, and, if need be, to bail her our of Newgate prison. As "for any practize of getting her out of Bridewell by reason of this cause," as the keeper of the BCB clumsily put it, "that shee should be sent before Sir Stephen Soame," Lord Mayor, "for suspicion of ffelony and therby to be committed by him to Newgate, wherby she myght be bayled forth out of that place, she is ignorant of the same, and otherwyse she will not aunswer" (BCB 4, fol. 249v). Mary Newborough was banking on silence being the best self-defense, but therein she was mistaken.[152] She was sentenced to wear the prison uniform, a blue gown, and set to spinning wool or flax for the rest of her detention in Bridewell except for the seven months in 1602 when the hospital was turned into a bawdy house. Spinning had once been a genteel occupation for gentlewomen; it was now menial labor for poor women and for female detainees.

Bridewell boasted a modern system of correction. On the one hand, the governors pursued the policy that all comers should be trained in a trade which would enable them to make a living on their releases; on the other, they still adhered to the practice of meting out corporal punishment as the best measure to reform miscreants, thieves, and prostitutes. Thus cloth-making became one of the cornerstones of the governors' policy. They had "the oversight and charge of . . . all things that in any wise shall or do appertain and belong to" cloth-making.[153] Their order to commit Mary Newborough to the spinning house and to subject her to the surveillance of its three overseers and there to spin in the company of vagrants, thieves, and whores must have been a painfully humiliating experience to endure. So was the order to exchange the trappings of a prostitute for a blue gown.[154] A fictional refashioning of the mortifying impact of this punitive measure has been inscribed by Dekker in the last scene of *The Honest Whore,* part 2. The first Master of Bridewell answers the Duke's questions why the whore Dorothea Target is set to spinning in a "blue Gowne" (5.2.302–4): "Being stript out of her wanton loose attire, / That garment she puts on, base to the eye / Onely to cloath her in humility.[155]

Besides the oversight of cloth-making in Bridewell, the governors also had the right to control the market, the demand, distribution, and purchase of cloth. This regulation was violated, in connivance with one of the four undertakers, by Mary Newborough's cohorts during the Bridewell scandal. Lawrence Hill's examination, dated 4 September 1602, brought to light that Susan Adams, Mary's maid, smuggled a "peece of Tufte taffeta" into Bridewell, which she wrongfully passed on to Katherine Arden who left the valuable fabric in the safe hands of Nicholas Bywater. A week later, on the occasion of the official inquiry into Bywater's "misdemeanours," he confessed that he still had the taffeta in his "custodie and keepinge." There is not the least doubt that the villany of this piece was plotted by Bywater, who had spent the revels in Katherine Arden's arms, or rather, bed, viciously subverting the reformatory policy the governors had pledged themselves to pursue. He must have asked his Bridewell paramour to procure for him, or rather for his wife, the taffeta through the service of Susan Adams, who had free access to her mistress and whose husband, a haberdasher, was the likely supplier (BCB 4, fol. 318r, 318v–319r).[156]

The *habituées* of the late medieval spinning rooms, whether marriageable girls or loose women, engendered a tradition of spinning songs which were spiced with sexual puns and double entendres. Bearing in mind that George Handford was to be inspired by Mary Newborough's sensational volte-face, which she performed in the style of a repentant magdalen in January 1603, to set her repentance to music, it is justified to argue that the detention of a bevy of notorious prostitutes in the late 1590s such as Elizabeth Holland, Luce Morgan, Nell Bedford, Mary Digby, Katherine Arden, and Mary Newborough must have given writers and composers new impetus to churn out spinning song and ballads. In fact, one such ballad brought fourth by the social energy of the Bridewell hemp house is the "Whipping Cheeare. Or the wofull lamentations of the three Sisters in the Spittle when they were in the new Bride-well. To the tune of hempe and flax" (published ca. 1625 in two parts, single sheet folio, STC 25353).[157] To the same European crop of crude folk ballads and sexually offensive spinning and weaving songs belongs, I think, the song that Orsino would like Feste to sing a second time, but which the jester leaves unsung, perhaps because he does not wish to disillusion the lovelorn Orsino. On the first offstage audition, Orsino apparently did not realize that, "The spinsters and knitters in the sun, / And the free maids that weave their threads with bones / Do use to chant it: it is silly sooth, / And dallies with the innocence of love, / Like the old age" (2.4. 44–48) can be understood as being wanton girls, standing in for their unblemished counterparts, or as being respected girls, standing in for their tarnished counterparts.[158]

As a spinner Mary Newborough was subjected to a strictly regulated diet. At dinner her ration was eight ounces of bread, the fifth part of a pound of beef, "a messe of porredge," and a quart of beer for the whole day. At supper the portions were eight ounces of beef and the like quantity of bread.[159] This fare did not agree with Mary Newborough who, as shown, had tasted the private haute cuisine of her patron Tomas Marini. Her mother, therefore, appealed to the governors, and on 8 August 1601 she and Susan Adams were granted the privilege to see Mary in the presence of a governor and to arrange for "the sicke dyett" provided her mother "pay for the same euery weeke before hand" (BCB 4, fol. 250v). The agreement they reached concerned both board and lodging. Mary's privileged treatment lasted until 11 December 1602, when by orders of the Lord Chief Justice it was revoked. Thenceforth she was "to be vsed in dyett and lodging as the rest" (BCB 4, fol. 338v).

Mary Newborough's complaint about the quality of prison food in Bridewell must also be seen as expressing her struggle to come to terms with her prison conditions and her anxiety about a bleak future. She was now a long-term resident facing a sentence of imprisonment that was to last nineteen months. Deprived of a private space, disregarded as an individual, caught in a rigid schedule, and presumably preoccupied with her body image under the restricted food intake and penal labor, she may well have developed eating disorders which were, in all likelihood, aggravated by the lack of variation in the dietary regime and the lost freedom in individual menu choice. To what extent food provision in total institutions shaped and is still shaping the prisoners' plight is an emerging field of research.[160]

The Bridewell Scandal of 1602

The brief outline of the Bridewell scandal given in O'Donoghue's history is so perfunctory and awry that the event must be assessed afresh. I propose to address those aspects of the scandal that O'Donoghue has ignored, played down, misread, and withheld. He has above all drawn a prudish veil of secrecy over the actual role played by the prostitutes and their patrons, pretending that no sexual transgressions were committed in Bridewell. Moreover, he has hushed up the brutality and physical violence perpetrated against the prostitutes. I shall marshal my arguments under the following headings: farming out Bridewell; Bridewell under the sway of the prostitutes; chastisement and resistance; and plots to escape.[161]

Farming Out Bridewell in 1602

The court of aldermen agreed, on 29 March 1602, to farm out Bridewell Hospital for a term of ten years to four "undertakers" or lessees: Thomas Stanley, gentleman, of London; Nicholas Bywater, tanner, of Southwark; Thomas Brownlow, draper; and Thomas Daniel, weaver. The civic authorities covenanted to pay this motley quartet, whose sole incentive was the lure of filthy lucre, the sum of £300 a year provided they honored Bridewell's social policy.[162] The four contractors took over the management of Bridewell on 20 April and settled in the best rooms, their leader Thomas Stanley, residing in the neighboring precincts of St. Bride's Church.[163] Within three months, the institution once hailed as Christ's holy hospital was in a complete shambles. A committee was then set up by the Lord Mayor, on 31 July, to investigate the gross violations of the agreement and the brazen disrespect for the authorities; and on 16 October, the four contractors surrendered their lease.

Information on the contractors is hard to come by. Thomas Stanley's identity remains shrouded in darkness. His appointment as promoter of a dubious business venture raises a host of intriguing questions. A biographical note, appended to the unpublished "Letter to Sir Edward Wingfield, Knt, from Thomas Stanley, a notable Thefe, whoe broke the Castell of Cambridge & departed from the same with 6 more of his Companions 4. June Anno xxxix [1597] in the Tyme of Anthony Cage, esquire, Sherife" and written in a different hand from the rest of the manuscript, discloses that "after much Serche" Stanley was captured in Worcestershire and taken to Newgate prison in London. He was condemned to be hanged but was then "by the means of the *Lord Chefe Justice* pardoned & by hym preferred to be one of the *Overseers or Maysters of Bridwell.*" He was hanged "att *West Chester* 1630 when he was lxx yeares at the least for a Robberie done by his man & hymself." The letter Stanley is supposed to have addressed to Sir Edward Wingfield is, to all appearances, a forgery or rather an audacious attempt to mythologize Thomas Stanley as a criminal, whom the sheriff Anthony Cage "doth Fret & rage & offereth thousandes to bringe me in the Compasse of an Egg Pie." The appended biographical note, on the other hand, can claim to be authentic.[164]

The news that a gentleman turned highwayman was pardoned by the Lord Chief Justice, Sir John Popham, about 1597, sounds quite credible. The previous year, as we know, he had pardoned George Newborough, another gentleman turned highwayman. What strains our credulity is the statement that the Lord Chief Justice recommended Thomas Stanley as the head contractor of Bridewell in 1602. How could Stanley have hoodwinked the Lord Chief Justice, the twenty-six aldermen of the city of London, and the thirty governors of Bridewell into believing that he was not a crook, but an expert qualified to run a renowned social institution as a capitalist enterprise that would yield an annual profit? He did so by assuming the air of a serious projector. Two publications bearing his name have come down to us. One is an undated broadside addressed in form of a *Petition* to King James, the House of Lords, and the House of Commons.[165] The other is a posthumous publication known as *Stanleyes Remedy* (1646).[166]

These two ideological publications provide a glimpse into the circumstances which in 1601/1602 moved Lord Chief Justice Popham to persuade the civic authorities of London to lease Bridewell to a set of four undertakers under the leadership of Thomas Stanley. Popham, apparently taken in by the repentance, social background, and intellectual level of a highwayman who, on the authority of the editor of the posthumous *Remedy,* had once been an Inns-of-Court gentleman, saw in Stanley the right man for the task to improve the financial difficulties besetting an institution that was endowed by the guilds and the citizens of London. He may also have seen in him a projector promising to work toward settling the contested issue of the governors' questionable right to arrest vagrants, delinquents, idlers, prostitutes, and their patrons.[167] Popham, as Stanley noted in his undated *Petition,* had been lecturing to him on "all the Motiues and Causes of the true discouery of the Foundation of *Bridewell*" under Edward VI and had been "commanding" him to "exhibite" the causes to Parliament, "for that he could thinke of no assured way but by Parliament rightly to establish the two Hospitals of *Bridewell* and *St. Thomas.*" This crucial statement made by Stanley one or two decades after Popham's death reveals that by 1601/1602 there was an ingrained disagreement between the Lord Chief Justice and the civic authorities of London over the legal status of Bridewell. This ideological disagreement, I think, lies at the root of the Bridewell scandal of 1602; it provides the key to the scandalous behavior of the contractors that shook Bridewell as a civic institution to its very foundations. The political and criminal dimension precludes any possibility to place the 1602 scandal among the frequent financial irregularities and embezzlements of funds that used to plague Bridewell.[168]

The civic authorities in their petition addressed to King James in 1603 played down the matter as being a purely financial issue. Sir John Popham, they argued, had put forward a motion "for a contribucion for stock and maintenance to be made by this citty towardes" the erection of two new houses of correction." The mayor and the aldermen were willing "to further the said motion," but the House of Commons refused to support the project for financial reasons. Despite the refusal of the Commons, "it was thought inconvenient" that every alderman should in person raise money in his ward. However, the aldermen failed to strike the charitable chord of "priuate persons." In view of this public refusal it "was agreed that Stanley and the rest" of the undertakers "should take the charge of the Hospitall of Bridewell, and yf the business sorted to that good successe, as was pretended and promised by the vndertakers, yt would then be a good meanes to induce the Commons to yeald to that contribucion or otherwise moue particuler persons of their charitable disposicion to contribute soe much as was requested."[169]

The scheme that Stanley submitted to the Lord Chief Justice and the civic authorities of the city of London proved a radical departure from the social policy to which Bridewell had been committed since 1552. Stanley and his three associates pledged themselves to set "four hundred poor people to work at new and profitable trades." The number given in the *Remembrancia* is "500 Vagrantes." However, the committee, set up by the Lord Mayor, Sir John Garrard, on 31 July, to investigate what was couched in a euphemism the "Inconveniences that have grown to the house of Bridewell by the disorder of the undertakers," found, to their dismay, that instead of four hundred inmates engaged in the workshops the undertakers were actually cutting down the number under sixty (BCB 4, fol. 313v–314v). By way of comparison, in 1601/1602, out of 2730 persons who passed through Bridewell, 172 were kept and set to work.[170] In point of fact, there were just sixty-two inmates left, that is, twenty-four men and boys at work; thirty-eight women, eight of them gentlewomen or rather prostitutes, and only eighteen of the poorest sort were at work. The day after the investigation, on 1 August, the undertakers "were so ymportunate with the governors . . . that they gott some of" the inmates "discharged." Thus the number fell under sixty (items 1,8, and 9 of the "Inconveniences"). Moreover, the undertakers settled in the best rooms and contrary to the rules of the agreement converted the empty workshops into tenements, letting them out to families of their friends and relatives (item 7).

The contractors had gone so far as to take "some sort of absolute government" in releasing vagrants and "prisoners" without the consent of the treasurer and governors (items 2 and 3). They kept the poor "naked," recklessly reducing the quality and quantity of the poor and sick diet so that some of the poor and sick died, bringing "discredit to the City." Some of them had to be taken to St. Thomas's Hospital to recover (item 4 and fol. 313r). The provocative policy of the Lord Chief Justice to direct his prison warrants to the contractors virtually undermined the authority of the treasurer and the governors. The contractors' refusal to let the governors inspect the prisoners practically amounted to their disempowerment (item 5). The four were so "remisse and carelesse in their charge" that they did not know the prisoners' identity nor their number (item 12).

The upshot of the scandal was that it was benevolently laid to rest. What looks like another scandal to us, who think in modern categories, was simply a matter of fraud, not a felony, and as such was ill provided for in the procedural law and tended to be left to the discretion of the magistrates. Hence the four contractors, though "at variance" with each other (item 11), were not taken to task for their breach of contract. On the contrary, when they surrendered the lease on 16 October, the governors, conscious of the fact that the infamous quartet was shielded by the Lord Chief Justice, agreed "in kindnesse and courtesy" to defray the debts accumulated by the undertakers to the amount of £265. They had maliciously neglected to pay the clerks, workmasters, and tradesmen, who were now going to be paid by Sir Stephen Soame "out of such money as was lately collected of the severall companies [guilds] within this cittie."[171] Finally, to top a series of scandalous misdemeanors with one more scandal in the modern sense of the word, the criminally minded undertakers broke the terms of their contract with impunity, while the female accomplices, the prostitutes felt the fury of the (un)even-handed justice descend upon them.

Bridewell under the Sway of the Prostitutes

The transmutation of Bridewell into a commercial venture resulted, as we have seen, in reducing the number of the inmates to one third of what it had been before. The workshops were converted into tenements for the friends and relatives of the undertakers, and the residential quarters were sequestered by the four contractors and the eight gentlewomen prostitutes who were "lyving at their owne pleasure" (item 9 of the Inconveniences). Within three months, the house of correction and rehabilitation of loose and lewd women became a site of unconcealed sexuality, a haunt of incontinence, for anyone who could afford to pay the gentlewomen. The working conditions in the historical setting of the ancient palace of Bridewell were favorable to an all-encompassing pattern of transgression. The spacious rooms on the waterfront of the Thames and those along Fleet Ditch, originally built as a royal palace and refurbished by Henry VIII for the reception of the emperor Charles V and his retinue in 1522, provided high-class gaming facilities for the undertakers, the prostitutes and their patrons.[172]

Sir John Popham does not seem to have been aware of the irony of the new situation. His misguided support of Stanley's project was doomed to end up in a débâcle. It brought about the disempowerment of the civic authorities and thereby he unwittingly played into the hands of the female prisoners he used to commit to Bridewell for correction. Instead of being disciplined, the gentlewomen arrogated the right to resume their former trade unhindered and unmolested. The investigating committee, set up by the Lord Mayor at the end of July, was quick to realize that the governors had lost the "oversighte" of the women prisoners or prostitutes. They reported that the "women prisoners beinge of lighte and lewde behauior" were suffered to indulge in sartorial impropriety and excess, "to weare their gorgeous apparrell" and "to enterteyne all men of their acquaintaince to come unto them, liberallie to walk and talk in the fairest roomes in the house and sometymes to shutt themselves vpp togeither privatly in chambers" (item 5). The committee's wording is coded in euphemistic understatements. However, the terse summary recorded in the *Remembrancia*, is quite outspoken: "such lewd women as weare committed vnto them for their wicked lyfe, and should haue bene kept hard at woorke and had the Dyett of the howse, weare suffered to intertaine any that would resorte vnto them in as great loosenes as they wold haue done abroad in their lewd howses."[173]

Under the auspices of Stanley's regime, commercial prostitution reigned

in the sexualized space of Bridewell. The social highlights of the bond between the undertakers and the prostitutes were the parties and entertainments
given both in Stanley's and Bywater's rooms. Bywater, called to account by
the governors on 16 July, admitted that the women "Prisoners that are sent
in by the Lo. Cheife Justice did sometymes diet at the table with him and his
wife and paide sometimes vjd and sometimes viijd a meale." The governors
found this practice intolerable, warning Bywater to put an end to it and issuing the order that dieting in Stanley's rooms at St. Bride's Church house
across the street should also be stopped (BCB 4, fol. 310v). A fortnight later,
the investigating committee struck the same note, finding fault with the daily
recourse of "gentlemen" into the house who came to "speake" with the
women prisoners who were, as of old, clad in "brave apparell" and "kepte at
an excessive dyett of viijd" (BCB 4, fol. 313r–313v). Elizabeth Fey, one of
the prisoners, incriminated Bywater, testifying that diverse times "sundry
gentlemen" resorted to his house and there "had the companye of the women
prisoners" and supped very sumptuously with them on "Crabbes, lobsters,
artetichoques, pyes and gallons of wyne at a tyme" (Court held on 11 August
1602, BCB 4, fol. 315). Aphrodisiac powers were traditionally attributed to
alcohol, marine food, and vegetables, and it is evident that the revellers con-
sumed the crabs, lobsters, and artichokes as a calculated prelude to the post-
prandial sexual intercourse in the *chambres séparées* of the former palace.[174]

For Mary Newborough, who had developed food disorders for being maintained at a dietary level below that of a person of her status, the banqueting
and reveling with the undertakers, her patrons, and one or two select prostitutes was a heaven-sent opportunity to recover her self-confidence. A gour-
met attuned to the refined kitchen of Tomas Marini, the malnourished Mary
must have relished the supposedly erotic marine food mentioned by Elizabeth
Fey and, as the *Remembrancia* put it, they "weare feasted with varietie of
wines and delicate meates, besides a common Tapphouse of stronge beere
which they had their [sic] sett upp to the great scandale of the said Hospitall."[175] The attention lavished by both the male and female revelers on the
food was brought into play as a vehicle for commensality and socialization.
It gave Thomas Stanley, the gentleman turned highwayman who had repented
but was about to lapse back into crime, and the still unrepentant gentlewoman
turned prostitute, whose husband was still kept in prison under the warrant of
Sir John Popham, a hold on each other. Mary Newborough "supped" in "Mr.
Stanleys howse," as Nicholas Bywater confessed, in the company of Mr.
Laugher and Mr. Cobb, who "have . . . seene the gentlewomen . . . often-
times," in his and his wife's presence, and in Mrs. Godfrey's, one of the
gentlewomen prostitutes, and Thomas Daniel's wife, one of the undertakers.
Bywater's confession, made on 11 September, confirms Mary Newborough's
uncontested status among the "imprisoned" gentlewomen. Mrs. Godfrey,

alias Mrs. Miles, attended the supper only because she was championed by the Bywaters for greasing their palms (BCB 4, fol. 318v.–319v).

The Bywaters were a wicked couple determined to leave no means unturned in exploiting what was for them a business venture. They prided themselves on their new role as a many-headed Cerberus, guarding the entrance to the tarnished territory of Bridewell and exacting an obulus which granted access to the prostitutes. Every gentleman that "resorted" to Mr. Bywater's house to have "the companye of the women" paid "Mrs. Bywater 5d" (BCB 4, fol. 315r) and Mr. Bywater, the self-imposed brothel keeper, two to five shillings. Sir Anthony Ashley paid 2s and "a gentleman that said he was the Lo. Cobhams kinsman" paid 3s 4d (BCB 4, fol. 319v). Mary Newborough, in her capacity as leader, is likely to have sold her "bele chose," to borrow a term from Chaucer, for 10s to both Sir Anthony Ashley and George Brooke, Lord Cobham's youngest son.

It was unrestrained sexuality that drove Sir Anthony Ashley (1551–1628) and George Brooke (1568–1603), two members of the political elite, the first aged fifty-one, the second thirty-four, to partake in the debaucheries which threatened to engulf Bridewell into a state of anarchy. Endowed with many intellectual accomplishments, both embarked upon what looked like brilliant public careers. Both were gifted linguists with several foreign languages at their command, Ashley winning much acclaim as the translator of a naval treatise and Brooke as supporter of the arts and patron of musicians.[176] Both had close ties with the public and private stage, Ashley as landlord of the Blackfriars theater and brother-in-law of Francis Langley, the builder and owner of the Swan theater, and Brooke as a reveler in court masques. But both were seriously flawed human personalities. Brooke went so far as to commit incest and an act of treason, for which he paid with his life. He was executed on 5 December 1603. Greed and ambition impelled Ashley to get embroiled in fraudulent activities. After his return from Cadiz, he was imprisoned in the Fleet (August/October 1596) and suspended in his function as clerk of the Privy Council until 1603 for his undeclared Spanish loot and for his protracted duplicity in pretending to retrieve for Her Majesty's government a diamond of twenty-six and a half carats valued at £2600, which had been stolen from the Portuguese carrack Madre de Dios in 1592, and at the same time plotting to secure it for Francis Langley and for himself.[177]

The conversion of Bridewell into a haunt of pleasure under the supervision of Thomas Stanley, who in all likelihood was an old Inns-of-Court acquaintance of Ashley's, served Sir Anthony Ashley as a welcome vehicle for redefining his disordered sexuality. He had conventionally married Jane, daughter and heir of Philip Okeover, of Staffordshire, about the early eighties and was the father of a daughter Anne. His wife, who was "in danger of death" in January 1592, must have died that year. As a widower, he was obviously struggling not to lose his sexual orientation. In 1602, he seized upon Bridewell to live out his sexuality as a heterosexual, but before he married his second wife, the young Philippa Shelton, in 1622, he fell to homosexual debauchery with boys.[178]

A client who took advantage of his acquaintance with Thomas Stanley was the London goldsmith Robert Smith. The first time he went to Bridewell to see Eleanor Lewes, alias Hawkins, whom he had known for one year and a half, he was accompanied by James Wright, dwelling in Cheapside. The second time he repaired to pay his respects to Eleanor Lewis, as he confessed to the governors on 13 October, he was on his own. He was let in through the back door, obviously without knowledge of the Bywaters, and taken to the rooms occupied by the Stanleys. Eleanor Lewes, on being examined in turn, admitted that when James Wright came to see her, she was in the company of Mary Newborough and the matron. The reason why the Lord Chief Justice had committed her to Bridewell was that she had been surprised in flagrante delicto with James Wright and some other men she did not know. Wright had also been detained for some time in Bridewell. Making a clean breast of her transgressions, she let the governors know that she had also "faulted" three years before. She had given birth to an illegitimate child, the father being one "Mr. FFountaine, a straunger" (BCB 4, fol. 324). The father's name was La Fountaine; he must have been one of the many French Huguenots living in London at the time.[179]

Chastisement and Resistance of the Prostitutes

The emancipated female prisoners did not surrender the freedom and power the undertakers had accorded them without putting up concerted resistance. When summoned to appear before the investigation committee on 31 July, they took collective action to defend their newly acquired privileges. The civic authorities, surprised by the fighting spirit of the prostitutes and the energy of their group solidarity, were taken aback. They had to send for the sheriffs to quell the unarmed palace revolt instigated by the women. The official report downplayed the female defiance, qualifying it as one of the inconveniences that beset Bridewell. "By reason of" their "ouer muche libertie and superfluous dyett," the report reads, the said women prisoners are growen so peremptorye and stout that they haue refused to come vpp to the courte" before the Lord Mayor and the aldermen, "but haue taken the keyes into their owne custodie and haue locked them selues vpp vntill the Shreifes officers haue ben reddie to breake open their chambers (BCB 4, fol. 313v–314v, item 5).

The contest between the female prisoners and the authorities dragged on for about a month. The duty of disciplining the women and restoring the old order fell to Nicholas Bywater. He fought a brutal and vicious battle against them in which he seemed to be getting the upper hand had not Mary Newbor-

ough remained unyielding in her oppositional stance. She proved the main-
stay of female resistance, fuelling a combative *esprit de corps* among her
fellow prisoners. Undaunted by Bywater's cruelties and iniquities, they did
not hesitate to raise their individual voices against his inhuman aggression
and savagery. Their protests disprove the current view that the authentic
voice of a prostitute in early modern England is undocumented and irrecoverable.

Mary Newborough informed the governors on 28 August that she had
raised her voice in protest against Bywater because he had "verie cruellie
beaten" some women and a "maid prisoner." Bywater, stung to the quick by
her protest, "came vnto her and called her whore, wherevpon" she parried
his slanderous attack, calling "him cuckoldie knave and his wife whoore."
Mary's abusive counterattack knocked Bywater out of countenance. Fuming
with rage, he seized a "cudgell" and "beate her with" it. Eleanor Lewes,
alias Hawkins, and Nell Bedford, Mary's roommates, confirmed that Bywater
dealt Mary three or four "blowes," adding that Mary "rann at him with the
sheeres" in self-defense when he was about to wield the cudgel. Mary Newborough, who is likely to have been hardened by the career of her husband
as a gentleman-turned-highwayman, remained undeterred by the cruel attack
launched by a member of lower standing. She instinctively rose to the situation, defending herself with a pair of scissors, the cutting instrument she was
adept at handling as a spinster in the Bridewell workshop and which now
stood her in good stead as a weapon. When on 11 September, Bywater was
called upon to account for what was styled "his misdemeanours," he did not
deny that "he did beate and evill entreat diuers weemen prisoners in this
howse, viz., Mrs. Newberry & Bridgett Winnicombe, Elizabeth Cam," who
was pregnant, "and Welgiver [Welgwer?] Gravener." He must have been confident that beating prostitutes and female criminals was not punishable by
secular law (BCB 4, fol. 318v–319v).

The new position as a projector running the country's most prestigious
house of correction brought out the beast in Nicholas Bywater, the tanner of
Southwark. Thus he struck the pregnant Elizabeth Cam several blows with
his fist and when he had "felled" or floored her, he "beat her . . . body . . .
black and blew" with "a bedstaff;" in proof whereof her bruised body was
displayed to the governors in the court session of 11 August. In the same
session, Welgiver Gravener testified that she, too, had been beaten, first by
the matron Mary Bate, then by Bywater's man, and finally by Bywater himself. And Bridget Winnicombe insisted on giving testimony that she had been
beaten by Bywater for having caught him in bed with Katherine Arden. As
she was climbing the flight of stairs in Charity Hall, presumably the banqueting hall of Henry VIII, leading to "Mrs. Newberris lodginge," she could tell
by the noise coming from an adjoining room that "Bywater was then vpon
the said Mrs Arden." She had the courage to raise her voice and tell the adul-

terous Bywater that "he had occupied" Katherine Arden, whereupon he beat her up (BCB 4, fol. 316v).[180]

Despite Bywater's heavy-handed method of imposing the old law and order on the women prisoners, Mary Newborough kept enjoying a privileged status for another four and a half months. The Lord Chief Justice had unwittingly abetted her regime when Bridewell, on 14 March, was leased out to the four undertakers; and he had not seen to it that her freedom was bound to terminate with the surrender of the lease on 16 October. It was only on 11 December, after her attempt to escape, that he issued a warrant to put an end to her privileges. It was his Lordship's "pleasure" that "Mall Newberrye and Nell Bedford," her roommate, "shalbe brought downe and sett to worke as others the common prisoners are, and to be vsed bothe in dyett and lodging as the rest" (BCB 4, fol. 338v). The wording of the warrant makes it unmistakably clear that Mary Newborough had never been an ordinary prisoner and had been treated with overindulgence. Her privileged treatment casts doubt on Sir John Popham's integrity and impartiality as a judge whose hostility to prostitution had earned him a reputation for prosecuting "poor pretty wenches out of all pity and mercy."[181]

Plots and Attempts to Escape from Bridewell

Organized rebellions were not infrequent in bridewells, but none assumed the subversive dimension of the London upheaval in 1602, which came close to a fundamental change of the whole system. Escapes, too, were nothing out of the ordinary; but escapes from the London Bridewell were always spectacular and sensational. Thus, in 1579, Jane Trosse, a "horrible strompet," escaped through the window, roping herself down the façade by means of bed sheets knotted together. To escape from Bridewell during the rule of the undertakers required no longer an athletic feat performed by a single woman; it became rather an interaction of money and sex staged by the prostitutes as a bribe and framed by a conniving gaoler.[182]

There is a brief entry in the report submitted by the investigation committee to the aldermen of London which draws their attention to the fact that the emancipated female prisoners have become "so their owne keepers" that two of them, Katherine Arden and Mrs. Miles, alias Godfey, "haue latelie thorowe their default escaped awaie" (BCB 4, fol. 313v–314v, item 5). The aldermen and governors, following up the findings of the committee and relying on the testimonies given by four female prisoners, Elizabeth Fey, Isabel Bradley, Bridget Winnicombe, and Anne Truelove, succeeded in reconstructing the circumstances leading to the escape. It emerges from their examinations that the villain of the plot was Nicholas Bywater. The author pulling the threads was Mrs. Miles. She went about Bridewell practicing "charmes" to unlock doors and urging her fellow prisoners to join the game. She used to

dine in the house of the Bywaters in the company of one Mr. Godfrey who
had free access as a fee-paying customer. The sociable setting lent itself to
making overtures to Mrs. Bywater. Mrs. Miles let her know that if her husband could contrive her liberty, she would procure him the keeping of a park
"which should be better worth unto him" than his being in Bridewell. She
was also willing to give Bywater £100 "to set her at liberty."

Mrs. Miles was also working on Bywater's weakness for clothes and rich
fabrics. She must have known that Katherine Arden with the help of Mary
Newborough's maid had got him a piece of taffeta. Thus she gave him "a
pair of breeches, a night cap and a pair of sweet gloves" for the day he was
to ride out of town. His absence from Bridewell was a ruse to blur the traces
of his complicity. He had arranged with Katherine Arden, after he had gratified his passion with her, to go out of London and leave the gate open. As
Bridget Winnicombe testified before the court, he had told Katherine Arden
"I goe out of Towne and then the doore shalbe left open, then doo what you
will." It was actually Bywater's servant who opened the gate of Charity Hall
for Katherine Arden, Mrs. Miles, "and the rest" to escape. No sanctions seem
to have been taken against the lawless and adulterous Bywater, nor against
his wife (courts held on 11 and 15 August 1602, BCB 4, fol. 315–317v).

Mary Newborough, Nell Bedford, and some other female prisoners, presumably encouraged by the successful escape of Katherine Arden and Mrs.
Miles, "laid . . . a plott & confederacye" in early December 1602. They were
wise enough to rely on their own resources, but their scheme, nonetheless,
was doomed to failure. Joan Thomas, for whatever reason, revealed it to the
matron and reported it to the governors. The plotters, as Joan put it, "pur-
posed to make an escape first by breakinge vpp the lockes and so to haue
gone out of the windowe in the Roome nexte to Charitie Hall and to gett
downe by hanginge sheetes out of the said windowe." The method was reminiscent of Jane Trosse's escape in 1579. In case of failure, their daring alternative was to climb up the "ten-pennye nailes," that is, nails of very large
size obviously driven into the chimney for the sweeper, "to gett out of the
chimney Topp" (BCB 4, fol. 337v, court held on 8 December 1602). This
foolhardy scheme underlined Mary Newborough's determinacy and unbroken spirit of adventure; the idea of climbing up the chimney on iron pegs was
not more daunting for her than wielding a pair of scissors as a weapon. The
news reached Sir John Popham with alarm, and on 11 December he suspended Mary Newborough's privileges.[183]

Mary Newborough's (Mock) Repentance and Release

The contest between Mary Newborough and the authorities, which had
been gathering momentum in December 1602, was brought to a close in Janu-

ary 1603. After the failure of her attempt to escape and the loss of her status as a privileged prisoner, she staged an unexpected coup. Conspiring with Nell Bedford, the two prisoners hatched the scheme to leave Bridewell as repentant magdalens. The coup de théâtre worked. It was rather easy for them to hoodwink some of the reform-minded governors into believing that they repented the life they had been leading as sinful sex workers. One of them was Mr. Newman. Overwhelmed by what must have been for him an act of God, he immediately sent for Mr. Egerton, "a reverend preacher of godes work" to officiate at the ceremony of conversion. Mr. Egerton, accordingly, repaired to Bridewell "and myndinge the conversion of Marye Newboroughe and Ellen Bedford, twoe famous harlottes remayning prisoners in this house, gave them good instruccions" to follow the path of virtue. The two dissimulating converts "seemed to geve a good eare vnto" Mr. Egerton's words, but some of the governors, if I am correctly interpreting the meaning of the record, had some doubts about their conversion. They somehow sensed that Mary Newborough was a good dissimulator who "in outward shewe seemed to haue the more repentinge and meltinge hart as partlie by her teares appeared" (BCB 4, fol. 346r, court held on Monday, 10 January 1603). The tears, I think, were not a sign of contrition, but were rather a mark of joy and relief.

After the self-scripted act of conversion, the alleged magdalens, the treasurer, and some of the governors moved the Lord Chief Justice to deliver a warrant of release. Sir John Popham agreed to discharge Mary Newborough on condition, as was the rule, that she paid "her charges", expenses made for special services, and submitted "surtie" of good behavior. Thus, in compliance with Sir John Popham's orders, the court sitting on Monday, 17 January, ruled that Mary Newborough should be "presentlie" released and given 5s "for releife" (BCB 4, fol. 348r). As a supposedly reformed prostitute, Mary Newborough qualified for temporary financial relief designed to ease her reintegration and resocialization. Bridewell was a charitable institution that somehow continued the tradition of the medieval religious orders. Taking care of repentant prostitutes and providing them with dowries so that even poor prostitutes could marry was no longer part of Bridewell's elaborate machinery, but its policy to reform the prostitutes and reintroduce them into the Christian community was still in force.[184]

We can take it for granted that Mary Newborough's repentance was not the work of the transforming power of God's grace on her sinful soul; and it is hard to believe that the pardoned Mary would now launch herself into a new career as a paragon of regenerate sexuality venerating the example of Mary Magdalene. What induced Mary Newborough to put on a show of repentance must have been the deteriorating health of her imprisoned husband and her fear to lose her inheritance. Let us bear in mind that her mock conversion was staged on 10 January or one or two days prior to this date. Her husband George died within seven months on 10 August 1603. Had she remained a prisoner in Bridewell, she would have forfeited her claim to her husband's property in Berkley, which, in fact, was granted to John Kevile of Crediton, Devon, on 22 September, because her husband obviously died intestate. She was then fighting a legal battle over the husband's estate which was settled in her favor. The grant to John Kevile, as already mentioned, was revoked on 21 November 1604. She returned to Berkley a dispossessed and displaced woman, but was reinstated in her legal rights and presumably settled there. Whether there was a reunion between husband and wife before 10 August 1603 is not known.

The question arises why Lord Chief Justice Popham pardoned husband and wife, but released only the female transgressor. The reason is that Mary was prosecuted for having committed a misdemeanor, whereas George was prosecuted for having committed a felony, which usually carried the death penalty. In the thinking of the day, Mary did not commit a crime, but a sin, an offense against God, not man. Sin, as G. R. Elton has argued, lacked the strictly criminal element of deliberate and malicious intent against another person's rights. Therefore, Mary's was a case of transgressive sexual consumption to be settled by the Bridewell governors and their court. George, however, had committed a legal crime in attacking two husbandmen and their personal property, which was punishable by death.[185]

George Handford's Song about "Mall Newberry her Repentance" (1609)

The life, repentance, and conversion of Mary Newborough seem to have made little impact on the body of Elizabethan literature. Presumably the reason for the lack of a literary response is that the conversion of a prostitute was a cultural phenomenon that had become a commonplace in Elizabethan drama since Lewis Wager's interlude *The Life and Repentance of Marie Magdalene* was performed in 1566 and Robert Greene's fictional crime biography *The Conversion of an English Courtesan* had come out in 1592. The only contemporary artist to respond to Mary Newborough's pretence to being a penitent magdalen was the little known composer George Handford (1582/85–1647). In December 1609, he presented his "Newly composed" *Ayres to be sunge to the Lute and Base Vyole,* bound in vellum with gold tooling, to Prince Henry. The manuscript consisted of twenty-eight folio leaves and twenty songs. Unfortunately, the leaf containing the bass and possibly further stanzas of number 16, "Mall Newberry and her Repentance," is missing. The text of one stanza, the first, and the treble and lute tablature have been preserved.

The wording of the anonymous verses reveals the satiric nature of the composition. It was clearly not cast in the vein of a contrite convert, but rather in the mood of a mock penitent. The final couplet has the ring of truth:

> Come teares and sighes, woes constant wofull mates,
> and cloude the luster of lasciuious eyes:
> and tare this yelding hart that oped the gate
> to sin and shame to endles mysery:
> my teares exhaust, and all my sighes be spent,
> teares, sighs, doe fayle me when I shold lament.[186]

The traditional song of repentance used to be sung in a mood of melancholy. Whether Handford, who was not a particularly distinguished composer, was endowed with the artistic sensibility to catch the ironic mood of a mock penitent is a matter for the musicologists to decide. As for the number of the stanzas, several must have perished or been removed for reasons of propriety. Bearing in mind that the penitent prostitute was expected, in compliance with the lyric tradition, to review her sinful past, we may hazard the view that the text was found to be offensive.[187]

Contemporary drama features a number of prostitutes singing songs. Yet a song of mock repentance sung by a false magdalen may have been a novelty. It can claim to be a hybrid derivative between a conventional song of repentance and a burlesque dirge that lent itself to bashing prostitutes. Talboys Dymoke provides an instance of such dirges. On the last Sunday in August 1601, he staged an interlude "for sporte and merriment at the setting up of a Maypole in South K[e]yme," Lincolnshire. Talboys and some of the actors sang burlesque dirges aimed at satirizing "moste of the knowne lewde and licentious women in the Cities of London," Lincoln, and Boston. Every dirge ended with the name of a prostitute and the Latin tag "ora pro nobis."[188]

The inclusion of "Mall Newberry her Repentance" in a collection of songs dedicated to Prince Henry demonstrates that even seven years after her mock conversion Mary Newborough's notoriety as a prostitute was still fresh in the minds of the Londoners from commoners (composer and song writer) to courtiers and royalty. They remembered her not as a model of regenerate sexuality, but as the incarnation of a wicked and sinful life. Philip Gawdy, as mentioned above, held her to be more infamous than Mrs Fowler, who in 1600 figured in a notorious case of bawdry.[189]

City Scandal or Court Scandal: A Topical Allusion to a Dark Lady in Shakespeare's *Twelfth Night*

The present investigation has thrown up some hitherto unknown aspects of the workings of higher-class prostitution at the close of sixteenth-century

London; it has also opened up new insights into the personal vicissitudes of some prostitutes, bringing to life the pregnant Katherine Arden and the fashion-conscious Elizabeth Reignoldes; and it has yielded a sizeable body of documentable evidence about a gentlewoman turned prostitute. Mary Newborough has emerged from the past as a real-life prostitute with the self-assertive voice and the unique experience as the wife of a gentleman-turned-highwayman which scarred her for life. She cut a prominent figure in one of the city's service industries that was geared to the sexual gratification of all classes, in particular to the sexual gratification of the leisure class. She was the talk of the Londoners on more than one occasion as when she rode in an open coach to watch the muster of the soldiers in St. James's Park or when she was carted and stoned on three consecutive days through the streets of the city. Her tribulations, her sense of solidarity, and her spirited resistance to male brutality commanded the respect of her Bridewell inmates.

The sensational record of Mary Newborough's London intermezzo may help settle the Shakespearean controversy over the identity of "Mistress Moll" in *Twelfth Night.* Sir Toby Belch manipulates Sir Andrew Aguecheek into believing that he is endowed with the physical and intellectual accomplishments that go to the making of a reveler. Goading Sir Andrew Aguecheek into displaying his dormant talents as a reveler, that is, as a dancer, linguist, lover, and ultimately wooer of Olivia, he raises what must be a rhetorical question in view of Sir Andrew's lack of natural endowments and sexual potency: "Wherefore have these things a curtain before 'em? Are they like to take dust, like Mistress Mall's picture?"[190] John Dover Wilson was the first to suggest in the Cambridge edition of 1930 that this might be a topical allusion to Mary Newborough. All he knew about her life was Philip Gawdy's reference to her carting. But then Leslie Hotson came out with an identification that has the ring of historical authenticity about it. With unflagging verve he delved into English and Continental archives to uncover the historical occasion for which Shakespeare wrote the comedy. The documents he unearthed led him to believe that Sir Toby's dig is aimed at the Sir William Knollys/William Herbert/Mary Fitton court scandal.[191] Mary Fitton, aged seventeen, had been admitted as one of the Queen's maids of honor in 1595. Sir Edward, her father, entrusted Mary to the special care of his friend Sir William Knollys, Controller of the Royal Household, aged forty-seven and married to a widow who was his senior. Despite his promise to see to her safety, Sir William kept urging Mary to marry him when his wife would die. His doting pursuit, documented in his correspondence with Mary's sister Anne Fitton, Lady Newdigate, was of no avail. His wife did not do him the favor of dying in time, and Mary bestowed her favors upon the young William Herbert, third earl of Pembroke. Early in 1601, she bore him a short-lived son, but the philandering earl declined to marry her.[192]

In his wide-ranging historical pursuit, Leslie Hotson failed to notice that while a maid of honor (Mary Fitton) was raising a court scandal, a maid of Venus (Mary Newborough) was bringing a city scandal to the boil. While the court scandal led to the private shaming of Mary Fitton, the city scandal led to the public shaming and carting of Mary Newborough. The reading of "Mistress Mall's picture" as being a topical allusion to the city scandal triggered by a gentlewoman turned prostitute is all the more plausible in view of the fact that Sir Toby's allusion was not offensive to the Court. Critics have deconstructed Hotson's self-contradictory theory. Alone its incompatibility with the rules of the court censorship renders it untenable. The Master of the Revels, by virtue of his office, would have objected to Sir William Knollys, the Controller of the Royal Household and the Queen's cousin, being lampooned as Malvolio and to Mary Fitton's scarred image being exposed to ridicule in a public play.[193]

Leslie Hotson, moreover, put forward a controversial date for the play. In his view, Shakespeare wrote the play in ten days' time for the visit and exclusive entertainment of Don Virginio Orsino, Duke of Bracciano, and the Chamberlain's Men staged it at Whitehall Palace on 6 January 1601. This in itself is a preposterous assumption. Internal evidence suggests that the play was written in 1601, that is, in the months following the Duke of Bracciano's departure from England and while Mary Newborough, condemned to wear a blue uniform, was spinning wool in Bridewell Hospital.[194] A topical allusion to the city scandal argues for the later date. The first known performance, and most likely the première, was staged before the Gentlemen of the Middle Temple on Candlemas Night, 2 February 1602.

Candlemas Day was one of the two major annual festivals celebrated at the Middle Temple and the other Inns of Court. On this day, the Feast of the Purification of the Blessed Virgin Mary, the legal dignitaries, the current and former members of the society of the Middle Temple, among them the law students, the sergeants, and their friends, would come together in the Great Hall for the celebration and entertainment. Illustrious guests, courtiers, noblemen, and Knights of the Garter used to be invited to the dinner and to the performance of a play or masque.[195] Among the audience watching the players, presumably the Lord Chamberlain's Men, perform *Twelfth Night* on 2 February 1602 must have been Sir John Popham, who had begun his professional career as a Reader, that is, tutor in 1568 and 1572, and had held the office of Treasurer of the Middle Temple from 1580 to 1587. In July and October 1601, he compounded the quarrel that had broken out between John Davies and Richard Martin, the Prince d'Amour of the 1597/98 Christmas revels at the Middle Temple. And if one may hazard a guess, he is likely to have met there during the Christmas revels of 1601/1602 his protégé and former law student Thomas Stanley, to whom he was about to hand over the management of Bridewell in March 1602.[196]

The reveller who is likely to have caught the full meaning of Sir Toby's gibe was, no doubt, the Lord Chief Justice. Considering that the cases of Mary and George Newborough lay in his jurisdiction, it is evident that Sir John Popham was the person who knew best to what extent the image of this gentlewoman turned prostitute had been disfigured by her immoral life. An allusion to the court scandal mounted by Mary Fitton would have been out of place and stale on 2 February 1602; an allusion to Mary Newborough, who had sullied her reputation and was chafing in Bridewell under malnutrition and hard labor, was highly topical. Sir Toby's dig does look like being one of the intramural jokes pregnant with legal and bawdy implications in which the play abounds.[197]

The view advanced by Henk Gras that *Twelfth Night* was written with a Middle Temple performance in mind adds further weight to the present argument that Sir Toby's Elizabethan perplexity bears the stamp of those *nugae* or sexual jests about legal issues that the prominent wits of the Middle Temple were known to indulge in.[198] Fascination with sexual transgression was one of the main sources of the Inns of Court holiday culture.[199] Thus bawds and brothels were a standard feature of the holiday kingdoms ruled by the Prince of Love and the Prince of Purpoole. Four bawds had the honor of being specially listed as "Tributaries" of Henry Helmes, the Gray's Inn Prince of Purpoole, and as holding properties in his mock kingdom during the Christmas revels of 1594/95. One of them was the notorious real-life Lucy Negro, the "Abbess de *Clerkenwell*" who was running the "Nunnery of *Clerkenwell, with the Lands and Privileges thereunto belonging.*" Lucy Negro and her "Choir of Nuns, with burning Lamps" officiated ''on the Day of His Excellency's Coronation," chanting "*Placebo* to the Gentlemen of the Prince's Privy-Chamber."[200] The love "Traffick" to Clerkenwell was given out to be in full swing during the revels until the 10 January 1595 when John Puttanemico [whore enemy] informed the Prince in a mock letter written "*From the Harbour of* Bride-well" that the Prince's "Merchants . . . began to surcease their Traffick to *Clerkenwell* . . . and such like Roads of Charge and Discharge"[201] As for the Prince of Love, he, too, prided himself on keeping a seraglio within his mock kingdom. It was the duty of the "Captain" of his brothels to display his sexual potency and to see to it that the ladies "humble, and submit themselves to his Higness pleasure."[202]

The unsavory topicality in *Twelfth Night* harks back to the presence of prostitutes in the Inns-of-Court scenarios scripted in terms of a festive world-upside-down burlesque. What makes the intertextual link between the allusion to mistress Mall and the reference to Lucy Negro all the more plausible is the fact that behind the prostitute nicknamed Lucy Negro was one of Mary Newborough's notorious sisters: Luce Morgan, alias Parker, one of the queen's gentlewomen from about 1579 to 1582, who was dismissed from court service for committing a misdemeanor, presumably a sexual transgression displeasing the queen. She survived her disgrace working as a prostitute in the 1580s and as a bawd in the 1590s. Her establishment in Clerkenwell was a favorite haunt of the Inns-of-Court students and lawyers. The two gentlewomen turned prostitutes shared the amenities of Bridewell Hospital for some days in early January 1600. They were released together on the same day, 31 January 1600 (BCB 4, fol. 142r).[203]

The view that the presence of Luce Morgan and Mary Newborough in metropolitan London and the subversive code of love affected by the officers of the Prince of Purpoole (Henry Helmes) and the Prince of Love (Richard Martin) proved a catalyst for generating the cult of immoral or dark ladies, does not seem to be far-fetched. Luce Morgan, after her royal disgrace nicknamed Lucy Negro, became a paragon of the fallen woman. The process of fashioning the stereotype of a dark woman called Black Luce had already been launched in the 1570s.[204] Moreover, the figure of the dark lady has also the trappings of being an Italian import and might ultimately be deflated as a construct brought into being by the pornographic tradition of Aretino and his followers in England. It should be borne in mind that Luce Morgan, celebrated as Lucy Negro in the Gray's Inn revels, has a Venetian counterpart, one Bianzifiore Negro, whose charms have been disparaged in some obscene lines attributed to Antonio Cavallino and published in the handbook *La tariffa delle puttane di Venegia*. Resorting to pornography and bawdiness was a strategy pursued to subvert Petrarchan notions of love.[205] It is, therefore, hardly conceivable that Luce Morgan was the Dark Lady of Shakespeare's sonnets as some critics, among them Leslie Hotson, have come to believe.[206] The latest theory advanced by postcolonial criticism transmutes Lucy Negro into a black woman, thereby deflecting the scandal of the *Sonnets* from alleged homosexual orientation to an interracial union.[207]

In conclusion, it remains to be pointed out that, although *Twelfth Night* is studded with rhetorical gems that are concessions made to the sophisticated Middle Temple audience, reading the play only in terms of the Middle Temple revels would mean turning a blind eye to its dramatic strategies and multifarious organization. Sir Toby's quip, besides being loaded with ephemeral topicality, takes on an added dimension when geared to the play's moral frame, and its deeper meaning can only be grasped by drawing on all the registers of the play's dramatic imagery. Thus the topical allusion to a real-life prostitute serves as a foil to the noble Olivia. The record of a London gentlewoman given to commercial sex and uninhibited self-display is suggested as being in sharp contrast to the fictional Olivia who stands for romantic love and filial self-effacement. In terms of the play's moral frame, Mistress Mall's image or reputation has taken "dust" (1.3.124), exemplifying Feste's dictum that "pleasure will be paid, one time or another" with pain (2.4.70–71). Mistress Mall is the sort of woman whose immorality infects society, whereas Olivia, for the infatuated Orsino, is an antidote, a deity who "purg'd the air of pestilence" (1.1.20).

In terms of the play's dramatic imagery, the curtain and picture image of Sir Toby's conceit anticipate their symphonic flowering in the first crucial encounter between the veiled Olivia and Viola cross-dressed as Orsino's messenger Cesario. The encounter is orchestrated as a mockery of romantic courtship conventions and as a parody of the Petrarchan sonnet tradition. Cesario at first abides by the court etiquette in delivering Orsino's formal encomium, but then he steps out of his role as messenger, urging that the veiled Olivia show him her face. Olivia, pretending to doubt that he has "any commission from" his "lord to negotiate with my face," is nonetheless willing to "draw the curtain and show" him "the picture" (1.5.233 ff). Cesario's response to Olivia's unveiling her face/picture is astonishment and doubt as to the quality of its beauty. Olivia, therefore, hastens to reassure the messenger that the face's beauty is "in grain . . . 'twill endure wind and weather" (1.5.240), implying that it will not wash away like the artificial paint on Mistress Mall's face. And finally cutting Cesario's compliments short, Olivia proceeds to defuse the emotional encounter. Performing a tactical shift from verse to prose, she delivers what reads like a prosaic anti-Petrarchan inventory or anti-blason catalogue of her feminine charms (1.5.247 ff).

Notes

1. Wallace Shugg, "Prostitution in Shakespeare's London," *Shakespeare Studies* 10 (1977): 291–313; Ian W. Archer, *The Pursuit of Stability: Social Relations in Elizabethan London* (Cambridge: Cambridge University Press, 1991); Paul Griffiths, "The Structure of Prostitution in Elizabethan London," *Continuity and Change* 8 (1993): 39–63; Ruth Mazo Karras, *Common Women: Prostitution and Sexuality in Medieval England* (New York: Oxford University Press, 1996); for a bibliography see Stanley D. Nash, *Prostitution in Great Britain 1485–1901: An Annotated Bibliography* (Metuchen: Scarecrow Press, 1994).

2. Ian Wallace Archer, *Governors and Governed in Late 16th-Century London ca. 1560–1603: Studies in the Achievement of Stability.* Oxford D. Phil. dissertation, 1988. G. R. Elton was one of the first historians to find fault with the concept of the "Elizabethan underworld" for being too readily written out of the imaginative literature of the day. See his "Introduction: Crime and the Historian" in *Crime in England 1550–1800,* ed. J. S. Cockburn (London: Methuen, 1977), 1–14.

3. The Bridewell Court Books are the property of Witley Grammar School, Surrey, but were transferred to Bethlem Royal Hospital, Beckenham, Kent, to be microfilmed and since then have been housed there. A microfilm copy of poor quality, covering the years up to 1642, is kept at the Guildhall Library, London. Thus the entries from May to July 1602 are illegible (BCB 4, fol. 299–309v). Unfortunately, not all of the original volumes of this important depository have survived the ravages of the Civil War and the Great Fire of London. There are several gaps in the records. Nine volumes have come down to us: BCB 1 (covering 1559–62), BCB 2 (1574–76),

BCB 3 (1576–79), BCB 4 (1597–1604), BCB 5 (1604–10), BCB 6 (1617–26), BCB 7 (1627–34), BCB 8 (1634–42), BCB 9 (1642–58).

4. Carol Kazmierczak Manzione, "Sex in Tudor London. Abusing their Bodies With Each Other," in *Desire and Discipline: Sex and Sexuality in the Premodern World,* ed. Jacqueline Murray and Konrad Eisenbichler (Toronto: University of Toronto Press, 1996), 87–100.

5. Jyotsna Singh voices the opinion that female resistances to patriarchal ideology are irrecoverable at the level of a prositute's experience. See her essay "The Intervention of History: Narratives of Sexuality," in *The Weyward Sisters: Shakespeare and Feminist Politics,* ed. Dympna C. Callaghan, Lorraine Helms, Jyotsna Singh (Oxford: Blackwell, 1994), 3–58.

6. The fictional fashionings of prostitution have also misled critics into believing that London's sexual geography was consigned to the suburbs. On the term "spaces beyond" see Bruce R. Smith, "L[o]cating the sexual subject" in Terence Hawkes and John Drakakis (eds.) *Alternative Shakespeare* (London, 1996) ii: 95–121. On the concept of sexual geography relegating prostitution to the confines of the underworld see also Paul Griffiths, "Overlapping Circles: Imagining Criminal Communities in London, 1545–1646," in Alexandra Shepard and Phil Withington (eds.), *Communities in Early Modern London* (Manchester: Manchester University Press, 2000), chap. 7.

7. *Twelfth Night,* The Arden Shakespeare, ed. J. M. Lothian and T. W. Craik (London, 1975), 1.3.122–24; all subsequent quotations from *Twelfth Night* are taken from the Arden edition.

8. *Calendar of State Papers, Domestic, Elizabeth, 1595–97,* p. 303.

9. The early items have been printed by the Somerset Record Society, vol. xxiii (London, 1907); they contain no reference to George Newborough.

10. Frederic Thomas Colby (ed.), *The Visitations of the County of Somerset in the Year 1623. Publications of the Haleian Society* 11 (London, 1876), 78–79; John Hutchins, *The History and Antiquities of the County of Dorset,* vol. 1 (Westminster, 1861), 419. The Somerset Record Office in Taunton holds no material relating to the Newboroughs of Berkley apart from a manuscript pedigree which records the dates of Jane Bodenham's marriage and death. I am indebted to D. M. M. Shorrocks, County Archivist, for kindly supplying the information. He has also drawn my attention to the fact that George Newborough had a cousin of the same name. He was baptized in 1568 as the son of John Newborough, resident at Berkley. We can, however, be confident that he was not the future highwayman, for in 1579 when the future criminal married Jane Bodenham, he was not of marriageable age. George had a younger brother Roger who may have been identical with the Roger Newborow of Berkley, esquire, who was summoned to appear before the Privy Council on 27 June 1587 and again on 21 July 1587 together with Thomas Turbervill, esquire, possibly his cousin. Philip Goughe charged Roger and Thomas with being "accessaries to felonie and maintenance of fellons." They were dismissed but enjoined to appear before the Justices of Assize in Dorset. See John Roche Dasent (ed.), *Acts of the Privy Council of England. Vol. XV. A.D. 1587–1588* (London HMSO 1897), 134–35, 164–65.

11. Marriage settlements were the rule among the aristocracy and gentry, but they were also frequent among the lower classes. See Amy Louise Erickson, *Women and Property in Early Modern England* (London: Routledge, 1993), 101, 222.

12. J. S. Cockburn in "The Nature and Incidence of Crime in England 1559–1625: A Preliminary Survey" has found that highway robbery was most often perpetuated by young gentlemen seeking an easy living (65). See J. S. Cockburn (ed.), *Crime in England* (1977), 49–71.

13. For a short discussion of the real-life highwayman see A. L. Beier, *Masterless Men. The Vagrancy Problem in England 1560–1640* (London: Methuen, 1985), 137–38.

14. Charges for accommodation and food were on a sliding scale adjusted to the prisoner's social rank. See Clifford Dobb, "London's Prisons," *Shakespeare Survey* 17 (1964): 87–100. On the gaoler's profession and charges for board and lodging at Newgate see E. D. Pendry, *Prisons and Prison Scenes,* Salzburg Studies in English Literature, Elizabethan and Renaissance Studies 17 (Salzburg: Institut für englische Sprache und Literatur 1974), i. 7, 8, 133.

15. St. Katherine's was one of London's hospitals. There William Lacke's daughter Elizabeth was christened on 28 July 1594. See A. W. Hughes Clarke (ed.), *The Registers of St Katherine by the Tower, London, 1584–1625. Publications of the Harleian Society* 75 (1945): 13.

16. John Stow has chronicled the history of St. Katherine's. "The parish church," he noted, "standeth in the cemetery of the late dissolved priory of the Holy Trinity, and is therefore called St. Katherine Christ Church. This church seemeth to be very old, since the building whereof the high street hath been so often raised by pavements, that now men are fain to descend into the said church by divers steps, seven in number. . . ." See John Stow, *A Survay of London . . . Written in the Year 1598,* ed. Henry Morley (London: Routledge & Sons, s.a.), 162–63.

17. For church seats reflecting social hierarchy and for mismanagement in allocating pews see Martin Ingram, *Church Courts, Sex and Marriage in England, 1570–1640* (Cambridge: Cambridge University Press, 1987), 111–12, 120–21.

18. G. R. Quaife in *Wanton Wenches and Wayward Wives. Peasants and Illicit Sex in Early 17th-Century England* (London: Croom Helm, 1970) refers to Robert Wolfall, who headed a circuit of private whores servicing the clergy (pp. 148, 150–51); F. G. Emmison in *Elizabethan Life: Disorder. Mainly From Essex Sessions and Assize Records* (Chelmsford, 1970) to Richard Halywell, rector of Twinstead (1555–57), who together with his wife was keeping a brothel (pp. 143–45); Gamini Salgado in *The Elizabethan Underworld* (London: J. M. Dent & Sons, 1977) to parson Checkyn of St. Nicholas in Old Fish Street, London (p. 52); and A. L. Rowse in *The Case Books of Simon Forman* (London: Pan Books, 1976) to Dean Owen Wood from Anglesey, who fornicated with his maid and with the wife of the Dean of Rochester (chap. 7).

19. For the meaning of "thing" see E. A. M. Colman, *The Dramatic Use of Bawdy in Shakespeare* (London: Longmans, 1974), Glossary, 218; Gordon Williams, *A Dictionary of Sexual Language and Imagery in Shakespearean and Stuart Literature,* 3 vols (London: Athlone, 1994) iii: 1379–81.

20. See Joseph Foster, *Alumni Oxonienses . . . 1500–1714* (Oxford, 1891) i: 463.

21. Archer, *The Pursuit of Stability,* 231–33.

22. On the income and taxes of the brothel keepers in the 1570s see Archer, 214–15. On fines see Emmison, *Elizabethan Life: Disorder.* Emmison records that two brothel keepers of Middlesex were fined £20 and £40 respectively (201).

23. William Shakespeare, *Measure for Measure,* The Oxford Shakespeare (1991), ed. N. W. Bawcutt, 1.2.106–7.

24. The number is not great compared to the bawds Jane Fuller and John Shaw who in the 1570s can be linked with at least thirteen and twenty-three prostitutes respectively. See Griffiths, 44. The most sophisticated brothels appear to have housed up to nine prostitutes. See Archer, 213.

25. For the importance of pimps see Griffiths, 45, 48.

26. For the Levant Company see Alfred C. Wood, *A History of the Levant Company* (Oxford: Oxford University P., 1935); T. S. Willan, "Some Aspects of English Trade with the Levant in the 16th Century," *The English Historical Review* 70 (1955): 399–410; and for the text of the charter and the names of its members see Richard Hakluyt, *The Principal Navigations, Voyages, Traffiques and Discoveries of the English Nation* (London: George Bishop, Ralph Newberie, and Robert Barker, 1599) ii: 295–303.

27. *Calendar of State Papers, Domestic, Elizabeth, 1598–1601* (London, 1869), 388.

28. See Robert Brenner, *Merchants and Revolution. Commercial Change, Political Conflict, and London's Overseas Traders, 1550–1653* (Princeton, 1993), 72, n.58. I am indebted to Guy Grannum, Reader Information Services, Public Record Office, Kew, for supplying me with the date of Robert Offley's marriage.

29. As much as 2300 tons of currants was said to be imported annually at this time and to yield a profit to the company of £11,500. See Wood, 24.

30. Henry Boyer, one of the most active pimps and keepers in the 1570s, received 5s for "carrying" Elizabeth Donnington's maidservant to the Portuguese ambassador. Jane Trosse, a "horrible strumpet," lifted £7 pounds from a Spaniard in Stephen French's brothel as a supplement to her 20s fee; and the "Spanyard" who in May 1559 frequented John Hall's brothel and had sex with Hall's wife and other prostitutes, offered Hall £10 to take Jane Starkey, a skinner's daughter, away with him as his mistress. See Griffiths, 49–50. Mrs. Sefton accused Simon Forman, on 9 May 1599, of taking Mrs. Bestow to two Spaniards in the warehouse, obviously two Cadiz prisoners, where they occupied her. See A. L. Rowse, *The Case Books of Simon Forman,* 154–55. Alvise Pavanella, a worker in the "glasshouse," the glass factory in Crutched Friars run by the Venetian Giacomo Verzellini, used "the body of Jane Parker for euery Saterdaie he comes to her and goes vp vnto a chamber to eate and drink" (BCB 4, fol. 380r–381r; court meeting of 26 May 1603).

31. See Archer, 213.

32. For the identification of Peter van Lore and his wife Myne see Irene Scouloudi (ed.), *Returns of Strangers in the Metropolis 1593, 1627, 1635, 1639. A Study of an Active Minority. Huguenot Society Publications,* Quarto Series, 57 (1985), 215. For the scale of his business under James I see John Hayward, "The Arnold Lulls Book of Jewels and the Court Jewellers of Queen Anne of Denmark," *Archaeologia* 108 (1986): 227–37.

33. In 1586, the Earl of Rutland bought from him a "brooch of her Majestie's picture in an agatt" set with fifty-three diamonds, and in 1621 he advanced, with two partners, £30,000, secured by Queen Anne's jewels, to support the claim of the Elector

Palatine to the throne of Bohemia. See Diana Scarisbrick, *Tudor and Jacobean Jewellery* (London: Tate Publishing, 1995), 61 and 35. In June 1595, Robert Devereux, earl of Essex, chief host of foreign visiting dignitaries in succession to Leicester, borrowed £500 from Peter van Lore in order to finance the return to France of Antonio Pérez, the former secretary to Philip II, who had resided in Essex House since his surprise arrival in England in the spring of 1593. See Paul E. J. Hammer, *The Polarisation of Elizabethan Politics. The Political Career of Robert Devereux, 2nd Earl of Essex, 1585–1597* (Cambridge: Cambridge University Press, 1999), 132, n. 113. For the princely accommodation of Pérez and the enormous amount of money Essex showered on his Spanish guest see Gustav Ungerer, *A Spaniard in Elizabethan England: The Correspondence of Antonio Pérez's Exile* (London: Tamesis, 1974) i: 295–97.

34. For their returns see R. E. G. Kirk and Ernest F. Kirk (eds.), *Returns of Aliens Dwelling in the City and Suburbs of London From the Reign of Henry VIII to that of James I. Huguenot Society Publications,* Quarto Series, 10 (1907), part 3: 1598–1625, p. 70.

35. For Dorothy Powell see A. L. Rowse, *The Case Books of Simon Forman,* 220.

36. For the Marini of Southampton and London see chap. 10 in Alwyn A. Ruddock's *Italian Merchants and Shipping in Southampton 1270–1600* (Southampton, 1951). Tomas was probably a cousin of Giorgio Marini (George Maryne) who is on record as a citizen and grocer of London (252).

37. On the authority of Thomas Vicary's *The Anatomie of the Bodie of Man* (London, 1577), ed. F. J. Furnivall and P. Furnivall (London: N. Trübner, 1888), blood was the "instrumental" fluid "whereof is made the sparme by the labour of the Testicles" (83).

38. Similarly, the "Laws of Love," to which the new Knights of the Quiver (female pudendum) in the Kingdom of the Prince d'Amour, i.e., the Middle Temple Chrismas revels of 1597/98, bound themselves, required a gastronomic change. They were administered a new "diet" that was "now suitable to the worth of" their love "service". See Benjamin Rudyerd (ed.), *Le Prince d'Amour, or the Prince of Love* (London, William Leake 1660), 53–54.

39. London: A. Islip for W. Barley, 1598; entered to John Wolfe on 30 April 1591; STC 10433.

40. For a cultural history of food see Stephen Mennell, *All Manners of Food: Eating and Taste in England and France from the Middle Ages to the Present* (Oxford, Blackwell, 1985), 62ff.

41. For Castelvetro's treatise and career see Kathleen T. B. Butler, "An Italian's Message to England in 1614," *Italian Studies* 2 (1938), 1–18 and "Giacomo Castelvetro 1546–1616," *Italian Studies* 5 (1950), 1–42. See also Luigi Firpo's entry in *Dizionario biografico degli italiani,* vol. 22 (Rome, 1979), 1–4, and for his importance as bookseller and importer of Italian books see R. J. Roberts, "New Light on the Career of Giacomo Castelvetro," *Bodleian Library Record* 13 (1990), 365–69. I have quoted the title of the treatise from BL, MS Sloane 912. Gillian Riley has published his English translation under the title *Fruit, Herbs and Vegetables in Italy* (Viking, 1989). There is no reference to Castelvetro in Mennell's study.

42. For Gondola's correspondence see G. S. Gargano, "Il mercatore Paolo Gondola 1590–1592" in his *Scapigliatura italiana a Londra sotto elisabetta e Giacomo I*

(Firenze, 1923). Gargano has expurgated Gondola's text, deleting the bawdy pun on "fichi" (figs) and "fiche" (female genitals). Gondola's original reads: ". . . et se hauete mangiato dell fichi io ho asagiato delle fiche che ancor non vi cedo" (Archivio di Stato di Firenze, Fondo Panciatichi, filza 126, fol. 370r). For the paradoxical encomia as practised by the members of the Roman Accademia dei Vignaiuoli and Niccolo Franco's collection of sonnets (1541) in praise of figs (cunts), melons and apples (buttocks), peaches (assholes) and string beans (cocks) see David O. Frantz, *Festum Voluptatis. A Study of Renaissance Erotica* (Columbus: Ohio State University Press, 1989), 29, 30, 33–38, 106.

43. For the diet in Bridewell see Salgado, *The Elizabethan Underworld,* 192.

44. Although the governors saw to it that the rules concerning diet were strictly observed, they could not prevent frequent infringements of the regulations. Thus Matron Alice Millett, presumably bribed by an inmate, was supected of having broken the rules "sett downe for the dyett or other matters," and the court meeting on Wednesday, 11 April 1599, debated whether to dismiss her or not (BCB 4, fol. 77v).

45. If Sergio Rossi can be trusted, only two hundred Italian citizens resided in Elizabethan England, the majority of them obviously in London. See Sergio Rossi, "Italy and the English Renaissance: An Introduction" in Sergio Rossi and Daniella Savoia (eds.), *Italy and the English Renaissance* (Milan: Unicopli, 1989), 9–24. The presence of Mediterranean merchants in late Elizabethan London remains regrettably neglected. Thus, for instance, historians have completely ignored the fact that Venice, in an attempt to renew the former diplomatic relations with Elizabethan England, sent the young patrician merchant Giovanni Battista Basadonna as agent to the Elizabethan court (1593–99). He kept his own miniature court in London at a time when Shakespeare wrote *The Merchant of Venice.* On his commercial, political, financial, and cultural activities see Gustav Ungerer, *A Spaniard in Elizabethan England,* ii, chap. 7, "The Intelligence Service" built up in Italy for the Earl of Essex.

46. Paolo Gondola's *Sturm und Drang* period in Nicolò de Gozzi's office and in London taverns and brothels is the subject of Gondola's letters addressed from 1590 to 1594 to his former colleague Gualtieri Panciatichi. See Gargano, "Il mercatore Paolo Gondola 1590–1592." Gondola's letters in the Archivio di Stato di Firenze, Fondo Panciatichi, filza 126, are, in fact, dated from 1590 to 1594; henceforth ASF, FP. The authority on Anglo-Ragusan commerce and Nicolò de Gozzi is Veselin Kostic, author of *Ragusa and England 1300–1650.* The Serbian Academy of Sciences and Arts, vol. 488 (Belgrade, 1975). The work contains a useful summary in English, pages 565–600. De Gozzi and Gondola did not sever their personal ties in 1592. Gondola was one of the witnesses of de Gozzi's will, dated 17 January 1595, in which the deceased left £30,000 to his heirs and church in Dubrovnik. De Gozzi died on 21 January 1595. See Kostic, 531, 589. For more information on the patrician families of the Gozzi (Gozze) and Gondola see Barisa Krekic, *Dubrovnik: A Mediterranean Urban Society, 1300–1600* (Aldershot: Ashgate, 1997).

47. In 1588, Nicolò der Gozzi and Sir Haratio Palavicino each subsribed £300 to a loan charged by the city to the Queen. See Kirk, *Returns,* part ii, 415. Nicolò's subsidy payment for 1589 was assessed at £350, Sir Horatio's at £400 and Filippo Corsini's at £160. See G. D. Ramsay, "The Undoing of the Italian Mercantile Colony in 16th Century London" in N. B. Harte and K. G. Ponting (eds.), *Textile History*

and Economic History. Essays in Honour of Miss Julia de Lacy Mann (Manchester: Manchester University Press, 1973), 22–49.

48. M. E. Bratchel, "Regulation and Group Consciousness in the Late History of London's Italian Merchant Colonies," *Journal of European Economic History* 9 (1980): 585–610.

49. Gualtieri Panciatichi, son of Nicolò di Gualtieri and Maria, daughter of the senator Luigi Altoviti, was born on 11 April 1563. After his formation in London, he traded as a merchant in Naples where he held the office of consul of the Florentine nation. On 14 December 1604, he was buried in the church of San Giovanni at the foot of a marble statue erected in honor of San Bartolommeo at his own cost. See Luigi Passerini (Orsini de Rilli), *Genealogia e storia della famiglia Panciatichi* (Firenze: M. Cellini, 1858), 213, Tavola XIV.

50. See Gargano, 23. Panciatichi andGondola would have fared no better under the supervision of Filippo Corsini. Corsini was for Panciatichi a terrible man who used to give terrible answers ("uomo terribile e che dà le risposte terribili"). See Gargano, 23. The business correspondence of Filippo Corsini was up for auction at Christie's in 1984, 1985, 1986, 1987, 1988; a microfilm is available at the Guildhall Library, London. See Robson Lowe, *Historical Letters to Gratious Street, London, 1570–1601* (London: Christie's, 1988).

51. For the organization of the Italian colonies in early modern England see M. E. Bratchel, "Alien Merchant Colonies in 16th-Century England: Community Organization and Social Mores," *Journal of Medieval and Renaissance Studies* 14 (1984): 39–62.

52. See Gargano, 36–37. He managed to hear mass in the residence of Dom Antonio, the exiled pretender to the Portuguese crown, some thiry miles outside London, presumably in Eton. Another venue was the private chapel of an English friend of his (ASF, FP, 126, fol. 252 v). It will come as a surprise to English musicologists that he also heard mass in the house of an English lady on the recommendation of John Bull, the organist: "Jo per mezo di quell Bull, organista della Regina, che con il Filichaja voleua passare in Italia, in casa di una gentildona, molto richa, . . . ho comodità della messa, ma nesuno non lo sa" (Letter to Panciatichi, dated 1 August 1590, ASF, FP, 126, fol. 287r). Bull's open adherence to the Catholic faith dates from 1613 when he fled to the Spanish Netherlands.

53. In his will, Nicolò de Gozzi left him £30 per every year he had been in his service. Simonelli was in his early thirties. See Kostic, 520.

54. Maruo Berti, of Lucca, was born about 1563. He was of the same age as Gualtieri Panciatichi and Paolo Gondola. When on 7 February 1596 he was summoned to appear before the High Court of Admiralty, the clerk noted that "Mauro Barti, mercator italus, Londini residens, vbi per sex annos morans fecit, annos agens xxxiij vel circa." See PRO, HCA, 13/32/59v. Nicolò de Gozzi left him £30 per year. See Kostic, 520.

55. Orazio Franciotti was somewhat older. He was twenty years old when he came to England in 1574 and was a member of de Gozzi's office until the latter's death in January 1595. However, he was also working on his own account when on his father's death in 1590 he inherited some money. See Irene Scouloudi (ed.), *Returns,* 177; and ASF, FP, 126, fol. 287. Nonetheless, Nicolò de Gozzi left him £50 per year. See Kostic, 520.

56. In the letter addressed to Panciatichi on 1 August 1591, Gondola wrote: ". . . ogni dominica giochiamo al palone insieme e poi andiamo in tauerna a cantare. Con questo colisone (sic) si caricha la balestra, e ua discorendo tal che si diamo bell tempo" (ASF, FP, 126, fol.368v). The word "colisone" seems to be a slip of the pen for "collisione," contest, fight. On the phallic meaning of "caricha la balestra," that is, with the game/contest the cross-bow/stone-bow is loaded [to be discharged on women], see Salvatore Battaglia, *Grande dizionario della lingua italiana* (Torino, 1962), under "Balestra. 4. In senso osceno." Gondola's companion "il Vani" used to meet his moll, facetiously called Piero del Giardino, at the Elephant: "Il Vani va più che mai al suo Piero dell Giardino et se homo lo vol trouare, bisogna che vadi là ho in casa dell Elefante" (ASF, FP, 126, fol. 250r).

57. The authorities objected to football games because encounters often ended in fatal casualties. See. F. G. Emmison, *Elizabethan Life. Disorder,* 225–26. For a discussion and illustration of the strategic and tactical football game as played in Florence at the time, which was in stark contrast to the warlike game as practiced in England, see A. Forbes Sieveking, "Games" in *Shakespeare's England. An Account of the Life and Manners of his Age* (Oxford, 1916, rpt. 1926) ii: 451, 462–63.

58. He placed the order in the letter addressed to his friend Panciatichi on 18 June 1592. "In la proxima cassa che manderete per noj," he wrote, "ui piacerà metter una dozzina di paloni da giochare tanto grandi quanto costà si usa, ma che siano dogni bontà e perfectione, dandoci debito dell costo" (ASF, FP, 126, fol. 433r).

59. That the Elephant catered to Italian customers has been noted by S. Schoenbaum in *William Shakespeare. A Documentary Life* (Oxford, 1975), 127. The inn's association with Italians is evoked in *Twelfth Night.* Antonio, the sea captain, knows that "In the south suburbs, at the Elephant, Is best to lodge" (3.3.39–40).

60. John Florio, *A Worlde of Wordes or most copious and exact Dictionarie in Italian and English* (London: A. Hatfield, 1598; rpt. Hildesheim, 1972). Florio was acquainted with Nicolò de Gozzi.

61. Obviously an augmentative of "potta," the cunt, in Ragusan parlance.

62. "Manello sta bene," Gondola wrote to his friend Panciatichi on 24 May 1590, "et l'altro giorno fumo insieme in burdelo, et è più che mai inamorato dell Potone; la vorebbe futere, et il choglione non lo sa fare; ma io diuerse volte ne li ho detto il modo che ha da tenire. Non so quello farà, ma mi par troppo vergognoso, et se, come l'o detto, non la lassa, non farà mai nulla" (ASF, FP. 126, fol. 250r; for the whole letter see Gargano, 42–47).

63. Gargano, 34.

64. "E ui prometto che alle spese mie," Gondola reported to Panciatichi on 10 October 1590, "ho imparato come ua hora il mondo e cambiatomi di assai, cioiè (sic) tanto in el spendere quanto in andare in burdelo, perchè adesso non ci vado più nè ponto nè pocho; et sino hora ho ateso sempre a spendere, hora bisogna andare a guadagnare qualcosa come farò quest'anno delle prouigioni" (ASF, FP, 126, fol. 332 v).

65. "Pawle de Gandell," servant to Nicholas de Gozzi, figures in a certificate which the commissioners levying subsidies dated 10 June 1590. They assessed his possessions at £10 and the tax amounted to 33s 4d. Gondola was then living in the Tower Ward. See Kirk, *Returns,* part ii (1902), 423. On the projected profits in 1591, see Gargano, 27, n.1.

66. Apparently, Gondola and his Italian companions were customers of the Dolphin. It was "a common inn for receipt of travellers" on the east side of Bishopsgate Street, near the end of Houndsditch. See John Stow, *A Survay of London,* 386.

67. The relevant passage in Gondola's letter addressed to Gualtieri Panciatichi on 14 May 1590 reads as follows. "Et la causa è che ui dirò dal oste dell Dolfino, cioè marito della nostra Gioanna, sendo in quelle parti doue il suo padre sta per alcuni— dicho il padre di lei—per alcuni sua affari, li disse che io ero per partirmene fra 15 giorni di questo Regno. Et lei, subito inteso questo, con lisentia di sua madre et senza saputa dell padre, montò con dua sua seruitori a cauallo con intentione di seguitarmi, secondo d'altri mi è stato detto; et mi hano detto ancora che non faceua altro che scapigliarsi e pi[a]ngere, e quando che ariuò a Londra, mandò un suo homo per cercharmi, il qual non sapendomi trouare, li riferì che ero ito via. La qual non credendoli, vene al Dolfino piangendo e scapigliandosi; doue pregò la nostra Gioanna per l'amor de Dio che li dicesse il vero. Doue lei li disse che non era così; et subito vene per me pregandomi per l'amor di Dio da parte sua che la vadi a uedere. Doue quando arivai, non potresti imaginare quante carezze mi fece e quanti basci mi dette. E starà qui in Londra una settimana, doue spero, auanti che vadi via, dormir con lei una ho due volte. E ui asicuro que è più bella di quello che quando voi la uedeste di un gran pezzo, sendo diuentata grassa e più grande e fatta; però ui ho volsuto dire questo a ciò che vediate se mi porta amore et che entriate in sugo. Et veramente tutto questo è verissimo, e non potresti imaginare quante carezze mi fa quando vado da lei. Il suo padre è qui in Londra, ma non già che sapia niente della sua venuta. La qual poichè me ha visto, se ne torna, come ho detto, fra dui giorni, et ui prometto che è gentildona di molto bona casa et adesso molto braua e denarosa. Di queste cose non ui è nesuno di questi nostri forestieri che lo sapia, perche mi ha pregato che non lo dichi a nesuno et che non vole si sapia che sia venuta in la terra" (ASF, FP, 126, fol. 250r–v; a modern transcript can be read in Gargano, 45–46).

68. ASF, FP, fol. 252r. The letter to Panciatichi is dated 20 June 1590.

69. See Thomas Coryate's "Observations in Venice" in his *Crudities* (London, 1611; rpt. Glasgow, 1905) i:403.

70. Gondola's aggressive foul-mouthed roughness comes out in his early letters. By way of illustration I have chosen the letter dated 5 July 1590, which ends with the current formula "e per fine me ui racomando Wd al mei hart" (and to end I commend myself to you with all my heart). But he cannot help adding an ironic comment coded for male consumption: "and so god chipe you and prosper you, et se non intendete questo inglese per essere fuor di parole ordinarie, datte falta a uoi stesso, e questo son sicuro che intendete: you hor sun gus and you hor sun cheneue adio' (and if you do not understand this English for being beyond ordinary words [that is, no tavern terms], you will have yourself to blame for it, and this I am sure you will understand: you whoreson goose and you whoreson knave good-bye). (ASF, FP, 126, fol. 262r).

71. In 1593/94, he entered into a partnership with Bartholomew Huggett, a London merchant, and Constantin Episcopopulo, a Greek merchant, whose father was trading in Candy (Crete). They were co-owners of the Constantin of London, Gondola and Huggett owning each one fourth, and Episcopopulo one half (PRO, HCA, 13/32/ 1–3). In 1596, Gondola and Huggett owned the St Paul of London. Gondola appeared in person before the High Court of Admiralty to defend himself against Thomas Pipe

who on behalf of the English crew accused Gondola and Huggett of owing them wages, a total of £21 17s 8d (PRO, HCA, 24/64/unfoliated). He was also in touch with Lodnon businessmen-bankers such as John Byrd, brewer, of Southwark, and Henry Stradling, draper, who in 1594 sold three ships, the Elizabeth of London, alias the Golden Noble, of 240 tons, the Bona Speranza, a "royally furnished ship," of 280–300 tons, at a price of £650, and the Hopewell, to Giovanni Battista Basadonna, the patrician merchant-banker, official agent of the Republic of Venice (1593–99), honorary MA of Cambridge University (February 1595) at the request of the earl of Essex. Gondola was no longer able to look after his booming enterprise on his own. Thus he relied on Henry Hungerford as his chief factor, and so did Basadonna (PRO, HCA, 13/31/349v–350).

72. Gondola was back in Dubrovnik by 1602 when Mary Newborough was in Bridewell. On his departure he sold the Sta Maria and the Elizabeth of Venice to Tommaso Manelli. In 1617 he commanded a naval expedition; he married about 1625 and died and about 1641. See Kostic, 301–4.

For Shakespeare scholars the value of the heavily understudied presence of Mediterranean merchants in the last decade of Queen Elizabeth's reign resides in the light it sheds on the conception of Antonio as one of the key figures in *The Merchant of Venice*. His status as a noble Venetian merchant, magnate, and bachelor is scripted in terms of the experience made, and reputation carved out in England, by the Mediterranean "bachelor uncles," to use Bratchell's coinage, or rather patriarchs, who were wedded to their family businesses in London and strongly committed to the personal running of their enterprises, to wit, Nicolò de Gozzi, Ragusan, residing in London from 1552 until his death in 1595; Filippo Corsini, Florentine, dwelling in Gratious Street from 1560/61 until his death in 1601. The patrician Giovanni Battista Basadonna, born in 1562, agent of the Republic of Venice, from 1593 to 1599, owned three English merchant vessels flying the Venetian flag and manned by English and Venetian mariners. The three were also active as merchant bankers. Nicolò de Gozzi and Filippo Corsini were the wealthiest London-based foreign merchants and, together with Sir Horatio Palavicino, the highest taxpayers. Their careers provide the key to decoding Antonio's status as a bachelor merchant.

73. The protection of prostitutes extended by patrons of high position and influence is well documented. See Archer, *The Pursuit of Stability*, 233.

74. See Alfred B. Beaven, *The Aldermen of the City of London*, 2 vol. (London, 1908 and 1913). Banning died on 30 September 1616. I have not been able to check John Able's identity. He has presumably nothing to do with John Abel (ca. 1578–1675), the master carpenter from Herefordshire. One Jean Abeels, obviously a wealthy Huguenot merchant, had a Privy Seal directed to him for a government loan of £100 in February 1601. See Kirk, *Returns of Aliens,* 109.

75. Alarms and rumors that the Spaniards had landed on the Isle of Wight and in Southampton generated a series of musters in London. The first on 8, the second on 22, the third on 25 August 1599. From then on there were musters every day until 4 September in expectation of an attack on the Thames by the Spanish galleys. On Sunday, 26 August, before 6 a.m., 3000 soldiers were all in armour in the streets and were being mustered and trained by their captains till past 7 p.m; and the following Monday, 30,000 citizens showed up at Mile End Green, the training ground for the citizen

forces of Lodnon situated a mile from Aldgate, where they were trained all day. See
G. B. Harrison, *A Last Elizabethan Journal . . . 1599–1603* (London, 1933),
32,33,34,36,38. Simon Forman entered in his Diary under 1599: "This year was the
great muster in August at St. James's. I bought much harness, and weapons for war."
Quoted from A. L. Rowse, *Simon Forman.*, 296. On the Spanish threat and the assembling of the national army in London see Lindsay Boynton, *The Elizabethan Militia
1558–1638* (London, 1967, rpt. Newton Abbot, 1971), 198–206.

76. See A. L. Rowse, *The Expansion of Elizabethan England* (London: Macmillan, 1955), 354.

77. The Lord Chamberlain, Henry Carey, first Lord Hunsdon, who maintained
Emilia Lanyer "in great pomp," as Simon Forman noted, received £40 a year; so did
Christiane Hobson, the-17-year-old "concubine" of a 56-year-old knight." See A. L.
Rowse, *Simon Forman*, 99, 222.

78. For the female "blakamores" in Paul Banning's household see Irene Scouloudi (ed.), *Returns of Strangers* (1985), 149. Three black servants was indeed an
exceptional number in an Elizabethan household; a few privileged households kept
just one black servant. The other households known to me which kept more than one
black servant were headed by converted Jews. Dr Hector Nuñez kept at least two,
Gratia and Elizabeth Anegro; Fernandes Alvarez had several, one of them called
Grace Anegro. See C. J Sisson, "A Colony of Jews in Shakespeare's Lodnon," *Essays
and Studies* 23 (1938): 38–51. This information supplements the Introduction of Kim
F. Hall's *Things of Darkness. Economics of Race and Gender in Early Modern England* (Ithaca: Cornell University Press, 1995).

79. Luce Morgan had been committed to Bridewell on 15 January 1600. See Les-
lei Hotson, *Mr. W. H.* (London: Hart-Davis, 1964), 254.

80. There are likely to be many more instances recorded in the BCB. Imaginative
literature took some years to respond to this social novelty. The first fictional prostitute to boast that she owned a coach was, as much as I know, the prostitute in Samuel
Rowlands's "The Courtezan," a poem in ballad type quatrains published in *Democri-
tus or Doctor Merryman his Medicines against Melancholy Humours* (1607). Laxton,
in Middleton and Dekker's play *The Roaring Girl* (1611), ed. Paul Mulholland (Manchester: Manchester University Press, 1987), on his ride to meet Moll at Marylebone
Park reminds the coachman that "any coached velvet cap or tuftaffety jacket" keeps
"a vile swaggering in coaches nowadays -the highways are stopped with them"
(3.1.13–16). Henry Peacham facetiously reports in *Coach and Sedan* (London, 1636)
that the mythic Dol Turn-up and Peg Burn-it used to go to the theater by coach. Peacham's reference is taken from Ann Jennalie Cook, *The Privileged Playgoers of Shakespeare's London* (Princeton: Princeton University Press, 1981), 204. For Elizabeth
Reignoldes as a theatergoer see below.

81. On transport in Elizabethan London see Charles Hughes, "Land Travel," in
Shakespeare's England, i, 198–223. Shugg in *Prostitution,* 299, realized the importance of this new transport facility for prostitutes, but placed it in the seventeenth
century.

82. For Laxton's assignation with Moll Cutpurse in Marylebone Park, see note
80.

83. Black Luce of Clerkenwell and Gilbert East helped their "harlottes" to

"tryme vp with swete water and calles [head-dress] and cotes and thinges for the purpose fitt for the degree of them that use them." Quoted from Archer, *The Pursuit of
Stability,* 213–14.

84. If Mrs. Wilkinson can be relied upon, Edmond Reignoldes was an elderly husband. When she took Elizabeth "vpp into a chamber" where a client was waiting to
be sexually gratified, she used to say to him: "I haue brought here a gentlewoman that
wanteth occupying for that she hath an old man to her husband." Then "Mrs Wilkinson would go downe agayne at what tyme the gent. had th'vse & carnall knowledge"
of Elizabeth's "body" (BCB 4, fol. 100r).

85. For a certificate of the receipt of plate from John Cotton, Keeper of the Standing Wardrobe of Westminster, by the master of the jewels (Sir William Herrick, a
Cheapside jeweller), dated 24 December 1617, see British Library, Add. MS 5751,
fol. 282.

86. On John Cotton's rank as page see *Calendar of State Papers, Domestic, Elizabeth, 1595–1597* (London, 1869), p. 9; as groom see John Roche Dasent (ed.), *Acts
of the Privy Council of England . . . A.D. 1597–1598* (London, 1904, p. 205; on his
insolvency, on 1 May 1599, see *Calendar of State Papers, Domestic, Elizabeth, 1598–
1601* (London, 1869), 190.

87. John Cotton, "the Lord Chamberlines man," was, in all likelihood, identical
with John Cotton, the theatrical speculator, who was given permission to build an
amphitheater for shows and sports, but the permission was withdrawn on 14 September 1620. See Gerald Eades Bentley, *The Jacobean and Caroline Stage* (Oxford,
1941) ii: 414. On the interaction between the three Offices of the Royal Household in
staging dramatic entertainments at court see John H. Astington, *English Court Theatre 1558–1640* (Cambridge: Cambridge University Press, 1999). Cotton was still
Keeper of the Standing Wardrobe of Westminster in 1617. A certificate of the receipt
of plate from him by the Master of the Jewels, Sir Henry Carey, is dated 24 December
1617. See BL, Add.MS 5751, fol. 272, old foliation 282.

88. Andrew Gurr in Appendix I of his study *Playgoing in London* (Cambridge,
1987) has listed Mary Frith as the earliest woman and prostitute/playgoer (1611).
Mary Frith, however, was a cross dressed cutpurse and entertainer, but not a prostitute. See my essay on Mary Frith in the 2000 issue of *Shakespeare Studies.* I am confident that a search through the BCB is likely to yield the names of other prostitutes
frequenting the playhouses. A source disclosing further information on women's presence in playhouses is being explored by Loreen L. Giese in "Theatrical Citings and
Bitings: Some References to Playhouses and Players in London Consistory Court Depositions, 1586–1611", *Early Theatre,* 1 (1998), 113–28. Thus Elizabeth Hattrell, a
domestic servant of Joan Waters, aged nineteen or twenty, testified that she saw John
Newton, the player of Prince Charles's Company, act "a parte" at the Curtain playhouse in 1611 (p. 118).

89. A petition, submitted to the authorities of the city of London in December
1537 to expel the whores from the stews in Southwark, found fault with their "excess-
yve and gorgious apparill" without specifying the garments. See Archer, *The Pursuit,*
250. Thomas Nashe in *The Choise of Valentynes* (1592) sticks to the stereotype: "And
mistris Francis in her veluet goune's / And ruffs, and periwigs as fresh as Maye / Can
not be kept with half a croune a daye." See *The Works of Thomas Nashe,* ed. Ronald

B. McKerrow (London: Houghton, Mifflin and Company, 1905) iii: 403–13, lines 64–66. So does Shakespeare: "taffeta punk" in *All's Well,* 2.2.22, ed. Susan Snyder in The World's Classics, (Oxford, 1994); "a fair hot wench in flame-coloured taffeta" in *Henry IV Part 1,* 1.2.8, ed. Herbert and Judith Weil in The New Cambridge Shakespeare (Cambridge, 1997). Robert Greene in *A Notable Discovery of Coosnage* (1591), however, rhapsodizes about the sartorial splendor, breaking the restrictions of the stereotype: "Oh, might the justices send out spials in the night! They should see how these streetwalkers will jet in rich-guarded gowns, quaint periwigs, ruffs of the largest size, quarter-and-half deep, gloried richly with blue starch, their cheeks dyed with surfling water-thus are they tricked up." Quoted from Salgado, 62.

90. For a detailed discussion of a gentlewoman's dress see Virginia A. La Mar, *English Dress in the Age of Shakespeare.* Folger Books (Washington: Folger Shakespeare Library, 1958). According to La Mar, the term petticoat is synonymous with kirtle, p. 11; according to Marie Channing Linthicum, *Costume in the Drama of Shakespeare and His Contemporaries* (Oxford: Clarendon Press, 1936), it is a woman's underskirt (187).

91. Sleeves, slashed to show the fabric under it, came into vogue in the 1590s. Petruchio makes fun of Katherine's gown with its slashed sleeves: "What's this? A sleeve? 'Tis like a demi-cannon. / What, up and down carved like an apple tart? / Here's snip, and nip, and cut, and slish and slash." *The Taming,* 4.3.86–92, ed. H. J. Oliver in The World's Classics (Oxford: Oxford University Press, 1994). The OED lists the term "hare-brain" or "hair-brain" in the sense of newfangled "harebrayne boyes" (1588). In 1602, Henslowe bought black satin at 12s a yard. See Gerald Eades Bentley, *The Profession of Player in Shakespeare's Time 1590–1642* (Princeton: Princeton University Press, 1984), 88.

92. Henslowe paid as much as £6 13s for a gown. See Jean MacIntyre and P. J. Garrett, "'Clothes worth all the rest': Costumes and Properties," in *A New History of Early English Drama,* ed. John D. Cox and David Scott Kastan (New York, 1997), 269–85. By way of comparison, the velvet, satin, and taffeta which the Admiral's Men bought in 1601 to make the cardinal's robes for the lost play on Wolsey cost £21 (ibid, 279).

93. For the rage of wearing ruffs in Elizabethan England see the section on "Costume" by percy Macquoid in *Shakespeare's England,* ii, 91–118. Even Doll Tearsheet is wearing a ruff which Pistol swears he will rip off her neck. See *Henry IV Part 2* (Oxford Shakespeare, ed. René Weis, 1997), 2.4.130.

94. In December 1596, Henslowe paid £3 10s for a headtire and rebato. See G. E. Bentley, *The Profession of Player,* 89.

95. Extravagant costuming was also one of the chief items of expenditure of dramatic entertainments at court. See Astington, *English Court Theatre,* 155.

96. On the social importance of the sumptuary laws see Marjorie Garber, *Vested Interests: Cross-Dressing and Cultural Anxiety* (London: Routledge, 1992), 21–17. Dressing up as people of rank above their own station was "a practice the prostitutes shared with the players." See Anthony Dawson and Paul Yachnin, *The Culture of Playgoing in Shakespeare's England: A Collaborative Debate* (Cambridge: Cambridge University Press, 2001), 40.

97. See Ruth Mazo Karras, "The Regulation of Brothels in Late Medieval En-

gland," *Signs* 14 (1989): 399–432, resp. 417. The articles of the regulation of the stews on Bankside can be read in Thomas Dekker's *The Dead Teame or Westminsters Complaint* (1608), sig. C1v–C2v. The book is dedicated to Sir John Harington.

98. In the reality of imaginative literature, the price of whores was typed. There was, with a few exceptions, a standard price of sixpence prevailing in Thomas Middleton and Thomas Dekker's plays. Curvetto, an old courtier in Middleton's *Blurt Master Constable* (1601), offers Simperina sixpence (3.3.3). See *The Works,* ed. A. H. Bullen, vol. 1 (Boston, 1885). Roger, the pimp in Dekker's *The Honest Whore,* Part 1 (1604), is "a slaue to sixpence" (3.2.48). Mrs Fingerlock, the bawd, offers Roger "sixpence a lane" (3.2.80–81), that is, 6d per lay. See *The Dramatic Works,* ed. Fredson Bowers, vol. 2 (Cambridge, 1964). Bellafront, the honest whore, is for Matheo "A sixe-penny Mutton Pasty, for any to cut vp" (5.2.149). The whore Catherina Bountinall denounces Bots as "a Dog that will licke vp sixe pence" (5.2.402). See *The Honest Whore,* Part 2 (1605). Justiniano in Dekker's *Westward Ho* (1604) calls the suburbs "the place of sixe-penny Sinfulnesse" (5.4.248–50); and in *Northward Ho* (1605) Mistress Dorothy expostulates the Drawer: "the rotten toothd rascall, will for sixe pence fetch any whore to his maisters customers (1.2.41–45). See *The Dramatic Works,* ed. Fredson Bowers, vol. 2. Sir Andrew Aguecheek sends Feste 6d for his "leman" (*Twelfth Night,*2.3.32). An exception is Witgood in Middleton's *A Trick to Catch an Old One* (1605). He raises the question: "Why should a gallant pay but two shillings for his ordinary that nourishes him, and twenty times two for his brothel that consumes him?" (1.1.5–7). See *The Works,* ed. Bullen, vol. 2 (Boston, 1885). Another exception is Katherine Bountinall. Detained in Bridewell, she accuses the bawd Horsleach of her trade and sliding price structure: "how many twelue-penny Fees, nay two shilings Fees, nay, when any embassadours ha beene here, how many halfe crowne Fees hast thou taken?" (5.7.374 ff.) See *The Honest Whore.* Part 2, ed. F. Bowers, vol. 2.—The stereotype also intruded into rogue literature. Pierce Penilesse urges the Devil to keep all London whores in hell "and not let our ayre bee contaminated with their six-pennie damnation any longer." See Thomas Nashe, *Pierce Penilesse His Supplication to the Divell* (1592), ed. McKerrow, *Works* (1904), i, 217.—The prostitute in John Taylor's poem *The Whore* sells her body "For sixe pence" to any "honest man or knaue". See *All the Works* (1630), facsimile rpt by Scolar Press (Menston, 1973), sig. Kk.1.v

99. The Knights of the Quiver in the Kingdom of Love, which was ruled by the Prince d'Amour during the Middle Temple Christmas revels of 1597/98, had to take similar precautions. It was one of the duties of the Lord Admiral to guarantee "Traffique into the Gulfe of *Venus*" and to see to it that the vessels "be well washt afore and after for fear of infection." See B. Rudyerd (ed.), *Le Prince d'Amour* (1660), 27. As early as 1547, the physician Andrew Borde had recommended "whyte wyne" as a disinfectant to men and women "burnt" by a venereal disease. A man "burnt of an harlot as sone as he hath done his carnal and fylthy concupiscence," should "washe al his scret places with white wine," three or four times, "as sone as the matter is done lest at length the guttes fall out of the bely." See his *The Breuiary of Helthe.* The English Experience, No. 362 (Amsterdam: Da Capo Press, 1971), a facsimle rpt., fols.XVv and xlr.

100. On prunes as a preventative and laxative see *Measure for Measure,* The Oxford Shakespeare (1991), 2.1.86 ff and n. 87.

101. On contraception see Paul Griffiths, *Youth and Authority: Formative Experiences in England 1560–1640* (Oxford: Clarendon P., 1996), 246; and on the danger midwives were facing see John M. Riddle, *Eve's Herbs. A History of Contraception and Abortion in the West* (Cambridge: Harvard University Press, 1997), 134–37.

102. *Pericles,* The Arden Edition, ed. F. D. Hoeniger (1963), 4.6.84. For Gordon Williams, *A Glossary of Shakespeare's Sexual Language* (London: Athlone, 1997) "herb woman" is a "quibbling title." Doreen DelVecchio and Antony Hammond comment in The New Cambridge Shakespeare (1998) that it means "a woman who deals in herbs" (169 n. 80). For the "comic exorcism of gross sexuality" in this brothel scene see Alexander Leggatt, "The Shadow of Antioch: Sexuality in *Pericles, Prince of Tyre,*" ed. Louise and Peter Fothergill-Payne in *Parallel Lives, Spanish and English National Drama 1580–1680* (Lewisburg: Bucknell University Press, 1991), 167–79. The case of Mrs. Miller supplements the findings of Margaret Pelling concerning the irregular female medical practitioners. See her essay on "Defensive Tactics: Networking by Female Medical Practitioners in Early Modern London" in A. Shepard, *Communities in Early Modern London,* chap. 3.

103. Archer, 213; Griffiths, "The Structure," 45.

104. Archer, 213; Griffiths, 45.

105. The Arden Shakespeare (1963), 4.6.5–7. Philip Edwards in The New Penguin Shakespeare (1976) glosses "kindness" as meaning a "natural act of goodness."

106. Archer, 214.

107. For Ann Morgan see G. R. Quaife, *Wanton Wenches and Wayward Wives,* 150.

108. For Aemilia Bassano and Chritiane Hobson see A. L. Rowse, *The Case Books of Simon Forman,* 222; for Elizabeth Compe see Griffiths, 47.

109. For Thomasin Breame see Griffiths, 46.

110. Sara Mendelson and Patricia Crawford, in *Women in Early Modern England, 1550–1700* (Oxford: Clarendon Press, 1998), argue that consumption decreased a prostitute's value (336) whereas Deanna Shemek in *Ladies Errant: Wayward Women in Early Modern Italy* (Durham: Duke University Press, 1998) is of the opinion that it increased its value (30).

111. Griffiths, 46–47. Sir Walter Whorehound assesses "the maidenhead" of Moll Yellowhammer as "Worth forty" pounds; but it is doubtful that in reality a virgin-prostitute could command as much as £40. See Thomas Middleton, *A Chaste Maid in Cheapside* (1613), ed. Bryan Loughrey and Neil Taylor in *Five Plays,* Penguin Classics (London: Penguin Group, 1988), 4.3.60–61.

112. In January 1579, Horatio Palavicino ordered Gilbert Periam, as recorded in the BCB, to search for "some mayden to abuse who had not been dealte with all before." See Archer, 232. It is tempting to suspect a connection between the frantic search for a virgin in London and in Guildford brothels and the birth of Palavicino's illegitimate son Edward about 1578–80. His mother, a "very mean person" (DNB), has remained unidentified. On Edward's illegitimacy and his father's obscure liaison see Laurence Stern, *An Elizabethan: Sir Horatio Palavicino* (Oxford: Clarendon Press, 1956), 26,27.

113. *Ben Jonson,* ed. C. H. Herford, Percy and Evelyn Simpson (Oxford, rpt 1966), vol. 4.

114. For women's networks see Jean E. Howard's "Afterword" in *Maids and Mistresses, Cousins and Queens: Women's Alliances in Early Modern England* (Oxford: Oxford University press, 1999), ed. Susan Frye and Karen Robertson. None of the contributions deals with women's networks in prostitution. On the benefits of occupational solidarity among Roman prostitutes see Elizabeth S. Cohen, "Seen and known: prostitutes in the cityscape of late sixteenth-century Rome, *Renaissance Studies* 12 (1998): 392–409.

115. Archer, 213–15; Griffiths, 44.

116. The danger that "the one" inmate "will infect the other" was known to the officials of Bridewell. See A. L. Beier, *Masterless Men,* 168. It was also known to Thomas Middleton. In *Your Five Gallants* (1605), Bungler defends the Boy from being sent to Bridewell by his master Pursenet: "Nay, I tell you true, sir; there's none goes in there a quean, but she comes out an arrant whore, I warrant you" (3.5.137 ff.). See *The Works,* ed. A. H. Bullen, (Boston, 1885), vol. 3.

117. On childbirth and female support networks see Linda Pollock, "Childbearing and Female Bonding in Early Modern England," *Social History* 22 (1997): 286–306.

118. For both quotations see *Ben Jonson,* ed. C. H. Herford, Percy and Evelyn Simpson (Oxford: Clarendon Press, 1963) 8: 87, 209. The Hospital of Bridewell stood along Fleet Ditch from its entry into the Thames to Bride Lane. For a revised reading of Jonson's mock-epic account of London's sewage system polluting the Fleet Ditch see Bruce Thomas Boehrer, "The Ordure of Things: Ben Jonson, Sir John Harington, and the Culture of Excrement in Early Modern England," ed. James Hirsh in *New Perspectives on Ben Jonson* (London: Associated University Press, 1997), 174–96.

119. For "basket" meaning female pudend check under "basket-making" in Gordon Williams, *A Dictionary of Sexual Language* (1994), vol. 1.

120. See Griffiths, 52.

121. If the father was unknown and the mother unable to support a child, the charge fell on the parish. See A. L. Rowse, *The Elizabethan Renaissance. The Life of the Society* (London, 1971), 156.

122. The best historical study of the Brookes is David McKeen's *A memory of Honour: The Life of William Brooke, Lord Cobham.* Salzburg Studies in English Literature, Elizabethan and Renaissance Studies 108 (Salzburg, 1986); see also the biographical entries in the *DNB* and in P. W. Hasler (ed.), *The History of Parliament. The House of Commons 1558–1603. Members* (London: HMSO, 1981). On the divided loyalties of the Brookes vis-à-vis the earl of Essex see Paul E. J. Hammer, *The Polarization of Elizabethan Politics. The Political Career of Robert Devereux, 2nd Earl of Essex, 1585–1597* (Cambridge: Cambridge University Press, 1999), passim.

123. See BCB 4, fol. 8r, 8v, 9r, that is, the courts held on Saturday, 4 March, Monday, 6 March, and Wednesday, 8 March 1598.

124. See McKeen, 439–40; Hasler, ii, 97; and BCB 4, fol. 10r.

125. On the incest see McKeen, 440.

126. For biographical information on Margaret Hoby (1567–1605), third daughter of Henry Carey, Lord Hunsdon, see under Sir Edward Hoby (1560–1617) in the *DNB* and Hasler, ii, 320–23; for her consultations of Simon Forman see Rowse, *Simon Forman,* 143, 240.

127. On the economic and sexual exploitation of young servingwomen see Keith

Wrightson, *English Society 1580–1680* (New Brunswick: Hutchinson, 1982), 42, 68, 146; Ann Rosalind Jones, "Maidservants of London: Sisterhoods of Kinship and Labour" in *Maids and Mistresses,* ed. Susan Frye and Karen Robertson, 21–32.

128. On "partridge" meaning prostitute see Gordon Williams, *A Dictionary of Sexual Language,* 999–1000. Mrs. Wilkinson's onomastic objections antedate the earliest examples given by Williams.

129. The common practice of pawning clothes is mirrored in drama. Mrs. Quickly is ready to lend Falstaff some more money even if she has to "pawn" her own "gown." See *Henry IV, Part 2* (Oxford Shakespeare, ed. René Weis, 1997), 2.1.154–55.

130. E. A. J. Honigmann, "Sir John Oldcastle: Shakespeare's Martyr" in *"Famed and Winnowed Opinions": Shakespearean Essays Presented to Harold Jenkins* (London: Methuen, 1987), 118–32.

131. Leslie Hotson, *Shakespeare's Sonnets Dated and Other Essays* (New York, 1949), 156. If Lord Cobham had recognized mother and son, they would have left some record. His bitter enemy, the philandering earl of Essex, fathered an illegitimate son in 1591. However, Essex, unlike Cobham, acknowledged his son, named Walter, who was looked after by the earl's mother, the countess of Leicester. Walter's mother was Elizabeth Southwell, a maid of honour and, ironically, first cousin of Cobham. See Hammer, *The Polarization of Elizabethan Politics,* 95, 96, 320.

132. See Charles Nicholl, *A Cup of News. The Life of Thomas Nashe* (London: Routledge and Kegan Paul, 1984), chap. 16: "The *Isle of Dogs* Affair." Alice Lyle Scoufos in "Nashe, Jonson, and the Oldcastle Problem," *Modern Philology* 65 (1968): 307–24, offers a brilliant analysis of Nashe's satire on the Cobhams in *Lenten Stuffe,* but her guess that Launcelot Gobbo and his purblind father in *The Merchant of Venice* (1596) are also cast in terms of the Cobham satire is beside the point. In her study *Shakespeare's Typological Satire. A Study of the Falstaff-Oldcastle Problem* (Athens: Ohio University Press, 1979), Scoufos ventures into the slippery ground of wild speculation, arguing that some events of Oldcastle's life are "subtly suggested in the action and characterization of Falstaff" and that these are fashioned to expose the questionable loyalty of Lord Cobham who had been involved in the diplomatic machinations of the adherents of the imprisoned Queen of Scots to set her free.

133. I am following the chronology of the plays as given by Giorgio Melchiori in *Shakespeare's Garter Plays: "Edward II" to "Merry Wives of Windsor"* (Newark: University of Delaware Press, 1994) and by Gary Taylor, "William Shakespeare, Richard James and the House of Cobham," *Review of English Studies* 38 (1987), 334–54. On Falstaff's role as misleader of youth see David Bevington's Introduction to *Henry IV, Part 1* (Oxford, 1987).

134. Isaac Herbert Jeayes (ed.), *Letters of Philip Gawdy of West Harling, Norfolk, and of London to Various Members of His Family 1579–1616,* Roxburghe Club (London, 1906), 108–9.

135. On this kind of physical mutilation of bawds see Valentin Groebner, "Losing Face, Saving Face: Noses and Honour in the Late Medieval Town," *History Workshop* 40 (1995): 1–15.

136. Thomas Vicary, *The Anatomie of the Bodie of Man,* 168–69.

137. John Stow, *A Survay of london,* 200.

138. Salgado, *The Elizabethan Underworld*, 52.

139. John Cordy-Jeaffreson (ed.), *Middlesex County Records*, vol. i (London, 1886/87).

140. Ibid., i, 287. Young women were also carted for abandoning their infants. Laura Gowing reports the carting of three women who exposed their illegitimate infants in the Royal Exchange in 1579. See her essay on "'The freedom of the streets': Women and Social Space, 1560–1640" in Paul Griffiths and Mark S. R. Jenner (eds.), *Londinopolis: Essays in the Cultural and Social History of Early Modern London* (Manchester: Manchester University Press, 2000), chap. 7.

141. Jeayes, *Letters of Philip Gawdy*, 99–101.

142. Norman Egbert McClure (ed.), *The Letters of John Chamberlain.* The American Philological Society (Philadelphia: University of Pennsylvania Press, 1930), i. 98.

143. McClure, i, 139, 369.

144. Stow, *A Survey of London*, 200.

145. The sentences of both Prudence Crispe and Elizabeth Holland can be read in John Cordy-Jeaffreson (ed.), *Middlesex County Records*, i, 234, 235.

146. For a map and discussion of the civic processional routes for major civic observances see Lawrence Manley, *Literature and Culture in Early Modern London* (Cambridge: Cambridge University Press, 1995), 226–27.

147. On shame punishments in charivaris and on the use of rough music see Martin Ingram, "Ridings, Rough Music and the Reform of Popular Culture in Early Modern England," *Past and Present* 105 (1984): 79–113. For the First Master of Bridewell the ringing of "the Bason" by the Beadle "is an emblem of" the whores' "reuelling." See Thomas Dekker, *The Second Part of the Honest Whore* (written 1604/5), 5.2.434–35. *The Dramatic Works of Thomas Dekker*, ed. Fredson Bowers (Cambridge: Cambridge University Press, 1964) ii: 217.

148. Jeayes, *Letters of Philip Gawdy*, 108.

149. Vicary, *The Anatomie of the Bodie of Man*, 169.

150. Caroline Barron, Christopher Coleman, Claire Gobbi, "The London Journal of Alesandro Magno 1562," *The London Journal* 9 (1983), 136–52.

151. On Overbury, see the courts held on 2 June 1599 (BCB 4, fol. 87v); on 22 April 1601 (fol. 231 r); on 28 July 1601; and on 14 May 1603 (fol. 376r). On Layton see the Lord Mayor's conscription of 78 inmates, on 27 April 1599, for service in the Low Countries (BCB 4, fol. 80r). Captain Crofts, in August 1601, received the commission to take up another batch of some 200 vagrants and masterless men. They were, first, to be taken to Bridewell, whipped and corrected, and then, if they agreed, to be sent to Ostend. See G. B. Harrison (ed.), *A Last Elizabethan Journal . . . 1599–1603*, 195.

152. The practice of bailing out prostitutes was endemic among the wealthy patrons. Dekker seized the opportunity to expose the social iniquity of this custom to the laughter of the theatregoers in the last scene of *The Honest Whore*, Part II (1605), which is set in Bridewell. Penelope Whore-hound entreats the Duke of Milan and his courtiers to bail her out (5.2.320). See *The Dramatic Works*, ed. Fredson Bowers, vol. 2 (Cambridge: Cambridge University Press, 1964).

153. Thomas Bowen (ed.), *Extracts from the Records and Court Books of Bridewell Hospital* (London: 1798), 11.

154. The "Ouerseers of the Artmasters & workes" of Bridewell were elected for three months. The three overseers of the spinning-house "chosen" by the court on 13 January 1601 were Mr. Crowch, Mr. Hickman, and Mr. Craford. The overseers of the knitters were Mr. Rumney, Mr. Kevall, and Mr. Skales, etc. (BCB 4, fol. 205v).

155. *The Dramatic Works,* ed. Fredson Bowers, vol. 2 (Cambridge: Cambridge University Press, 1964).

156. Irregularities of this sort were endemic. In 1599, the auditors of the hospital found that Thomas Box, the treasurer, had committed some financial irregularities besides diverting four pieces of cloth, the hospital's property, to his private residence. See Edward Geoffrey O'Donoghue, *Bridewell Hospital, Palace, Prison, Schools from the Death of Elizabeth to Modern Times* (London: John Lane, 1923) i: 188.

157. The text has been published by H. E. Rollins (ed.), *A Pepysian Garland. Black-Letter Broadside Ballads of the Years 1595–1639, Chiefly from the Collection of Samuel Pepys* (Cambridge: Cambridge University Press, 1922), 39–43.

158. Quoted from *Twelfth Night,* The Arden Shakespeare (1975). Compare Orsino's innocence with Vindice's sarcasm: "And careful sisters spin that thread i'th'night / That does maintain them and their bawds i'th'day." See Thomas Middleton, *The Revenger's Tragedy* (1606), ed. Loughrey and Taylor (1988), 2.2.141–42.

159. This was the diet approved by the governors on Saturday, 31 January 1601. The diet for the hemp-house was identical with the exception of beer. Those condemned to beat hemp were entitled to "a pottle of beere" a day (BCB 4, fol. 212v).

160. See Stephen Mennell, Anne Murcott, and Anneke H. van Otterloo, *The Socialogy of Food, Eating, Diet and Culture* (London: Sage, 1992), 112–14.

161. See Edward Geoffrey O'Donoghue, *Bridewell Hospital. Palace, Prison, Schools from the Death of Elizabeth to Modern Times,* 2 vols (London, 1923 and 1929) i: 190–92, 236. Salgado, *The Elizabethan Underworld,* 191, and E. D. Pendry, *Elizabethan Prisons and Prison Scenes, Salzburg Studies in English Literature,* Elizabethan and Renaissance Studes, 17 (Salzburg, 1974), vol i, follow O'Donoghue's historical inaccuracies.

162. Corporation of London Record Office (CLRO), Repertory Books of the Council of Aldermen, vol. 25, fol.372, session of 24 April 1602.

163. In March 1602, a committee had been set up headed by Sir Henry Billingsley and Sir William Ryder to "consider what roomes and places are most fit and conveny-ent to be allotted and layed out for the vndertakers." CLRO, Repertory Books of the Council of Aldermen, vol. 25, fol. 366v, session of 12 March 1602. The undertakers seem to have overruled the findings of the committee.

164. British Library, Add. MS. 5821, fol. 207–10. The document is superscribed "Extracts & transcripts from an old manuscript lent the owner by his friend Thomas Martin of Palgrave in Suffolk, Esq., 1752."

165. Its title reads: *To the Kings most Excellent Maiesty, the Lords Spirituall and Temporall, and Commons in the present Parliament assembled. The humble Petition of Thomas Stanley* (London, single sheet, folio, STC 23228.5). The only copy preserved is in the Guildhall Library, Broadside 24.40. The date 1621, suggested by the STC, seems quite plausible considering that the petitioner was "of great age" and had "small time to continue in this world." In any case, the *Petition* was written after the death of Sir John Popham in 1607. He is also the author of another petition touching breweries, dated 1619. See British Library, Add. MS. 12496.

166. The full title reads: *Stanleyes Remedy: or, The Way how to reform wandring Beggars, Theeves, high-way Robbers and Pick-pockets. Or, An Abstract of his Discoverie: Wherein is shewed, That Sodomes Sinne of Idlenesse is the Poverty and Misery of this Kingdome* (London, Printed for the good of the Poore, 1646). There are three copies in the British Library, shelfmark 1027.i.16 (1 and 2), E. 317 (6).

167. On these ideologicla issues see W. K Jordan, *The Charities of London 1480–1660* (London: George Allen and Unwin, 1960), 186–96; A. L. Beier, *Masterless Men,* 151, 164–69; P. Griffiths, 42–43. Presumably, Thomas Stanley, the projector, was identical with Thomas Stanley, the law student, who was admitted to Gray's Inn in 1552. See Joseph Foster, *Register of Admissions to Gray's Inn 1521–1887* (London, 1887), 23.

168. Sir John Popham took a lifelong interest in setting rogues and vagabonds to work and in helping the poor. He sat in several committees debating the penal and reformatory issues of delinquents. In his will, dated 4 September 1604, he provided for a hospital to be erected at Wellington, Somerset, for the maintenance of twelve poor and aged people, six men and six women, and for two poor men's children. He had a stake in several commercial and colonial ventures. Thus, in 1586, he was appointed undertaker in the plantation of Munster and invested £1200 in the project, importing workers from England. As Reader of the Middle Temple (1568, 1572), Serjeant-at-law, Solicitor General (1579), Attorney General (1581), and Treasurer of the Middle Temple (1580–87), he was lecturing law to the students of the Inns of Court, and when he met Stanley, an alleged student of an Inn of Court, he fell back into his former academic routine. As Stranley put it in the *Petition,* Popham "deliuered vnto him . . . the Causes of . . . the Foundation of Bridewell." For Sir John Popham's biography see Anthony Wood, *Athenae Oxonienses* (London: B. Knaplook, D. Midwinter, J. Tonson, 1721) i: 258–61, 342; *DNB;* and P. W. Hasler, (ed.) *The History of Parliament. The House of Commons 1558–1603,* vol. 3.

169. "The Humble Peticion of the Mayor, Alldermen, and Cominaltie of your H. Cittie," CLRO, *Remembrancia,* vol. ii, fol. 124–25, item 254.

170. Thomas Bowen (ed.), *Extracts,* 25.

171. On the settlement of the debts and the resumption of the old order see the court of aldermen which sat on 19 October 1602 (CLRO, Repertories of the Court of Aldermen, 26, fol.37). I single out the matron Mary Bate who received 40s despite having viciously beaten some of the prostitutes. O'Donoghue, apart from withholding vital information, is not careful about numbers. The number of inmates left in Bridewell is given as sixty-three, the debts as £250 (pp. 191, 192).

172. On Bridewell's history as a royal palace see J. Stow, *A Survay of London,* 362–63.

173. CLRO, *Remembrancia,* ii, fol. 124–25, item 254.

174. On crabs as restoratives or aphrodisiacs see John Marston, *The Malcontent* (1603) as quoted in James T. Henke, *Renaissance Dramatic Bawdy (Exclusive of Shakespeare): An Annotated Glossary.* Salzburg Studies in English Literature, Jacobean Drama Series 40 (Salzburg: Institut für engliche Spache und Literatur, 1974), vol. 2, p. 254. As for marine food and artichokes, the duty of the Archflamen, one of the Prince d'Amour, was "To enjoyn Penance to Lovers impotent in performance, that they fast upon dry Alegant," that is, Spanish wine from Alicante, "cold Lobsters,

Oysters, and Hartichokes, and such like tamers of the flesh." See Benjamin Rudyerd, editor of the Middle Temple revels of 1597/98, whose text was published posthumously as *Le Prince d'Amour, or the Prince of Love* (London: William Leake, 1660), 23.

175. Thomas Stanley had a vested interest in breweries. On 4 February 1619, he and Jeffrey Duppa were to address to King James some "Considerations and reasons, indusive for the planting and erecting of common Brewhouses in all citties, corporacions, Markett Townes and other fitt places . . . for avoyding the detestable sinne of drunkennes to gods glory, the good of common wealth in generall, and to the honor and great yerely revenew" (BL, Add. MS. 12466, fol. 187r–v, old foliation 176).

176. Thomas Weelkes (1576–1623) dedicated to George Brooke his *Canto. Madrigals of 5. and 6. parts, apt for the Viols and Voices* (1600, STC 25206), according to David Brown one of the most important works issued by an Englishman, and Charles Tessier, who in 1597 moved in the Essex circle, dedicated to him a manuscript collection of twenty-nine French songs, to which a different hand added twenty-three songs in French, Italian, and Spanish. See David Brown's entry in *The New Grove Dictionary of Music and Musicians,* ed. Stanley Sadie (London: Macmillan, 1981); see also Frank Dobbins, "The Lute Airs of Charles Tessier," *The Lute Society Journal* 20 (1978): 23–50. Dobbins has reproduced Tessier's dedication to "Giorge Brouc" (plate 5), but has made no reference to the two introductory sonnets written by "George Brooke Gent. in prayse of the Author." As much as I know, these are the only poems by George Brooke that have come down to us. The first two stanzas of the first sonnet read: "Sol neuer dived into faire Thetis bed / Yeelding Luna his ingendring shine / Twice seaven moones, but in my hammering head / Still haue I sought this triple worke of thine // Seene much, heard more, turned ouer many a Lyne / Till Mercury in me such fury bredd / As with the Planetts wholy overspread / I thought my earthlie partes transformed divine" (Quoted from Bodleian Library, MS. Mus. Sch. d. 237, fol. 11). The verses on alchemy (Bodleian Library, MS Ashmole 1445, vii, 11–12), attributed to him in Cooper's *Athenae Cantabrigienses,* were written by George Brooke of Norton, Cheshire. See McKeen, 166, n. 3. It is most unlikely that George Brooke of Norton was the dedicatee of Weelkes. See David Brown, *Thomas Weelkes. A Biographical and Critical Study* (London: Faber and Faber, 1969), 20, 96.

177. His biography, though still incompletely known, can be pieced together from the entries in *DNB* and in *The History of Parliament* (1981), ed. P. W. Hasler; Gerald E. Bentley, *The Jacobean and Caroline Stage,* IV (1968); William Ingram, *A London Life in the Brazen Age: Francis Langley 1548–1602* (Cambridge: Harvard University Press, 1978); and William Ingram, "The Closing of the Theatres in 1597: A Dissenting View," *Modern Philology* 69 (1971): 105–15.

178. On his homosexuality see Alan Bray, *Homosexuality in Renaisance England* (London: Gay Men's Press, 1982), 70, and Bruce R. Smith, *Homosexual Desire in Shakespeare's England. A Cultural Poetics* (Chicago: University of Chicago Press, 1991), 178. Thomas Stanley, in all likelihood, was an Inns-of-Court acquaintance of Ashley's.

179. At least five La Fountaines are eligible. Guillaume (William), Clement, Peter, Nicholas, Erasmus (de la) Fountayne (Fountaine) are recorded between 1598 and 1602 in Kirk, *Returns of Aliens,* 2, 12, 34, 66, 68, 81, 85, 87, 88, 109, 111.

180. The legal form for sexual intercourse was "to know a woman"; the ecclesiastical term "to occupy a woman."

181. The quote is taken from Archer, *The Pursuit of Stability,* 229. Sir John Popham's integrity as a judge and projector did not go unnoticed by Ben Jonson, who seems to have satirized Popham's greed in *The Devil Is an Ass* (1616). Julie Sanders argues that Sir Paul Eitherside's involvement in the financial venturing and the projections of Meercraft and Lady Tailbush is probably a take-off of Sir John Popham's unpopular undertaking and projection of fen drainage in Somerset and Cambridgeshire in 1605. See Julie Sanders, "A Parody of Lord Chief Justice Popham in *The Devil Is an Ass,*" *Notes and Queries* 44 (1997): 528–30.

182. On Jane Trosse and on rebellion in other bridewells see Griffiths, 49, and Beier, 168.

183. James Sheppard, the most famous criminal of the eighteenth century besides Dick Turpin, made his spectacular escape from Newgate prison through the chimney. For the broadsheet illustrating his escape made on 15 October 1724 see Gerald Howson, *Thief-Taker General. The Rise and Fall of Jonathan Wild* (London: Hutchinson, 1970), plate 10.

184. On the relief work for prostitutes see Ruth Mazo Karras, "The Regulation of Brothels in Later Medieval England," *Signs* 14 (1989): 399–432.

185. G. R. Elton, "Introduction: Crime and the Historian" in *Crime in England 1550–1800,* ed. J. S. Cockburn (London: Methuen, 1977), 1–14.

186. For the text see Edward Doughtie, "George Handford's *Ayres:* Unpublished Jacobean Song Verse," *Anglia* 82 (1964), 474–84, and *Lyrics from English Airs 1596–1622* (Cambridge, Mass.: Harvard University Press, 1970), 304–14. There is a biographical entry by Diana Poulton in *The New Grove Dictionary of Music and Musicians,* ed. Stanley Sadie. The original MS is at Trinity College, Cambridge, shelfmark R.16.29.

187. On the song of repentance and its form see Elizabeth Garke, *The Use of Songs in Elizabethan Prose Fiction* (Berne: Francke Verlag, 1972), 52–53.

188. On Talboys Dymoke's Summer Lord games see C. L. Barber, *Shakespeare's Festive Comedy. A Study of Dramatic Form and Its Relation to Social Custom* (Princeton, 1959), chap. 3, and Norreys Jephson O'Conor, *Godes Peace and the Queenes. Vicissitudes of a House 1539–1615* (London: Oxford University Press, 1934), part 6.

189. See Jeayes, *Letters of Philip Gawdy,* 99.

190. Quoted from The Arden Shakespeare, 1.3.122–24. On Sir Andrew Aguecheek's missing qualities as a reveller and lover see Gustav Ungerer, "Sir Andrew Aguecheek and His Head of Hair," *Shakespeare Studies* 16 (1983): 101–33

191. Leslie Hotson, *The First Night of Twelfth Night* (London, 1954, rpt. 1961, 1977), chap 5, p. 106.

192. For more information on Mary Fitton and the speculation about her identity as the Dark Lady of Shakespeare's sonnets see Sidney Lee's entry in the *DNB;* Charlotte Carmichael Stopes, *The Life of Henry, Third Earl of Southampton, Shakespeare's Patron* (Cambridge: Cambridge University Press, 1922), chap. 16; Ivor Brown, *The Women in Shakespeare's Life* (London: The Bodley Head, 1968), chap. 11; A. L. Rowse, *The Elizabethan Renaissance. The Life of the Society* (London: Macmillan,

1971), 51–54; S. Schoenbaum, "Shakespeare's Dark Lady: A Question of Identity" in *Shakespeare's Styles. Essays in Honour of Kenneth Muir,* ed. Philip Edwards et al. (Cambridge: Cambridge University Press, 1980), 221–39.

193. See the review of Hotson's book by William T. Hastings in *Shakespeare Quarterly* 6 (1955): 128–29; Josephine Waters Bennet, "Topicality and the Date of the Court Production of *Twelfth Night*", *South Atlantic Quarterly* 71 (1972): 473–79. Roger Warren and Stanley Wells in their Oxford ed. of the play (1994) still hold Mary Fitton as the likeliest target for the allusion.

194. For the listing of internal evidence and topical allusions substantiating the suggestion that Shakespare wrote the play in the course of 1601 see Stanley Wells and Gary Taylor, *William Shakespeare, A Textual Companion* (Oxford, 1987), 123. For a critical discussion of the date see The Arden Shakespeare (1975), xxvi–xxxv.

195. See Robert Parker Sorlien (ed.), *The Diary of John Manningham of the Middle Temple, 1602–1603. Newly Edited in Complete and Unexpurgated Form from the Original Manuscript in the British Museum* (Hanover, NH: The University Press of New England, 1976), 312–13.

196. G. P. V. Akrigg has taken the presence of Sir John Popham for granted. See his note "*Twelfth Night* at the Middle Temple," *Shakespeare Quarterly* 9 (1958): 422–24. In July 1601, Sir John Popham had taken great pains to bring about a reconciliation between Richard Martin, the Prince d'Amour of the 1597/98 revels, and John Davies, who had been made fun of as Stradilax because of his awkward carriage and clumsy gait. On 30 October, the society of The Middle Temple and Sir John Popham in person accepted Davies's apology for having assaulted his old friend Martin. On their quarrel, Davies's expulsion, and reconciliation see Robert Krueger and Ruby Nemser's Introduction to *The Poems of Sir John Davies* (Oxford, 1975).

197. The debate about the identity of "Mistress Mall" has also focused on Mary Frith, commonly called Moll Cutpurse. But Mary Frith simply does not qualify as a candidate. As I have shown in an essay to appear in volume 28 of *Shakespeare Studies,* she began her career as a pickpocket about 1600, and her notoriety as a cross-dressed indoor and outdoor popular entertainer, who was playing on her lute and singing bawdy songs while working hand in glove with a gang of pickpockets, reached a peak as late as 1611. For the dispute over the identification waged by nineteenth-century editors and critics of the play see the New Variorum, ed. Horace Howard Furness (New York: J. B. Lippincott, 1901), 49–50.

198. Henk Gras in "*Twelfth Night, Every Man Out Of His Humour,* and the Middle Temple Revels of 1597–98," *Modern Language Review* 84 (1989): 545–64, argues that Shakespeare's comedy was written with a Middle Temple performance in mind, which, of course, does not mean that the play was exclusively written for an Inns-of-Court audience. The leading Middle Temple wits were the following lawyers: Richard Martin (The Prince d'Amour), John Hoskyns, rhetorician, Benjamin Rudyerd, editor of the printed revels, and John Davies, poet. In his study *Shakespeare and the Prince of Love. The Feast of Misrule in the Middle Temple* (London: Giles de la Mare, 2000), Anthony Arlidge, a barrister of the Middle Temple, makes the same point as Henk Gras. The essay of Gras is a powerfully argued piece of scholarship unknown to Arlidge, whose study turns out to be a painstaking but unconvincing compilation of circumstantial evidence in support of the theory that *Twelfth Night* was conceived as an Inns-of-Court play and saw its première in Middle Temple Hall on 2 February 1602.

199. See Philip Finkelpearl, *John Marston of the Middle Temple. An Elizabethan Dramatist and His Social Setting* (Cambridge, Mass., 1969). To what extent mock academic learing, linguistic misrule, double entendres, scatology, and mock encomia were poured into the Inns-of-Court Revels can be gathered from W. R. Elton's magisterial study *Shakespeare's "Troilus and Cressida" and the Inns of Court Revels* (Aldershot: Ashgate, 2000).

200. Henry Helmes, *Gesta Grayorum,* ed. W. W. Greg, The Malone Society Reprints, 41 (Oxford, 1915), 12.

201. Ibid, pp. 49–50. The naval imagery prevalent in the Gray's Inn and Middle Temple revels of 1594/95, resp. 1597/98, is strongly redolent with sexual double entendres which spilled over into the naval imagery of *Twelfth Night.*

202. Rudyerd (ed.), *Le Prince d'Amour,* 30.

203. For Lucy Morgan's biography see Leslie Hotson, *Mr. W. H.* (London, 1964), chap. 11. She had been committed to Bridewell for the nth time prior to 5 January 1601. See CLRO, Repertory Books of the Council of Aldermen, vol. 25, fol.29, session of 5 January.

204. Mrs. Baynam, the most prominent bawd in the 1570s, had also been called Black Luce of Clerkenwell. See Archer, 231; Paul Griffiths, *Youth and Authority: Formative Experience in England 1560–1640* (Oxford: Clarendon Press, 1996), 161.

205. On Antonio Cavallino and anti-Petrarchism in bawdy literature see David O. Frantz, *Festum Voluptatis. A Study of Renaissance Erotica* (Columbus: Ohio State University Press, 1989), 101–4, and chap.5. The women in Aretino's *Sonetti Iussuriosi* (Sonnets of Lust), written in 1524), are prostitutes. See Frantz, 47–57.

206. On the Dark Lady and the ever-increasing catalogue of identifications see Marvin Hunt, "Be Dark but Not Too Dark. Shakespeare's Dark Lady as a Sign of Colour," ed. James Schiffer in *Shakespeare's Sonnets. Critical Essays* (New York: Garland Publishing, 1999), 369–89. I cannot endorse the latest hypothesis that Shakespeare's Dark Lady may have been an African beauty even though there were many more African women working in late Elizabethan households than is currently known to scholars. I will address, in a forthcoming article, the presence of blackamoor slaves in Tudor households abroad (in Spain) and at home and in foreign households in Elizabethan London.

207. Imtiaz Habib in the first chapter of his ideologically trenchant study *Shakespeare and Race. Postcolonial Praxis in the Early Modern Period* (Lanham: University Press of America, 2000) argues that "a historical black woman such as Lucy Negro represents, among competing contemporary scholarly claims, a compelling possibility from a postcolonial standpoint of being the woman mentioned in the poems" (pp. 11–13, 23 ff). Lucy Negro, however, was a real-life white woman.

Leaning Too Hard Upon the Pen: Suburb Wenches and City Wives in *Westward Ho*

MICHELLE M. DOWD

NEAR the end of his *Points of Housewifery* (1573), Thomas Tusser offers the following advice to housewives:

> Ill housewifery moveth with gossip to spend.
> Good housewifery loveth her household to
> tend.
>
> Ill housewifery wanteth with spending too fast
> Good housewifery canteth the lenger to last.

(SigX2^v)

Tusser's rhyming couplets wittily capture his attempt to define housewifery. Using the rhetorical technique of antithesis, Tusser separates housewifery into "ill" and "good" varieties. He clearly connects and good housewife with frugality (her ability to "cant" or portion out supplies) and a desire to remain at home. The bad housewife, on the other hand, gossips, strays outside the home, and spends away the family resources. In his attempt to define the good housewife, Tusser exposes his own concerns about the proper enclosure and proper spending habits of wives, topics that garnered attention from numerous early modern conduct writers and moralists.

Writers such as Tusser, Richard Braithwaite, Gervase Markham, and William Gouge set out guidelines for proper housewifery that were tailored to their specific audiences. In *The English Housewife* (1615), Markham directed his eminently practical advice toward wealthier rural wives who would have had households of servants to run. Braithwaite also writes for a wealthy rural audience in *The English Gentlewoman* (1631), though he gives much more attention than does Markham to the socialite woman concerned with fashion and manners. Gouge, perhaps the most popular of the conduct writers, wrote for both the gentry and the literate middling sort, but the key difference between his *Of Domestical Duties* (1622) and the works of Markham and Braithwaite was its specifically urban audience. A minister in London's

Blackfriars district, Gouge aimed his sermons and writings at those living in London's vibrant market economy.

Like Gouge, I wish to turn my attention to London as a specific urban site where "ill" and "good" housewifery could be defined, negotiated, and acted out. Scholars have long been interested in London as central to the political, economic, and cultural life of early modern England. However, recently critics have been focusing more particularly on the urban history of London and its market economy. The essays in A. L. Beier and Roger Finlay's *London 1500–1700: The Making of the Metropolis* (1986) analyze the specific consequences of London's population growth, commercial centralization, and changes in the social landscape. Lena Cowen Orlin's *Material London, ca. 1600* (2000) presents essays that demonstrate the many specific ways in which London became the "English national lodestone" at the turn of the seventeenth century (3).

The same economic changes that made London the "national lodestone" also had dramatic impact on urban housewives and their connections to the market. By 1600, the decline of home production and the increasing presence of a domestic market meant that English families were becoming more dependent on goods produced outside the home.[1] The increased demand that this dependence created, combined with the mercantile expansion of the period, led to a rise in imports, including luxury goods.[2] As Joan Thirsk has demonstrated, the seventeenth century offered English consumers a much wider selection of goods than had the sixteenth century. Although the rise in imports and home markets was a gradual one, English consumers could notice a significant increase in the number of available goods as early as 1600.

This increase in goods altered the nature of the urban housewife's tasks. A wife of the middling sort would have needed to be proficient in housewifery, the performance of basic but labor-intensive household tasks such as baking, managing the household, and making clothes for family members.[3] Of course she would also be having babies and taking care of children. However, wealthier urban wives would also have been expected to be proficient in consumption. Wealthier middling households in London contained an increasingly wide range of household goods, including status items such as fine linens or table cloths.[4] Natasha Korda in her work on women and consumerism in the early modern period emphasizes the increased purchasing power of urban wives:

> [w]ith the decline of the family as an economic unit of production . . . the role of the housewife in late sixteenth-century England was beginning to shift from that of skilled producer to savvy consumer . . . The housewife's duties were thus gradually moving away from the production of use-values within and for the home and toward the consumption of market goods, or cates, commodities produced outside the home.[5]

The city housewife in this period thus had more frequent access to money and purchasing power than was previously true.

I am interested in the ways in which the urban housewife as consumer became a fixture not just in London, but on the London stage. Where conduct writers like Tusser and Gouge set out prescriptive guidelines for early modern women to follow, London's flourishing entertainment industry spun new ideas about women and money into dramatic narratives. The London theater presented vivid illustrations of both the pleasures and dangers of "ill housewifery" and the different ways in which "good housewifery" could be acted out. The housewifery that conduct manuals prescribed could come alive with more variety and pleasure on the early modern stage. Of course, some early modern plays were more concerned with women and housewifery than were others. Appearing on London stages first around 1598, city comedies took as their main focus the activities of the urban middling sort and concerns about economics and sexuality in London.[6] Particular attention to urban middling women, including their practice of housewifery, was likewise more sustained in city comedies than it had been in the romantic comedies and history plays common on public stages in the 1590s.[7]

At its inception, city comedy showed concern for the difficulties of regulating female sexual and economic activity in an urban context. William Haughton's *Englishmen For My Money* (1598), perhaps the earliest English city comedy, dramatizes the wayward activities of three daughters of a wealthy Portuguese merchant living in London. The play frequently conflates the sexual desire and transactions of the daughters with economic exchange. Their three English suitors indeed seek marriage with the daughters in part to erase the debt they owe to the girls' father, Pisaro; the sex act does literal economic work in this text. Though the three daughters do take action on their own behalf, the plot is largely driven by the plans of the English male suitors and their friend Anthony, who uses the guise of schoolmaster to serve as pander. And though the daughters participate in sexual and economic machinations throughout the play, the text does not show us their activities once they become wives. Haughton's play is interested in maids, not housewives, and in the manipulations of courtship, not the work of housewifery.

Thomas Dekker's *The Shoemaker's Holiday* (1599) shifts the focus to a citizen wife, and one, moreover, centrally concerned with both production and consumption. If the women of *Englishmen For My Money* are largely contained in patriarchal exchange, Margery is allowed more scope in her economic activities. Wife to Simon Eyre, Margery both works in her husband's shoemaking shop and buys status items, such as a French hood. But Margery's consumption, her desire for the trappings of the middling wife, is viciously satirized in the play; the servants poke fun at her eagerness to "enlarge her bum" with new fashions (10.35–57). Concerns about the troublesome nature of Eyre's quick rise in status get displaced on to Margery and her spending habits. Margery is not a site of anxiety about wayward female sexuality in the way that Pisaro's daughters are, but the ridicule that accompanies her economic pretensions introduces to city comedy a new anxiety about women who have money to spend.

By the time Ben Jonson wrote *Volpone* in 1606, city comedies had a more dense focus on a nexus of issues, including urban wives and their spending habits. In Jonson's play, Celia, wife to the merchant Corvino, throws her handkerchief down to Volpone, disguised as a mountebank, in order to "buy" the potion that he is selling. Furious, Corvino locks her up, complains that she is easily distracted by trinkets, and accuses her of being a whore. He even punishes her open sexuality by allowing her only "backwards" pleasure, or anal sex (2.5.61). In this play, the (mute) economic exchange that Celia makes exposes her to direct attacks on her chastity. At least in Corvino's mind, public spending sprees open the doorway for illicit sexual sprees. And though *Volpone* ultimately exonerates Celia, while *Shoemaker* persists in satirizing Margery, it nevertheless holds out to the audience a titillating moment of female economic and sexual self-assertion.

Thomas Dekker and John Webster's *Westward Ho* (1604) takes this titillating moment and shapes an entire plot around it. Like *Volpone* and *Shoemaker*, *Westward Ho* draws attention to spending habits of urban wives. Indeed, unlike many other city plays, including *Shoemaker*, *Westward Ho* presents wives who seems to do nothing but spend; they do not participate in productive labor in their husband's shops or elsewhere. The wives of *Westward Ho* also spend much more time onstage than do city wives in other plays; they are not only the play's main characters, but they are also allowed unusual freedom in the text to roam around London and even beyond its walls. For a female spectator, this freedom could have offered the titillating pleasure of housewifery gone wrong, while at the same time offering male and female spectators alike an anxious caution about female economic control. *Westward Ho* offers both unusual pleasures and an unusually sustained focus on typical city comedy fears about women and money; as such, it is a prime site from which to begin an investigation into the ideological representation of housewives in city comedy.

In what follows I will argue that *Westward Ho* offers the reader or spectator a seductive yet cautionary fantasy about urban women and their purchasing power in early modern England. Such power, within the logic of this play, allows these wives to escape the patriarchal confines of the family and pursue illicit desire in the suburbs. However, the freedom that money allows these wives is ultimately disciplined by the wives' own self-regulation. As I will argue, *Westward Ho*, unlike some other city comedies such as *Every Man in His Humor* (1598), *Volpone*, and *Chaste Maid in Cheapside* (1613), eschews physical force as a means of restricting its wayward female characters. Drawing on work by Norbert Elias and Michel Foucault, by contrast, I will argue that *Westward Ho* dramatizes the emergence of the self-disciplined middling subject in early modern England. And though Dekker and Webster's text cannot be read as a direct means of access to the real lives of early modern women, it can offer us access at the level of representation to the illicit pleasure associated with female mobility and buying power and to real anxieties about this freedom.[8]

In the main plot of *Westward Ho,* Mistress Honeysuckle, Mistress Wafer and Mistress Tenterhook, three citizen wives, develop elaborate schemes in an effort to escape their husbands and homes in London and to rendezvous with a group of gallants in Brainford. Meanwhile, Justiniano, an Italian merchant, has spread a rumor that he is in dire financial trouble, and he believes that his wife will soon give her sexual services to an old, but wealthy, earl. Justiniano decides to disguise himself as a schoolmaster and assist the wayward wives; by doing so he hopes to force their husbands into the same position that he finds himself. The plots that Justiniano and the three women concoct are often contingent upon the ability of these wives to take control of money and to use it as they wish. For example, in act 2, Justiniano attempts to convince Mistress Honeysuckle to join Mistress Wafer and Mistress Tenterhook and to meet one of the gallants, Sir Gosling Glowworm, in the Steelyard. When she asks, "What excuse shall I coyne now?", he replies:

> Fewh! excuses: You must to the pawne to buy Lawne: to Saint Martins for Lace; to the Garden: to the Glass-house; to your Gossips: to the Powlters: else take out an old ruffle, and go to your Sempsters: excuses? Why, they are more ripe than medlers at Christmas. (2.1.213–18)[9]

Here Justiniano suggests several possible "excuses" that a city wife's normal shopping routine could provide for sexual rendezvous. He includes shopping for luxury items (lawn, lace) alongside more basic items (poultry). These wives clearly have regular access to money, which they use to buy both provisions and status items. However, such access potentially poses a danger to the patriarchal family. As Korda has argued, a wife's consumption and management of household property could become "potentially threatening to the symbolic order of things".[10] That is, a wife's managerial skills could give her partial control over the family economy, which could in turn seem to threaten traditional household order. *Westward Ho* dramatizes such fears about wifely control of money; Justiniano in effect suggests that the wives misuse their purchasing power as shoppers to provide an excuse for sexual misconduct. As we will continue to see, this manipulation of their purchasing power takes the women outside of family structures and, eventually, outside of the city itself.

The wives' purchasing power also allows them to buy sex more directly through the act of writing. Mistress Honeysuckle and Mistress Wafer first come to Mistress Tenterhook to announce, "we are come to acquaint thee with an excellent secret: we two learne to write" (1.2.120–21). Though reading skills seem to have been shared fairly equally between early modern men and women, women were far less likely to know how to write.[11] As Amy Erickson has demonstrated, the prevalence of reading-only literary in women began with the education of young girls, who often left school to work in the household before age six or seven, when writing was usually taught.[12] Thus, though it is likely that the three wives learned to read in their childhood, it is hardly surprising that they do not know how to write. Learning to write in adulthood could very well have been a common, even desirable activity for the wives of city merchants. As Erickson also notes, the inability to write "may . . . have hindered the ability of marketwomen or shopkeepers to keep track of customer's debt and credit, and of women in general to transact exchanges which involved written instruments."[13] Learning to write could allow city wives to participate directly in their husbands' businesses.

However, women who handled "written instruments" were often accused of handling sexual "instruments." Eve Sanders notes that the "eroticization of female writing" resulted in the assumption that women who knew how to write were "likely to engage in illicit affairs."[14] Because they focused attention on the pen/penis pun, dramatic representations of women's writing held out the possibility of sexual, as well as textual, misconduct. Mistress Honeysuckle underscores this possibility when she describes "Parenthesis," the writing master: "thou mayest send him of any arrant, and trust him with any secret; nay, to see how demurely he will beare himselfe before our husbands, and how jocund when their backes are turn'd" (1.2.125–28). Like Anthony in *Englishmen for My Money,* who served as both schoolmaster and pander, Parenthesis explicitly links the purchasing of writing as a skill with the sexual deception of husbands "when their backes are turn'd."

Mistress Honeysuckle is not the only one to recognize this connection. In one of the most memorable and humorous scenes of the play, Justiniano and Master Honeysuckle exchange loaded sexual comments when they discuss Mistress Honeysuckle's writing abilities:

Hony. And how does my wife profit under you sir? hope you to do any good upon her?
Just. Maister *Honisuckle* I am in great hope shee shall fructify: I will do my best for my part: I can do no more than another man can.
Hony. Pray sir ply her, for she is capable of any thing.
Just. So far as my poore tallent can stretch, It shall not be hidden from her.
Hony. Does she hold her pen well yet?
Just. She leanes somewhat too hard uppon her pen yet sir, but practise and animadversion will breake her from that.

(2.1.69–79)

Justiniano gloats about his own "poor talent," but it is clear (perhaps all too clear to Justiniano) that the true sexual prowess belongs to Mistress Honeysuckle. Her writing abilities are here comically rewritten as sexual abilities. Justiniano's description of Mistress Honeysuckle's leaning "too hard upon her pen" wryly emphasizes her sexual prowess as well as her developing writing skills. Mistress Honeysuckle herself asks Justiniano, "have you a new pen for mee Maister, for by my troth, my old one is stark naught, and will cast no inck" (2.1.121–22). Fully aware of the pen/penis pun, she uses the language of writing to suggest illicit sexual desire. For the three citizen wives, money and leisure buy writing skills, and writing skills open up sexual possibilities. Women's writing figuratively represents sexual promiscuity, but Justiniano as Parenthesis also physically enables these wives to leave the city and their husbands' control. The link between consumer power and illicit sexuality is thus not merely figurative but also clearly instrumental in this play. The city wives' mastery of language provides the urban audience with a titillating hint of female sexual mastery, but it at the same time literalizes the feared "eroticization of female writing" and reveals an underlying anxiety about women and money in the urban environment.

Writing is only one of the skills that the three wives are able to purchase as they plan their escape from London. While gossiping about their husbands, Mistress Wafer tells the others that her husband would like her to breast-feed her youngest child rather than hire a wet nurse. Mistress Honeysuckle calls this unfortunate request "the policy of husbands to keepe their Wives in" (1.2.116–17). In fact, she gladly provides specific details of the cosmetic effects of breast-feeding on women's breasts to buttress her claim against Master Wafer: "I doe assure you if a Woman of any markeable face in the Worlde give her Childe sucke, looke how many wrinckles be in the Nipple of her breast, so many will bee in her forheade by that time twelve moneth" (2.1.117–20).

The debate between Wafer and his wife over breast-feeding is a fictional rendition of a very real debate during the early modern period. As Valerie Fildes has demonstrated, religious and humanist discourses encouraged maternal breast-feeding, though in practice, "women with any status in society rarely breastfed their own children".[15] Wet nursing was an explicitly class-coded choice; only those families "with any status" could afford the luxury.

Though Mistress Wafer disobeys her husband, her refusal to breast-feed simultaneously marks her submission to the dictates of the wealthy patriarchal family. As Dorothy McLaren has demonstrated, the contraceptive effects of lactation and the general taboo against sexual intercourse during lactation meant that lower-class women who *had* to breast-feed reduced their fertility, often resulting in smaller families. Upper-class women who hired wet nurses often found themselves facing more pregnancies and more of the risks associated with pregnancy, including infant and mother mortality.[16] Thus Mistress

Wafer's decision seems to indicate that she will continue to produce babies for the Wafer family, returning herself immediately to sexual relations with her husband and guaranteeing her family's lineage.

But her decision simultaneously indicates that she will be able to maintain a degree of personal freedom. She will be able to travel outside of the home to socialize and to purchase goods at the marketplace. Gail Paster writes: "To make herself [the mother] totally available to nurse an infant on demand—the most common form of breast-feeding in the period—was to remove herself from social circulation, and to risk the premature aging and wrinkling that was commonly associated with suckling."[17] These are the exact same complaints that preoccupy Mistress Wafer and the other wives: the "wrinkles . . . in the nipple of her breast" and the "policy of husbands to keep their wives in." Elizabeth Clinton, in *The Countesse of Lincolnes Nurserie* (1622) specifically describes these complaints as indicative of "unmotherly affection, idlenesse, desire to have liberty to gadd from home, pride, foolish finenesse, lust, wantonnesse, & the like evils" (13). For Clinton, the decision to hire a wet nurse signifies illicit sexual desire and a rejection of traditional family roles. Thomas Tusser's *Points of Housewifery* even makes explicit the link between hiring a wet nurse and being a spendthrift. Tusser writes: "But one thing I warn thee, let housewife be nurse, / least husband do find thee too frank with his purse" (W4). These same fears about illicit sexuality and immoderate spending underscore Webster and Dekker's narrative. By refusing to breast-feed, Mistress Wafer mitigates her own reproductive function in the family. But instead of staying home and producing more babies, she rejects the confines of her home and the licit sexuality of the marriage bed. That is, Mistress Wafer gets to have it both ways; she alienates herself both from breast-feeding and from her reproductive function in the family. Her ability to purchase a wet nurse buys her own freedom from household enclosure, the freedom to pursue illicit pleasure outside of London.

Mistress Wafer also uses her purchasing power to facilitate the trip to Brainford, allowing all of the wives to escape the confines of London. In act 2, scene 3, we learn that the child has been sent out of London to a wet nurse. The wives devise a "clenly excuse" and decide to pretend that the Wafer child is sick and that they must go and visit it at the nurse's home. They thus gain an excuse to leave London without arousing their husbands' suspicion (2.3.79–111). The nursing child becomes plot device; the "policy of husbands to keepe their Wives in" is dramatically overturned. The women make use of the wet nurse to help themselves get out—both out of London and out of their individual families. Mistress Wafer's decision suggests that consumer power can enable wives to absent themselves from reproductive sexuality, pursue illicit desire, and evade traditional household duties. Anxiety about female control accompanies the sense of joyful escape that the scene provides; the wives are essentially able to buy themselves illicit sexuality, thereby turning sex into a market commodity seemingly no different from onions or eggs.

Possessing money and wit thus allows the three wives of *Westward Ho* to remove themselves from patriarchal control. Through these characters, Dekker and Webster cautiously acknowledge the dangers posed by urban wives who have control of money. But the three wives are not the only women in the play who involve themselves in economic transactions, nor are they the only ones who control financial resources. Mistress Justiniano contemplates betraying her husband for an explicitly economic reason: she thinks that he is bankrupt. In despair, she asks him:

> What would you have me do? all your plate and most part of your Jewels are at pawne, besides I heare you have made over all your estate to men in the Towne heer? What would you have me do? would you have mee turne common sinner, or sell my apparell to my wastcoat and become a Landresse? (1.1.175–79)

Instead of turning "common sinner," Mistress Justiniano decides to offer her sexual services to a rich earl.[18] In this case, her act of prostitution is driven, in her understanding, by acute financial need. She acts out of a position of financial dependence, while the play's other city wives act out of positions of consumer control.

The character that links these two positions is Birdlime, the bawd. Birdlime appears throughout the play as the wives' ally and as their go-between for sexual liaisons; she introduces Mistress Justiniano to the earl, and she helps arrange for Mistress Tenterhook's rendezvous with Monopoly. She is also fully aware that money buys power. In the first scene, she suggests that city wives' control of money allows them to trick their husbands. She tells the tailor that city wives "have as pure Linnen, as choyce painting," as wealthy ladies, but that ladies learn from city wives how to "awe their Husbands, to check their Husbands, to controule their husbands" (1.1.27, 31–32). Birdlime argues that the upward mobility of city wives, their ability to afford the same goods that wealthy ladies buy, informs their ability to manipulate their husbands. This bold claims underscores the play's anxieties about women and purchasing power; Birdlime verbalizes the implicit threat of the three wives.

In her own right, Birdlime is a threatening figure because she is never enclosed in a patriarchal household. As a bawd, she not only sells sexual transactions, but she works as a brothel keeper, a sexual entrepreneur.[19] When Sir Gosling Glowworm asks her on the way to Brainford, "how many of my name . . . have paid for your gurr'd Gownes, thou Womans broker," she responds, "No Sir, I scorne to bee beholding to any Glo-worme that lives uppon Earth for my furre: I can keep my selfe warme without Glowormes" (5.3.42–46). Birdlime highlights her financial independence, her ability to keep herself "warme." As a brothel keeper, Birdlime demonstrates how a woman

could exist as an entrepreneur, a *feme sole* in a market economy. Because of
her status, she gets to enjoy the power, mobility, and control over access to
female sexuality that accompany the role of entrepreneur, a luxury that a simple prostitute like Luce, who works for Birdlime, does not have. As bawd and
brothel keeper, Birdlime explicitly offers sex as a commodity that can be
bought and sold.

However, Birdlime is also a midwife. She does not simply sell sex; she is
intimately involved with the reproductive consequences of sexual activity,
just as the citizen wives are. In act 2, scene 3, we find Mistress Wafer defending Birdlime's reputation to Sir Gosling. When he asks, "Zounds whats she?
a Bawd, bith Lord Ist not?" Mistress Wafer replies, "No indeed, Sir *Gozlin,*
shees a very honest woman, and a Mid-wife" (2.3.118–20). Later Birdlime
herself says that she is "going to a womans labour" (2.3.128). whether or not
we take Birdlime's claim at face value, and despite the fact that historians
such as Cressy argue that "[M]ost midwives were respectable married women
or widows . . .",[20] we should recognize the associations that contemporaries
did draw between midwives, bawds, and witches, at the level of representation.[21] Regardless of its historical accuracy, the ideological link between
bawd and midwife is explicit in *Westward Ho.*

Birdlime as both bawd and midwife links two kinds of women's labor in
this play: the sex act that Birdlime sells and the pregnancy and birth that the
wives must endure. But she also occupies a precarious space between consumer power and financial powerlessness. She takes control of the activities
of Luce and Mistress Justiniano, who finds themselves at the bottom of the
financial ladder. However, she also sells sex and midwife services to others,
in contrast to the three city wives who are in a position to buy sex and reproductive services (such as wet nursing) from others. The class difference here
is crucial; the wives' control of money allows them to buy Birdlime's services, but she does not seem to have reciprocal control over the wives.
Though the wives' activities at times come dangerously close to prostitution,
they do not actually sell their own sexual services for money. Indeed, when
Mistress Tenterhook arranges to have Monopoly arrested by Ambush and
leaves "two Diamonds . . . worth two hundred pound" with Ambush so that
she can take Monopoly "alittle Way out of Town," she essentially purchases
his sexual services (3.4.33–35). Here it is Monopoly, the earl's high-ranking
but impoverished nephew, who prostitutes himself out of financial need. Monopoly, like Luce and Mistress Justiniano, seeks sex because of need; the
three citizen wives seek sex because of desire. Birdlime is able to align herself with both of these positions.

Birdlime does not have the same relationship to sex and money that the
wives do, but she nevertheless facilitates their fully funded desires and serves
as a reminder that *all* services can be bought and sold. This, I would argue,
explains her promiscuity in this text. By promiscuity I mean both her sexual-

ity and her physical pervasiveness in the play. She is the first figure to speak onstage, and she takes part in both of the play's plots, the city wives plot and the Earl/Mistress Justiniano plot. That is, her sexual promiscuity requires her textual promiscuity. By professionalizing sexuality, she fully enacts the commercialization of sex that the city wives merely suggest.

The consumer fantasy that Birdlime facilitates and that the three citizen wives initially desire does not actually materialize in the play. Though the wives' control of money has put them in a position to either buy or sell sex, in the end they do neither. Instead, they decide to refuse the gallants in time to humiliate their own husbands by their virtuous behavior. Mistress Tenterhook tells the other wives that "the Jest shall be a stock to maintain us and our pewfellowes in laughing at christnings, cryings out, and upsittings this twelve month" (5.1.171–73). Instead of enjoying sexual pleasure with the gallants, these women plan to store up a "stock" of pleasure in stories that can last the entire year. However, the translation of actual activity into narrative diffuses the danger of Mistress Tenterhook's proposal. Though the women create an idealized female space through storytelling, the threatening potential of this space dwindles with its idealization. The wives have consciously decided to reduce their potentially threatening activities to a more easily contained act of storytelling. Dekker and Webster have converted action into narrative; the wives voluntarily choose to abandon the dangerous consumer fantasy of the play's first four acts.[22]

I would argue that this voluntary abandonment is a symptom of the consumer savvy that brought the wives out of their homes in the first place and a fulfillment of the self-regulation that the play ultimately advocates. These wives have the consumer power to buy themselves sexual services, yet they choose to practice thrift instead. Mistress Tenterhook enjoins the other wives, "tho we are merry, lets not be mad." When Mistress Wafer says, "[w]eele eate and drinke with em," Mistress Tenterhook responds:

> O yes: eate with em as hungerly as souldiers: drinke as if we were Froes: talke as freely as Jestors, but does as little as misers, who (like dry Nurses) have great breastes but give no milke . . . tho we lye all night out of the Citty, they shall not find country wenches of us: but since we ha brought em thus far into a fooles Paradice, leave em int. (5.1.164–71)

Tenterhook here compares the rejection of the gallants to the offering of a dry breast, an image that immediately recalls Mistress Wafer and her decision not to breast-feed. However, whereas Mistress Wafer's decision earlier signified her financial wantonness, here the women present themselves as frugal "misers" who control their bodily functions just as they control their finances.

In *The Mothers Counsell* (1630), one of the female-authored advice books that appeared in the first half of the seventeenth century, M.R. advises her reader to "keepe a narrow watch over your heart, words, and deeds continually," warning also that "[f]rugalitie is the stave of chastitie" (A3r, A4v). M.R.'s advice is very similar to that found in Tusser's *Points of Housewifery,* where he writes, "If thrift by that labor be honestly got, / then is it good housewifery, else it is not." (R4v) Both writers explicitly connect frugality with good and chaste housewifery. The wives in *Westward Ho* choose to follow this advice. They break the link between spending and wantonness by demonstrating that it is possible, at least at the level of representation, to spend money and still be in control of one's sexuality. Partly this involves a recognition on the wives' part that buying sex is indeed very different from buying onions or eggs. It is one thing to hire a wet nurse, it is quite another to buy sex. Mistress Wafer, for one, understands the "ground[s]" that accompany childbirth (3.3.64), and Mistress Tenterhook recognizes the difference between being "merry" and being "mad." In essence, the women prove themselves to be savvy sexual consumers; in the words of Monopoly, they have "savde themselves" (5.4.195). They freely choose to abandon their illicit sexual desires, and in so doing they demonstrate thrift and good housewifery, despite the warnings of the conduct manuals. Their self-disciplining is therefore directly related to their class position as citizen wives.

Norbert Elias argues in *The Civilizing Process* that the early modern period saw a gradual but clear change in people's behavior, what he terms the growth of "civilite." He writes that in the centuries following the Middle Ages, "with the structural transformation of society, with the new pattern of human relationships, a change slowly comes about: the compulsion to check one's own behavior increases."[23] Elias further reads the behavioral self-discipline that began to develop in the sixteenth century as a practice of class discipline that worked to distinguish the properly disciplined elite and middle classes from the improperly disciplined vulgar. In the second volume of *The Civilizing Process, Power and Civility,* Elias goes on to argue that individual self-control ultimately becomes an efficient mechanism of social regulation.[24]

Michel Foucault makes a similar argument in his famous section on Panopticism in *Discipline and Punish.* Foucault argues that the Benthamian Panopticon, a prison in which everything is exposed, creates a situation in which the prisoners become the agents of their own discipline. As he writes, "[h]e who is subjected to a field of visibility, and who knows it, assumes responsibility for the constrains of power; he makes them play spontaneously upon himself; he inscribes in himself the power relation in which he simultaneously plays both roles; he becomes the principle of his own subjection."[25] Self-discipline once again becomes an effective method of social control.

The self-discipline of the city wives in *Westward Ho* can thus be seen in light of the increasingly self-disciplined middling subject in early modern England. As Elias and Foucault suggest, proper social control in this play is most dramatically demonstrated by the wives' choice to discipline themselves. And though neither Elias nor Foucault speak at all about the way in which specifically *gendered* bodies are disciplined (see the proliferation of the word "he" in the Foucault passage I cited), *Westward Ho* dramatizes the ways in which self-discipline works to create a properly ordered body that is both citizen class *and* female. Further, as I have been arguing, the female citizen that self-discipline creates is clearly also a consumer. Frugality, as Tusser and M.R. suggest, thus becomes a key component of the self-disciplining of the early modern citizen wife.

The last scene of the play, however, reveals the fragility of this self-discipline. The witty aggressiveness of the wives throughout the play provides the audience with the illicit pleasure of wanton behavior, while simultaneously indicating that the wives could at any time break into new antics of subversiveness. Chastity and frugality are conscious choices; the wives could choose differently another time. Furthermore, their self-disciplining is only secure as long as their own class positions are secure. After the wives are reconciled with their husbands, Justiniano centers his attention on Birdlime and reveals her duplicitous activities. He describes Birdlime's operations within the city of London by saying: "Shee has tricks to keepe a vaulting house under the Lawes nose." Yet his description of these tricks is specifically class-inflected:

> For either a cunning woman has a Chamber in her house, or a Phisitian, or a picture maker, or an Attorney, because all these are good Clokes for the raine. And then if the party that's cliented above-Staires, be yong, Shees a Squires daughter of lowe degree, that lies there for phisicke, or comes up to be placed with a Countesse: if of middle age, shees a Widow, and has sutes at the terme or so. (5.4.257–66)

Justiniano's description of Birdlime highlights her ability to disguise whores as more respectable citizens, to use "good Clokes for the raine" to hide her unsavory business. But Justiniano also reveals to the three wives the dual role that Birdlime has been playing all along. That is, she has not only been assisting the wives, but she has been operating in her own right as a bawd on behalf of "female parties" that include Mistress Justiniano. By recognizing Birdlime's position as a *feme sole,* Justiniano confuses the power alignment the three wives assumed was operative. His revelation collapses the economic difference between Mistress Justiniano, who sought Birdlime's services because of financial need, and Mistress Tenterhook, who sought Birdlime's services as a consumer demand.[26] We might also recall that it is Birdlime who ultimately gets the "two Diamondes" that Mistress Tenterhook paid for Monopoly's release; she "save[s] the Gentlewomens credit" by taking possession of the diamonds that represent both sexual and financial control (4.1.229). The wives have less control over Birdlime than they initially thought, and this loss of control brings their actions dangerously close to prostitution. No wonder Mistress Tenterhook immediately tells Justiniano, "O, fie upon her, burne the witch, out of our company" (5.4.267).

Birdlime's class fluidity, her ability to negotiate between desire and need, threatens the wives' carefully won self-discipline by disrupting their own class positions. At the end of the play, this class fluidity gets physically mapped onto the city itself so that Birdlime can be literally removed from the scene. Justiniano tells Birdlime at the end of the play to "go, saile with the rest of your baudie-traffikers to the place of sixepenny Sinfulnesse the suburbes" (5.4.248–50). While Mistress Tenterhook exclaims, "[l]ets hem her out of *Brainford*, if shee get not the faster to *London*," Mistress Wafer quickly rejoins, "O no, for Gods sake, rather hem her out off *London* and let her keep in *Brainford* still" (5.4.268–71). That is, Justiniano and the wives eventually agree that Birdlime must remain outside the city proper, staying in the areas already acknowledged as sites of sexual vice. The city wives clearly distinguish themselves from "sub-burbe wenches," the term that Mistress Honeysuckle applies to women who dwell immediately outside of London's walls (5.1.114). With the line, "[q]uickly shall wee get to Land," the play's final song adds to the sense of hasty departure, and Justiniano further attempts to resolve the situation swiftly by calling it "but a merriment" and "all but a May-game" (5.4.278). He verbally substitutes the maypole dance, a heterosexual fertility festival, for the female activities that have dominated the play.[27]

But this hasty substitution is ultimately ineffectual. The phallic interference of the maypole can only be described as comically impotent; we are hardly likely to believe that the erotic escapades of the wives have been "all but a May-game." And even if we did take Justiniano at his word, Birdlime refuses the geographical separation that Justiniano and the wives propose. In doing so she brings to the forefront the problematic historical relationship between prostitution and city jurisdiction that existed at the beginning of the seventeenth century. Ruth Karras notes that an ordinance of 1393 attempted to "segregate whores, prohibiting them the city except for one street (Cock's Lane), banishing them to the areas of the stews or bathhouses in Southwark, outside the city proper."[28] Concern about this area and the connection between prostitution and crime led eventually to Henry VIII's closing of the stews in 1546.[29] This did not, of course, end prostitution, (and Edward VI later reinstated the stewhouses), but it arguably intensified the geographic problem and threat that prostitution posed. Further, as Wallace Shugg has noted, the appearance and great popularity of coaches by the early seventeenth century led to an increased mobility of prostitutes, who could now "range easily throughout the City and solicit customers at any public places".[30]

Ian Archer makes this point clear in *The Pursuit of Stability*. In his chapter on crime, Archer discusses prostitution in early modern London. He includes a map on which he locates bawdy houses in the period and marks their positions relative to the city walls.[31] Writing about this map he notes: "The unsavoury reputation enjoyed by areas like Clerkenwell, St. John's Street, Whitechapel, and Shoreditch is confirmed, but it is also striking just how many establishments operated within the supposedly much better governed areas under the City's jurisdiction."[32] Thus, when Birdlime responds to Justiniano by saying, "I scorne the Sinfulnesse of any suburbes in Christendom; tis well known I have up-rizers and downe-lyers within the Citty, night by night, like a prophane fellow as thou art . . . you cannot hem me out of *London*" (5.4.251–53, 272), she explicitly calls attention to the sexual fluidity of London's boundaries.[33] She refuses an easy geographical mapping of her own sexuality and the class threat that she poses to the wives as a *feme sole*; instead she serves as a living reminder that all services, including sex, can be bought and sold. Birdlime's rewriting of the map of London simultaneously reveals a sexual and a class fluidity that threaten the chastity and the economic stability of the city wives. In doing so it reveals the fragility of their self-discipline, suggesting that their consumer savvy is neither guaranteed nor predictable.

In *Westward Ho,* Dekker and Webster allow female spectators to flirt with the pleasures of "bad housewifery" while simultaneously cautioning those same spectators (and their male counterparts) about the potentially subversive effects of pleasures left unchecked. Though the play's end holds out the promise of female self-discipline and a return to order, the play also demonstrates that women are literally able to buy their way out of patriarchal control and that female self-discipline cannot always be counted on. By 1604, when the play was written, urban wives were increasingly expected to use their skills as consumers to provide goods for their households. The instability of the housewife's consumer role meant that she must use her consumer savvy to manage the household properly. However, Dekker and Webster create a fictional account in which women take this consumer savvy too far and use it to purchase the wrong goods. Though the wives ultimately choose sexual frugality and self-discipline, this containment is superficial and temporary at best. The urban wife may be able to discipline herself, but she nevertheless remains a potential threat to household order because she maintains purchasing power in the urban environment. Later city comedies will continue *Westward Ho*'s focus on economic and sexual self-regulation. In a play like Heywood's *The Fayre Mayde of the Exchange* (1607), the heroine, Phillis, both works in a shop in the Exchange and commissions a handkerchief in her attempt to attract a suitor. Phillis is at once productive, consumptive, and desiring, yet she is ultimately also self-regulating; she adjusts her desires to suit her parents' wishes and social decorum. Similarly, the excessive consumption of characters like Gertrude in *Eastward Ho* (1605) and the gossips in *Chaste Maid* (1613) are ridiculed, while self-restraint and thrift are championed. These later plays thus continue much of the ideological work done by *Westward Ho,* though Dekker and Webster's play arguably places greater emphasis on the seductive yet dangerous potential of the city wife. Economic resources combined with exceptional wit allow the wives of *Westward Ho* to evade traditional duties in the home and "gadd" about town with other women. And maybe tomorrow they will go ahead and add sex to their shopping lists immediately under butter and cheese.

Notes

Citations are derived from the following editions:

Richard Brathwait, *The English Gentlewoman* (London, 1631); Elizabeth Clinton, *The Countesse of Lincolnes Nurserie* vol. 720, *The English Experience* (Amsterdam: Walter J. Johnson, Inc., 1975); Thomas Dekker, *The Shoemaker's Holiday,* edited by A. Parr (London: A. & C. Black, 1990); Thomas Dekker and John Webster, *Westward Ho!* edited by F. Bowers, Vol. 2, *The Dramatic Works of Thomas Dekker* (Cambridge: Cambridge University Press, 1955); William Gouge, *Of Domestical Duties* (London, 1622); William Haughton, *Englishmen For My Money,* edited by A. C. Baugh (Philadelphia: University of Pennsylvania Press, 1917); Thomas Heywood, *The Fayre Mayde of the Exchange,* vol. 2, *The Dramatic Works of Thomas Heywood* (London: John Pearson, 1874); Ben Jonson, *Every Man in His Humour,* edited by R. N. Watson (London: A. & C. Black, 1998); Ben Jonson, *Volpone,* edited by P. Brockbank (London: A. & C. Black, 1997); Ben Jonson, George Chapman, and John Marston, *Eastward Ho!,* edited by C. G. Petter (London: Ernest Benn, 1973); Gervase Markham, *The English Housewife,* edited by M. R. Best (Kingston: McGill-Queene's University Press, 1986); Thomas Middleton, Thomas, *A Chaste Maid in Cheapside,* edited by A. Brissenden (London: A. & C. Black, 1997); M. R., *The Mothers Counsell Or, Live within Compasse* (London, 1630); Thomas Tusser, *Five Hundred points of good husbandry united to as many of good housewifery now lately augmented* (London, 1573).

    1. Robert Brenner, *Merchants and Revolution: Commercial Change, Political Conflict and London's Overseas Traders, 1550–1653* (Cambridge: Cambridge University Press, 1993), 40–41; Joan Thirsk, *Economic Policy and Projects: The Development of a Consumer Society in Early Modern England* (Oxford: Clarendon Press, 1978), 177.

    2. For England's mercantile expansion, see Karen Newman, *Fashioning Femininity and English Renaissance Drama* (Chicago: University of Chicago Press, 1991), 131–32, and Brenner, *Merchants and Revolution,* 39–50. For the increased desire for luxury goods, see Susan Cahn, *Industry of Devotion: The Transformation of Women's Work in England, 1500–1660.* (New York: Columbia University Press, 1987), 42–43.

    3. The "middling sort" is perhaps the best term we have to describe a very diverse and continually shifting group of people. For a good description and analysis of this group see Theodore B. Leinwand's, "Shakespeare and the Middling Sort," *Shakespeare Quarterly* 44.3 (1993): 284–303, especially 284–95. See also William Harris-

on's *Description of England* book 2, chapter 5, where he divides the English into four groups: "gentlemen, citizens or burgesses, yeomen, and artificers, or laborers." William Harrison, *The Description of England,* edited by G. Edelen (New York: Dover, 1994), 94.

4. Sara Mendelson and Patricia Crawford, *Women in Early Modern England 1550–1720* (Oxford: Clarendon Press, 1998), 307.

5. Natasha Korda, "Household Kates: Domesticating Commodities in *The Taming of the Shrew,*" *Shakespeare Quarterly* 47.2 (1996): 109–31 (here cited from 111).

6. Theodore B. Leinwand, *The City Staged: Jacobean Comedy, 1603–1613* (Madison: University of Wisconsin Press, 1986), 51.

7. We should not forget that poorer urban women would have worked as textile producers, domestic servants, or retailers and would have been far less concerned with buying status items. Katrina Honeyman and Jordan Goodman, "Women's work, gender conflict, and labour markets in Europe, 1500–1900," *The Economic History Review* 44.4 (1991): 608–28 (cited from p614); Peter Earle, "The female labour market in London in the late seventeenth and early eighteenth centuries," *The Economic History Review* 42.3 (1989): 328–53 (here cited from 339–44). However, city comedy tends to focus on the upper echelons of the urban middling class and thus frequently associates city wives with consumption. Karen Newman's groundbreaking *Fashioning Femininity and English Renaissance Drama* (1991) provides an early analysis of the ways in which the relationship between woman and consumption took on new importance in London and in Jonson's city comedy, *Epicoene* (1609).

8. For a similar understanding of the link between history and representation, see Frances E. Dolan, *Whores of Babylon: Catholicism, Gender and Seventeenth-Century Print Culture* (Ithaca: Cornell University Press, 1999), 2, 4, 84.

9. Dekker, Thomas and John Webster, *Westward Ho* (1607), *The Dramatic Works of Thomas Dekker,* vol. 2, ed. Fredson Bowers (Cambridge: Cambridge University Press, 1955). All citations will be from this text.

10. Korda, "Household Kates," 119.

11. Eve Sanders, *Gender and Literacy on Stage in Early Modern England* (Cambridge: Cambridge University Press, 1998), 169. See also Margaret Spufford, *Small Books and Pleasant Histories: Popular Fiction and its Readership in Seventeenth-Century England* (Athens: University of Georgia Press, 1981), 34–36, and Jonathan Barry, "Literacy and Literature in Popular Culture: Reading and Writing in Historical Perspective," in *Popular Culture in England c. 1500–1850.* edited by T. Harris (New York: St. Martin's Press, 1995), 77.

12. Amy Louise Erickson, *Women and Property in Early Modern England* (London: Routledge, 1993), 56–57.

13. Erickson, *Women and Property,* 58–59.

14. Sanders, *Gender and Literacy,* 171.

15. Valerie Fildes, *Wet Nursing. A History from Antiquity to the Present* (Oxford: Basil Blackwell, 1988), 83; Gail Kern Paster, *The Body Embarrassed: Drama and the Disciplines of Shame in Early Modern England* (Ithaca: Cornell University Press, 1993), 199.

16. Dorothy McLaren, "Marital Fertility and Lactation 1570–1720," in *Women in English Society 1500–1800,* edited by M. Prior (London: Methuen, 1985), 46; Paster, *The Body Embarrassed,* 201–2.

17. Paster, *The Body Embarrassed,* 202.

18. In the end, Mistress Justiniano is celebrated by her husband because she escapes the earl's advances "without paying" (4.2.191). The play never holds out the threat of Mistress Justiniano as a consumer. In fact she not only retains her chastity, but she gets the earl's proffered jewels too, in a move that resembles Dekker's *Shoemaker's Holiday,* scene 18, in which Jane escapes Hammon and gets his money to boot.

19. See Ruth Karras on medieval prostitution and female entrepreneurship in *Common Women. Prostitution and Sexuality in Medieval England* (Oxford: Oxford University Press, 1996), 44.

20. David Cressy, *Birth, Marriage & Death: Ritual, Religion, and the Life-Cycle in Tudor and Stuart England* (Oxford: Oxford University Press, 1997), 60.

21. For the link between prostitutes, midwives and witches see: Newman, *Fashioning Femininity,* 55–58 and Thomas Rogers Forbes, *The Midwife and the Witch.* (New York: AMS Press, 1966), 112–38. For the very negative (and largely outmoded) view of midwives as incompetent see Forbes and Lawrence Stone, *The Family, Sex and Marriage in England 1500–1800,* abridged edition (New York: Harper, 1979), 59. For the more general connection between women, midwives and occult healing as well as the replacement of midwives by male physicians, see Anthony Fletcher, *Gender, Sex & Subordination in England 1500–1800* (New Haven: Yale University Press, 1995), 223–39.

22. For a good account of the subversive female alliances that develop in this play, see Simon Morgan-Russell, "'No Good Thing Even Comes Out of It': Male Expectation and Female Alliance in Dekker and Webster's *Westward Ho,*" in *Maids and Mistresses, Cousins and Queens: Women's Alliances in Early Modern England,* edited by S. Frye and K. Robertson (Oxford: Oxford University Press, 1998), especially 80–83. See also Jean Howard's recent article on the play and her analysis of the wives' commitment to chastity in relation to "definitions of English womanhood", Jean E. Howard, "Women, Foreigners, and the Regulation of Urban Space in *Westward Ho,*" in *Material London, ca. 1600,* edited by Lena Cowen Orlin (Philadelphia: University of Pennsylvania Press, 2000), 161.

23. Norbert Elias, *The Civilizing Process,* translated by Edmund Jephcott (Oxford: Blackwell, 1994), 66.

24. Norbert Elias, *Power and Civility,* translated by Edmund Jephcott (New York: Pantheon, 1982), 239–42.

25. Michel Foucault, *Discipline & Punish: The Birth of the Prison,* translated by Alan Sheridan (New York: Vintage, 1995), 202–3.

26. The fact that Justiniano is not really impoverished does not alter the situation. What is important is the fact that Mistress Justiniano thought she was acting out of need, and Mistress Tenterhook thought she was acting out of desire *unlike* Mistress Justiniano.

27. For critics who accept Justiniano's rendition of the ending of the play, see Alexander Leggatt, *Citizen Comedy in the Age of Shakespeare* (Toronto: University of Toronto Press, 1973), 132) and Charles R. Forker, "*Westward Ho* and *Northward Ho:* A Revaluation," *Publications of the Arkansas Philological Association* 6.2 (1980): 8–9. For the maypole festival as a celebration of the heterosexual norm, see Peter

Burke, *Popular Culture in Early Modern Europe* (London: Temple Smith, 1978), 194. See also Howard, who argues that the play's ending complicates the "ideology of purity" that the play tries to offer ("Women, Foreigners," 163).

28. Karras, *Common Women,* 15.

29. Karras, *Common Women,* 37–43.

30. Wallace Shugg, "Prostitution in Shakespeare's London," *Shakespeare Studies* 10 (1977): 299. See also E. J. Burford, *The Orrible Synne: A Look at London Lechery from Roman to Cromwellian Times* (London: Calder and Boyars, 1973), 217, for the high number of bawdyhouses during James I's reign.

31. Ian W. Archer, *The Pursuit of Stability: Social Relations in Elizabethan London* (Cambridge: Cambridge University Press, 1991), 212.

32. Archer, *Pursuit of Stability,* 211. See also E. J. Burford and Joy Wotton, *Private Vices—Public Virtues: Bawdry in London from Elizabethan Times to the Regency* (London: Robert Hale, 1995), 15, and Karras, *Common Women,* 75–76, where she notes that whores had a good deal of geographical mobility.

33. The men already know that she operates a brothel within the city walls because they have gone to her London brothel in Gunpowder Ally, located about two hundred yards north of Tower Hill (1.1.8; 4.1; see Shugg, "Prostitution in Shakespeare's London," 300).

Songs by Aurelian Townshend, in the hand of Sir Henry Herbert, for an Unrecorded Masque by the Merchant Adventurers

PETER BEAL

In the National Library of Wales, Aberystwyth, in a composite volume of papers of the Herbert family (NLW MS. 5308E), is a bifolium (fols. 12r–13v) containing copies of three songs apparently relating to an early-seventeenth-century masque. The "first song" (comprising twenty lines), "second song" (comprising fifteen lines), and ".3. song" (comprising six lines) are written on both sides of the first leaf (fol. 12r–v.). The cursive, rounded hand responsible for this copy can be identified as that of Sir Henry Herbert, Master of the Revels, many of whose autograph papers appear in NLW MSS. 5295–5313. The first page of the second leaf of the bifolium (fol. 13r) is left blank; while the verso of that leaf (fol. 13v) is endorsed in Herbert's hand, "Townsends Verses Vpon the Masque." The paper bears a clear armorial watermark comprising three diagonal lines (the "Strasbourg Bend") within a slightly frayed crowned shield. This watermark is not, however, readily dated from standard sources and is of a type found in paper produced in Strasbourg from ca. 1540 to ca. 1640, but imitated by various other European papermakers.[1] Each page of the bifolium measures 310 × 200mm. Before being bound up with other papers in the NLW volume, the bifolium was evidently kept folded in half and in half again in the form of a small packet measuring 80 × 200mm., as is evident from the worn folds and dust-staining of the exposed outer panel.

Even if the words "Maske" and "Masquers" appeared nowhere in this manuscript, it would be evident from their style and allusions that the songs belonged to some kind of Jacobean or Caroline entertainment. The reference to "Townsend" in the endorsement also establishes a clear attribution of authorship—at least of the songs, if not of the whole masque with which they are associated.

The Text

Before any further commentary is offered, the full text of the songs as they appear in the manuscript (complete with erratic punctuation) is printed here, with line numbers supplied.

The subject of ye Maske
expressed in the first song.

After this Rabble whom the sea hath taught
To dance Levoltoes; & sharpe winds have brought
T'obey their whistles, to the shore are come
And reel'd in consort to their Kettle-drum.
You shall perceive this barke of mine containes
fraught, that deserves y purchaser & my paines
Gold such as Colchos, & Arabia riche
Never in mine or farr fam'd Fleece possesse
Diamonds wher fier & water are so mett
They rather lightninge then a light begett
Pure Cutchenecle not such as fades & dies
But growes the richer for the chapmans eyes
Rawsilke: so smoothe, so glossy & so white
Merchants may venture on such ware by night
Sugars, so perfect as those lips that meete
But with a taste, itt makes their whole lives sweete
Thinke not in Canes, in Jngots or in Bales
To see this treasure, but scarfes & vailes
And when this route is all disperst & gonn
The tyme, the place, the goods are all y owne.

12

Three songs by Aurelian Townshend in the hand of Sir Henry Herbert: Aberystwyth, National Library of Wales, NLW MS 5308E, fol. 12r–v. (Original size of each page 310 × 200mm.) Reproduced by permission of the National Library of Wales.

The second song to call
out the Masquers.

Faire suretys of my truthe appease
And Lett the Merchant royall see
There is no fraude in you nor mee
Which hauing once made Cleere
noe priuse can make you deere.

They cannot thinke I meane to gaine
yf I should aske their whole estats
for who leaues you att any rates
May with sadd lookes maintayne
His wealth is in the Mayne.

But they will growe as poore as I
As soone as they haue seene your eyes
for all they haue will proue good prise
soe att your mercy Lyes
both those that sell & buye.

      The. 3. song to make them
            vnmasque.

Rise, rise, you cold spectators rise,
And if you cannot from yon skies
      driue those black cloudes away,
Inuoke this bright & glorious sunn
to rise; & with his Beames bewonn
      to turne our night to day.

[fol. 12r]

The subject of yᵉ Maske
expressed in the first song.

After this Rabble whom the sea hath taught
To dance Leuoltoe's;[1] & sharpe winds haue brought
T'obeye their whistles, to the shore are come
And reeld[2] in consort to their Kettle Drum.
5   you shall perceiue this barke[3] of mine containes
fraught,[4] that deserues yʳ purchase & my paines
Gold, such as Colchos,[5] & Arabia blest
Neuer in mine or farr fam'd Fleece possest.
Diamonds wher fier & water are so mett
10   They rather lightninge then alight[6] begett,
Pure Cutcheneele[7] not such as fad's & dies
But growes the richer for the chapmans[8] eyes,
Rawsilke: so smoothe, so glossy & so white
Merchants may Venture on such ware by night
15   Sugars, so perfect as those lips that meete
But with a taste, itt makes their whole liues sweet.
Thinke not in Canes,[9] in Ingats or in Bales
To see that treasure, but [in][10] scarfes & vailes
And when this route is all disperst & gonn,
20   The tyme, the place, the goods arr all yʳ owne.

---

[1] Leuoltoes] *levolto* is an obsolete form of *lavolta,* a lively dance for two persons consisting a good deal in high and active bounds (*OED*). This type of dance is cited frequently by contemporary authors and playwrights, including Ben Jonson.

[2] reeld] a *reel* is a lively dance, usually danced by two couples facing each other and describing a series of figures of eight, but *reeling* can also mean whirling or swinging about as a result of intoxication (*OED*).

[3] barke] *bark* or *barque*: a small sailing ship or rowing boat (*OED*).

[4] fraught] freight or cargo (*OED*).

[5] Colchos] Colchis (the Crimea), where Jason and the Argonauts captured the Golden Fleece.

[6] alight] a light.

[7] Cutcheneele] *Cochineal,* a Mexican dye, brilliant scarlet in colour, made from insects or cacti (*OED*). In the Privy Council's discussion on 9 July 1614 of the benefits of dyeing cloth in England rather than on the continent, "cochenilo" is cited as one of the necessary materials "easily brought hether": Astrid Friis, *Alderman Cockayne's Project and the Cloth Trade* (Copenhagen: Levin & Munksgaard; London: Humphrey Milford, 1927), p. 461.

[8] chapman] a merchant banker (*OED*).

[9] canes] cane sugar, presumably from the Caribbean.

[10] [in]] omitted from the manuscript, but necessary grammatically and to scan properly.

[fol. 12v]

The second song to call out the Masquers.

Faire suretys of my truthe appeare
    And Lett the Merchant royall see
    There is no fraude in you nor mee
Which hauing once made cleere[11]
5   noe prise can make you deere.

They cannot thinke I meane to gaine
    If I should aske their whole estats
    for who Leaues you att any rates
May with sadd lookes maintayne
10   His wealth is in the Mayne.[12]

But they will growe as poore as I
    As soone as they haue seene your eyes
    for all they haue will proue good prise
    soe att your mercy Lyes
15 Both those that sell & buye.

[fol. 12v]

The .3. song to make them
Vnmasque.

Rise, rise, yee cold spectators rise.
And if you cannot from yon skies
    Driue those black clouds away,
Inuoke this bright & glorious sunn
5 to rise; & with his Beames be wonn
    to turne our night to day.

Occasion of the Masque

From allusions in these songs it may be inferred that the masque featured a "Rabble" or "route" of mariners, who not only dance "to their kettle Drum" but also "reel," possibly in carousing or bacchanalian vein, and

---

[11] cleere] altered to *cleere* in the manuscript from *deere*.
[12] in the Mayne] a pun upon *main* as the principal or most important part of a business and *main* as the Spanish Main or high seas.

that—whether by verbal implication, actual display or symbolic representation—they bring "to the shore" from their "bark" a rich cargo ("fraught") of merchandise ("ware," "treasure," "goods"), including gold, diamonds, dye, silk, and sugar, which is associated with "Merchants" who "Venture." The first two songs at least are sung by someone who refers to "my" pains and who dismisses the notion that he intends to gain too much profit: the protagonist presumably being the sea captain or merchant in charge of the cargo brought ashore. The appeal of the second song to "the Merchant royall" presumably refers to the presence as spectator of the King himself, who is enjoined to perceive clearly that "There is no fraude" in the masquers, that they do not seek exorbitant gains, and that "Both those that sell & buye" lie at his "mercy." It is presumably the King to whom the third song urges the spectators to "Inuoke" as "this bright & glorious sunn" who will "turne our night to day."

Although the celebration of overseas trade and merchandise before a royal or noble audience is scarcely unknown in early-seventeenth-century entertainments (the recently discovered entertainment by Jonson for the opening of the New Exchange on 11 April 1609 being a case in point),[2] these combined allusions suggest strongly that the masque was presented before the King under the auspices of the Company of Merchant Adventurers—of "Merchants" who "Venture." While their principal export commodity was always cloth, the Merchant Adventurers were also heavily involved in the import of the kind of luxury goods mentioned here—such as silks from France, Italy and elsewhere—especially during the depression years of the 1620s.[3] The final invocation is not only an appeal to the King to bless the performance, but also, for the public good, to look favorably upon, and promote the interests of, the Merchant Adventurers, their company, and, by implication, their charter of rights and privileges itself.

In the long list of recorded masques and entertainments of this period[4] one presentation only is recorded as being specifically related to the Merchant Adventurers.[5] On 8 June 1616 Alderman William Cockayne (1560?–1626) entertained James I and Prince Charles at his house in Broad Street, London, with a lavish banquet by way of celebration and thanks to the King for granting a charter to his trading company under the title of the New Company of Merchant Adventurers. Besides presenting the royal guests with phenomenally costly gifts—namely, two basins of gold containing gold pieces, James's to the value of £1,000, Charles's to the value of £500, and the whole "feast" costing allegedly £3,100[6]—Cockayne laid on an entertainment for them written by Ben Jonson. According to George Gerrard, it took this form:

for the Kings better Contentment, they presented Dyers, Weauers wth theyre Shitles, and Cloth dressers; speaking by way of Interlude to grace themselues, and theyre indistrye; after thys, was presented certayne Hamburgians, wth great bellyed Dobletts, all druncke, wch spake such language as Ben Jonson putt into theyre mouthes, only for merriment.[7]

Although the King was sufficiently pleased with this entertainment to knight the Alderman with the City sword before departing, a complaint was made afterward to the Privy Council by the ambassador of the United Provinces, Sir Noel de Caron, who evidently objected to the caricaturing of the fat, drunken Germans, with their mock-German dialogue. However, so far as we can tell, the complaint seems to have fallen on deaf ears.

So could the present songs attributed to Townshend belong to this entertainment supposedly by Jonson? They do have certain points in common. The occasion, in each case, would seem to be an entertainment before the King to celebrate this actual or hoped-for patronage of the Company of Merchant Adventurers. Both feature a party of revellers, if not drunkards, of sorts—at least, if "this Rabble" who "reeld in consort" be taken as suggesting some measure of carousing as well as dancing—whether German or otherwise. And at least part of the goodly merchandise which is apparently landed on shore in the first song comprises "Rawsilke" and materials to produce "scarfes & vailes," if not the craftsmen to work them—the "Dyers," "Weauers," and "Cloth dressers"—who graced "themselues, and theyre indistrye" in the Cockayne entertainment.

On the other hand, do timing and circumstances coincide sufficiently?

The Merchant Adventurers

Originally founded in the thirteenth century, the Company (or Fellowship) of Merchant Adventurers had enjoyed the benefit of royal charters granted or renewed by Henry IV in 1407, Edward IV in 1462, Henry VII in 1505, Henry VIII, Edward VI, Philip and Mary, and Elizabeth in 1564 and 1586.[8] James I renewed the company's charter in 1604 and 1607, but within the next few years a series of disputes arose concerning their monopoly of the woollen cloth trade. The company controlled the export of undyed and undressed cloth, which was consequently dyed and dressed in the Netherlands for reimportation into England. This arrangement, which suited both the company and the Netherlands, provoked serious objections from critics who saw no reason why the dyeing and dressing should not be done in England. These objections prevailed upon the King sufficiently for him to revoke the company's charter on 2 December 1614.[9] In August 1615 James was pleased instead to grant a charter for a new company, entitled "The Governor Assistants and Fellowship of the King's Merchant Adventurers of the new Trade of London," to his great friend Alderman William Cockayne. This, then, was the context for the occasion on 8 June 1616 when, before receiving a knighthood, Cockayne feasted the King on so lavish a scale as a token of his unbounded gratitude—and also, in effect, as a huge bribe in face of the storm of criticism to which the new venture was subjected—giving him and Prince Charles gold to the value of £1,500: the equivalent of some hundreds of thousands of pounds today. The entertainment presented was especially relevant in that the English "Dyers," "Weauers," and "Cloth dressers" who featured—rather than merchants and traders in general—were the very people who supposedly stood to benefit most from the new company.[10]

As for the "Hamburgians," as Gerrard called them, the Merchant Adventurers had scored a major victory over their chief rivals, the Hanseatic League, in 1567 when they established a concordat with the Free City of Hamburg, which became their principal trading base on the continent. Although after 1578 their rights there were in abeyance, and the company made its headquarters instead in the Netherlands, they were invited back to Hamburg in 1611. This meant that for the next few years they were in an extremely strong position, possessing a lucrative trading monopoly which benefited both themselves and the Netherlands (which continued to control the dyeing business) and also the city of Hamburg. The King's revocation of their charter in favor of Cockayne's new company was accordingly viewed with dismay, not only by many of the old Merchant Adventurers themselves, but also by the Netherlands and Hamburg, both of which stood to lose serious revenue by the new arrangements. Besides all else, this may help to explain why those responsible for the Cockayne entertainment felt free to make fun of Hamburgians and why the ambassador of the Netherlands was so annoyed by it. Although the caricaturing of Hamburgians as fat drunkards was perhaps, as Gerrard implies, little more than harmless "merriment"—a piece of typically English, not to mention Jonsonian, bluff humor at the expense of foreigners[11]—the aggressive independence of Cockayne's new company, which rivalled rather than co-operated with Hamburg, allowed for a less circumspect indulgence in such horseplay than would have been likely with the old Company. De Caron's objections presumably stemmed from general hostility to the new Company—in view of its threat to Dutch interests—and because of the opportunity this entertainment presented to discredit Cockayne in the eyes of the Hamburgians, with whom, in this respect, the Netherlands shared common interests.[12]

In fact, as it turns out, Cockayne's new company would prove to be a disastrous failure. By 29 November 1616 a characteristic entry in the *Calendar of State Papers Domestic* reads: "Great distress in the cloth trade. The Hollanders and Alderman Cockayne blamed. The King purposes to make sumptuary laws for moderating excess in apparel. A proclamation is expected ordering the wearing of cloth, which causes great deadness in trade."[13] Because of the lack of experience and competence of its new members, and because the expected benefits for English cloth-workers and dyers failed to materialise (since the Netherlands and Hamburg retaliated by prohibiting the import of English dyed fabrics), the new company had, in Sir C. P. Lucas's words, only "a brief and most inglorious existence."[14] The result was James I's proclamation of 12 August 1617 "restoring the Ancient Merchantes Adventurers to their former Trade and Priviledges"[15] and his granting them a new, generous charter in January 1617/18. This, coupled with the formal enlargements of the company's rights in Hamburg in June of the same year, meant that, in due course, the old, renewed Company of Merchant Adventurers could become as strong as ever.

Even so, in the years after 1618 and before the Civil War, the company was obliged to withstand not only the general economic depression of the 1620s but also bitter opposition to its monopolies and restrictive practices from rival merchants, or "Interlopers" as they were called, who pressed for free trade. Influenced by these views, the House of Commons passed resolutions hostile to the company and its "patent" in 1624. After 1625 the new king, Charles I, was periodically bombarded by protests and petitions from bodies of rival merchants who opposed the company, and the Adventurers' refusal to consent to the King's imposition of tonnage and poundage so angered him that he seriously considered dissolving the Fellowship yet again in favor of a more compliant body of courtiers and noblemen. Nevertheless, the arguments in favor of the benefits of their traditional monopolies prevailed, and Charles—perhaps having learned some measure of caution from his father's ill-judged support of the disastrous new venture in 1615—was pleased to confirm the Company's rights in proclamations made on 7 December 1634 and 5 May 1639.

Therefore, if we are looking for an occasion after 1616 when the Company of Merchant Adventurers might have been minded to lavish attention upon the King, to remind him of the importance and usefulness of their trading, to argue for the fairness of their practices and profits, and to retain his support against their critics, or, indeed, to hail him as their great benefactor and protector, the range of possibilities is wide. Certainly reasons for laying on such an entertainment would have presented themselves throughout the 1620s and 1630s, even if no specific occasion would seem to be recorded in the annals of masques and shows for that period.

Aurelian Townshend

"Townsend" (however spelled) is not a particularly uncommon name, and there is at least one man of that name directly associated with the theater in this period: namely, John Townsend, patentee of a provincial acting company who flourished between 1611 and 1634.[16] Nevertheless, the obvious and pre-eminent candidate for the identification of the "Townsend" to whom the present songs are attributed in the manuscript must be the poet Aurelian Townshend (fl. 1583–1649). Even so, could Aurelian Townshend have written masque-songs as early as 1616?

In fact, this period of Townshend's life is the one about which we know the least. In the early 1600s Townshend travelled on the continent as a Queen's Messenger in the service of Sir Robert Cecil, and he may have been the "Master Townsend" who attended Sir Robert Cecil on his deathbed in 1612. But then, as Chambers notes, there "follows a long gap of twenty years in the history of Aurelian Townshend, during which his way of life is altogether obscure," until, in fact, "he was living and registering his children between 1622 and 1632 [actually 1634] in the parish of St. Giles, Cripplegate."[17] One autograph letter by Townshend himself, written to the English Resident at Brussels, William Trumbull, on 13 March 1620/21, adds marginally to this picture. Written from Hampton Court, and replete with the latest gossip about Buckingham and other prominent figures, Townshend's letter shows that he was connected with the court in some capacity, even though he was unable to revisit Trumbull in Brussels that summer ("because my pasporte from hence, must bee signed by too many handes, for I see a poore man that hath many frends, hath almost no tyme of his owne").[18]

All the same, we have no evidence that Townshend had any involvement in court masques until the 1630s, following the fall from favor of Ben Jonson. Townshend wrote the verses for two full-length masques for the King and Queen at Whitehall, both performed with scenery by Inigo Jones and afterwards published in full. One was *Albions Triumph,* performed 8 January 1631/32 (and Townshend refers to himself in his printed description as being "as loath to be brought upon the Stage as an unhansom Man is to see himselfe in a great Glasse," but that he obeyed the command of the King); the other the Queen's Shrovetide masque *Tempe Restor'd,* performed a month later on 14 February 1631/32.[19] There is evidence that Townshend was involved in other masques in this period.[20] These include what have been identified by Stephen Orgel as antimasques played after the French pastoral *Florimène* performed by the Queen's ladies on 21 December 1635, songs known from a five-page printed pamphlet, the apparently unique surviving exemplum of which is now in the Huntington Library (RB 13016);[21] and "A maske before their Majestyes, 1636," probably the court revival on 12 January 1636/37 of William Cartwright's *The Royal Slave,* to which Townshend contributed a "Baccanall Songe."[22]

All these masques were written in the period after Ben Jonson had fallen out of favor and lost the position he had held for many years as the principal writer of court entertainments (his last court masque being *Chloridia,* performed for the Queen on 22 February and ca. 2 May 1631).[23] Although he has been sometimes cited by biographers as a friend or colleague of Jonson's, there is no clear evidence that Townshend ever was associated with him in any way, either as friend or rival.[24]

As to whether the present songs conform stylistically to Townshend's known masque-songs, there is little to indicate one way or the other. Neither the diction nor the prosody would seem to be particularly distinctive. The songs vary in length, meter, and rhyme scheme. The first, and indeed best, song is in pentameter couplets throughout. The second has three stanzas each beginning with three tetrameter lines rhyming *abb,* followed in the first two stanzas by trimeter couplets and in the third stanza by trimeter lines rhyming *ba.* The brief third song is couched in a six-line medieval rhyme scheme in which the tetrameter couplets are balanced by medial and terminal trimeter *b* rhymes (*aabccb*).[25] Such variant forms are common enough in masques both by Townshend and his contemporaries, as, indeed, is the serviceable but largely undistinguished phrasing of the songs.

In other words, while there are no stylistic features here to suggest the authorship of Townshend specifically, neither is there anything to suggest otherwise. Moreover, the attribution is made by none other than Sir Henry Herbert.

Sir Henry Herbert

More than one member of the illustrious Herbert family had both serious literary interests and links with the court—the philosophical writer and diplomat Edward, Lord Herbert of Cherbury (1582?–1648), and his brother the poet George Herbert (1593–1633) being not the least prominent among them. Some Herberts had especially ready access to court entertainments—the courtier Philip, fourth Earl of Pembroke (1584–1650), associate of Ben Jonson and Inigo Jones, for instance, and his elder brother William, third Earl of Pembroke (1580–1630), poet, patron, Lord Chamberlain, and dedicatee of the First Folio of Shakespeare. None, however, had a closer association with court entertainments, or was better placed to acquire texts of them, than Sir Henry Herbert (1594–1673), brother of both Edward and George, and Master of the Revels from 1623 to 1642 (his office renewed in 1660).

As Nigel Bawcutt has explained, Sir Henry Herbert's job as Master of the Revels was to choose the plays and entertainments performed at court; to check their text; and to supervise rehearsals. It was his duty besides to license and censor plays for the public stage, as well as to license other "smaller shows" (troupes of conjurors, and the like).[26] Herbert was also himself a shareholder in several theaters, including the Phoenix or Cockpit Theater and, in 1631, the Salisbury Court Theater,[27] which led to his reading and passing judgment on dramatic scripts for yet further commercial considerations. Besides having other literary pursuits,[28] Herbert is even credited, though on dubious evidence, with being a playwright himself.[29]

As Master of Revels, Herbert would have received or had access to many synopses, or "programmes," of proposed masques, as well as texts of their "songs." One such example relating to Townshend is the pamphlet of anti-masques to *Florimène* (1635), including "A Song" and "The Subject of the Masque," mentioned above. This is unusual in being printed. But there seems to be no lack of evidence that copies of synopses and songs, if not full texts, of masques by such writers as Jonson were occasionally distributed in scribal copies to guests, spectators and other interested parties in this period.

Even so, why should Herbert have copied out these songs in his own hand? That the cursive, rounded handwriting is his is readily established by reference to known examples of Herbert's hand,[30] and by the fact that the Herbert collection in which this manuscript is bound (NLW MSS. 5295–5313) is full of comparable autograph papers by him. Although the docketing "Townsends Verses Vpon the Masque" is written in a more cursive script than the main text—with, for instance, the word "the" appearing in a scribbled form not found in the text of the songs—and the endorsement also refers to "the Masque" rather than the main text's heading "ye Maske" (though the third song's heading has the word "vnmasque"), the handwriting is clearly all one and the same: witness in each case, for instance, the flourished majuscule *T*, the characteristic forms of *v* and terminal *s*, the abortive secretary form of the terminal *e,* and the common tendency towards leaving gaps between the letters within words, as well as other general similarities in the flowing, rounded script. It would seem, then, that rather than its being a casual relic of his routine professional activities, Herbert's copy—one he took the trouble to write out himself—was a product of his personal literary interests. This is a general dimension to which the Herbert papers—containing, as they do, copies of many works in verse and prose by authors besides the Herbert family itself—bear ample witness. The heterogeneous and composite NLW MS. 5308E itself includes, for instance, a quarto booklet of sixteen poems by Donne (fols. 1–9), as well as a variety of later Restoration poems. Bound as folios 10–11, immediately before the Townshend songs, is a bifolium containing a copy of Francis Beaumont's "An Elegy vpon the death of the Countess of Rutlande," the main text written in an unidentified angular italic but endorsed on fol. 11v in the familiar docketing hand of Henry Herbert. Originally written in 1615, this elegy was first published in 1622, but circulated widely in contemporary manuscript copies.[31] Thus we see that, besides all else, Herbert was a collector, as well as an amateur writer and professional licenser, a man apt to pick up and retain manuscript verse circulating among the educated classes in this period, even if composed earlier, and whether directly relating to his personal or professional interests or not.[32]

However, the manuscript contains yet another interesting clue. Herbert's endorsement attributing the "Verses" to "Townsend" is followed, evidently in his hand as well, by two notes, the second in a darker ink, reading: "Troye

Endorsement in the hand of Sir Henry Herbert: Aberystwyth, National Library of Wales, NLW MS 5308E, fol. 13v. (Original page size 310 × 200mm.; inscribed panel 200 × 80mm.). Reproduced by permission of the National Library of Wales.

$^{165}/_{114}$ - waight |16. Marche.| The wine was frenche". These may, of course, be random jottings which bear no relation to the masque in question. Alternatively, if Henry Herbert, Master of the Revels, were annotating his copy with further particulars of the occasion on which the songs were presented we might deduce three things about it: (i) that it occurred on a 16 March; (ii) that the wine—presumably served to the guests—was French;[33] and (iii) that something on the occasion weighed a substantial amount. Troy weight (the name derived from the French town Troyes) was a measure used primarily for gold and silver, and also for precious stones. An ounce in Troy weight was approximately 31 grams, as opposed to ca. 28 grams per ounce by the more common *avoir du poids* measurement. The figures here, $^{165}/_{114}$ expressed as a fraction, might well mean 165 ounces plus 114 grains (= 7.387 grams) in Troy weight.[34] Thus they could well refer to one or more items of gold or silver weighing over ten pounds—a sizeable piece of treasure. Such a thing might relate to the "Gold" or "Diamonds" mentioned in the first song (lines 7, 9) or else (if it were not the same thing) to a present made to the King ("... the goods are all y^r owne": line 20). Here again one recalls the "Basen and Eure of Gold" filled with gold pieces which the New Company of Merchant Adventurers presented to James I and Prince Charles at the Cockayne entertainment on 8 June 1616.[35]

Finally, whether coincidental or not, there is also some evidence of a direct connection between the Herbert family and Aurelian Townshend himself. In 1608–1609 Townshend accompanied Sir Edward Herbert on his travels to France, being described by Herbert in his *Autobiography* as "a Gentleman That spake the Languages of Frensh, Italian and Spanish, in greate Perfection."[36] Chambers suggests that "It may be that this was not the end of Townshend's connexion with Sir Edward Herbert, for in a letter of 8th April 1615, Herbert's stepfather, Sir John Danvers, states that he has repaid himself £50 'about soe much wch I had disbursed for you towards the hundred pounds imployed for Mr. Townsend and your other occasions'".[37] Whether or not this "connexion," such as it was, helped to induce Henry Herbert to copy out songs by Townshend at a later date can only be a matter of speculation.[38]

Conclusion

Even with the clue that the masque may have been presented on a 16 March, we cannot pin down as yet the precise occasion for which the present songs were written. Nevertheless, the combined evidence enables us to make a number of inferences. The likelihood is that the songs (if not the whole masque) were composed, as Herbert implies, by Aurelian Townshend; that, accordingly, they were written not only during the period when Herbert was

Master of the Revels (1623–42) but also probably when Townshend was actively engaged in court masques (1631–37); that the entertainment was presented before Charles 1, whether at court or in a private house; and that it was put on by the Company of Merchant Adventurers, as, in effect, a propaganda exercise to secure or retain the King's support of their charter at a time when their privileges and monopolies were under threat from their critics and rivals. That it was presented in a period well after the collapse of the Cockayne project in 1617 is also evident because the songs refer unashamedly not to the home manufacture of cloth but to the import of luxury foreign goods such as silk for veils and scarves. "The general wearing of silks and foreign stuffs instead of cloth" was one of the supposed causes for the decay of trade which a committee of the Privy Council adumbrated in their report on 22 June 1622,[39] and the import of such "stuffs" was for a time prohibited in a misguided effort to boost the home textile industry. By the time this masque was presented, clearly the climate of opinion had changed.

For all its economic uncertainties, the 1630s proved to be a period of recovery and consolidation for the Merchant Adventurers. Townshend's "Verses" were evidently made as a small contribution toward the support and celebration of that progress.

Notes

1. Examples of this family of watermarks can be found, notably, in Briquet 988, Heawood 135–40 (dated 1611–35), and Gaudriault 206–7. I am grateful to Ruby Reid Thompson for help on this matter.

2. See James Knowles, "Cecil's Shopping Centre," *TLS* (7 February 1997), 14, and "Jonson's *Entertainment at Britain's Burse*" in *Re-Presenting Ben Jonson,* ed. Martin Butler (Basingstoke: Macmillan, 1999), 114–51; also Janette Dillon, "Court Meets City: The Royal Entertainment at the New Exchange," *Research Opportunities in Renaissance Drama,* 38 (1999), 1–21.

3. B. E. Supple, *Commercial Crisis and Change in England 1600–1642* (Cambridge: Cambridge University Press, 1959), 90–91.

4. See C. E. McGee and John C. Meagher, "Preliminary Checklist of Tudor and Stuart Entertainments," *Research Opportunities in Renaissance Drama* 27 (1984), 47–126 [1603–13]; 30 (1988), 17–128 [1614–25]; 36 (1997), 23–95 [1625–34]; 38 (1999), 23–85 [1634–42].

5. McGee and Meagher, *RORD* 30 (1988), 39. The documentary evidence for this entertainment is discussed most notably in N. W. Bawcutt, "Ben Jonson's Drunken Hamburgians: An Entertainment for King James," *Notes & Queries* 242 (March 1997), 92–94. The present account of this occasion is greatly indebted to this article.

6. John Chamberlain to Sir Dudley Carleton, 22 June 1616, cited in Bawcutt, "Ben Jonson's Drunken Hamburgians."

7. George Gerrard to Sir Dudley Carleton, 14 June 1616: PRO SP 14/87/57, cited

in Bawcutt, "Ben Jonson's Drunken Hamburgians." Jonson's text for this entertainment is not known to survive.

8. My account here of the history of the Merchant Adventurers is based on relevant material in Friis, *Alderman Cockayne's Project;* Supple, *Commercial Crisis;* George Cawston and A. H. Keane, *The Early Chartered Companies* (London and New York: Edward Arnold, 1896), Chapter 3 and Appendix 2; W. E. Lingelbach, *The Merchant Adventurers of England: Their Laws and Ordinances with other Documents* (Philadelphia: University of Pennsylvania Press, 1902); Sir C. P. Lucas, *The Beginnings of English Overseas Enterprise* (Oxford: Clarendon Press, 1917), chapter 3; Charles Grey, *The Merchant Venturers of London* (London: H. F. & G. Witherby, 1932); Rudolf Robert, *Chartered Companies and their Role in the Development of Overseas Trade* (London: G. Bell & Sons, 1969), Chapter 2; and Theodore K. Rabb, *Enterprise & Empire: Merchant and Gentry Investment in the Expansion of England, 1575–1630* (Cambridge: Harvard University Press, 1967).

9. The text of James's proclamation is printed in Cawston & Keane, pp. 296–99.

10. It is possible, incidentally, that Jonson was not the only dramatist to write in celebration or defence of Cockayne's new company. As Grace Ioppolo explains in her forthcoming Oxford University Press edition of *Hengist, King of Kent,* a play which she dates ca. 1616–19, Middleton's subplot involves a satirical depiction of the weaver Oliver, who is perceived as treacherous because he works in "fustian," a worsted cloth made of cotton and flax which was imported from those enemies of the Cockayne project the Low Countries and Germany.

11. Jonson was scarcely averse to mocking foreigners in his poems and plays, the "Dutch" (meaning both Germans and Hollanders) among them. In his *Epigramme* cvii ("To Captayne Hvngry"), for instance, he makes slighting reference to "the grosse *Dutch,*" and in *The Devil is an Ass* of 1631 (III.iii. 22–33) Meercraft tells Everill that, instead of wearing "Scarlet, gold lace, and cut-works', he could have been contented "With cheese, salt-butter, and a pickled hering, / I' the Low-Countries," where he might also have worn "cloth, and fustian!" (I am grateful to Ian Donaldson for these references).

12. My suggestions here are prompted by N. W. Bawcutt's puzzlement as to "why the ambassador of the United Provinces should have reacted so strongly to an insult to the inhabitants of Hamburg ("Ben Jonson's Drunken Hamburgians").

13. *Calendar of State Papers Domestic, James I,* IX (1611–1618), 410.

14. Lucas, 99.

15. The text of this proclamation is printed in Cawston & Keane, 300–303.

16. See Gerald Eades Bentley, *The Jacobean and Caroline Stage,* 7 vols (Oxford: Clarendon Press, 1941–68), II, 602–4; N. W. Bawcutt, *The Control and Censorship of Caroline Drama: The Records of Sir Henry Herbert, Master of the Revels 1623–73* (Oxford: Clarendon Press, 1996), p. 86 and nos. 84, 150, 188, 325.

17. E. K. Chambers (ed.), *Aurelian Townshend's Poems and Masks* (Oxford: Clarendon Press, 1912), p. xvi. See also the forthcoming entry on Townshend by Peter Beal in the *New DNB.*

18. British Library, Add. ms. 72360, fol. 136. See the reproduction of part of this letter in Sotheby's catalogue of "The Trumbull Papers," 14 December 1989, pp. 80–81 (lot 36).

19. Chambers, pp. 55–100; *The Poems and Masques of Aurelian Townshend,* ed. Cedric C. Brown (Reading: Whiteknights, 1983), 75–108.

20. Bentley, V: 1226–31.

21. Brown, 109–14.

22. Chambers, 7–8, 104–5; Brown, 115–16.

23. McGee & Meagher, *RORD* 36 (1997), 53–57. Jonson was effectively paid off with £40 "in Consideracion of his paynes taken in her Ma^tes service vpon severall occasions in Masques, and otherwise as by her highnes Warrant dated the third of November 1631": entry in the household accounts of Queen Henrietta Maria kept by her Treasurer Sir Richard Wynn (National Library of Wales Wynnstay MSS. 174–186); and see also the Queen's signed warrant and Jonson's receipt signed by him on 12 November 1631 in the Public Record Office (LR5 64), cited in N. W. Bawcutt, "New Jonson Documents," *Review of English Studies,* NS 47 (1996), 50–52.

24. See Chambers, pp. xiv, xvii, xxiii

25. I am grateful to Steven May for his comments on the prosody of these songs.

26. Bawcutt, *Control and Censorship,* 27–87.

27. Bawcutt, *Control and Censorship,* 40.

28. Such as writing two devotional works in 1621–1623/24: see *Herbert's Golden Harpe or His Heauenly Hymne,* ed. Chauncey Wood (Fairfield, Conn.: Sacred Heart University, 1998). Although none of the three manuscripts of "The Broken Heart" and "Herbert's Golden Harpe" (Bodleian Library MSS. Don. f. 26 and 27, and Huntington Library HM 85) is in Herbert's hand, the grounds for attributing these writings to Sir Henry Herbert are strengthened by the set of "Praiers and Meditations in Old Age" which Herbert wrote in 1672: see N. W. Bawcutt's review of Wood's edition in *Review of English Studies,* NS 50 (1999), 379–80.

29. Among the various poems and prose works in the Herbert Papers is a full-length tragedy entitled *The Emperor Otho* (NLW MS. 5302B). This heavily revised working manuscript is recorded in the NLW catalogue of manuscripts as being in Sir Henry's hand. Comparisons of handwriting made from microfilm print-out of two sample pages prove inconclusive. Nigel Bawcutt has suggested to me that the writer may well be the second Sir Henry Herbert (1654–1709), whose verse-collecting activities are also represented in NLW MS. 5303. Moreover, the style of the play seems to be later, echoing that of the rhyming couplet heroic tragedies of the 1670s. An edition of this tragedy by Dr Herbert G. Wright, which was offered to publishers in 1928 but remains unpublished, is preserved in typescript among his papers at the University of Wales, Bangor (Bangor MS. 17725).

30. Cf., for instance, the example of Herbert's writing reproduced in W. W. Greg's *English Literary Autographs 1550–1650,* 3 vols (Oxford: Oxford University Press, 1925–32), I, No. xxx.

31. See Peter Beal, *Index of English Literary Manuscripts,* Volume I, *1450–1625,* Part I (London: Mansell; New York: R.R. Bowker Company, 1980), 70–72 (BmF 27–55).

32. NLW MSS. 5300B and 5303E in particular contain poems by or probably collected by Sir Henry. The propensity of members of the Herbert family in general to collect, or even transcribe, manuscript poems in this period is well attested by the many verse manuscripts to be found in the Herbert and Powis family papers now in the National Library of Wales.

33. Nigel Bawcutt kindly points out to me that Herbert would seem to have been generally interested in wine: for instance, he wrote on 5 May 1630 to Endymion Porter enquiring, on behalf of his kinsman Philip, Earl of Pembroke, for particulars of the merchant who had supplied Porter with some particularly good French wine, and the subject of wine also features in Herbert's letters to John, Viscount Scudamore: see Bawcutt, *Control and Censorship*, 7, 110.

34. For explicating these figures to me I am grateful to Paul Wood.

35. Gerrard to Carleton, 14 June 1616, cited in Bawcutt, "Ben Jonson's Drunken Hamburgians," 93.

36. *The Life of Edward, First Lord Herbert of Cherbury Written by Himself,* ed. J. M. Shuttleworth (London: Oxford University Press, 1976), 41; the autobiography cited in Chambers, xv. Townshend also served as Herbert's go-between in issuing a challenge to an impertinent French courtier, and he rode with him on a hunt in which Herbert was nearly gouged by a boar (*Life,* ed. Shuttleworth, 42, 47). Chambers speculates (xvii–xviii) that one of the other members of Herbert's 1608 party to France, Edmund Taverner, secretary to Philip, later Earl of Pembroke, may have played a part in Townshend's later introduction to court masques.

37. Chambers, xv, citing a letter by Danvers to Edward Herbert in the Powis Papers.

38. One other possible connection between Townshend and the Herbert family is the frustratingly unverifiable report of the existence of an inscription attributed to Philip Herbert, Earl of Pembroke, in a book dated in or after 1642, referring to the "poore & pocky Poett" Townshend, "but a marryed man & an howsekeeper in Barbican" who would have been "glad to sell an 100 verses now at sixepence a piece, 50 shillinges an 100 verses." This unlocated inscription is reproduced by Alexander Dyce in his edition of *The Works of Beaumont and Fletcher* (11 vols, London: Edward Moxon, 1843–46), I, xvii; and see Chambers, xxiii–xxiv.

39. *Calendar of State Papers Domestic, James I,* X (1619–1623), p. 410.

Reviews

Queer Virgins and Virgin Queans on the Early Modern Stage, by Mary Bly. New York: Oxford University Press, 2000. Pp. viii + 213. Cloth $55.00.

Reviewer: PATRICIA CAHILL

Because scholarship on same-sex desire in early modern literature has largely been limited to inquiry into canonical, and primarily Shakespearean, texts, much about representations of sexuality on the Renaissance stage remains unexamined.[1] It is thus a welcome event to come upon Mary Bly's thoroughly researched and elegantly written book, which goes a long way toward remedying this lacuna. Bly offers a comprehensive view of the first Whitefriars (also known as the King's Revels), a debt-ridden boys' company that operated in London for eight or nine months in 1607–1608 and whose eight known dramas showcased heroines with a penchant for sexual humor, "the queer virgins and virgin queans" of her title. Examining this ribald repertory, Bly looks in detail at John Mason's *The Turk*; Robert Armin's *The Two Maids of More-clacke,* Lording Barry's *Ram Alley,* John Day's *Humour out of Breath* and *Law Tricks,* and Edward's Sharpham's *Cupid's Whirligig.* While these plays are likely to be familiar only to the most intrepid of contemporary readers, Bly makes a strong case for their importance, a case that has little to do with their "literary merit" (about which she seems to be dubious) and much to do with their value as cultural artifacts (29). She argues that the Whitefriars' company structure—an alliance of shareholding and first-time playwrights—was unusual; that its mode of humor was strikingly different from the satirical and political wit associated with the other children's companies; that its works were the product of collaborative ventures rather than, as is usually assumed, of single authorship; and that its managers, playwrights, and players catered to and helped to create a "self-aware homoerotic community" of men in early seventeenth-century London (6). This last claim is perhaps her boldest and her most subtle: rightly alert to the dangers of anachronism, Bly is at pains to indicate that what she wishes to resurrect for readers is *not* a version of the protogay subculture of the late seventeenth-century molly houses, which Alan Bray has described in his pioneering study, *Homosexuality in Renaissance England.*[2] Rather, what she wishes to flesh out is a more inchoate kind of male fellowship: in Bly's nuanced account, the Whitefriars' playhouse is a place where the bawdy wit of cross-dressed players enables members of "an early modern erotic minority"— writers, actors, and theatergoers alike—to forge bonds with each other through laughter (17).

Bly's historical narrative—which calls upon a wealth of archival material about the business of playing and also includes engaging narratives about actors turned thieves and playwrights turned pirates—would on its own make

Queer Virgins a compelling read. But what makes Bly's book innovative as well as compelling is that Bly weds her research into company structure to an investigation of matters both narrowly aesthetic and broadly cultural: her study thus ranges from consideration of the chain of signifiers evoked by various now-obsolete words to consideration of the cultural work that lewd performances may have done in early modern London. In the five chapters of her book, she develops a number of disparate arguments about the Whitefriars, engaging in dialogues with Patricia Parker's recent study of wordplay in Shakespearean drama, with Jeffrey Masten's work on collective authorship, and with work on sodomy and homoeroticism by critics such as Gregory Bredbeck, Mario di Gangi, and Jonathan Goldberg. Arguing that "Whitefriars plays were read *for* their puns, which constitute their primary characteristic as a group" (30), she indicates that her goal is "to recreate the audience of the Whitefriars theatre . . . to turn readers[of her book] into that audience" (39). Although one might quibble with some of her analysis or wish that she had explored matters even more widely, it is clear that Bly has gone a long way toward meeting her goal. In short, this relatively slim volume represents an original and important contribution both to the study of Renaissance erotic discourse and to the scholarship on non-Shakespearean drama.

In the first chapter, Bly calls attention to the commodification of wit in the Jacobean theater as well as the varieties of linguistic playfulness in evidence elsewhere in the culture, identifying an early modern taxonomy of wordplay, which encompassed such forms as jests, quibbles, clinches and clenches (11). Investigating the production and reception of what critics have tended to dismiss as mere vulgarity, she focuses on the "queer puns" of the Whitefriars, which she variously defines as puns that "carry homoerotic resonances and speak to homoerotic desires" (2) and that "construct the male body as a site for the sensually celebratory appetite" (2). Through this wordplay, she suggests, we may gain insight into the workings of desire in a culture in which erotic identities were less fixed than they would become under modern regimes of heteronormativity.

In chapters 2 and 3, Bly argues that what distinguishes the Whitefriars repertory from that of other companies is its reliance on a recurring character: a marriageable heroine who delights in sexual puns—who is in fact obsessed with penises—and who never gets punished for voicing her lust. How, she asks, might we interpret the Whitefriars' use of seven such women in less than a year? How might we understand the company's departure from what she, perhaps too quickly, describes as the period's typical romantic comedy plot in which the heroine is marked by her chastity in word and deed? The answer, for Bly, is that these plays—in which the woman who can't resist phallic puns is also the cross-dressed boy player who speaks *his* desire—are all, literally, invested in queerness, in the breaching of normative erotic codes. Moreover, so Bly contends, the similarities between differently authored Whitefriars plays cannot simply be seen as coincidence; rather, she suggests, the proliferation of such characters must result from the growing awareness, on the part of the cash-strapped Whitefriars' management, of the commercial viability of its particular brand of sexual humor (32).

In addition to this suggestive, if ultimately unprovable, hypothesis about the Whitefriars' marketing strategies, Bly offers in chapters 2 and 3 a series of dazzling close readings, identifying networks of puns that link the different plays and interpreting a variety of Jacobean slang terms, such as *dog-fish, mutton, water-works,* and—my personal favorite—*pantofles.* Much of her analysis is devoted to double entendres spoken by the virgins, puns whose meanings turn on "the figurative undressing of the speaker" and thereby remind audiences of the sexual organs of the boy player (116). Discussing these witty exchanges, Bly emphasizes their status as performances—the fact that the puns are both visual and linguistic—and suggests that "any bawdy pun can mutate between female and male bodies," as for example when male sexual parts are evoked through words like *case* or *sweetmeats* that are more commonly associated with female prostitutes and female genitalia (79). Such mutations, she suggests, not only define the male body as a penetrable one; they also link the theater to the brothels in their midst, tantalizing audiences with the thought that the sexual services of the boy players may be for sale.

Throughout these chapters, Bly wonderfully demonstrates the queerness of these puns, the ways in which the Whitefriars plays are marked by what Eve Sedgwick calls "the open mesh of possibilities, gaps, overlaps, dissonances and resonances, lapses and excesses of meaning when the constituent elements of anyone's gender, of anyone's sexuality aren't made (or can't be made) to signify monolithically"[3] From time to time, however, Bly appears to leave this realm of polymorphous perversity and return to more familiar binaries, suggesting, for example, that "it is difficult to see Whitefriars' heroines as female" (84), a comment that would seem to imply that, despite all the queer puns, the desiring bodies in this theater may always already be gendered male. While sympathetic to any critic whose attempt to separate sexuality from gender runs asunder and while aware, too, that Bly may indeed be dealing with a theater that is symptomatically blind to female-female desire, I nevertheless found myself wishing that she had expanded her commentary on the place of female libidos in this repertory or had engaged more explicitly with recent critical work on female masculinity. Her remarks on the place of female homoeroticism are intriguing, but too brief: one is left to wonder, for example, how she interprets the desire she uncovers, what, for example, she makes of the fact that in two of the five comedies, "the most provocative dialogues . . . occur between women, mediating between salacity and obscenity" (48).

In chapter 4, Bly offers a *tour de force* analysis of queer puns in circulation in other early modern literary texts—including love sonnets of Richard Barnfield; rarely examined homoerotic eclogues by Lewis Machin; historical poems about Piers Gaveston by Michael Drayton; and the steamier portions of Marlowe's *Hero and Leander* and *Edward II*. By uncovering a number of connections between these poets and the Whitefriars playwrights—she notes, for instance, that Machin was co-author with Gervase Markham of the Whitefriars's play, *The Dumb Knight* and that Drayton was the Whitefriars primary shareholder—and by tracing the migration of certain recurring images—such as that of wanton, longhaired boys who are naked except for the pearls that adorn them—from the poets' manuscripts to the Whitefriars stage, Bly persuasively argues that the Whitefriars must have targeted an already existing market for homoerotic texts. Bly also offers an extensive discussion of Marlovian influence on the anonymous and homoerotically charged play *Lust's Dominion*, which she persuasively argues may be a source for the even more explicitly homoerotic play *The Turk*, the Whitefriar's only tragedy. By bringing together these orientalist texts, Bly seems to hint at a relationship between discourses of sexuality and race, which might fruitfully be explored at greater length; in any case, what she clearly shows is that, by alluding to famous homoerotic images, the Whitefriars were slyly engaging an emergent discourse about male-male desire and winking at those audience members who were sharp enough to catch on.

In the final chapter, Bly's materialist critical bent emerges most fully, as she speculates about the original audience for these plays and most explicitly takes up a number of matters related to the geography and economics of the theater. Here, too, Bly turns attention to texts outside of the Whitefriars repertory—among them, *Grene's Tu Quoque*, *A Christian Turn'd Turk*, and *The Insatiate Countess*. Demonstrating that these plays may be read as adaptations of Whitefriars texts, she also notes that they are virtually devoid of the queer puns that marked the originals. Along the way she makes a strong case for our understanding the Whitefriars Company as a "syndicate" specializing in a particular brand of humor and appealing to a particular class of canny consumers.

Behind Bly's desire to shift the critical gaze from court records of sodomy cases to this queer theater, one can perhaps detect a utopian strain or, at the very least, a liberatory model of the drama: thus, for example, she writes that the erotic puns "inscribe a place within early modern culture in which homoerotic double talk is both erotic and celebratory, funny and profitable" (5). To attend to the Whitefriars theater, she suggests, is to encounter a lost world of sexual pleasures; further, she seems to intimate, an acquaintance with this repertory can remedy decades of homophobic—or simply prudish—criticism and "can temper a twentieth century wish to divest . . . subjects of their communities, their collaborations, and their intimacy" (144). There is of course, much to be admired in Bly's stance here and throughout this book, not least the intelligence and energy with which she works to "out" the truth of homoeroticism in this period's drama. But her polemical edge—her admirable wish to "glimpse a moment less burdened with anxiety and more potent with desire than are extant trial records addressing sodomy" (5)— seems to allow certain questions about the nature of this desire to remain unanswered, indeed unasked. More precisely, one might wonder whether the drama she explores may provide narratives about desire that are less celebratory than those she adumbrates: that is, one might wonder whether the bawdy wit she uncovers might be hooked into other narratives about early modern sexuality, narratives about such matters as aggressiveness, shame, and exposure. Early in her book, Bly distinguishes between "contemptuous" and "sympathetic" humor, suggesting the necessity for looking at plays "in which laughter resonates not with anger but with desire" (19–20) and contending that Whitefriars' puns are "used not to mock but to engage, not to condemn but to titillate" (20). Surely it is wise to distinguish, as Bly does, between a theater (in this case, so she suggests, most early modern theaters) "in which one erotic minority consistently served as the object of humor" and another (the Whitefriars) that talks back, as it were, providing a counterdiscourse that "reveals its own homoerotic, humorous pleasure" (21). And yet, following Freud's insights into the nature of jokes, one might also ask whether it is possible to sustain this absolute distinction between contemptuous and sympathetic humor: when the Whitefriars punsters bribe their audience with homoerotic delights, what hostile desires are being laid bare? Who or what is being hated, shamed, or exposed via their bawdy wit?

Laughter is a key word for Bly in this book, which makes a convincing case for the theater as a palace of pleasure. One measure of Bly's success— one of the things that makes *Queer Virgins* such an accomplished and valuable work—is that her labor of deciphering and explaining what was once outrageously explicit may make it hard to read the plays of this period without grinning broadly. And yet Bly's ambitious book—a book whose opening sentence echoes Stephen Greenblatt's famous pronouncement as she declares her desire "to laugh with the dead" (1)—also invites one to take the laughter seriously and to consider the possibilities of a less comfortable cathexis with the dead. In short, retrieving what's been lost may mean retrieving something more than the ludic moments of freewheeling eros to which Bly calls our attention; if one takes the Whitefriars puns as seriously as she suggests that we ought, then one might be inclined to see the need for yet more analysis, yet more close reading. Might the erotic wordplay she identifies also be bound up with anxieties about market or libidinal economies; with matters of social order, patrilineage, and inheritance; or with unease about bodies' gendered female as well as male? By opening a window into this world, Bly even invites us to ask whether the homoerotic humor she traces in these plays may be intimately connected with discourses of misogyny and homophobia. While she doesn't provide an answer to such questions, she performs what in the end may be a more valuable service: In ensuring that readers can no longer miss the obscenities that are the stuff of this drama, she offers us a wonderful model for a reading practice that recognizes historical alterity and welcomes the arduous task of learning a language whose queerness we have only begun to reckon with.

Notes

1. On this point, see, for example, Mario DiGangi, *The Homoerotics of Early Modern Drama* (Cambridge: Cambridge University Press, 1997).
2. See Bray, *Homosexuality in Renaissance England* (London: Gay Men's Press, 1982).
3. Eve Kosofsky Sedgwick, "Queer and Now," *Tendencies* (Durham, NC: Duke University Press), 8.

Re-Presenting Ben Jonson: Text, History, Performance, edited by Martin Butler. New York: St. Martin's Press, 1999; London: Macmillan Press, 1999. Pp. xii + 255. Cloth $55.00.

Reviewer: RICHARD FINKELSTEIN

The boom in Shakespearean editing has been trickling down to his contemporaries. Middleton and Chapman have gained new standard editions; new anthologies of Renaissance drama are replacing Fraser and Rabkin; the revolution in bibliographic theory is spreading to other early modern dramatic texts. Under the general editorship of Martin Butler, David Bevington, and Ian Donaldson, a *Cambridge Edition of the Works of Ben Jonson* is in process. Its editors, and the contributors to the volume under review, have an ambitious goal: supplanting the much revered if less loved eleven volume edition and commentary by Herford and Simpson. Indeed, one could now say that the Oxford edition (1925–52) dates back two centuries: Herford and Simpson began their research when Victoria still ruled England. It is a monument to nineteenth-century education and erudition, with its untranslated Latin and Greek, its rigorous concept of original spelling, its strict vision of final authorial intentions, and its visual likeness to facsimiles. The contributors to Butler's volume nod respectfully at their editorial predecessors but emphasize the problems of using, and misjudgments in, the Oxford edition.

Re-Presenting Jonson makes its argument by drawing on a rich store of pub-lishing history, bibliographical theory, stage history, and common sense. Butler and his contributors have manufactured an effective *prolegomena* for the new Cambridge Edition and also, an advertisement for the increased read-ing, performance, and rethinking of Jonson's works. True to their argument that people should know *more* of Jonson, they refreshingly give us two essays on *Every Man Out,* one on *Catiline,* much on the texts and their history, and nothing on plays commonly discussed.

The official evolution of both this volume and the Cambridge edition began in 1993 at a small conference, with members of Cambridge University Press, to review options for re-presenting Jonson. A larger conference, from which this volume derives, was held in 1995 at the University of Leeds.[1] The twelve included essays, largely by distinguished Jonson scholars, wonderfully make the inquiries which are today necessary when planning a new edition. As a group, the authors significantly revise our sense of Jonson's involvement with the publication of his works; of the best copy-texts for modern editors; of the provisionality of his career; of performance possibilities; and of Jonson's sources and influence. Although not led by any one theoretical orientation, they align themselves with current editorial theory by emphasizing the mate-rial record over Jonson's carefully organized authorial presence.

Butler, in his introduction, and Bevington, in his essay, lay out the rationale for replacing Herford, Simpson, and Simpson. Perhaps the greatest problem with the Oxford edition is that it has "not translated into a Jonson who is widely and intimately known" (3), particularly with regard to less read plays and peripheral texts. Bevington believes that "a well-informed, sensibly priced and accessible complete edition [would] encourage the survival of Jonson's plays in the theatrical repertory" (22). He wisely argues that this edition should modernize Jonson's spelling; provide modern, not Roman stage directions; and supply modern notes that clarify and translate refer-ences, elliptical language, and foreign phrases. In short, Jonson should be presented like Shakespeare, and not in Oxford's arcane forms. In addition to the visual and linguistic challenges posed by the Oxford text, there is the very dated quality of its introductions and its survey of Jonson's career. Bevington rightly points out that Herford, Simpson, and Simpson somewhat overstate Jonson's classicism in their philological speculations; in part, the Oxford edi-tors lacked information on the theaters, printing houses, and historical occa-sions that are now available to scholars.

Curiously, although the Swan Theater in Stratford has revived some of Jon-son's less read plays (such as *The Devil is an Ass, The New Inn,* and *Every Man In*), discussed by Lois Potter, productions have not proliferated for plays already in accessible editions, such as *Bartholomew Fair* and *Epicoene* (de-spite, for the latter, much academic writing about cross-dressing and cos-tume). Still, Bevington and Butler use forceful and logical arguments that lesser known plays could become more prominent with an updated *complete* edition. Certainly, the method of presentation in the new edition should stimulate interest. There will be an affordable print format for the works. Supplementary web materials will deepen Jonson's connection to his time and ours by supplying and constantly updating old-spelling versions, contextual, critical, and historical documents. Whatever its effects on popularization, this open-ended scheme will increase the quality not just of Jonsonian scholarship, teaching, and performance, but of early modern research in general.

Although this volume emphasizes a need to reconceive Jonson theatrically and stimulate performance, it lacks contributions from people based in drama departments or in professional theater. Potter and Helen Ostovich, however, inventively interpret or imagine performances to theorize editorial issues. Their projects challenge Jonson himself: they recognize that he would not have thought performance relevant to an ideal edition, given his antitheatrical prejudice and his desire to control our knowledge of him through the written record of the Folio. The productions Potter has seen remind us that there are a variety of Jonsons. This recognition shatters stereotypes that shape both editorial choices and textual interpretations. For example, Potter noticed that stage business she observed during silences in *Every Man In* (an updated Roman comedy) show it compatible with romantic elements like those seen by Anne Barton in late plays. Reading *Every Man Out* for its complex "choreographic" staging leads Ostovich to prefer the quarto as a copy text. Ostovich argues that when Jonson prepared the Folio, he chopped up and regularized vigorous scenes. If, in transforming performance into the Folio's written record, he diminishes the play's "witty combination of place and emblematic representation," why not privilege the early version in our own age, less antitheatrical than its author? Kevin Donovan's companion piece on *Every Man Out* similarly questions Jonson's manufactured illusion of final intentions. He sees Herford, Simpson, and Simpson seduced by Jonson's desire to give avant-garde comedy a humanist, neoclassical form in print. We can question whether early audiences thought *Every Man Out* as radical as do modern readers (Donovan is to some extent himself seduced by Cordatus, who insists the play is "strange," and not tied to "strict and regular formes" [*EMO* 231–70]). But *EMO* indeed provides the best argument for reading against Jonson's "final" decisions. As Donovan notes, it shows that the playwright deployed elaborate "bibliographic codes" to turn invention into a static record for study.

By implicitly revealing an alliance between Jonson and Herford, Simpson, and Simpson to "clean up" experiments, Donovan expresses one of this volume's central themes. As Bevington notes, the remarkable longevity and status of the Oxford edition have been bolstered by the belief that Jonson's texts are more stable than those of his contemporaries. However, Donovan's bibliographic analyses, the printing house studies of Gants and Bland, the performance thought of Potter and Ostovich, even the archival discoveries of James Knowles and Duncan-Jones, all destabilize the available record and show choice a greater factor than we thought.

For example, David Gants conducted an extraordinarily detailed examination of the Folio using collation technology unavailable to the Oxford editors. He found 1000 more variants than the 1500 they saw. Gants painstakingly reconstructs the process of printing to revise the legend of Jonson's obsessional oversight of Stansby's work on the Folio. Using a complicated set of assumptions, Gants persuasively shows that Jonson's involvement declined sharply over the course of printing. Nor does Gants believe that Jonson consistently read proofs at the printing house. Gants's analysis of several texts printed with the Folio shows that Stansby probably *sent* early pulls to Jonson for correction while leaving numerous pages standing. Because Herford, Simpson, and Simpson so privilege the Folio variants, they ironically give more credence to the errors of Stansby's house than they do to Jonson's choices.

Reconsideration of sources, influence, and chronology may not shape editorial choices as much as the above discoveries, but will have a significant impact on the commentary and scope of a new edition. In this volume, such rethinkings direct further attention to Jonson's range and relationship to his time. Blair Worden focuses on *Catiline* to emphasize that even Jonson's classicism was, like that of his contemporaries, mediated by early modern scholars. Worden adroitly delineates the influence of Justus Lipsius and Durantinus Felicius on Jonson's presentation of themes derived form Sallust and Tacitus in *Catiline*. Jonson's humanist *Catiline* explores "the conduct, within a vicious world, of virtue in action and in power" (170–71). This theme is not quite as unique to *Catiline* as Worden suggests: it is much pondered by Crites in *Cynthia's Revels*; travestied with Overdo in *Bartholomew Fair*; and depending how one defines politics, raised by the uses of Celia in *Volpone* and Lovel in *The New Inn*. Not surprisingly, like his peers, Jonson "anglicized Rome and romanized England."

For inexplicable reasons, the most direct records of Jonson's creative engagement with his London have largely been lost. Without them, another Jonsonian face is missing. Without his civic entertainments, we miss Jonson celebrating the kind of mercantilism—noise—criticized in so many of his plays. But there is now an exception—the rediscovered *Entertainment at Britain's Burse,* written at about the same time as *Epicoene.* The city entertainment praises the New Exchange's opening with a masque of "wondrous goods" that themselves generate the kind of activity frustrating to Morose. "Britain's Burse" contains much that we recognize: a sort of prologue (spoken by the key keeper), who at one time kept an inn and tavern (another Jonsonian "cook," appealing to our palate); an antimasque/masque structure; and long catalogues of stuff. James Knowles provides an edition of *Britain's*

Burse, traces the provenance of the text, and fully examines its original occasion and performance. He defers discussions of staging and critical issues to later essays. (He does, though, supply a letter from Thomas Wilson to the Earl of Salisbury that describes some of the *planned* staging for the event.) The festive attitude toward commerce taken by Jonson's entertainment gives us an author who seems increasingly distant from the Stoic, epideictic judge of his lyric verse.

Also unavailable to Herford, Simpson, and Simpson was the frequency analysis technology used by Hugh Craig to determine the chronological position of *A Tale of a Tub.* On a perennial battleground, Jonson scholars must choose between the Oxford editors' very early date, placing it first among Jonson's plays, and W. W. Greg's forceful argument for a late one. Identifying many layers, from Elizabethan to Caroline, Craig's conclusions benefit from our increasing emphasis on authorial revision. Because he believes that the text contains old material, revised material, and wholly new material, Craig speculates that *Tub* might have been Jonson's earliest *and* last piece for the stage. If so, we get even more of a native, romantic writer than we'd imagined: one who began his career with a festive and romantic comedy of village life; and towards the end, reused the same genre for the philosophically adorned *New Inn.* Although Jonson uses *The Magnetic Lady* to present his career as a circle returning to classically based humours comedies, his arc now seems more erratic. We will perhaps never untangle the riddle of *A Tale of a Tub.* The play's conscious archaisms, unique genre, and Jonson's likely revisions make it more difficult to compare to other plays than Craig would like, a problem he recognizes.

In different ways, both Michael Cordner and Robert Evans address the need to hear Jonsonian allusions and echoes better than the Oxford editors. Since the early twentieth century, the definition of influence itself has been revised—it now means much more than the strict source hunting of old historicists like Herford, Simpson, and Simpson. Somewhat peripheral to others in the volume, Michael Cordner's essay mainly studies John Wilson's Restoration play, *The Cheats,* which has a central character, Scruple, who descends from Jonson's Busy. *The Cheats* indexes late-century interpretations and expectations of Jonson. Cordner shows that Wilson depended on an audience well aware of *Bartholomew Fair,* even though they understood it in a Puritan cultural context. Indeed, we gain an amusing footnote to theater history when Cordner explains that, while planning a performance of *Fair,* the King's Company initially postponed performing the climactic scene in which puppets humiliate Busy. As in his other work on Jonson, Robert Evans provides a myriad of tantalizing references, and delineates provocative questions that they raise. He asks all the right editorial questions—about how an edition should define "allusion"; about why allusions should be in an edition; on how they should be organized; and about where to find new ones.

Evans closes the volume by wisely demonstrating ways in which facts and details shape research; yet Evans also sees the limitations of facts when he points out that they give us mainly "directions for future research" (241). New *complete* editions enable particular directions in scholarship. However, scholarship depends in part on accidental recognitions which allusions, source studies, and contexts only partly determine; interpreting their figuration within specific works is always a tough task. At least during the last half century or more, theory, too, has driven scholars' questions and shaped portraits of early modern authors and cultures. The new Cambridge editors smartly know that their work will not give us a *final* edition of Jonson, or his final character. Much as new theories help us see Jonson in context, so will they someday help us see this new edition in the context of its own assumptions—surely in a manner that will invigorate our use of it. And if we translate the vocabulary of Herford, Simpson, and Simpson with the right application of theory, their insights also will continue to enrich our knowledge of Jonson and his age. Rereading their introductions sometimes shows them less dated than using dated language. Their notes and attitudes certainly make connections that seem peripheral to us, but like a good library, may enable as yet undiscovered areas for study. Indeed, even as the methods of some writers in this volume mark our distance from the old historicism, others erase distinctions between old and new. We all have good reason to look forward to a re-edited Jonson: updated prefatory matter; increased attention to cultural context; cleaned up texts; modernized type; a better chronology; and dynamically updated records of history, performance, and much else. We can look forward to teaching a wider range of plays and genres. We will hear Jonson in the best twenty-first-century terms, if not for all time.

Notes

1. See Ian Donaldson, "A New Text of Ben Jonson?" *Ben Jonson Journal* 2 (1995): 223–31. Two essays which are largely interpretive in nature appear outside the volume under review. See Stephen Orgel, "Marginal Jonson," in D. Bevington and P. Holbrook, eds., *The Politics of the Stuart Court Masque* (Cambridge: Cambridge University Press, 1998), 144–75; and Ian Donaldson, "Jonson's Duplicity," in his *Jonson's Magic Houses: Essays in Interpretation* (Oxford: Oxford University Press, 1997), 46–65. Two other essays important for bibliographical work but not in the volume are Mark Bland, "William Stansby and the Production of the *Workes of Benjamin Jonson,* 1615–16," *Library* (6th series) 20 (1998): 1–33; and Katherine Duncan-Jones, "'They Say a Made a Good End': Ben Jonson's Epitaph on Thomas Nashe," *Ben Jonson Journal* 3 (1996): 1–19, the first version of which appeared in the *TLS* of 7 July 1995.

Shakespeare: The Comedies, by R. P. Draper. New York: St. Martin's Press, 2000. Pp. xii + 265. Cloth $55.00. Paper $19.95.

Reviewer: ANNETTE DREW-BEAR

This volume in the *Analysing Texts* series is an eminently sane, sound, and useful book, refreshingly free from trendy theory and strong in skillful, informed, and revealing textual analysis. Nicholas Marsh sets out the purpose of this series in his "General Editor's Preface." To "demystify" "the study of literature," each volume provides the reader with the "tools" or "samples of close, detailed analysis, with an explanation of the analytical techniques utilised," and "at the end of each chapter" provides "useful suggestions for further work" that the reader can practice (xi). In part 2 of each volume, "there are chapters about the rest of the author's work, assessing their contribution to developments in literature; and a sample of critics' views are summarised and discussed in comparison with each other" accompanied by suggestions for further reading (xi). This is an ambitious plan, but R. P. Draper fulfills these objectives with admirable flair.

Draper begins his book by defining "The Nature of Shakespearean Comedy" as transcending usual definitions because of its "kaleidoscopic" variety (4) and complex "happy confusion of characters, genres and contrasting styles" (6). As Draper puts it, "various facets of this complex comic process will be explored by close analysis of passages" from four comedies, *A Midsummer Night's Dream, Much Ado About Nothing, As You Like It,* and *Twelfth Night* (5). In his initial chapter on "Atmospherics," Draper establishes "Methods of Analysis" involving both "language" and "speaker, speech and dramatic context." Under language, Draper advises his readers to "look closely at (a) choice of words, including puns, (b) use of rhetorical devices and the structure of sentences, and (c) the use of figurative language. In verse also pay particular attention to (d) metre, rhythm, pauses and the use of end-stopped or run-on lines" (20). This is sound advice, rooted in rhetorical analysis and in new critical "intrinsic" or text-based analysis that contemporary students need to learn to truly "read" or comprehend the text. Recent works like Russ McDonald's *Shakespeare and the Arts of Language* (Oxford University Press, 2001), which reprises part of the title of Sister Miriam Joseph's significant *Shakespeare's Use of the Arts of Language* (Columbia University Press, 1947), testify to the resurgence of interest in rhetorical analysis. Draper may be asking a bit much of typical Shakespeare students, however, in his advice on recognizing metrical variations: "Hearing both the underlying metric pattern and the surface variations from it, and gauging the extent of the disruptive effect of these variations, should become a natural part of your response to Shakespeare's verse" (22). The second topic, "speaker, speech and dramatic context" acknowledges the play as a performance text containing "clues" for interpretation in the tradition of John Barton's video-tapes and his book *Playing Shakespeare*.

Draper's chapter on "Sympathetic Criticism" analyzes passages from *As You Like It* to illustrate how Shakespearean comedy balances "sympathy and criticism" (35). The chapter on "Illusion" examines passages from all four comedies to show how "illusion takes on a multiplicity of forms" (38). Similarly, in "Romantic Sentiment," Draper shows how passages from each of the four plays display Shakespeare's "double-visioned awareness of love and romance" (69), his "awareness of the ambivalent nature of romance" and his "delicate counterpoint between sympathy and criticism" (70). The chapters on "Wooing," "Fools (1): Dupes," "Fools (2): Clever Fools," and "Manlike Women" are particularly accessible to students since they focus on specific issues that readily engage our interest. Draper excels in "teasing-out of the implications" of passages in the plays (157) and in demonstrating how "a more than usually heightened awareness is needed of linguistic devices and their tonal implications" (159). With Draper's good examples as models, one would surely hope that students who are asked to do some of the intriguing "Suggested Work" at the end of the chapter on "Wooing" and on "Fools (2): Clever Fools" would also excel. Students would also enjoy the chapter on "Manlike Women" which demonstrates how "these boy-represented hero-ines reveal manlike qualities which challenge conventional ideas of woman-hood" (163). The chapter on "Odd Men Out" convincingly argues that "Odd men out" "are a prophylactic against complacency; they inoculate a comedy against its own necessary, yet potentially harmful, sense of what its destiny should be" (191). "Set Pieces" provides exemplary analyses of how the part relates to the whole and offers good ideas for "Suggested Work" for students to pursue. In "Endings" Draper productively applies his analytical method to the closing scenes of all four comedies.

In "Part 2: The Context and the Critics," Draper briefly relates the four comedies to other Shakespearean comedies, poems, and then to the histories, tragedies, and last plays. One might add to his necessarily brief account of Henry's wooing of Katherine in *Henry V* the fact that Henry's wooing skill-fully utilizes the very rhetorical strategies that he pretends to eschew (using eloquent *occupatio,* for example, to plead his cause), illustrating once again the multifaceted nature of the language. Draper's chapter on "Theories of Comedy and Criticism of Shakespeare's Comedies" presents a judicious ac-count of the theoretical context refreshingly free of jargon and of the need to endorse one theory at the expense of others or at the expense of the plays. In fact, Draper wisely recognizes that "Shakespeare is also, as a man of the theatre, very much seized by what works on the stage; and what works may (fruitfully) disrupt the patterns and structures perceived by the critic" (256). In keeping with his stress throughout the book on the multiplicity of the com-edies, Draper concludes by pointing to the "openness of the imagination which is the distinguishing mark of Shakespearean comedy, and the thing that makes it at once so lastingly entertaining and so endlessly capable of disturbing" (257). Draper's own openness to the infinite variety of Shakespeare's comedies provides a welcome model for analysis. The suggestions for further reading are necessarily selective but sound. One might question why Draper chooses to use Peter Alexander's 1951 edition of the plays when, as he himself acknowledges, recent well annotated editions exist. Also, Draper misquotes Ben Jonson. In his *Discoveries* Jonson said, "Speak that I may see thee" not "Speak that I may know thee" (122). These cavils aside, I would enthusiastically recommend this book to anyone who wishes, in the general editor's words, to read a book "designed to stimulate and encourage your critical and analytic faculty, to develop your personal insight into the author's work and individual style, and to provide you with the skills and techniques to enjoy at first hand the excitement of discovering the richness of the text" (xi).

The History of Morris Dancing, 1458–1750, by John Forrest. Toronto and Buffalo: University of Toronto Press, 1999. Pp. xviii + 439. Cloth $65.

Reviewer: SKILES HOWARD

As John Forrest observes in his exciting investigation of *The History of Morris Dancing, 1458–1750,* "there was never a time when one could speak of *the* morris dance," since "morris" might have referred to a mass procession, a solo jig, a wooing "ring dance," a country couple dance, a martial sword dance, or the familiar pantomime with the hobby horse and Maid Marian (xvii). Expanding and extending his earlier publication with Michael Heaney, *Annals of Early Morris* (accessible in Appendix A, "Methodological Issues: The Early Morris Database and Archive"), *The History of Morris Dancing* presents with impeccable detail and clarity the development of the practice in all its variety. Supported by a wealth of lively quotations from a spectrum of sources, the work provides a timely and enthralling addition to the contemporary scholarly discussion on popular culture in early modern England. For, as Forrest emphasizes, his work is not only a record of the evolution of the morris dance but encompasses the social history, transformations, and conflicts of its contexts as well (xviii). Beginning with the first known reference to the morris, a bequest in 1458 of silver cups decorated with the image of a morris dancer (48), and culminating in a detailed study of the history of Aynho House, Northants, and the morris teams that, according to household records, performed there between 1696 and 1792, the work promises to be an invaluable resource for specialists in Shakespeare and Renaissance drama, dance history, and cultural studies.

Forrest, an anthropologist, productively enlists the methodologies of his discipline to interpret the profusion of references to the morris in early modern texts as diverse as plays, court masques, chronicles, household accounts, and ecclesiastical records, as well as in an extensive array of more recent works from dance reconstructions, to studies of the festive calendar, to social histories of the Reformation in England. In this boldly revisionary work which "challenges a number of cherished ideas concerning English culture at critical junctures" (xviii), Forrest disputes the cherished and persistent "origin" theories of antiquarians and folklorists such as Sharp and Chambers—all, as he rightly emphasizes, with political, social, or ideological agendas of their own (3)—who claimed to have discovered the single genesis of morris dancing. Instead, he merges developmental analysis with a text-in-context approach to trace the evolution over three centuries of the various dances subsumed under the designation "morris," based not on the anachronisms that have marked genetic studies but on primary materials rigorously examined in the contexts of time, place, and participants—the latter particularly relevant to developmental issues of transmission over time and between classes (xvii). But the work has a broader purpose, as Forrest explains, which is

to use the fine-grained details of the developmental history of Morris dancing as a case study for reflections on a much more general and analytic plane concerning the cultural transmission of ideas over time and space, evolution in the arts and aesthetic forms, the sources of creativity and innovation, and the interplay between aesthetics and other arenas of cultural life. These reflections permeate the work and are drawn together at the end. My hope is to show, in principle, how the most exacting dissection of the smallest events on the most local of scales can open out into visions of the universal. (xviii)

The first three chapters—"Theories of Origin," "The Contexts," and "Earliest References"—and the last, "Endings," review traditionalist genetic theories, explain the assumptions and methodology that ground Forrest's work, and discuss the first few allusions to the dance, found principally in wills and account books. Did the morris dance originate in classical antiquity, pagan rites, or court masque? Did it arrive in England from Morocco via Spain, or perhaps from France? Did it derive from old English festival, or Moorish revelry? Or was it actually the invention of the devil himself? Forrest dismisses antique and modern speculations alike as deficient in solid documentary evidence, or, alternatively, as based on tenuous premises, such as the "morris / Moorish" cognate. In contrast with the genetic model, which, he asserts, emphasized essential and unchanging pattern (11) and grounded present practices in the past (15), the evolutionary model focuses on diffusion, on change over time, and the mechanisms of change: "[c]ontemporary physical anthropology," Forrest insists, "suggests that there are few, if any, monolithic origin points or events, but rather identifies nodal points in a general evolutionary process" (11). Together with the concept of a bidirectional flow of ideas (353) and a non-Hegelian dialectical model of dissemination (355ff.), the evolutionary model, Forrest asserts, accommodates important transformations of meanings over time (11).

Additionally, the text-in-context approach expedites an investigation of the complexities of dancing practice with the assumption that "cultural forms derive meaning from the ways in which they are structured into a particular culture, and [that] every form has multilayered metaphoric and metonymic connections to other parts of the culture" (25). Consequently, in building typologies, Forrest has privileged context over form and used it as a frame to analyze what he calls the "dance event," a category that embraces elements of form such as costume and gesture as well as contextual factors such as venue, patrons, and performers (26). *The History of Morris Dancing* is structured by the major categories of what Forrest terms "venue" in which the dance was documented to occur—the royal court, urban streets, church property, the public stage, the countryside, the country dance hall, and private houses or estates. Events in each of these contexts are prolifically documented with energetic and appropriate textual selections, which Forrest situates, analyzes, and interprets with scrupulous lucidity. The sequential predominance of each of these contexts over time is vividly portrayed by Forrest's use of the seriation technique to show the peak textual occurrences of the morris dance in each venue—royal venues, for example, peak first (1480–1510), followed by urban streets (1541–70), church property (1571–1600), village (1601–90), and private houses (1721–50); stage morrises, at once representation and event, resist, Forrest notes, the limits of seriation.[1]

According to Forrest in chapter 4 on the "Royal Court," account books and chronicles testify that the most active royal patronage for the morris occurred in the early Tudor courts of Henry VII and Henry VIII. He argues that during this era, although morris dancing exhibited "general continuities," there are indications that it was "not a single, simple phenomenon" (58), and he classifies morris references into two groups based on context: the opulent "disguising" and the less spectacular festival event (58–59). Forrest disputes the tenacious notion of the dances' folk origins—the theory that the court morris was an elite version of a rustic dance—for lack of documentary evidence (60), and suggests that the courtly disguising, with which the morris was strongly associated, demonstrated links with the earlier forms of tournament and mumming (62). These links, he speculates, may, in turn, explain aspects of the form and developmental trajectory of the morris—its martial flavor, courtship plots (or parodies), and gestural characteristics.

In chapter 5, Forrest discusses the occurrences of the morris on "Urban Streets" and its subtle differences in a variety of celebration, specifically the Midsummer Watch, the Lord-of-Misrule processions, guild processions outside London, and May Games. Popular in the city throughout the early modern era, the morris was particularly so between 1520 and 1580 as an element of the Midsummer Guild processions and the May games (92), as guild records of expenditures and contemporary descriptions of the spectacles by chroniclers and observers such as John Stow and Henry Machyn attest. Sources for the arrangement of the Midsummer Watch, a festival of civic order, suggest that the sequence of the quasi-military procession was well established, and that the morris dancers performed a kind of heralding function (103). The accounts, Forrest argues, suggest that the dancers enjoyed a relatively high social status, liverymen who were paid commensurately with minstrels, above the level of the unskilled participants in the processions (109), and were—perhaps uniquely among the elements in the processions—a preexisting group hired, not assembled, for the occasion (106). The morris was also associated, perhaps as a kind of free-floating festive element (115), with what Forrest calls the mirror image of Midsummer celebrations, the winter Lord-of-Misrule processions that celebrated the breakdown of order (111) with mock tournaments and other parodic enactments of aristocratic order. Finally, in the May Games, morris dancers were both part of the procession into the country and back, and performed with other traditional festive personages such as hobbyhorse and maypole in the unbridled revels that followed.

May games were, of course, much excoriated by Puritan sympathizers (138), and Chapters 6 and 7 deal with the performance of the morris on church property and its subsequent proscription and prosecution. Unlike the expensive courtly and urban spectacles of which the morris was an important element (171)—and ironically in the light of later prosecutions—the morris was initially sponsored by the church in fund-raising ales (140), where it became "entangled" with Robin Hood (146), Friar Tuck, and Maid Marian (156–57). Morris dancing at the ales, Forrest speculates, may well have begun as a parody of the courtly morisk, which comprised a series of quite different dances based on either competition and combat or symbolic wooing, and which, in rural settings during the sixteenth century adopted ideas and figures from country dancing (167). However, the church turned against dancing on its property, and the morris dances took their revenues elsewhere, depriving the churches of needed income at a time when they bore the cost of successive Protestant, Catholic, and Protestant renovations (175–76).

The loss of revenue, Forrest speculates, may have intensified ecclesiastical hostility toward morris dancing. Church prosecutions reached their zenith in the period between 1601 and 1630, which led to a precipitous decline in dance events between 1631 and 1660, Forrest reports. Church opposition to morris dances—ostensibly moral but covertly ideological (186)—took three primary forms: sermons and polemics, episcopal injunctions, and prosecutions. Forrest examines each of these during the reigns of Elizabeth, James I and Charles I, the Interregnum, and the Restoration, supporting his discussion with the tabulation of Visitation Articles in Appendix B. Ultimately, he points out, in banning the festivities of which morris was a part, the Church destroyed an important occasion for social cohesion in the countryside, and a force for the maintenance of the status quo (214).

On the public stage, Forrest emphasizes in chapter 8, morris dances presented special complications in terms of evolution and diffusion (30–31), since they were simultaneously dance and enactment (217), and took place in two discrete venues—the world of the play, and the world of stage and audience (216). They were employed in plays, usually to add a rustic touch, from the late Elizabethan era to the Restoration, and especially around the time that prosecutions were taking place in the countryside (215). Surprisingly, although the morris exerts a strong imaginative presence in the modern imagination, Forrest points out that only fourteen plays had a morris dance in them, eleven of these staged during the years of greatest incidence (215). The best known of these plays are *The Shoemaker's Holiday, The Witch of Edmonton,* and *Two Noble Kinsmen,* but Forrest's stimulating exposition of the morris in each of the plays in which it appeared will illuminate new dimensions of the plays for readers of Renaissance drama. Although not a major venue for the dance, the stage did, Forrest notes, bring together strands from court, rural, and urban dance, elite and popular culture, and professional and amateur performance (257), often functioning as a class marker onstage (257) and a rustic pleasure as seen through the eyes of townsmen (258).

Chapters 9 through 11 deal with the morris in rural locations, country dance halls, and on private estates. Forrest sees the rural morris as a continuation and development of the church-sponsored morris, taking both the forms of a processional and a general dance (275), and representing the simple, wholesome pleasures of the country people in contrast to those of the city and court, the old ways as opposed to the new (292). However, under the influence of country dancing, Forrest discerns a general shift from individual, competitive movements to patterned group action, including the longways set and elaborate figures (277) familiar from Playford's *English Dancing Master,*[2] the first English dancing manual. Elite adaptations by dancing masters of "country" dances became the "new bourgeois taste" (295): an example of their elaborate choreography and intricate floor pattern is supplied by Allan Terry's transcription from Feuillet notation of *Mr. Isaac's Morris,* in Appendix C. Finally, Forrest examines morris dancing on private premises, from the Oxford colleges to the estates of the country gentry. What was a source of revenue for the churches became a "secular vehicle for largess from the gentry" (331), and the culmination of Forrest's work is a lengthy and detailed examination of manor economies and morris dances at Aynho House, Northants. "Following the many threads [of each dance idea] and their contexts reveals a rich tapestry woven into England's history," Forrest writes in the introduction (xviii), and this impressive book examines the morris and its settings in luxuriant and compelling detail.

Notes

1. In Appendix D, a graph of all extant churchwardens' accounts from Ronald Hutton's data in *The Rise and Fall of Merry England: The Ritual Year 1400–1700* (Oxford: Oxford University Press, 1994), Forrest is careful to qualify a rise in the mention of a custom as a possible artefact of extant sources in a way that a decline is not.

2. John Playford, *The English Dancing Master: or Plaine and Easie Rules for the Dancing of Country Dances, with the Tune to Each Dance* (London, printed by Thomas Harper, 1651). (London: DanceBooks Ltd., 1984).

Staging in Shakespeare's Theatres, by Andrew Gurr and Mariko Ichikawa. Oxford and New York: Oxford University Press, 2000, Pp. vi + 181. Cloth $39.95.

Reviewer: ROSLYN L. KNUTSON

According to the description on the book jacket, the "Oxford Shakespeare Topics" series is intended for students and teachers; the entry in that series, *Staging in Shakespeare's Theatres* by Andrew Gurr and Mariko Ichikawa, combines theater history, staging conditions, and performance issues. In the opening chapters, the authors subordinate theater history as defined by playing companies and their business to issues such as the experience of the playgoer in the physical and emotional environment of the playhouse, the flexibility of texts and playing venues, and the architecture of indoor and outdoor London playhouses. The middle chapters focus on aspects of staging and stage movement: costumes, properties, entrances, exits, and the openings in the stage façade. The final chapter is "a detailed account of how one play, *Hamlet,* might have been staged at the Globe in 1601" (2).

This final chapter is the practical application of the generalities of the previous chapters. It therefore ought to demonstrate how moments in the performance are enhanced by the choice of one text over alternatives, one playhouse over other possible venues, and one rule of thumb for the use of entry and exit doors with variations only as necessitated by textual considerations. Instead, the conjectural performance of *Hamlet* often demonstrates that generalizations have little force in theater history. As the authors concede, most of their claims about stage conditions, texts as performance guides, and use of the stage doors yield to "the best-guess principle" (122), a principle impossible to differentiate from the authors' directorial preferences. The

1601 text is the first to go. Gurr and Ichikawa choose the First Folio text, "adding stage directions from Q1 and Q2 whenever they appear to add anything significant to the F text" (125). They acknowledge that their reconstruction is therefore "an optimal performance" (122), that is, longer than any 1601 performance is likely to have been, but that acknowledgement does little to alter the sense that the performance is being imagined for Wanamaker's Globe, not Shakespeare's.

The choices made by Gurr and Ichikawa for the first act illustrate the problem of turning generalizations into specific practice. Launching the performance, the authors interpret the stage direction in F, "*Enter Barnardo and Francisco two Centinels,*" as the entry of Barnardo through the door on the left and Francisco through the door on the right. This decision may appear inconsequential, yet it looks back to a lengthy discussion in chapter 5 about the openings in the stage façade (called the *frons* by the authors) and conventions that might have "governed the use of the stage doors" (97). In that discussion, Gurr and Ichikawa designate Bernard Beckerman's suggestion that one door was used for entrances and one for exits as the "O" rule and propose ten situational exceptions to it, the first of which is simultaneous entry. Yet in a discussion of that exception, the authors point out that two characters may enter from the same door and be unaware of each other; they cite as evidence the opening stage direction of 1.3, *Julius Caesar*: ". . . *Enter Caska, and Cicero.*" Preceding the discussion of act 1 of *Hamlet,* the authors formulate the "S" rule, by which actors exit by their entry door, and the "L" rule, by which one door represents interior space, the other the outdoors; but neither applies to the case of Barnardo and Francisco. Gurr and Ichikawa decide that the first exception to the "O" rule does apply. Francisco will exit by Barnardo's entry door, through which Horatio and Marcellus are entering, thus invoking exception "iv" to the "O" rule, which allows exiting and entering characters to meet and exchange greetings. Thus, by their choices in stage movement for the opening lines of the play, Gurr and Ichikawa waive the constraint of generalizations such as the "O" rule, finding permission in exceptions to the rule to make their own directorial choices.

Gurr and Ichikawa use the entry of Horatio and Marcellus to raise another topic they introduced in earlier chapters, namely, the issue of class in Elizabethan times. Many in the projected audience of the Oxford series may be relatively unfamiliar with the degree to which Elizabethan dramatic texts exploit the decorum of dress and certain deferential behaviors; therefore, it is genuinely helpful and audience-sensitive for Gurr and Ichikawa to indicate moments where the texts invites or stage business permits these issues to resonate. For example, in their conjectural production, Horatio wears velvet; his hat is feathered; his weapon is a rapier. As the authors explain, such a hat, weapon, and suit mark Horatio as a gentleman. Marcellus, by contrast, is dressed more soberly; he carries a partisan, a weapon that marks him as a junior officer, superior to the sentinels with their halberds. In addition to the contrast above of Marcellus with Horatio, and both with the sentinels, Gurr and Ichikawa point out instances where decorum may be indicated ironically, as when Hamlet behaves indecorously during Claudius's ceremonious scene of courtly togetherness, and when he continues to greet Rosencrantz and Gildenstern as friends even though he knows they are spies. The authors also explore the comic possibilities of violating protocol, e.g., the *faux pas* of Osric with his hat in the scene where he invites Hamlet to the fencing match.

To open scene 2, Gurr and Ichikawa have the court party enter through a third door in the stage façade, a "central doorway or aperture" (96), which is curtained and "exceptionally broad" (123), thus making it easy for a dais with chairs for the monarchs to be thrust out onstage. As used by the authors, the central opening is a valuable interpretative dimension of the performance. It enhances the status of the king, and his ceasing to use it in later scenes is a visual signal of his fall. The players appropriate the king's power in little by using his entrance as their stage, and the ghost "reflects his kingly status" by using it to enter and exit Gertrude's bedchamber (144). In chapter 5, "The Three Openings in the *Frons,*" Gurr and Ichikawa claim that scholars generally agree "that Shakespeare's playhouses had three entryways" (96), and they discuss situations where the players "might have benefited from the use of the central opening" (105). Few scholars would dispute the *benefit* of such an opening, but there is not similar accord on its nature and availability at various theatrical venues. Scholars seem to agree that a third opening was most likely at a private playhouse such as the Blackfriars and least likely at touring venues (as the authors themselves acknowledge [25]). The debate seems to be on the nature and presence of a third central opening on London public stages such as the Globe where the authors' conjectural performance of *Hamlet* takes place. The Swan drawing does not show a middle door, but that drawing as evidence of the design of the public playhouses is increasingly being disputed. Addressing the issue, scholars have suggested various possibilities. For the staging of *Sir Thomas More* at the Rose, Scott McMillin suggests a "removable pavilion, curtained below for discoveries and interiors, its roof affording ample space above" for scenes involving more than a few characters who engage in busy and prolonged action.[1] In *Enter the Whole Army,* a gathering of his drawings from the New Cambridge Shakespeare series, C. Walter Hodges depicts a third opening as an interior "discovery space" large enough to accommodate a three-tiered tomb (fig. 13, *Romeo and Juliet*), as a raised set of stairs or a pulpit adjoining but separate from the façade (fig. 11, *Richard II*; fig. 15, *Julius Caesar*), and as an extension of the upper balcony into a porch (fig. 46, *The Tempest*).[2] Alan Dessen and Leslie Thomson find only one stage direction in some five hundred plays that names "*three several doors*" and one that could be so interpreted.[3] Therefore, by taking the third opening in the façade as fact and following the "best-guess principle" as to use, Gurr and Ichikawa gloss over the hypotheses on central entry spaces that scholars are still testing with argument and evidence.

   The treatment of King Hamlet's ghost is another example of generalization modified by practice. Discussing costuming in chapter 3, Gurr and Ichikawa say that ghosts "wore a recognizable shroud" (53).[4] Yet as they point out, the inventory lists in the memorandum book kept by Philip Henslowe at the Rose list "j gostes sewt, and gostes bodeyes."[5] And, in their reconstructed performance, the ghost dresses in armor when he appears on the battlements (as the text suggests he should); in Gertrude's bedroom, he wears a nightgown (as the stage direction in Q1 indicates he should). The authors also consider the ghost's means of entry and exit. In 1.1 of their performance, the ghost enters through the trapdoor, exits and re-enters through the stage door at the right, and exits through the trap. When he meets Hamlet in 1.5, the ghost enters by way of the trap, exits with Hamlet by way of the door on the right, re-enters with him through the door on the left, then exits through the trap. In the bedroom scene (3.4), the ghost enters and exits through the central curtained opening, "stepping over a corpse [Polonius's] . . . and ignoring it entirely" (144). Bernard Beckerman, in his study of stage practice at the Globe, offered a simpler stage movement. His ghost used the doors at left and right for all entrances and exits, and he used the trap only as a space beneath from which to cry "Swear" (Beckerman points out that the ghost has plenty of time—fifty-seven lines—after his exit through the door to get to the trap under the stage).[6] The point of these differences is, in one sense, often Gurr and Ichikawa's point: stage directions that provide nothing more than "Enter" and "Exit" leave it to scholars to determine the common denominators in Elizabethan staging practice. However, in a putative reconstruction, it can be confusing when choices are driven by the authors' interpretation of significant themes in the play instead of some principle of Elizabethan practice.

   An informative, interesting, but questionably germane aspect of the reconstructed staging of *Hamlet* is the attention to stage business. No one would question that there *was* stage business on the Elizabethan stage, but it is debatable whether a description of exemplary Shakespearean staging is the place for such interpretation. One instance of authorial interpretation that arguably goes beyond a consideration of sixteenth-century stage practice is the commentary on Hamlet's reaction to the ghost (1.5). Gurr and Ichikawa imagine that he "uses both hands to make a vivid visual gesture, putting his hands to his head as he says, 'Remember thee? / I, thou pore Ghost, while memory holds a seate / In this distracted Globe'" (131). The authors explain further: "The gesture affirms the fourfold visual and verbal pun of clutching his head, an orb driven to distraction" (131). The stage business of Hamlet's clutching his head leads to a digression on another dimension of the "head/ orb" pun, the comparison Hamlet makes of himself with Hercules. There follows a micro-essay on the aptness of such a comparison, its frequency, and metathetricality. A second instance of interpretation is the micro-essay on "Hamlet the Dane" (153). The authors have discussed the textual-theatrical moment earlier (e.g., 50), and the digression on Hamlet's identification of himself to the mourners at Ophelia's gravesite is interesting but arguably irrelevant to stage practice in a reconstructed performance of the 1601 *Hamlet.*

Few readers will find serious fault with the specific choices made by Gurr and Ichikawa in their direction of *Hamlet* in entrances, exits, costuming, and even such imagined stage business as Ophelia's stumbling approach to Hamlet in the "nunnery" scene, carrying a "small fabric package [of love tokens], which she extends to him with a brief curtsey, but which he rejects with a casual wave" (138). The issue is the degree to which the Gurr-Ichikawa reconstruction can be put forward as an illustration of Elizabethan stage practice. In chapter 2, the authors acknowledge the difficulty of recognizing a generalization about performance behind a specific piece of evidence such as a stage direction: "In this kind of study there are many areas of uncertainty, and a related danger that too much weight can be put on individual instances as a mark of general practice" (47). There is also a danger in setting forth generalizations, then constructing an exemplary performance that is not covered by them. The concept of moving from evidence on stage practice to generalizations about that evidence to practical application of the generalization to a performance is an attractive one (even if an entire chapter is given to a discussion of how many lines it takes for a character to enter or exit the stage), but it is inevitable that the choices of the authors will require an air of authenticity despite interjected reminders that the imagined performance is largely guesswork. Students and teachers for whom *Staging in Shakespeare's Theatres* is supposedly a handbook on Elizabethan staging will have to read closely to sort out Gurr and Ichikawa's directorial preferences from documentary evidence.

Notes

1. Scott McMillin, *The Elizabethan Theatre and "The Book of Sir Thomas More"* (Ithaca: Cornell University Press, 1987), 133.

2. C. Walter Hodges, *Enter the Whole Army* (Cambridge: Cambridge University Press, 1999). Hodge's fig. 20 shows five views of the tiring-house wall, each with a different design for the conjectured third opening.

3. Alan Dessen and Leslie Thomson, *A Dictionary of Stage Directions in English Drama, 1580–1642* (Cambridge: Cambridge University Press, 1999), entry for "several, severally." The direction, *"three several doors,"* occurs in *The Maid's Metamorphosis,* which was played at the indoor playhouse at Paul's. The stage direction that possibly indicates a third door occurs in *Patient Grissil,* a play given at the outdoor Fortune, by which two characters enter "at severall doors" and a third enters "in the

mid'st"; Gurr and Ichikawa cite it but not the one from *The Maid's Metamorphosis* (105).

4. Though the authors do not say, their authority is probably the prologue of *A Warning for Fair Women* (King's Men, Globe, 1599), in which Comedy accuses Tragedy of bringing in "a filthie whining ghost, / Lapt in some fowle sheete, or a leather pelch" to cry "Vindicta."

5. R. A. Foakes and R. T. Rickert (eds), *Henslowe's Diary* (Cambridge: Cambridge University Press, 1961), 318, 321. Henslowe also listed "j gostes crown" (321).

6. Bernard Beckerman, *Shakespeare at the Globe, 1599–1609* (New York: Macmillan, 1964), 202. Beckerman quotes John C. Adams as arguing that the use of the trap is usually accompanied by the sounds of thunder in order to disguise the noise of the trap machinery.

King Henry VIII, or All is True, by William Shakespeare and John Fletcher, ed. Jay L. Halio, The Oxford Shakespeare (Oxford: Oxford University Press, 1999). Pp. x + 230. Cloth $72, paper $7.95.

Reviewer: MICHAEL A. WINKELMAN

What vaileth trouth?

—Sir Thomas Wyatt

King Henry VIII harbors several problems for students, advanced scholars, or theater companies to work out. Questions of authorship and title may keep literary critics busy, while juicy roles and spectacular scenes can occupy those involved with practical staging decisions. Thematic matters, too, such as the tragic *de casibus* pattern of nobles falling, can involve the mental exertions of sundry interested parties. A favorite onstage through the nineteenth century, this play full of pomp and pageantry was first performed in 1613. Of late it has attracted sustained academic interest for its "shifty" re-presentations of Henry's reign. Shakespeare's last history makes for gripping theater.

Jay Halio's modern-spelling *Henry VIII* succeeds in providing a reliable text of the play, with sufficient background to guide a great variety of readers. This volume for the Oxford Shakespeare series is solid, informative, and easy to use. Like other recent critical editions, this *Henry VIII* presents the script with glosses, references, and brief historical explanations at the bottom of the page. A collation of significant variants appears between the dialogue and the notes in tiny type. There is also a useful, wide-ranging introduction (1–61), an index, and a short but helpful guide to previous editions and important studies of the play or its subjects (63–67).

The Oxford title page draws attention to two major concerns facing redactors: what is this work entitled, and who wrote it? Halio's answers suggest multiplicity:

King Henry VIII, or All is True
By William Shakespeare and John Fletcher

The First Folio (1623) actually calls it *The Famous History of the Life of King Henry the Eight,* perhaps to align it more linearly with the earlier sequence of English histories. Originally, though, it seems to have been known as *All Is True,* a title with intriguing thematic significance (16–18). Sound external evidence, such as a letter by Sir Henry Wotton quoted by Halio (17), supports this appellation. The authorship question may be a bit more slippery (partly because collaboration between early modern stagewrights is itself not understood in great detail). No attribution to anyone other than Shakespeare survives from the seventeenth century. Critics since 1850, however, beginning with James Spedding and Samuel Hickson, have theorized that John Fletcher wrote a share (exactly how much has remained a topic of disagreement). Various linguistic and stylistic analyses, more or less rigorous or objective, all point to Fletcher's hand. Halio comments: "The work of scholars summarized here establishes if not 'historical fact,' then at least 'various probability.' . . . [Evidence] help[s] to establish Fletcher's role in the composition of *King Henry VIII*" (24). The claims of the title page, then, seem justified.

Most readers will find the critical apparatus useful; supplementary information is supplied in good measure. Shakespeare's depiction of the cataclysmic middle years of Henry's reign, 1520–1533, routinely alters chronology to suit other aims. The editor provides a short summary of this history, Henry's "Great Matter" (1–11), and knowledgeably shepherds readers through the sources the authors turned to (11–16). Because of borrowings and overlapping between accounts of Henry's reign, precise attributions for many events cannot be made. The most important sources are Holinshed's *Chronicles of England* (1587); Foxe's *Acts and Monuments* (1596), and Samuel Rowley's *When You See Me, You Know Me.* (The last item, a play from 1603, furnishes the King his characteristic speech tic "Ha!") One of Halio's strengths is his subtle understanding of the creative process, the translation of chronicle to stage, and his ability to discern likely causes for both including and excluding material. Halio also devotes a paragraph to a probable Stuart context: the marriage in February 1613 of Prince Frederick, a leading European Protestant, to Princess Elizabeth, King James's daughter (16). Like *Perkin Warbeck* by John Ford (1634), *Henry VIII* can be viewed as historically dualistic—an interpretation of early Tudor times meant to comment obliquely on the current Stuart monarchy.[1]

The fame of this drama derives from its spectacular aspects: "The Globe burned down on 29 June 1613" during one of its earliest performances (16–17). In his letter a week later, Wotton writes of:

> many extraordinary circumstances of pomp and majesty . . . sufficient in truth within a while to make greatness very familiar, if not ridiculous. Now King Henry making a masque at the Cardinal Wolsey's house, and certain chambers being shot off at his entry, some of the paper, or other stuff . . . did light on the thatch, where . . . it kindled inwardly, and ran round like a train, consuming within less than an hour the whole house to the very grounds. (17)

After hearing of the lavish Field of the Cloth of Gold (1.1), audiences are treated to visual presentations of the aforementioned masque at Cardinal Wolsey's (1.4), the showy Divorce Trial of Queen Katherine (2.4), the Coronation of Queen Anne Boleyn (4.1), Katherine's "Vision" (4.2), and finally, the show-stopping christening of Princess Elizabeth (5.5).

For four centuries, *Henry VIII* has remained popular in London playhouses, often in increasingly grand productions ("Each following day / Became the next day's master, till the last / Made former wonder its" [1.1.16–18]). In tracing out its performance history (45–61), Halio is particularly good on the eventual shift away from excessive artifice: "Mrs Siddons is responsible for a revolution in the representation of *King Henry VIII,* restoring the balance among principal characters that earlier eighteenth-century productions had lost in their emphasis upon the male leads and, even more, the spectacle provided by the pageant scenes" (49–50). Several women and men have won great acclaim in the leading roles: Thomas Betterton as Henry in the Restoration, Sarah Siddons as Katherine starting in 1788, Henry Irving as Wolsey a century later.

Built around over-the-top set pieces, apparently co-authored, and in places wildly anachronistic, *Henry VIII* frequently faces the charge of lacking cohesion. The reported title, *All Is True,* then becomes a debate topic; the prologue's acknowledgment of "chosen truth" admits as much. "Truth" gets bandied about rather shabbily throughout the proceedings, acquiring a resonance like other key terms in Shakespeare (e.g., "emulation" in *Troilus and Cressida,* "blood" in *Richard II,* "conscience" in *Hamlet* and this play), a point Halio might have done more with (cf. 28n.4, 59–61). "Truth" also registered as a specifically loaded religious concept during the Reformation, with peculiar applicability to the Queens: the Catholic Katherine and the Lutheran Anne, mother of Elizabeth. In fact, the playwrights tend to present viewers dueling truths. Anne Boleyn is and is not ambitious, Wolsey is and is not overly worldly, Elizabeth is and is not a baby boy (5.1.162–67; see 30n.2). Authorial religious viewpoints do not take center stage; even the schismatic undertones surrounding the attainder engineered by Gardiner of the Protestant Archbishop of Canterbury Cranmer (an event derived from

Foxe) seems curiously muted. Halio rightly points out that "Issues of theology or the politics that became involved with theological controversy are not raised, except perhaps indirectly" (6). Other tropes do get foregrounded. The apologetic epilogue anticipates that the "expected good" reaction will come only from "The merciful construction of good women," that is (apparently), the rehabilitation of the two queens, both eventually cast away (Anne's later disgrace is not of course dramatized). More than one commentator has noted that the miscellaneous agendas pursued here leave the royal title character rather marginalized.

But Halio does not subscribe to this view. He posits that Henry *is* the central figure and that his play treats his political coming of age: "for all its pomp and splendour, *King Henry VIII* focuses mainly on the use and abuse of power. . . . By the end of the play, [Henry] has learned from his erstwhile servant how to play the power game—and win—better than anyone else" (25, 27). In this argument, both the *de casibus* pattern (the falls of Buckingham, Wolsey, and Katherine) and the pageantry serve to reveal (sometimes by contrast) the King's "growth in stature" or "emergence into authority."[2] This reading aligns *Henry VIII* with sixteenth-century court interludes such as Skelton's *Magnyfycence* and Lindsay's *Ane Satyre of the Thrie Estaits,* and also with Shakespeare's Romances. It is a good fit in many ways, a helpful lens for comprehending Henry's personal and political development. In sinking Wolsey or saving Cranmer, the monarch demonstrates his maturation:

He has begun to know himself and those around him and to take charge at last. . . . [In 5.2–3] Henry takes command of the situation, scolding the lords for their behaviour and restoring Cranmer to his position of honour at the table. He reads the Councillors a lesson in humility and in the proper service of their sovereign. Through it all Henry shows them—and us—that he is now not only a king who reigns, but a king who rules. He is himself at last. (31, 36)

Well. This is a nice theory, at any rate. By the rules of the game, an editor is obliged to offer an original interpretation, and it would not be fair to expect the kind of textual and rhetorical persuasiveness as in a stand-alone essay meant to make a single point. Rather, the exegetical section of a good introductory essay should suggest, should open up paths of inquiry. Still, even with those caveats registered, I must say I find Halio's hypothesis unconvincing. The irony and ambivalence present throughout, coupled with the spotlighting in performance of victimized characters antagonistic to Henry the monarch, undercut Halio's oddly pro-King cheerleading. This is but a matter of opinion, and I should reiterate that Halio clearly and succinctly covers a lot of valuable terrain in setting up the play; readers can glean much here, especially if they consult the footnotes.[3]

So what of this *Henry VIII* as an "edition"? Halio, like all other editors, uses the First Folio as copytext. He has also tended to follow the *Oxford Complete Works* (1986), edited by Stanley Wells and Gary Taylor, with John Jowett and William Montgomery, especially with stage direction expansions but not slavishly in all cases.[4] Halio has been liberal in amplifying and adding stage directions. Most of his decisions in this regard either provide subjects and objects where F1 is content with verbs (e.g., [*The King*] *walks* [*with Gardiner*] *and whispers* [*with him*], 2.2.120.1), or rely safely on gestic indicators:

> *King Henry. (embracing Campeius)*
> And once more in mine arms I bid him welcome.
>
> (2.2.98)

Yet the edition here too is happily conservative (except for 1.1.0.1, treated below).

There is widespread agreement that *Henry VIII* was set from scribal transcript, not a prompt book or authorial "foul papers." The text is mostly unproblematic; where emendations are made, the reasons are explained by clear notes and collations. For example, at 5.2.12, Cramer's "sound" is changed to "found": "Pray heaven he found not my disgrace." The gloss below, which I quote in full, reads:

> **found**   Rowe's emendation of F 'sound' is not generally accepted, but long *s/f* confusions are not uncommon. Maxwell justifies the metaphorical sense of 'sound' = fathom as well as the medical sense = probe. Foakes glosses 'sound' = make known; in NCS and Riverside 'sound' = proclaim.

I do not concur with this specific change. Usually, though, Halio treats the dialogue conservatively. He retains, for instance, "too blame," i.e., "too blameworthy" (OED v. 6), where many switch to "to blame" (4.2.102). He also sticks with the F2 reading, *glad* (as does everyone else) at 3.2.143, where Henry is dismissing Cardinal Wolsey:

> You have scarce time
> To steal from spiritual leisure a brief span
> To keep your earthly audit. Sure, in that,
> I deem you an ill husband and am *glad*
> To have you therein my companion.
>
> (3.2.140–44, my emphasis)

Lines 143–44 are glossed thus: "Henry is not, as Foakes suggests, coupling himself with Wolsey as an 'ill husband' (he to Katherine, Wolsey to his earthly affairs); he is saying (with disguised irony) that he is glad to have so spiritual and unworldly a person as his fellow." This seems a mite ingenious. Why should not the F1 reading, "gald," stand? *Galled,* or rubbed the wrong way, seems more like the point the King is trying to make, and Wolsey's apologetic response suggests as much (ll. 144–50). Moreover, "gall" is a word Shakespeare uses in *Twelfth Night, Othello, Hamlet,* and *Henry V.* Gabriel Harvey spelled the past participle *gald* in 1573: "So that I have not yit bene so courst and *gald* in our own Hous, as I am like hereafter to be pincht and nipt in the Regent Hous" (OED, vb. [6]). Might we have here a cease of "editorial fossilization," as Margaret Kidnie calls it?[11] *Galled* is still sarcastic, and may be edgier yet clearer. What do people think? In general, notes, whether glosses, references to proverbs, scripture, other plays, or historical clarifications, help in comprehension.

At stake in the Oxford *Henry VIII,* therefore, is not the text per se; you will read almost exactly the same lines whichever copy you choose. So to whom might this new book appeal, and what differentiates it from the competition? To those questions we now turn. The introductory material covers the ground more closely, and the notes provide more detail than can be found in standard classroom anthologies such as the Riverside or the Norton.[5] However, the same basic themes, and frequently annotations to the same alleged cruxes (linguistic convolutions, literary allusions, historical obscurities, etc.) occur in the various complete works as in this Oxford. In addition, having all of Shakespeare between one set of covers allows for instant cross-referencing, a handy feature. Of course, anthologies run pretty heavy (the old Riverside, 1927 pages; the Norton, 3420 pages), so the portability of the lightweight 230 page Oxford has its merits. For acting companies then, this tome would fit. Halio reaches out to his crowd in his preface: "A special effort has been made to include information that may be useful to actors and directors engaged in staging the play" (v). Two elements in his presentation affect theatrical utility. First, the editorial stage direction "*A cloth of state throughout the play*" (1.1.0.1) seems needlessly imperious in foreclosing scenic decisions. Even if that was an original, "authorized" intention (or actuality in June 1613), surely a director today, influenced by Ian McKellan's *Richard III* or Baz Luhrmann's *Romeo + Juliet,* might wish to exercise more creative control. Related to this conundrum, I find the lack of specified locations irritating. (Most scenes take place around the Court.) This omission is felt most strongly in Katherine's big trial scene (2.4). The trial took place in June 1529 at the Blackfriars, which eighty years later had become the "private" theater of the King's Men. Thus it is possible that the play had its debut there, giving a metadramatic flavoring to this action. A note at 2.2.138 mentions this setting, but a reference for 2.4 would have been even nicer. The aforementioned anthologies, in contrast, do provide locations for the reader's benefit.

For undergraduate students who do not need other Shakespeare plays, this edition is more than adequate. Likewise, scholars engaged in comparative work, with, say, seventeenth-century dramas about Henry VIII (e.g., Calderón, *La Cisma de Inglaterra*; Vernulaeus, *Henricus Octavus*; or Banks, *Vertue*

Betray'd) will find Halio's tome practical. I imagine full-fledged Shakespeareans will have previously absorbed much of Halio's general account, and will stick with their personal preferences; if that entails the sharp Oxford volume, this addition to the ranks will be welcome (but expensive in hardcover).

Among similar products, how does Halio stack up? An examination of one short interchange indicates that there is not much to choose between them. The downcast Wolsey hears about his replacement:

> *Cromwell.* The next is that Sir Thomas More is chosen
>   Lord Chancellor in your place.
> *Cardinal Wolsey.*   That's somewhat sudden.
>   But he's a learned man. May he continue
>   Long in his highness' favour and do justice
>   For truth's sake and his conscience, that his bones,
>   When he has run his course and sleeps in blessings,
>   May have a tomb of orphans' tears wept on him.
>
>   (3.2.394–400)

Among the New Cambridge, Arden 1, Arden 3, and Oxford, the latter two adapt the Folio punctuation of a period after "sudden" (F1: "Sodain."), while the former two use a comma. All note the compression of chronology in this scene, the bringing together of events ranging from More's appointment to the Chancellorship in 1529 to Anne's crowning in 1533 (ll. 403–7). They also all explain that Chancellors were guardians of orphans. All but Cambridge go so far as to provide a parallel to an elegy for Prince Henry (died 6 November, 1612 [DNB]), another tomb of tears.[6] These glosses seem innocuous.[7] Yet annotation is (according to Ralph Hanna III) an aggressive intervention aimed at constructing text and reader, and More's post-play fate draws out "real" editorializing, in a subjective sense. Compare

Oxford, note to ll. 396–400:	*and Arden 3, note to 395–96:*
The irony of these lines may be unintentional. Unable to support Parliament's bill, 'Submission of the Clergy,' More resigned as chancellor in 1532 (see Ridley, 205). He later died a Catholic martyr.	The audience would, of course, hear heavy irony in these lines, knowing as they did of More's martyrdom in 1535.

This reviewer judges the irony here to be deliberate and thinks it would have been picked up readily enough by many late Renaissance readers and auditors—the *de casibus* emphasis certainly invites speculation on characters who fell after 1533: More, Queen Anne, Cromwell, Crammer. This minor plaint aside, Halio's edition does a lot, and it does it well.

It is not, however, the best *Henry VIII* available. The aforementioned

Arden 3, edited by Gordon McMullan, is simply formidable, the one thing to own for serious study.[8] McMullan provides the most thorough glosses, plus nifty appendices with various attribution and doubling schemes, plus a chronology of Henry's life, 1491–1547. McMullan has also written what is less an introduction and more an insightful, nuanced book-length essay on a play he knows through and through. The way *Henry VIII* is related to the romances, and the examination of how the authors conflate aspects of the two queens, strikes me as brilliant. All this work takes some space: McMullan runs 506 pages, a length some potential readers might be put off by. Nonetheless, Arden 3 is a treasure.

Whether of an age or for all time, in love or out, Shakespeare nowadays has transmogrified into an industry. To complain about this stage of affairs risks disingenuousness: liberal Ivory Tower humanists like us certainly *should* favor the continuation of culture represented by Shakespeare's survival, while to be economically honest, for many a professor of Renaissance literature (myself included), teaching the Swan of Stratford-upon-Avon during the school year (itself not unpleasurable) pays the bills for summers spent publishing, attending theater . . . or editing Shakespeare and his lesser known contemporaries.[9] Yet I still feel compelled to address the obvious point: cranking out new editions of "Shakespeare" is a practice done because of its profitability and cultural cachet, not because of a "critical" lack (as might be the case for Early English Text Society volumes or many of the Revels Plays). And this bugs me. Having a choice can be a good thing, and the level of intellectual acumen is very high; enthroning Shakespeare, nonetheless, means ignoring (suppressing?) other worthwhile activities and artists, means inefficient duplication and mindless perpetuation of notions of authority not entirely unproblematic.

You now have no less than ten *Henry VIIIs* (Oxford, New Cambridge, Ardens 1 and 3, Pelican, Bedford, Bantam Classic, Viking Penguin, Wadsworth, Folger) plus several complete works to choose from, and they would be indistinguishable to 99 percent of the general population.[10] If you want to read Rowley's fascinating *If You See Me, You Know Me,* on the other hand, you will have to track down either an early printing, the Tudor Facsimile Text, or the Malone Society Reprint, none widely available. Ha!

Notes

1. Halio could have provided more contemporary secondary sources in his de facto bibliography (65–67), e.g., Garrett Mattingly, *Catherine of Aragon* (Boston: Little and Brown, 1941).

2. Foakes qtd. 36n.1

3. No doubt Halio faced constraints of space; nevertheless I imagine that neophyte or nonspecialist users might have benefited if he had fleshed out his discussions of, e.g., the Reformation and the complications and motivations for the king's first two marriages.

4. This reviewer would have preferred more on editorial methodology; see p. 63.

5. See the review essay of the Norton; Riverside 2d ed.; and Bevington's Complete Works, 4th ed., by Martha Tuck Rozett, in *Shakespeare Quarterly* 48 (1997): 465–72.

6. George Steevens is cited as the source for this information, for his edition of the *Plays* with Samuel Johnson, 1773.

7. Let me also mention how curious I find it that nobody thinks it worthwhile to report Shakespeare's involvement with another collaborative drama—Munday and crew's *Sir Thomas More* (ca. 1593). See Anthony Munday et al., *Sir Thomas More: A Play*, eds. Vittorio Gabrieli and Giorgio Melchiori, The Revels Plays (New York: Manchester University Press, 1990).

8. William Shakespeare and John Fletcher, *King Henry VIII (All Is True)*, ed. Gordon McMullan, The Arden Shakespeare, Third Series (London, 2000). Hardcover: $45, paperback, $13.95.

9. See David Scott Kastan, *Shakespeare After Theory* (New York: Routledge, 1999), Ch. 3, "The Mechanics of Culture: Editing Shakespeare Today": "Everyone seems to be doing it these days, or thinking about doing it, or most often—it is the nineties, after all—thinking about why he or she is not doing it. Editing, that is. Editing has suddenly become hot, or, if not exactly hot as an activity to undertake (it does, after all, involve a lot of very tedious, numbingly cold work), at least a hot topic (arguably *the* hot topic in Shakespeare studies) to debate. Never has the materiality of the texts we study seemed so compelling, so unavoidable, and so exhilaratingly problematic" (59). Cf. Leah Marcus, *Unediting the Renaissance: Shakespeare, Marlowe, Milton* (New York: Routledge, 1996): "If we do not feel that our standard editions satisfactorily transmit the cultural imbeddedness and malleability we find in literary materials of the Renaissance or of any other era, we would do well to stop grousing about the shortcomings of past editors and become editors ourselves" (227).

10. The most interesting is a transcription of the First Folio, *Henry VIII*, The Folio Texts, ed. Neil Freeman, (New York: Applause, 1999).

11. Margaret Jane Kidnie, "Text, Performance, and the Editors: Staging Shakespearean Drama," *Shakespeare Quarterly* 51 (2000): 456–73.

Shakespeare Performed: Essays in Honor of R. A. Foakes, ed. Grace Ioppolo. Newark: University of Delaware Press, 2000. Pp. 315. Cloth $47.50.

Reviewer: ARTHUR F. KINNEY

R. A. Foakes is one of the foremost scholars of early modern drama in England, and one would be hard put to find other scholars, critics, teachers, or students who have not turned to his work for their own. His editions of plays are exemplary in their precision of detail and perception of judgment; and they include *The Revenger's Tragedy, The Comedy of Errors, Henry VIII,*

Much Ado About Nothing, A Midsummer Night's Dream, Macbeth, Troilus and Cressida, and *King Lear* found in all the standard series. His literary study on *Shakespeare: The Dark Comedies to the Last Plays* is a fundamental study of the development of Shakespeare's art while, conversely, *Hamlet versus Lear: Cultural Policies and Shakespeare's Art,* shows our own cultural progression on the two major tragedies, our shifts in values and attitudes causing a shift in the play we feel most importantly speaks to us in our own times. (He is not a latecomer to cultural perspectives; his book about *Coleridge on Shakespeare* had already shown how different ages reread Shakespeare's plays; in a sense, then, he predicted the present concern with the cultural reshaping of texts.) But this interest in Shakespeare's plays themselves never isolated them from their own times and their own material conditions. More than forty years ago, in 1961, he co-edited with R. T. Rickert the text of *Henslowe's Diary,* now a basic text for any historian of Shakespeare's theatrical age, and then went on, alone, to edit the two-volume *Henslowe Papers.* Both works have been foundational; our theater history always begins with these firsthand documents on the Lord Admiral's Company and the Rose Theater. More recently his comprehensive collection, with commentary, of all reliable *Illustrations of the English Stage, 1580–1642* has reminded us once more, this time visually, of those material conditions playwrights wrote to and actors responded to in the great age of English drama. This insistent bridging of historical performance (insofar as we can recover it) and critical reception continually characterizes his work, drawing on deep reservoirs of knowledge and appreciation that rarely show in the lightness of his critical touch and the sureness of his editorial choices. In a way, then, Foakes is a scholar's scholar, one who has taught some if not most of us along the way; while, in another way, his comments are accessible to anyone who wants to know more about the English Renaissance plays he or she is reading. In his full career of teaching—starting as one of the first three junior Fellows at the Shakespeare Institute at Stratford-upon-Avon (the other two, who supply their own tributes here, were John Russell Brown and Ernst Honigmann), to his later classes at Durham, at Yale, at the University of Toronto, at the University of Canterbury in Kent, and, longest and most recently, the University of California at Los Angeles—he has sought to instill this range of interest and clarity of judgment in those who are now his colleagues. Many of them contribute to this overdue *Festschrift* meticulously and creatively edited by a former student at UCLA, Grace Ioppolo, and as she notes acutely what their work displays is what Foakes's work has long demonstrated: the fundamental inseparability of and insistence on the recognition that "a dramatic text should first be seen as a *performing* and *performative* text and second as a *literary* and *reading* text" (8): long before the recent surge of interest in theater history, Foakes was doing that too. "Whether teaching Shakespeare and Renaissance drama or the Romantics, his other major field of study," Ioppolo notes, "his lectures were infused with a brilliant command of an astonishing range of material that captivated his audience, and his seminars and tutorials with that endless energy, quizzical look, and quiet authority that made his students want to work very hard to keep up with him" (7). In the opening essay, Jonathan Bate puts it another way; Foakes, he implies, found ways in his work to unify what "A rough survey of the overall terrain" of criticism these days seems to fall into—"one of two camps: those whose primary interest is *ideas* and those whose primary interest is *performance*." But he goes on to argue that "The idea—or ideology— camp put a high premium on theory, while the performance camp, being more interested in the nuts and bolts of theatre, respond more to practice. Idea-logues ask how we may link Shakespeare's plays to theories of gender, sexual orientation, race, class, history, nationhood, 'alterity' and so forth. Performers ask seemingly more mundane questions; in what ways did Shakespeare draw on an inherited set of theatrical conventions and traditions?" (17). A basic premise to Foakes's work is that he never made that dichotomy, and those who have leaned on him (and who at some time has not?) will know how one implicitly resides in the other. In some ways, in fact, Bate's own essay is one of the deftest exercises in just this tradition. "Shakespeare's Foolosophy" argues that theory and history are both embedded in performance. Turning to Jean Bodin's formative *Method for the easy Comprehension of History* (1565), which argues that "natural and divine history follow an 'inevitable and steadfast sequence of cause and effect,' whereas 'human history mostly flows from the will of mankind, which ever vacillates and has no objective'" (18), Bate contends that *Lear* is of all Shakespeare's historical and tragic work the one most concerned in its examination of human history with the natural and the divine; what sets it apart is its insistence that natural man—exposed on the heath—needs a divine dimension—as in the reconciliation with a reappearing Cordelia; the mere human philosophies after Bodin—that of Stoicism and Cynicism, taken from ancient and contemporary thought—are finally insufficient. But this is not merely a matter of ideas. It is the performative that makes it clear: Lear on the heath tests man's nature, as Cordelia's reappearance does. This is the elevating wisdom of foolish man, captured in the dramatic presentation of both the Fool and Poor Tom. "We are ruled by our passions and our bodies; we go through life performing a series of different roles of which we are by no means in control" (28). The attempts to face down adversity or surrender to it—by Gloucester, Edmund, even Albany—is displaced when Shakespeare, like Erasmus's Folly before him, realizes that the true nature of man is foolish wisdom and wise folly. But unlike Erasmus, Shakespeare does this theatrically. Foakes's method, and Bate's illustration of it, are confirmed by Stanley Wells in a brief but fitting afterword: the apparent contest between those concerned with ideas or theory and those concerned with facts is false, he says, because, "as literary theorists constantly reiterate, the objective search for truth is a chimera" (299). Facts are always open to reinterpretation; and performance makes that point even as it may suggest the outer limits of such possibilities.

This essential linkage between idea and action, the performative and the readerly, is at the basis in one way or another in every contribution to this important volume, but readers may find different ones more appealing. Michael Hattaway, in another provocative and perceptive essay, takes his hint from the title page of the 1607 Quarto of *Lear*—

> M[aster] William Shakespeare: his true chronicle history of the life and death of King Lear and his three daughters. With the unfortunate life of Edgar, son and heir to the Earl of Gloucester, and his sullen and assumed humour of Tom of Bedlam. As it was played before the King's Majesty at Whitehall upon St Stephen's Night in Christmas holidays. By his Majesty's servants playing usually at the Globe on the Bankside (quoted 200–201)—

that such a record of *performance* suggests not a parallel between Lear and Gloucester but between Lear and Edgar. "Both are conspired against, both go mad, both have to sound the base string of humility, expose themselves to what wretches feel. Both Lear and Edgar are detached from their possessions and, as a materialist critic writes, 'removing what a person *has* simultaneously takes away what a person *is*.' This double structure based on both symmetrical and asymmetrical father-child relationships is one of the many disconcerting things about the play" (201). But it is perhaps also one of the most useful. Edgar may be a key. But, then, how do we interpret Edgar? How does his role play out? He may find in madness a kind of curative therapy; he may act upon compulsion; he may be possessed by devils. In act 4 at Dover he may help to restore his blind father or, refusing to acknowledge his own life and forgiveness, may display instead or in addition unnecessary cruelty. In act 5, his duel with Edmund may bring a restoration of justice; it may also be fought out with the fierceness of revenge. Hattaway's point is that performance always illumines—but it also always interprets—texts. Each performance reinterprets. Guided by Shakespeare's script, actors interrogate and audiences respond—seeing, hearing, reading.

Another illustration of Foakes's legacy is Ian Donaldson's subtle examination of how Shakespeare's *Julius Caesar* and Ben Jonson's *Sejanus* "appear to be joined in a conversation" (88). They both draw on republican Rome in the late 1590s, when a succession of plots against the government seemed especially prevalent and dangerous; and both playwrights may be conscious of Tacitean history which argued the underlying forces in a politics of power and treachery. Both Cassius and Sejanus seem disciples of Tacitus. But as Donaldson shows, Cassius' ability to understand and control the forces of government is openly questioned by the end of the play, while judgments on

Tiberius and Sejanus, in Jonson, never are. Addressing a partially shared terrain, Shakespeare interrogates; Jonson judges. "Acts of misinterpretation, such as those made by Cremutius Cordus' accusers as they read his annals, derive from wickedness or plain stupidity. Misinterpretation in *Julius Caesar* [as with Brutus of Cassius; Cassius at Phillipi] occurs in simpler and more innocent ways, in which we as audience are often implicated. A shout or gesture or a dream is honestly misunderstood. The past, like the present, retains its hermeneutic puzzles, and its shape, though often glimpsed, is never perfectly understood" (105). Donaldson's interpretation is not simply that of the text—what is shouted or reported from a dream—but from performance— what is gestured. Other essays I found especially illuminating are those by Alexander Leggatt who finds in the deposition scene of *Richard II,* the fly-killing scene in *Titus,* and Hamlet's understanding of Horatio in the 4.4 of Q2 of *Hamlet* reflective scenes that interrupt the action and swerve from it, pausing onstage to assess, forcing viewers and readers to do likewise; and Philip Edwards' far-reaching observation that "A good deal of Elizabethan drama . . . dedicated to the detection of 'seeming,'" is in fact the work of disguise and counterfeit: 'Set a thief to catch a thief' (122). Richard III, Iago, Goneril, Angelo: "Shakespeare will all the time illustrate the pitfalls in [the] process of unmasking" (122). "Sincere speech is easily fabricated by the insincere" (123). "Falsehood comes in many guises. Malcolm is one of a whole array of good deceivers in Shakespeare, many of whom adopt a physical disguise as well as a verbal disguise—Rosalind and Duke Vincentio, Edgar and Kent, Paulina and Ariel," alongside others such as Macbeth, Antony, or the assumed confession of Hamlet to Rosenkrantz and Guildenstern (2.2.293– 310) that makes falsehood and irony "indistinguishable" (125). "Shakespeare recreates the confusion of life. The sharp edge of the conflict between right and wrong, true and false, good and bad becomes hopelessly blurred in the representation of misrepresentation. Shakespeare's plays are always arguing against their own right to exist. 'It is not good to stay too long in the theatre,' said Francis Bacon, but, as his essay on simulation and dissimulation so convincingly demonstrated, there is nowhere else to go" (130).

    Ioppolo divides this collection into two parts: Shakespeare performed in his own time, and in ours. She herself contributes to both, though she has chosen to be in the second section, working out from Sir Richard Eyre's Royal National Theater production of *Lear.* Her question seems simple: should a director choose the Quarto, the Folio, or a conflation—or should he take ingredients of the texts and conflate them in his very own way? It is of course a vexing question, even when, as Ioppolo notes, the conflated text is a modern invention itself, not, as the Oxford editors know, authoritative. Eyre's answer, however, was to conflate, by following Folio but adding the trial scene from the Quarto. But this was not a matter of simple choice, nor of expediency; Ioppolo works to extract how and why choices are—must be—

made. Eyre cut parts he thought "'theatrically dubious'" (187). This was in keeping with his premise that Shakespeare was a man of the working theater. But he also "cut to maintain and strengthen the narrative line of the play, his main concern" (188): that is, his sense of the working theater, now. She juggles his choices, his material, his logic, concluding, as Foakes might, that "Eyre validates the ideas of theatrical and textual revision expressed by the new revisionists, but he also demonstrates that literary editors and critics are not the sole or even the primary constructors, purveyors or interpreters of a Shakespearean text" (192).

In the liveliest, and in some ways the most invigorating essay, Carol Chillington Rutter points to the centrality of designers, "interpreters who translate Shakespeare into visual languages"; "They structure the audience's looking" (217). It is a matter of sets: *Richard II* against a medieval Book of Hours; *Richard III* among the tombs of Beauchamp Chapel. It is the place: *Much Ado* in the British Raj; *All's Well* during the Crimea; *Henry VI* in Bosnia. It is in costume: they are "legible, freighted with significance that is both iconic and performative" (222). Her attention focuses on *Troilus and Cressida*: the exchange of tokens; the import of battle dress; Sam Mendes' stage "littered with . . . junk" (232) and John Barton's production where "Combat was voluptuous, a form of homosexual seduction, and both sides desired it" (235). But the play provides internal meaning, too; and she is especially helpful in positing Cressida alongside Helen. Alan Brissenden, meantime, provides a comprehensive and amusing history of "Australian Shakespeare" beginning with *Henry VI* in Sydney on 8 April 1800—long before the founding and federation of the country—and continuing with the competing capital for Shakespeare, Melbourne, where in 1853 Conrad Knowles staged *Hamlet* in the Queen's Theater and "'an enthusiastic member of the audience was so "impressed" by the "jolly-good-fellowness" of Claudius, that he sent him down a bottle of brandy from the gallery by the thong of his stock whip'" (241). Shakespeare seems to have been the center of culture for the late-emerging country; "between 1855 and 1861 more of Shakespeare's plays were performed in Melbourne than in any comparable period in the twentieth century" (243); but the Australian stage was for a long time derivative of English production—until, in 1948, it merged with adulation of Hollywood when the British Council sponsored a tour of the Old Vic company led by Laurence Olivier and Vivien Leigh. In the last decades, however, confirmed with the establishment of the Bell Shakespeare Company in 1990, Shakespeare has become part of the national culture—and actors now speak with an Australian accent. A companion piece, on film, is provided by Peter Holland, who argues that even though filmic performances are frozen for all time as theater performances are not, the filmscripts that are published do not always record what stays in the final product: his chief exemplar is the Branagh *Hamlet*. Marliss C. Desens, in showing how women, contributing a supernatural and ritualistic discussion to *Richard III,* are cut by Olivier and by Richard Loncraine (in the Ian McKellen version) not only make the play more masculinist, but make it very different.

Just as Desens follows Foakes in putting modern productions against earlier ones, in part to measure loss as well as gain, so other contributors attempt to establish originary meanings to help us understand Shakespeare today. The most intriguing work of conjectural sleuthing for me is by Peter Davison who attempts to account for Shakespeare's company when it closed down in 1597 following the scandal over *The Isle of Dogs.* "The Chamberlain's Men had to do one of three things to sustain themselves. They could sell plays to printers (and they sold *Richard II* to Andrew Wise, who entered it on 29 August 1597); they could pawn or sell props and apparel as Pembroke's Men were 'feign' to do according to Henslowe's letter to Edward Alleyn of 28 September 1593 because they could not meet their touring charges; and they could tour" (58). They toured. Combining archival evidence with informed conjecture, Davison argues that the company must have walked on their tour and they must have spent, near the end of it, a longer period at Marlborough. But why Marlborough? Not the town, as with Bristol, but the possibility of performance at a manor house: Tottenham House in the Savernake forest two miles outside town, owned by the Earl of Hertford (Sir Edward Seymour), and Wilton, where the Pembrokes would entertain James VI and I in 1603. If Davison is right, we have more work to do in determining what great houses Shakespeare may have visited, and what connections the company may have had, through their owners, at court. There are other conjectures, too, about Shakespeare's work. M. M. Mahood reasons, with some probable evidence, that the two rear doors to Shakespeare's stage were always used as either a door to the outside world (OD) or to an inside venue (ID), and Honigmann argues that in the sonnets the Rival Poet is Ben Jonson and the Dark Lady is Mary Fitton, but I find these cases less persuasive.

Renaissance Clothing and the Materials of Memory, by Ann Rosalind Jones and Peter Stallybrass. Cambridge: Cambridge University Press, 2000. Pp. xiii + 368. Cloth $74.95, paper $27.95.

Reviewer: JEAN MacINTYRE

This book is filled with useful information about the fashion, fashioning, and fashions of Renaissance clothing. It makes us aware of how much "fabrics were central to the economic and social fabrication of Renaissance Europe and to the making and unmaking of Renaissance subjects," whether as garments worn in ordinary life, depicted in visual art, or worn by actors on the stage. A review can only hint at the book's wide range over a complex field and note some limitations and some authorial lapses that a publisher's reader or an editor should have caught.

The introduction prepares the reader for the breadth to come. It traces the development of the word "fashion" from a verb signifying creation or manufacture of anything to a noun signifying, as now, intentional novelty in dress, and develops the theoretical underpinnings of the chapters to follow. These chapters, grouped in the separately titled sections "Material Subjects," "Gendered Habits," and "Staging Clothes," examine ways in which fabric and fashion communicated class and gender roles in European society (not exclusively in English) and in the English theater.

"Material Subjects" contains three chapters. "The Currency of Clothing" concentrates on clothing as stored wealth, by pawn or sale convertible into cash and by redemption or resale back into clothing. It discusses what cloth was made of, how it was made and by whom, and "clothes as payment [i.e., livery] and as stored and circulated wealth." Livery, in its widest sense of clothing given as a perquisite of employment, was worth much more than the pay both of liveried servants and officeholders (e.g., Elizabeth's maids of honor and ladies in waiting) for whom the value of clothing given them as official dress substantially exceeded their traditional and often meager salaries.

"Composing the Subject: Making Portraits," focuses on the clothes chosen for depiction in a portrait memorializing, usually, a significant moment in the sitter's life. Conventionalized faces might be painted from no more than one sitting, but garments remained in the painter's studio to be meticulously delineated whether in a miniature or a large painting. The latter part of this chapter is devoted to the garments chosen for portraits of Thomas Lee, Sir Robert Shirley and William Feilding Earl of Denbigh. The Lee and Shirley costumes make political statements through what the authors call "hybridity." Lee's costume asserts his self-placement between English birth and Irish colonial status, intermediate between the "redshanks" wild Irish and the "civil" English.[1] Shirley's Persian attire, more nearly a livery in the modern sense, asserts his status as the Shah's ambassador to Christian Europe. Denbigh's portrait in Hindu dress records his 1631–1633 journey to Shah Jahan's temporary court at Burhanpore, and about a month each in the ports of Masulipatam and Surat; in Persia for no more than five weeks, he is unlikely to have gone far from the port of Gombroon. All three sitters donned their exotic attire to project an image to "now and after times," but this was less uncommon than the authors indicate. Others who sat for portraits in "unusual weeds"—masquing attire, parade armor, or Garter robes—were doing the same.

"Yellow Starch" discusses the feared "contagion of foreign fashion," epitomized in the Jacobean fashion of ruffs stiffened with starch colored with saffron or urine. Paradoxically associated with both "foreign" luxury and the "barbarous" Irish, the coincidence of the yellow starch fashion with the Overbury murder branded it with the mark of Cain because allegedly invented by Frances Howard's accomplice Anne Turner. In the 1650s it gained an antimonarchical afterlife through both reprints of earlier writings and revisionist versions of Jacobean history.

The second section, "Gendered Habits," centers on the relationship of spinning and needlework to ideals of femininity and to "the creation of social memory." Its three chapters include much information about the processes of clothmaking, tailoring, and textile ornamentation, particularly focusing on the restrictions imposed upon women in these manufactures. Texts and pictures are used to show the social ambivalence of the time to the most characteristic textile work women did, namely spinning and needlework. "Arachne's Web: Velasquez's *Las Hilanderas*" focuses on the foreground, where five lower-class women are turning fleece into thread. The background suggests a brightly lit stage set where female aristocrats in fashionable finery stand before a tapestry depicting Arachne and Minerva. The goddess gestures to initiate the change of the woman from a weaving rival to a spinning spider. "The Fate of Spinning: Penelope and the Three Fates," begins with the wool, linen, or silk yarn from which all fabrics were made, spun mainly by women working in "virtuous poverty," a euphemism for "cheap labor." Female saints and nuns might be praised for their industry in spinning, but in some parts of Europe spinning was associated with the sinister Three Fates, with witches, where "lasciviousness [was] linked to magic," and with female violence against men. In England and in the silk producing cities of Italy, weavers' guilds undertook to confine women to spinning, and penalized masters who employed women weavers even when men were unavailable. Some texts altered Penelope's weaving to spinning. The visuals illustrating these two chapters were created in Spain, Germany, and the Netherlands, but most texts used for their interpretation are English, without traceable links to pictures made not only in other places but years before or after the chosen texts.

"The Needle and the Pen: Needlework and the Appropriation of Printed Texts," discusses women's self-expression through needlework as a socially acceptable alternative to self-expression through writing. Among the upper classes needlework was advocated as a "remedy" against women's socially imposed idleness. Professional embroiderers who ornamented rich fabrics for pay were male professionals; "needlework" was the name for fabric decoration done by women, usually from male-designed patterns, even if the women freely arranged elements of these patterns in compositions, about which they were not apologetic as women writers tended to be whether or not their writing reached print.

The four chapters that make up "Staging Clothes" take up the sources and functions of stage costume, the problems of identity posed by cross-dressed boy actors (especially in scenes of undressing), the relation between property in clothes and property in women, and the "material mnemonics" of ghost costumes in plays and, for the living in both plays and life, of garments and accessories that memorialized their dead. These later chapters echo earlier, using different approaches to many of the same materials. "The Circulation of Clothes and the Making of the English Theater" revisits the themes of chapter 1 as they apply to the acquisition, accumulation, and disposal of theatrical costume. It notes that theaters were sites to display fine garments by both actors and audience. Rapid changes in Jacobean upper-class fashion increased the pawning and the sale of finery that was no longer fashionable. Unlike accumulated money, damned as avarice and linked to usury, the costly garments of elite display "shared the wealth" with those who supplied materials and fashioned them into garments. Such sharing continued when fashion changed or the first wearer abandoned a garment, as dealers in fashionable discards then profited, as did the acting companies who bought them. At the end of such secondhand usefulness, others benefited from recycling fabrics and trims.

Chapters 8 and 9, "Transvestism and the Body Beneath: Speculating on the Boy Actor" and "(In)alienable Possessions: Griselda, Clothing, and the Exchange of Women," deal with relationships between gender and clothing. The former speculates that during a performance audiences were conscious that characters in female dress were males underneath. I do not find this chapter convincing.[3] Indeed, it contradicts what the chapter on portraits says about clothes; that they, not the face or the body they covered, most truly represented the sitter.

Chapter 9 takes up the many versions of the Griselda story from Boccaccio on. In all versions the lower-class heroine is remade when stripped of her peasant dress and reclothed by her noble husband in upper-class finery, his to give and later his to take away. This conforms to "the lawes and customes" of England that everything a woman brought to or acquired during marriage was absolutely her husband's, so that she could not dispose even of the clothes she wore without his consent.[4] But Dekker and Rowley's late Elizabethan *Pleasant Comedy of Patient Grissel,* to which they add new characters and a contrasting subplot, uses costume and costume change expressing social status and its changes in complex, indeed subversive ways that this chapter does not acknowledge.

"Of Ghosts and Garments: The Materiality of Memory on the Renaissance Stage," deals with the problem of representing bodiless spirits by the bodies of living actors. Because most stage ghosts demand that living characters remember them, their costumes had to make them first recognizable to the audience as ghosts and to living characters as the ghosts of known individuals. But speaking ghost characters normally also name themselves or, if unspeaking, are named by someone else. Depending on the play, ghost costumes were variable, whether the special ghost bodice and ghost suit belonging to the Admiral's Men in 1598, the winding sheet in which most people were interred (e.g., the ghosts in *Richard III*), the garments in which they died (e.g., Banquo in *Macbeth*), or some characteristic garb of their lifetime (e.g., King Hamlet, in act 1 in armor and in act 3 in a night gown). The chapter concludes with an extensive analysis of the ghost role in *Hamlet*.

While I do not always agree with the authors' interpretation, I commend the range of factual information they have brought together in a conveniently sized package. Obviously any book that attempts as much as this one will be found wanting in some respects, especially when it handles matters distant from the authors' own expertise. Weak spots are notable in discussions of visual art, which the authors tend to read literally, as if they were verbal texts. Even if allegorical, a pictorial "text" is more open-ended for interpretation than a verbal one. There are also, alas, errors in historical fact connected with the pictures. The authors say that Anthony and Robert Shirley "accompanied the Earl of Essex on a mission to Persia" in 1598– 99, years when Essex, whose life is too well known for such a misstatement, was in England and Ireland.[5] Newham Paddocks in Warwickshire, not Hamilton in Scotland, was and is the Denbigh estate.[6] Other errors result from anachronistic readings and overgeneralization. For instance, Van Dyck's 1630s portrait could not show Denbigh as a "colonial official." I question any imperialist reading of this portrait, for in the 1630s the English in India were by East India Company policy simply traders, and were in a weak position politically. The shift from petitioning for trade privileges to the establishment of colonial enclaves began when Joshua Child determined to exploit weakness in the Mughal state after Aurengzebe's death.[7] The authors interpret Velasquez's version of the Arachne myth through George Sandy's English translation of the *Metamorphoses* rather than through the somewhat different moralized Spanish Ovid popular in seventeenth-century Spain. The account of Velasquez and the Order of Santiago errs about a court painter's social position. Velasquez was a royal counsellor, not a lowly artisan like the journeymen of the London Painter Stainers Guild. His consciousness of his high status is clear from his self-representation in *Las Meñinas,* a painting close in time to *Las Hilanderas.* Rubens, another Habsburg court painter, acted as a Habsburg diplomat and, like Van Dyck, received an English knighthood. Errors like these cast doubt on other statements beyond a reader's own knowledge.[8]

These criticisms do not, of course, impugn the book's importance or its impressive range and diversity. Even if a reader observes gaps or does not always agree with the ideas it advances, the book still provides valuable stimuli for research and thought. The bibliography (twenty-five closely printed pages) supplies a splendid map for "further reading." Cambridge University

Press is to be commended for issuing both a sturdy hardback for the book's surely heavy use in libraries, and a well-bound, affordable paperback for personal collections, even those of students.

Notes

1. James P. Myers Jr. interprets Lee's self-representation somewhat differently. "'Murdering Heart . . . Murdering Hand': Captain Thomas Lee of Ireland, Elizabethan Assassin," *Sixteenth Century Journal* 22 (1991): 47–60. Queen Elizabeth's retired champion Sir Henry Lee commissioned Gheeraerts to paint three symbolic likenesses: himself, his shirttail cousin Thomas, and the famous Ditchley portrait of Elizabeth.

2. My contextual study of Denbigh's journey and Van Dyck's commemorative portrait will soon appear in *Quidditas: The Journal of the Rocky Mountain Medieval and Renaissance Association.*

3. In productions of Renaissance plays that cast burly blue-chinned males as women and of baroque operas that cast plump sopranos in male roles written for castrati, the audience does of course notice gender incongruity. Will Fisher's recent "The Renaissance Beard" marshals textual and visual evidence that in the Renaissance the beard was the "sign" that distinguished men from women, so a beardless boy "was considered of a different gender from men." (*RQ* 54 (2001): 155). The universal "she" for female characters in stage directions, and their occasional shift to "he" for a female character disguised as a man, suggests that both playwrights and audiences thought the clothes mattered, not the body beneath.

4. In "The Single Self: Feminist Thought and the Marriage Market in Early Modern Venice," *RQ* 48 (1993): 513–81, Virginia Cox anticipates Jones and Stallybrass when she says "the real motive of censors of fashion is a desire to curtail women's liberty and freedom of expression," then adds that, for patrician women with large dowries, exaggerated clothing style was "a bid for visibility, a display of power, and in some cases a gesture of defiance" (553–54).

5. D. W. Davies' *Elizabethans Errant: The Strange Fortunes of Sir Thomas Sherley and his Three Sons, as well as in the Dutch Wars as in Muscovy. Morocco, Persia, Spain, and the Indies* (Ithaca: Cornell University Press, 1967) would have supplied the authors with more of a context for Robert Shirley's portrait than the brief biographical entry they quote.

6. Cecelia Feilding, Countess of Denbigh, makes this clear in her *Royalist Father and Roundhead Son: Being the Memoirs of the First and Second Earls of Denbigh 1600–1675* (London: Methuen, 1915). Her book is listed in the bibliography.

7. See K. N. Chaudhuri, *The English East India Company* (London: F. Cass, 1965).

8. I mildly cavil at another instance of hasty reading, the statement (in a note) that my *Costumes and Scripts in the Elizabethan Theatres* contradictorily calls copper lace both cheap and costly. But the text cited reads "a single purchase of £3 18s 4d (at 10d per ounce) was used on one suit and one gown." Indeed, in 1616 copper lace at 14s an ounce for Prince Charles's masquing clothing was over ten times more costly,

whether because more copper was used more elaborately or because dealers inflated the price for the Jacobean court.

The Romance of the New World: Gender and the Literary Formations of English Colonialism, by Joan Pong Linton. Cambridge Studies in Renaissance Literature and Culture. Cambridge: Cambridge University Press, 1998. Pp. xii + 268. Cloth $64.95.

Reviewer: Naomi C. Liebler

In *The Romance of the New World,* Joan Pong Linton offers a Geertzian "thick description" of a foundational moment when two cultures became permanently entangled and interdependent, despite the long subsequent history of military and cultural wars to separate them. Intelligently and perceptively, and in a style at once scholarly and engaging, she examines a wide variety of texts, some long neglected, emerging from the nexus of economic and political shifts on both sides of the Atlantic. The book delivers on both terms of the series title, "Studies in Renaissance Literature and Culture," balancing attention to both "literature" and "culture" evenhandedly and meticulously throughout. Linton illuminates the operations of discoveries and settlements on the American continent by shuttling the voyager-reader back and forth across the Atlantic (and in chapter 3, to the Pacific coast with Drake in California) with greater frequency and certainly greater security than those original settlers and profiteers must have experienced.

I learned much from every chapter. The author skillfully weaves a narrative not unlike those of her romance subjects, doubling back to an "episode" in an earlier chapter to pursue a different aspect of it in a later one, and reminding her readers from time to time of the inherent complexities in such a rich cultural narrative. She has set herself the challenging task of "reading" the exploration and appropriation of the New Found Land in the light of England's increasingly precarious economy in the sixteenth and seventeenth centuries, and of the establishment of colonies as corporations facing extraordinary hazards not only for survival but also for credibility back home. Careers and lives hung on the successes and failures of the settlements, their negotiations with and often rapacious domination of native tribes, and the similarly rapacious demands of English investors. The history of these settlements itself reads like a romance, at times picaresque, at other times heroic, and sometimes purely fantastic.

The popular romance genre was more than a fanciful allegory for a real story, and appropriately Linton does not stop at notice of generic similarities among facts and fictions. She offers a genuine interrogation of the relations between literary production and the life-and-death productions of hegemony on land and sea. Romance literature simultaneously fueled and reflected a deep hunger for property, honor, heroic reputation, and a good return on financial investments. The heroes of fictional romances endured the same risks, and often the same losses, as their inspired counterparts in the real world. At the same time, fictional figures (e.g., Spenser's Red Crosse Knight, Deloney's Jack of Newbury) become models for real-life adventurers such as Drake and Hakluyt. "Romances were stories about historical figures and events, and English voyagers and colonists were only the most recent makers of history" (1).

Three types of romance figures dominate the landscape of both fictive and real narratives of the period: the knight, the merchant, and the husbandman. The last-named is foremost among these, and Linton implies a teleology in both doctrine and praxis: after the explorations and discoveries by knight-adventurers, the land and those who live there were subdued, domesticated, and commodified. Once tractability was more or less established, the successful "master" managed his "household." This, of course, was a progression shared alike by practitioners of colonialism, slavery, economic monopoly, and gender repression: hence the book's subtitle, "Gender and the Literary Formations of English Colonialism." The will to power infected domains beyond the merely domestic and familial; hegemony was deeply embedded in early modern English culture. The history of English colonialism in the New World purposefully replicated the patterns of domestic domination seen not only *at* home but also *in* the home; these patterns were modeled and reinforced continually in the fictional narratives of the English romance genre. Constraint was not limited to women in households, nor were instances of resistance restricted to the domicile. The historical records Linton adduces show that the trajectory toward "husbandry" was not always direct. Native rebellions, the vagaries of weather and climate, illness, injury, and self-interest on the part of the colonists all conspired toward the occasional failures of the settlements.

Linton guides the reader through a comprehensive documentary history of English colonization and plantation in America. On this matter of comprehensiveness, I have to say that the single seriously distracting feature in an otherwise fascinating journey is the sheer enormity of the author's research combined with what is undoubtedly a requirement of the press's house style. Finally exasperated by too many superscripted directions to turn to the back of the book, I counted an average of three endnotes per page; this is cumbersome enough when absolutely necessary, but an avoidable irritation when the note only directs us to another note or to a fuller discussion in a preceding chapter. Lest this appear to be a cranky little cavil, I note that not a single page in the book escapes these hazards; surely even some of Linton's historical explorers managed a day or two of travel without stumbling over obstacles. Cambridge's endnote requirements offer a strong argument for universal adoption of MLA documentation style. A book this good deserves to be read without incessant challenges to the reader's concentration.

Linton's primary focus, to which she returns consistently, is on the operation of gender relations in every colonial venture and every romance she discusses. The pattern of the romance genre, she argues in her Introduction, always aims toward the rhetorical recuperation of successful (ad)ventures culminating in marriage and promises of domestic harmony. So too does the rhetoric of colonial ventures in text after text. "Both in textual and real-life situations, [gender] roles are the articulators of social values; they provide the means by which these values are negotiated in the course of exchange, or translated from one context to another. This formulation allows us to see how gender roles in the English romance, and the social values they articulate, can inform the construction of experience in the colonial narratives" (5). The land, its products (notably timber and tobacco, after repeated efforts to cultivate cotton failed to supply a profitable export and quests for gold failed), and its indigenous population were all "constructed" on the model of the malleable female. Reading this book, I realized that Donne's famous apostrophe to his mistress (which Linton does not invoke, perhaps because it's such an obvious connection)—"O my America! my new-found land. / . . . My Myne of precious stones. My Emperie / . . . Then where my hand is set, my seal shall be"[1]—was less a clever conceit than a commonplace analogy found in a wide variety of historical and fictional narratives.

The book's outstanding quality is its extraordinarily logical and progressive organization, which is no small achievement in a study that undertakes so much disparate material. Chapter 1, "Love's laborers: the busy heroes of romance and empire," establishes the connection between what Linton calls the "marriage-minded" romance and the rhetoric of colonial narratives, with particular attention to Gascoigne's *Adventures of Master F. J.,* Warner's *Albion's England,* Lyly's *Euphues,* and Lodge's *Rosalynde,* mapping out a trajectory on which narrative begins with courtly adventures for "love" and ends with love's ventures toward marriage. This pattern, she argues, fixed in the public imagination the connection between marriage and marketplace. To "follow the genre's expanding horizon is to trace the formulation of a cultural narrative in which courtly love and chivalric adventure are transvalued and appropriated to the aspirations of an age" (38). They also helped to invent those aspirations. It is, after all, impossible to distinguish the interpenetrations of literary praxis and national ideology.

This last point is evident in the deep study of the second chapter, "Sea-Knights and Royal Virgins: American Gold and its Discontents in Lodge's *A Margarite of America* (1596)." To set up her study of that little-known work, Linton explores links between Spenser's *Faerie Queene* and Raleigh's *Dis-*

covery of Guiana, and between the Spanish monopoly in gold-mining in the Americas and England's need to seek other means for economic health, namely an immensely profitable slave trade. Rivalry with Spain provided an opportunity for an interesting form of casuistry whereby England could assert its moral Protestant superiority over Spanish papists (also reputed rapists). Cargoes of precious metal were "liberated" for the queen's Armada campaign by Elizabeth's most successful pirates, Hawkins, Frobisher, Raleigh and Drake, who received knighthoods or higher titles for out-pillaging the enemy (45). Spaniards enslaved natives to work their mines; the English turned Indians into commodities, selling them at times even to the very Spaniards whose mining profits they would later attempt to steal through piracy. The English quest for the high moral ground relative to Spain in the treatment of Indians required a great deal of rhetorical maneuvering; poets such as Spenser and Raleigh were happy to supply the necessary allegorical "spin," at the same time that other writers such as Lodge and Chapman implied "a veiled critique of empire" (51) through satire, irony, and the deconstruction of the ideals and ideologies of romance. Linton is consistently careful to balance views of "the romance of the New World"; we follow throughout a double thread of the romanticized rhetoric of colonialism and a harsher recognition of its failures both practical and moral.

Chapters 3, 4, and 5 take up specific domains of commodification and marketing as the impetus and *raison d'être* of colonial monopoly. The critical strategy in these chapters is especially well considered. Though some readers may be well informed about the history of the cloth trade in England and American prospects for enhancing it (chapter 3), others about the instantiation of consumer capitalism through the "fetishizing" of trifles for sale to a gullible and largely female market (chapter 4), and still others about the history of the cultivation in America of tobacco and the equally assiduous cultivation in England of a profitable addiction to it (chapter 5), there cannot be many readers who are equally well informed about all three important components in the history of Indian subjection and land-appropriation on the American continent. Chapter 3, "*Jack of Newbury* and Drake in California: domestic and colonial narratives of English cloth and manhood," connects Deloney's prose romance about the rise of the cloth trade and Drake's introduction of cloth to Indians in California during his voyage around the world in 1579. "Both the prose romance and the colonial narrative are promotions for the cloth trade. . . . In focusing on Winchcombe and Drake—'founding' figures in the domestic and colonial enterprises—the stories of cloth are in fact stories of an ideal bourgeois manhood elaborated through the economics and politics of cloth-making" (62). Linton then turns to the genre Laura Stevenson O'Connell calls the "Elizabethan Bourgeois Hero-Tale," whereby writers such as Deloney, Richard Johnson, and Thomas Heywood, "three of the most popular second-rate Elizabethan authors,"[2] appropriated the valorized adventures of earlier aristocratic romances for the merchant/craftsman/ apprentice classes. Borrowing Norbert Elias's notion of the "civilizing process," Linton notes an articulated ideology that re-formulated not only class structures but also gender identities by modeling the civil state on the structure of the household, thus anchoring firmly the "bourgeois difference from feudal aristocracy" (63). That "difference" consisted largely in putting everyone to work in the production of cloth and clothing, especially those who otherwise contributed little or nothing else to a strained economy:

> Severall kindes of artificers, husbandmen, seamen, marchauntes, souldiers, capitaines, phisitions, lawyers, devines, Cosmographers, hidrographers, Astronomers, historiographers, yea olde folks, lame persons, women, and younge children. . . .
> (Hakluyt, quoted in Linton, 75)

Such a move shifts a fictional "bourgeois heroic" to a real-world "narrative of bourgeois manhood" (75), a Brave New World indeed. Augmented by a reported Indian penchant, like that ascribed to women back in England, for buying "trifles," the domestic narrative of bourgeois manhood may extend to the colonial area . . . [d]omesticating women at home, converting and civilizing savages abroad" (76).

Chapter 4, "Eros and Science: The Discourse of Magical Consumerism," extends logically the discussion of the preceding chapter to explore exactly how markets for trifles, and the manufacturing enterprises that produce them, were created in both the New and Old Worlds, drawing from materials as disparate as Marx's notion of fetishism as "a mystification of the commodity which conceals the value of labor," Spenser's narrative personifying Error as female (*FQ*, Book I), and early modern ballads extolling (and sometimes decrying) the peddler's trade. The (male) merchant cultivates his customer's (female in England, Indian in America) desire for fashionable, cheap, disposable goods as a magus manipulates his subjects, by mesmerizing the gaze of the consumer, whose rationality is thereby suspended (86), whereas the "culturally superior" male merchant is immune to such subjection (87). Eros and magic were already linked during this period in the discourses of courtly love and the dramas of paternally unacceptable suitors who could only have won the maiden's heart by witchcraft or magic (e.g., *Othello*). With such cultural structures in place, it is easy to see how, "Where erotic and commercial motives overlap, the result is the image of the merchant or pedlar who charms women with his trifles and his talk of love" (87). If somewhat educated Englishwomen could be turned so easily into trifle-fetishists, it was even easier to sell trinkets to Indians. Linton acknowledges the contradictions inherent in the real-life relations of trifle-marketing in America. Not all Indians could be gulled, and not all markets thrived. Furthermore, while sales reports sent back home seemed "good propaganda," the success they implied was starkly contested by very real failures of some settlements. Gold was not found, crops died, and colonists became increasingly dependent upon Indian hospitality, a situation which radically undercut confidence in many English notions of cultural superiority. Romantic idealism can wear thin when survival itself is threatened (90–91).

The next logical progression moves from the discourses and narratives of trifle-fetishism among women and Indians to the creation of a different kind of trifle-fetish among English*men*: the taste for tobacco. Chapter 5, "Gender, Savagery, Tobacco: Marketplaces for Consumption," follows on from the construction of Indians and women as gullible consumers, to unpack the ways in which tobacco-fetishism "rendered problematic the assumed superiority of the civilized English to the savage Amerindians" (107). Tobacco, too, was gendered feminine, in that tobacco was seen to provide what women provided: comfort, respite, and a way to spend both money and leisure. In fact, tobacco was used as currency to purchase women for the settlements, so that "the price of women fluctuated with the price of tobacco on the English market" (127); thus "the savage 'weed' can be said to manage racial anxieties by displacing Amerindian women as the object of exchange" (128).

Chapter 6, "Inconstancy: Coming to Indians through *Troilus and Cressida*," moves from the general to the specific by weaving together accounts of the cultural resonances of Shakespeare's play and the problematic negotiations between John Smith and Powhatan, using the currency of yet a different kind of trifle: colonial rhetoric itself. Against the backdrop of some quite astute observations about the play's representation of self-fashioned heroes and heroics, Linton sets John Smith's critique of fabricated reports of successes and worth by "ingenious verbalists" (152) that put the Jamestown settlement in serious jeopardy. Reading *Troilus and Cressida* and the history of the Virginian colonial enterprise as reciprocally contextual, Linton's notice of connections between historical and dramatic narratives is at its best in this chapter.

No analysis of works reflecting discovery and colonization in the New World would be complete without a chapter on *The Tempest*. Mindful of current studies of what its imaginary island "signified" in the seventeenth century, Linton resists the temptation to reinvent the critical and analytic wheel, and goes beyond earlier discussions of the play as a touchstone for discourses about colonial appropriations in the New World. Chapter 7, "*The Tempest*, 'Rape,' the Art and Smart of Virginian Husbandry," extends from the preceding chapter's focus on "ingenious verbalists," to include pandars and historiographers such as Purchase and Hakluyt, and situates the play among other narratives of power inhering in and emanating from words. Her specific analysis of *The Tempest* may not offer many new insights, but in the context of the preceding chapters it casts the play in a different and most interesting light.

The book ends with a six-page "Coda: The Masks of Pocahontas." It may be unfair to select one section from among so many that work well, but in my view this "chapter" is the most rewarding in the book, not least because it answers a question that is or should be implicit in any reader's mind: "So what?" Having escorted her readers through a long and complex history and literature of colonialism, mercantilism, and racial and sexual subjection, Linton examines our own contemporary appropriations (or misappropriations) of "history" into "myth," and why the past should matter. "Whereas the figure of the husband romanticizes history, the myth in rewriting colonial husbandry unhinges romance from history. In staging romance as a possibility never realized, the myth sustains a mirage of intercultural and interracial harmony that substitutes for a critical understanding of America's colonial history" (186). Her subject is Pocahontas, "the woman on the other side of history held hostage to romance, whose voice we have never heard nor ever will hear" (186), who emerges as the apotheosis of the entire historical/mythical narrative of colonialism in America. This narrative continues on television's History Channel and in Disney's cartoon versions, both modern forms of the early modern romance genre. "The 'corporate takeover' of Pocahontas raises questions of how we as scholars and teachers might define a critical practice that is responsible to history. . . . I am interested in a cultural conversation in which native as well as immigrant Americans can participate from our disparate historical positions and disconnections" (188). Students, as she observes, read literature as "made knowledge—knowledge that can be challenged and transformed, a process that transforms students into makers of knowledge for themselves. . . . For it is in recognizing their own historical agency that inhabits their fiction-making that students make of their learning ways of living and acting in the world that are critically responsible to the legacies of the past as well as to the possibilities of the future" (189). Ending a meticulously researched book with a reminder of why we as teachers and scholars read and write such books in the first place is a professionally responsible move worthy of wide imitation.

Notes

1. Elegie XIX, "To His Mistris Going to Bed," ll. 27–32. I follow Hugh Kenner's edition in *Seventeenth Century Poetry: The Schools of Donne and Jonson* (New York: Holt, Rinehart, and Winston, 1966), 38.

2. Laura Stevenson O'Connell, "The Elizabethan Bourgeois Hero-Tale: Aspects of an Adolescent Social Consciousness," in *After the Reformation: Essays in Honor of J. H. Hexter,* ed. Barbara C. Malament (Philadelphia: University of Pennsylvania Press, 1980), 267.

Plays on Women, edited by Kathleen McLuskie and David Bevington. Manchester: Manchester University Press and New York: St. Martin's Press, 2000. Pp. 416. Cloth $69.95. Paper $19.95. ISBN 0-7190-1646-0.

Reviewer: ALISON FINDLAY

The epilogue of *The Roaring Girl* fears that "the picture of a woman" drawn to the life on stage will be deemed imperfect according to the "several verdicts" of different audience members (lines 2–5). Given the range of woman-centered texts across the period, the editors of *Plays on Women* must, likewise, have felt the impossibility of satisfying students and teachers with a likeness of the early modern woman on stage within the scope of the volume. They devise an elegant, ingenious solution to the problem by returning to starting points. The book identifies four plays which "established the ways of representing women in contemporary settings which were to become the hallmark of the public theatres" (p. 1). The texts credited with such theatrical innovations are *A Chaste Maid in Cheapside* (for extending the dramatic space available to women), *The Roaring Girl* (for centering a city comedy on a woman), *Arden of Faversham* (for the development of "an entirely authentic and idiosyncratic personality" in Alice), and *A Woman Killed With Kindness* (for its more controlled tragic exploration of the emotional costs and social damage caused by adultery). While casually perusing this picture of "plays on women," our own "several verdicts" may identify what we feel are gaps for an undergraduate collection. My initial response was to welcome the presence of a cross-dressing play (something I missed in Kinney's larger anthology),[1] but to lament the absence of a fully developed tragic protagonist in a court drama, such as offered by Webster's *Duchess of Malfi.*

Any slight reservations about the lack of breadth are more than compensated for by the tightly structured logic of the selection, carefully thought through by the editors. By mirroring two city comedies against two domestic tragedies set in the provinces, the book is able to establish a clearly focused terrain through which to introduce ideas about the relationship between dramatic texts, circumstances of production, social history, and gender issues. *Arden of Faversham* and *A Woman Killed With Kindness* work neatly to offer a "tragic mirror image of the comic interaction between women, men, and the changing social world" (p. 28). Encouraged by the introduction, students will able to make critical connections between the fluid world of city comedy, and the rigidities of provincial tragedy, examining relationships between setting, gender, and genre. McLuskie rightly points out that generic appropriation is a two way process: comic promiscuity and changing economic and social relationships were recast into tragedy, but the moralistic pathos of plays like *A Woman Killed With Kindness* was also lampooned in *A Chaste Maid.*

The texts are introduced together by a substantial essay of sixty pages, divided into thematic sections. Given the title of the volume and McLuskie's pioneering feminist scholarship, it is perhaps surprising that gender is not the all-consuming focus of this introduction. Instead, McLuskie's mature understanding of women's positioning in early modern culture is interwoven with more generalized discussion of staging, props, settings, genre, plot, and character in order to "illustrate the ways in which both theatrical pleasures and social relations complicate the connection between women and plays in early modern drama" (p. 1). The overall effect is a beautifully subtle demonstration of how gender difference functions, often silently, as a foundation stone in the discourses and practices of early modern theater and culture.

In the opening section, student readers are given vital information about authors and playing companies. Succinct literary biographies point to further work by Heywood, Middleton, Dekker (although there is little attempt to compare their representations to work by other authors). McLuskie makes the important point that conditions of authorship were very different from our own. The inclusion of a collaborative and an anonymous text demonstrate that, to a theatre company, individual authorship of a creative work was "less important." Nevertheless, authorship is an important issue when it comes to women's power to represent themselves. By simply listing Elizabeth Cary's *Mariam* as "a private drama to be read by a coterie" (p. 3), the introduction unfortunately continues to exclude the aristocratic household or court as legitimate spaces for dramatic production (in which women could take part).[2] We must await Barker and Hinds's forthcoming anthology to innovate the integration of professional and nonprofessional arenas, by including Cary's play in its selection of *Renaissance Drama*.[3]

McLuskie alerts student readers to the "theatrical pleasures" of the texts in a lively analysis of stage effects. Her discussion of props and stage pictures playing an iconographic role in *A Woman Killed* offers a timely reminder to students to consider a text's nonverbal elements. The plays' use of geographical space also receives incisive critical attention. City and provincial locations are briefly contrasted to set up what is implicit in the following discussions of "Citizen Stories," dealing with the comedies, and "Country Matters," and "Love Stories I and II" dealing with the tragedies. Here, the plays are discussed individually, so that even though the volume is designed to be read as a whole, ideas for exploring each play are offered. The recommendations for further reading, which are all appropriate and up to date, are general rather than text-specific. (There is an interesting minor typo whereby Stephen Mullaney's study of the Liberties becomes *The Place of the Stage License*!) Teachers will need to draw up reading lists for individual plays in order to identify chapters in books or to encourage students to consult journal articles, which are not listed.

By highlighting matters of language and style, the introduction addresses another area in which student readers often need encouragement. The interactions of different linguistic registers in the plays are illustrated to show just how much can be gained by following up references in the texts' detailed footnotes. There is, for example, a fascinating reading of Alice Arden's inappropriate use of classical allusion as a telling moment of self-delusion, where language exposes "the gap between Alice's actions and her fantasies about them" (p. 50). In such moments McLuskie gives students an exemplary demonstration of the values of close reading. Some important points are glossed over. Having analyzed the rhetorical games through which Moll Cutpurse's sexual identity is rendered ambiguous, McLuskie refers to "the instability of early modern concepts of sexuality" (p. 54) but doesn't explicitly link this to Moll's cross-dressing to argue through the idea of gender being prosthetically constructed. I fear that my students would be unable to make this connection on their own.

One aim of the volume is to show how social relations complicate the connection between women and plays, and the introduction achieves a poised balance between historicist perspective and reminders that drama is a specific form of social and historical record with its own literary conventions and traditions. Detailed historicist focus opens up readings with clarity. For example, McLuskie draws on the work of Laura Gowing[4] to suggest that Alice and Arden's conflicting accounts of their failed marriage, a source of apparent inconsistency, can be read as dramatic versions of the "narrative of litigation" deliberately opposed in the church courts (p. 37). There is concise information on early modern physiology, social conventions, conduct book literature, and the relationship between economic change and status. In her discussion of the plays' stories, McLuskie highlights points of connection with students' own experiences of romantic fiction, and draws attention to important cultural differences. Her patient analysis of the subplot in *A Woman Killed* spells out the feudal gift culture in which Mountford feels enmeshed, and in which Susan becomes a gift. Oddly, McLuskie cites the stage direction specifying Susan's "*gentlewomanlike*" appearance, and ignores her even more significant words: "Brother, why have you tricked me like a bride?" (14.1). This is a curious blip; well-directed guidance for the student reader is a real strength of the book.

The texts of the four plays are based on the Revels editions by R. B. Parker (1969), Paul Mulholland (1987), M. L. Wine (1963) and R. W. van Fossen (1961). Although these are somewhat dated, their scholarship provides a very strong foundation. Working from this, the general editor, David Bevington, has carefully revised the texts and constructed a student-friendly commentary. In line with the book's view that these plays pioneered the presentation of men and women as recognizable contemporaries, the opening exchange of *A Chaste Maid in Cheapside* is set out, more credibly, as prose rather than verse (as in Wine's edition). Additional stage directions are included to help clarify the action for first-time readers (*Arden* 1.1.282, 359, 522, for example). Those relating to the use of props are another useful reminder to students about the use of nonverbal signifiers, as in Clarke's presentation of the poisoned crucifix (*Arden* 10.79).

Many of the footnotes have been made more accessible to a student readership. New footnotes providing helpful commentary, and linking back to McLuskie's introduction have been included, while others have been thoughtfully reworded or slimmed down. To some extent it is a simplification. One regrets the loss of biblical quotations in favor of paraphrase and reference since students are unlikely to recall the words which would undoubtedly have resonated through spectators' minds at moments like Frankford's sense of betrayal (*A Woman Killed* 8.102–3). In glossing words or phrases, the dictionary-like cross references to other contemporary texts are removed, but the loss of such broader literary contexts will be less keenly felt by the undergraduate audience. The meticulous attention to detail which is a hallmark of the Revels editions, is still in evidence. It is a pleasure, for example, to glance down from the text of *A Chaste Maid* to read the explanation of a tiny detail like '*eryngoes*] candied sea-holly root, considered an aphrodisiac, like the other foods in the list' (3.3.17). The richness of such annotation does help to excite wonder at an alien culture when it is laid so readily before the student reader. In crediting David Bevington for his work on the texts, McLuskie comments that his fine scholarship reminded her that "only the best is good enough for students" (vii). In this volume, students are offered the best in sensitive editing, clear explanation and finely tuned analysis. The menu of plays is selected with careful attention to that readership. Its focus on city comedy and domestic tragedy offers the chance to work within easily recognizable parameters. At the same time, the possibilities for developing richly complex analyses through the criss-cross of comparative readings are suggested in the introduction. The circulation of meanings from the four plays is imaged visually in the juxtaposition of illustrations which encapsulate the book's concerns with theater, geography, and gender. Reproduced are a map of London, De Witt's drawing of the Swan, Saxton's map of Kent, the frontispiece of the *Arden* Quarto, and, of course, the famous image of pipe-smoking, roaring girl, Moll. Across the canvas of early modern plays on women, this volume, the equivalent of a cameo portrait, shows just how multifaceted the image of woman can be.

Notes

1. *Renaissance Drama: An Anthology of Plays and Entertainments,* ed. Arthur F. Kinney (Oxford: Blackwell Publishers, 1999)
2. See S. P. Cerasano and Marion Wynne-Davies, ed., *Readings in Renaissance*

Women's Drama: Criticism, History and Performance 1594–1998 (London and New York: Routledge, 1998) and Alison Findlay and Stephanie Hodgson-Wright with Gwen Williams, *Women and Dramatic Production 1550–1700* (Harlow: Longman, 2000).

3. *The Routledge Anthology of Renaissance Drama,* ed. Simon Barker and Hilary Hinds (Forthcoming, 2002).

4. Laura Gowing, *Domestic Dangers: Women, Words and Sex in Early Modern London* (Oxford: Clarendon Press, 1996).

Elizabeth I: Collected Works, edited by Leah S. Marcus, Janel Mueller, and Mary Beth Rose. Chicago: University of Chicago Press, 2000. Pp. xxiv + 446. Cloth $40.00.

Extraordinary Women of the Medieval and Renaissance World. A Biographical Dictionary, by Carole Levin, Debra Barrett-Graves, Jo Eldridge Carney, W. M. Spellman, Gwynne Kennedy, and Stephanie Witham. Westport, CT and London: Greenwood Press, 2000. Pp. xviv + 327. Cloth $65.00.

Reviewer: MARGUERITE A. TASSI

As we near the fourth centenary of Queen Elizabeth I's death, it would seem that England's great and memorable queen has never been more popular. From director Shekhar Kapur's film *Elizabeth* (1998) to fantasy novels set in Elizabethan England to the never-ceasing publication of biographies and criticism, our cultural fascination with Elizabeth proves Shakespeare's poetry apt in her case: "age cannot wither her, nor custom stale / Her infinite variety." While many of these contemporary texts reflect a desire to re-invent Elizabeth in our own image, some scholarly work has been dedicated to making accessible Elizabeth's own voice and rhetorical efforts at self-representation. The most recent volume to do so, *Elizabeth I: Collected Works,* remarkably seeks to render a large portion of the Queen's writings and records of her speeches in readable prose or verse that stays true to the documentary evidence.

The achievement of *Elizabeth I: Collected Works* cannot be underestimated. Based on the extensive archival work of Leah S. Marcus, Janel Mueller, and Mary Beth Rose, all well-known new historicists with distinguished careers and notable publications in early modern studies, this project was conceived twelve years ago and has thankfully made its way into print. In this volume, the editors offer for the first time in a single publication a wide array of Elizabeth's writings that range across genres, from poetry and devotional writing, to letters and speeches. Their implicit argument is that Elizabeth is an author of merit who has failed to gain recognition as such because of ideological reasons: her gender and an "idealized aesthetics of timeless literary greatness" (xii) have barred her admission into the literary canon. According to the editors, the Queen is deserving of a secure position in the canon. They render Elizabeth's writings admirably accessible by translating all of her work, whether originally in Latin, ancient Greek, Italian, French, Spanish, or Elizabethan English, into modernized English. Recognition that this practice involves a degree of interpretation led them to include notes that clarify some of their choices. Scholars who wish to consult the texts in their original language, spelling, etc. are referred to another volume that Marcus, Mueller, and Rose will soon have published, *Autograph Compositions and Foreign Language Originals.* In a collegial spirit, they invite the discriminating reader to consult this volume in order to judge the success of their methods. The editors have clearly scrutinized the extant texts thoroughly and have made painstaking choices regarding inclusion, modernization, and annotation. Their archival scholarship deserves praise for the high standard they have maintained.

For those interested in early modern textual production, one of the most significant findings lies in the evidence that suggests that Elizabeth engaged in collaboration or "complex coproduction" (xii) with government officials in the composition of her speeches. In analyzing the multiple copies and variant texts of Elizabeth's speeches, the editors conclude that it was highly probable that Elizabeth delivered some of her speeches extemporaneously or from memory, then had them transcribed by auditors, later revising some of them herself. As is the case with memorial reconstruction, textual variants crop up due to the vagaries of memory, attention, and interest. "In such a situation," the editors claim, "there is no single trustworthy text, but rather a range of materials representing various stages of evolution—from the lost oral performance that so bedazzled her contemporaries through the finished public record of it" (xiii). In a number of cases, the editors provide variant versions of speeches. Their stated intention is "to call attention to the historicity of all elements of Elizabeth's text" (xx). To read the multiple texts one after another is to gain a very different sense of the textual situation from that which we have had from previous printings of speeches in which only one version or a conflated version appears as the putative "original." Another benefit of this method of providing multiple texts is that Elizabeth's various rhetorical maneuvers become clearer when one can inspect each text, as well as other supporting materials, which the editors provide, such as the petitions to which Elizabeth was responding.

This method of editing is what Leah S. Marcus has elsewhere called "unediting."[1] Instead of attempting to reconstitute an "original" text, Marcus holds that, as social artifacts, texts should be examined each in its own right as meaningful records. No single text, then, becomes the privileged text. The one major deviation Marcus made from her editorial principle of unediting was to alter spelling and punctuation through modernization of the texts; this was undoubtedly a difficult decision to make, but for the purpose of gaining a wider readership, it was absolutely the right decision. In a sense, Marcus, Mueller, and Rose have solved all the maddening technical problems presented by obscure handwriting, erratic spelling, and foreign language usage. Many scholars will undoubtedly be grateful for this service.

While the editors provided some explanatory annotations, they refrained from using introductory headnotes, or elaborating upon the historical circumstances of each of the writings (though some pertinent information is given when they thought it necessary). Some readers may wish for more in the way of explanatory text that reveals the political and interpersonal dynamics motivating and underlying each written piece. Yet the editors expressly wished to avoid that sort of apparatus in their edition; their aim was to give as little interpretation as possible so that the writings, enigmatic and difficult as some are, can speak for themselves and engage readers' own interpretive responses. Their intended readership is clearly an educated one, schooled in the period, its intricate politics, and Elizabeth's biography. While the editors' restraint may frustrate the reader at times, it is designed to provoke us to do our own surmising, perhaps even undertake our own investigations.

One wonders, however, why the editors did not include a complete list of Elizabeth's writings. They defend convincingly their decision to omit certain texts due to suspect attribution, routine and formulaic style, and lack of space; nonetheless, such a list would have been a helpful inclusion for the scholar who wishes to know precisely what the extent of Elizabeth's writings was. The omission of Elizabeth's translations, which spanned from her youthful forays inspired by and dedicated to Katherine Parr to her mature humanist efforts at Boethius, Horace, and Plutarch, is unfortunate, as well, particularly because they, of all her writings, establish Elizabeth as a true Renaissance writer. In a sense, they help make the case best for Elizabeth as a pioneering woman writer of the sixteenth century who distinguished herself as many humanist writers did, by trying her hand at translating the classical writers. It is understandable, however, that the editors would choose to have these works to former and future editors, for their 446 page volume already offers a variety of genres, each of which is valued as "literary" in its own right. Even without the translations, this collection verifies that Elizabeth was quite adept at representing her desires and thoughts in the available genres and major classical and modern languages of the period. In doing this, she is both representative of the Renaissance humanist writer and exceptional as a female writer.

This volume, in other words, shows us a well-educated woman adept at rhetorical acts in both private and public modes of writing. Her livelihood was, after all, dependent on such fluency, psychological astuteness, and grace (or when it suited her purpose, a highly contrived complexity and enigmatic quality) in expression, which she cultivated over a period of sixty years. Her letters to Queen Mary, for example, are models of assertive, yet tactfully humble, self-defense; Elizabeth walked a fine line with Mary, necessarily pleading her loyalty again and again. Letters regarding the unfortunate Seymour affair reveal the youthful Elizabeth assailed by ill-wishers, fearfully, yet again assertively, insisting on her innocence. After Henry VIII died, Katherine Parr hastily married Thomas Seymour, the ambitious Lord High Admiral, who had apparently aspired to marry Elizabeth. Living as she did with Seymour and Katherine, Elizabeth became unduly embroiled in an ambiguous domestic situation (a sort of *ménage à trois,* as some critics have called it), which became quite dangerous once Katherine died. Rumors ran abroad that Elizabeth was pregnant by Seymour. When Seymour was accused of treason, Elizabeth was implicated and therefore forced to defend her honor to the investigator, Edward Seymour, Lord Protector, Duke of Somerset and Thomas's older brother, which she did in a series of letters. Her insistence on a form of self-representation and justification, rather than relying on the interrogator's account, mark Elizabeth's earliest efforts at gaining control over her public image and reputation. The sordid affair ended with the execution of Seymour. Anxious to have her good name restored, Elizabeth boldly appealed to Edward in a letter dated 21 February 1549 "to send forth a proclamation into the countries that they refrain their tongues, declaring how the tales be but lies, it should make both the people think that you and the Council have great regard that no such rumors should be spread of any of the king's majesty's sisters (as I am, though unworthy)" (32–33).

The early letters give us a portrait of the young princess in formation: at twelve years old, she was, by all appearances, a sensitive, pious, and dutiful girl, devoted to her stepmother, Katherine Parr. Some of the letters preface translations she undertook for Parr, an effort that reflects Elizabeth's early training in arts and letters. Her most significant tutors, Sir John Cheke and Roger Ascham, gave her a rigorous humanist education that would distinguish her as an intelligent and quick-witted orator who could improvise in Latin, as she apparently did in her early speeches at Cambridge and Oxford (1564, 1566) and in her rebuke of the Polish Ambassador (25 July 1597). Her enthusiastic discovery of the power of rhetoric is quite apparent in her letter prefacing her English translation of John Calvin's *Institution de la Religion Chrestienne* (30 December 1545):

> And yet, especially among the aforesaid arts and sciences, the inventions of letters seems to be the most clever, excellent, and ingenious. For through their ordering not only can the aforesaid bodily features be declared, but also (which is more) the image of the mind, wiles, and understanding, together with the speech and intention of the man, can be perfectly known—indeed, traced and portrayed so close to artless and natural that it actually seems that his words that were spoken and pronounced long ago still have the same vigor they had before (11–12).

It is rather astonishing to discover this passage in the twelve-year-old Elizabeth's letter; at an early age Elizabeth had already formed a notion of the written word as representing "the image of the mind, wiles, and understanding." She would later learn how rhetoric could be employed to equivocate and to give an imperfect, opaque view of the mind. Her appreciation for the excellence of letters was clearly cultivated at an early age, in part under the tutelage of Katherine.

The Queen's speeches to Parliament are exercises in that famous rhetorical ploy Elizabeth herself described as the "answer answerless" (200). Particularly in her responses to Parliament's pressing demands regarding marriage, succession, and the execution of Mary, Queen of Scots, Elizabeth prevaricated at length, finally closing her speeches without in fact having given a satisfying answer. In response to the Common's petitions that she marry, Elizabeth masterfully refuses to entertain the question and then, shifts the terms of the argument so that she has the distinct advantage (28 January 1563):

> And though I am determined in this so great and weighty a matter to defer mine answer till some other time because I will not in so deep a matter wade with so shallow a wit, yet have I thought good to use these few words, as well to show you that I am neither careless nor unmindful of your safety in this case, as I trust you likewise do not forget that by me you were delivered whilst you were hanging on the bough ready to fall into the mud—yea, to be drowned in the dung (71–72).

Like an angered parent admonishing complaining, fearful children, Elizabeth refers to how she saved them from the "dung" of Catholicism and papal jurisdiction (as the editors' gloss claims). Her speech ends on a high note with the Queen declaring, "yet shall you never have any a more mother than I mean to be unto you all" (72). Elizabeth manages not only to evade Parliament's demand, but also in the end to render them as ungrateful children who have not sufficiently appreciated her maternal care.

Elizabeth was also quite adept at using religious rhetoric, not only in her prayers and poetry, but also most effectively in her public speeches. She manages to strike a balance between modest, Christian humility and bold assurance that she is protected and guided by divine will. Elizabeth's rhetoric always seems sincere and yet, at the same time, orchestrated brilliantly for effect. In a speech defending her passive response to Parliament's petitions urging the execution of Mary, Queen of Scots (24 November 1586), Elizabeth presents her years of experience, and her double devotion to God and her people as reasons that justify a prudent period of meditation.

> And now to say more unto you of myself, when I first came to the scepter and crown of this realm I did think more of God who gave it me than of the title. . . . I committed my cause unto Him for whose sake I did it, knowing He could defend

me, as I must confess He hath done unto this time, and doubt not but He will do unto the end. After that I did put myself to the school of experience, where I sought to learn what things were most fit for a king to have, and I found them to be four: namely, justice, temper [temperance], magnanimity, and judgment. . . . And now, as touching you, I must needs say and confess that there was never prince more bound to his people than I am to you all (197–98).

Elizabeth's self-proclaimed dependence on God and her desire to do God's bidding undoubtedly struck a pleasing note to her most pious Protestant parliamentarians, but as they must have perceived in time, the religious rhetoric barely masked the queen's absolute will to delay or circumvent the matter at hand. It is no wonder that Elizabeth was fond of relating the classical anecdote of the philosopher who ran through the alphabet before giving an answer.

Far less remains of Elizabeth's verse than of her letters and speeches. We remember George Puttenham's praise of the queen, "whose learned, delicate, noble Muse, easily surmounteth all the rest that haue writte[n] before her time or since, for sence, sweetnesse and sibtillitie, be it in Ode, Elegie, Epigram, or any other kinde of poeme Heroicke or Lyricke, wherein it shall please her Maiestie to employ her penne. . . ."[2] While this eloquent passage gives the impression of flattery, we should note that it also importantly reveals that Elizabeth was publicly recognized as a poet, and a practiced and varied one at that. As the extant poems do not reflect this variety, one suspects that much of the Queen's work has been lost. The poetry produced between 1572 and 1587 includes the Petrarchan lyric, "On Monsieur's Departure," thought to have been written about the Duke of Alençon (later Duke of Anjou), and "When I was Fair and Young," both of which have some literary merit. Primarily, however, the poems are valuable because they give insight into Elizabeth's political situation, as do the famous lines written on a window frame at Woodstock when Elizabeth was imprisoned by Queen Mary: "O Fortune, thy wresting, wavering state. . . . Much suspected by me, but nothing proved can be" (45–46). An assertive, even taunting, statement from the young Elizabeth, these lines indicate what will later blossom into Elizabeth's rhetorical ability to make authoritative assertions, while refusing to give an answer, make a commitment, or take an action.

The most remarkable of the poetry is the eccentric composition of twenty-seven stanzas in French written in Elizabeth's hand (ca. 1590). Since no text other than this one has been found, the editors conclude that this is Elizabeth's original verse. It records, in abstract terms, a perilous account of a monarch's spiritual journey that anticipates the visions of Emily Dickinson:

> Thus newly made,
> I saw the state of my heart,

> Which was so ruinous
> That reason, seated in my soul,
> Was most scornful of it.
>
> (416)

More than any of the previous volumes that have offered selected letters (G. B. Harrison), poems (Leicester Bradner), or speeches (John Neale, T. E. Hartley, Allison Heisch), this collection gives us a clear and complex image of Elizabeth I's mind, wiles, and understanding. The editorial juxtapositions provoke insight and new understanding. Though Elizabeth's style is often deliberately obscure, her rhetorical ploys can be grasped more readily with the variety of texts provided. The monumental efforts of Marcus, Mueller, and Rose represent one of the most significant editorial achievements of our time. Not only is their work meritorious and significant in its success at rendering an exceptional woman's voice audible, they have also provided an excellent foundation for further textual studies of Elizabeth's works and a model for superior archival scholarship.

Another notable effort to give visibility to exceptional women of the past can be found in the attractive biographical dictionary, *Extraordinary Women of the Medieval and Renaissance World,* compiled and written by Carole Levin, Debra Barrett-Graves, Jo Eldridge, W. M. Spellman, Gwynne Kennedy, and Stephanie Witham. We will not find Elizabeth I in this volume, however, nor are other famous queens and luminaries, such as Katherine Parr, Catherine de' Medici, and Hildegard of Bingen, given entries. Instead one finds such names as Levina Teerlinc, Shikibu Izumi, Jacqueline Félicie, and Akka Mahādēvī. The authors wisely decided to focus their volume on women whose lives have been "unsung"; thus, many of the names are surprisingly unfamiliar, even to long-time scholars who have worked on women in these periods. Levin notes in her introduction that information can readily be found on the well-known women of this period, as we can see in the case of Elizabeth I, whereas little scholarly work has been done on many of the lesser known or unknown, accomplished women of this time. Her purpose and that of her co-authors is to introduce into public discourse recognition of the lives of notable women "who frequently moved beyond the conventional ideology of the time that told women to be 'chaste, silent, and obedient'" (xiv). Over seventy distinguished women from a variety of cultural backgrounds, both eastern and western, are represented here for their bold literary, artistic, medical, religious, and political achievements. The authors attempted to represent women of all classes, but as Levin points out, "Because of the sources available to us we include more women who were literate and thus privileged" (xiv). This volume offers an important starting place for students and scholars committed to research that enhances the visibility and recognizes the significant cultural contributions of medieval and Renaissance women. Students especially will find this to be an indispensable and enlightening resource.

What the reader will find remarkable about many of these women is their will to represent themselves in their own artistic terms. The professional calligrapher and miniaturist, Esther Inglis, for example, includes in twenty-four of her manuscripts, a miniature self-portrait that serves not only as a signature, but also as "a sign of pride in her own artistry and an assertion of self-identity" (136), as her biographer, Jo Eldridge Carney, asserts. The painters, Lavina Fontana, Sofonisba Anguissola, and Artemisia Gentileschi, each left their images recorded in vivid self-portraits which are helpfully reprinted in this volume. Gentileschi's *Self Portrait as La Pittura* (ca. 1630) is perhaps the most striking for its allegorical boldness and Caravaggesque technique. As the personification of her art, Gentileschi appears in both a physically sensuous and symbolic manner. Her absorption in her work and the self-consciousness of such a representation of the self distinguish this painter as exceptionally fierce in her devotion to painting and in her will to compete with the great male artists of her time. These female artists received much acclaim in their time, accepting important commissions, and producing, in some cases, a considerable volume of work. However, as is the case with many artists from these early periods, lack of authentication and lost works distort their record. Fontana, we are told, apparently produced over one hundred works, yet only about thirty works can be attributed through signature or date to her. Some of Anguissola's paintings from the Spanish court cannot be verified as her work, and a seventeenth-century fire is thought to have destroyed other works of hers.

In many cases, the authors admit that little is known about their subjects, yet enough can be determined from existing records so that their biographies can be sketched with some authority. About Marguerite Portete (ca. 1250–1310), for example, "We possess very little biographical information" (241), but in 1946 she was verified as the author of the spiritual treatise titled, *The Mirror of Simple Souls.* This textual authentication provides a solid basis for Portele's biographer, W. M. Spellman, since he is able to draw reasonable conclusions about her education and spiritual beliefs from the style and substance of this text. A similar case can be made for Louise Labé, the French poet, who is known primarily through the evidence provided from her publication, *Euvres de Louise Labé Lionnoize* (Lyons 1555). "We know very little about Helen Kottaner" (157), a servant to Queen Elizabeth of Hungary during the fifteenth century, her biographer, Jo Eldridge Carney, states, yet we do have her memoir, which not only gives some documentary evidence for Kottaner's history, but also represents "the first memoir written by a woman in German" (157).

Many of the profiles celebrate the daring achievements of women who were the first of their sex, as was Kottaner, to accomplish something of note. At the very least, these women all warrant the title "extraordinary" in being exceptional in the ways that they were able to defy the strictures established for their sex in their given cultures. Collectively, the impression this volume gives the reader is that these women were pioneers in their respective fields and countries. To some extent, they were given recognition by their peers, as well. Many of these women were in a position to have their portraits painted one or more times, to be actively involved in social, political, and religious movements, and to witness the publication of their writings. Over thirty of the women distinguished themselves by writing drama, poetry, memoirs, and other kinds of works. Hrotsvit of Gandersheim (ca. 932–1001), for example, "is the first known nonliturgical dramatist of Christianity" and "the first female German poet and historian (125). Mary Wroth (ca. 1587–1653?) authored "the first original dramatic comedy written by a woman in English" (294). The Cooke sisters in Britain translated religious texts that received wide circulation, if not publication. As their biographer, Stephanie Witham, indicates, "Remarkably, these women found their voices in the ancient church text and were able to avoid attacks on their character because of their pious literary selections" (59). In an age when it was regarded by some as immoral, or at least indecent, for women to publicize themselves in any way, including through arts and letters, the Cooke sisters and the large handful of women writers profiled in this volume courageously raised their pens and voices in order to be heard.

The volume includes a helpful selected bibliography, which surveys the seminal works, primarily from the 1980s and 1990s, on medieval and Renaissance women. Individual bibliographies follow each entry, which offer a starting point for research on specific women. Advanced scholars may wish that the authors had provided more bibliographic material, but the works listed certainly give the reader some excellent sources to consult. In some cases, these may very well be the only scholarly publications on the particular woman. There is no doubt that *Extraordinary Women of the Medieval and Renaissance World* offers a unique and valuable resource for students interested in women's history. This is a collection of bibliographies designed not only to inform, but also to spur readers on to further investigation. As Levin states, "The purpose of this collection is to make the lives of these extraordinary women available to a wider audience and to encourage further studies of their lives and of the lives of other medieval and Renaissance women" (xvii). One wonders how many more extraordinary women from this period await discovery.

Notes

1. See Leah Marcus, *Unediting the Renaissance: Shakespeare, Marlowe, Milton* (New York: Routledge, 1996).

2. George Puttenham, *The Arte of English Poesie* (1589; Menston, England: The Scolar Press Limited, 1968), Iiir.

Shakespeare and Masculinity, by Bruce R. Smith. Oxford Shakespeare Topics series. Oxford: Oxford University Press, 2000. Pp. x + 182. Cloth $39.95; Paper $19.95.

Reviewer: CHARLES R. FORKER

This is an excellent book. As part of a series intended to be introductory (and written with students principally in mind), it is also likely to attract seasoned Shakespeareans and other scholars of the period for its learned, compact, well-written and deeply researched presentation of a wide diversity of Renaissance ideas on its subject. These Smith considers from both traditional humanist and historical perspectives as well as from more recent theoretical ones. Profoundly influenced, though by no means brainwashed, by feminist criticism, the author insists on a fundamental distinction between biological maleness and socially constructed concepts of masculine identity as disclosed in the plays and poems. For Shakespeare and his age, Smith argues, masculinity "is a matter of contingency, of circumstances, of performance" (4), a condition not merely conferred by nature but rather a status to be "*achieved*" (2) in respect of public behavior, of divergent and shifting moral and social codes, of more or less fixed or fluid class distinctions, of attitudes toward self and others, and of role-playing, both on- and offstage. Smith grounds his necessarily abstract discussion in constant and wide-ranging illustrations from Shakespeare's text—and impressively from *all* of it, not neglecting the minor and collaborative works. The volume is thus synthetic in a positive way, conveying a satisfying sense of wide, even "complete," coverage without intellectual superficiality.

Five chapters approach Shakespeare's concept (or concepts) of masculinity from different angles, using various topical coordinates. The first takes up "Persons," a term that embraces a man's definition of himself according to the dual perspectives of his unique relation to God (his soul) and of his relation to his body as conceived by Galenic physiology with its theory of balanced and unbalanced humours. The category of "persons" extends also to its cognates—"personage" (social importance or celebrity) and "personae" (actors, whether stage professionals or metaphorical role-players on the stage of life). Thus Prince Hal's achievement of manhood, his transformation from Eastcheap playboy to royal hero, can be seen as the healthy readjustment of his bodily humours, while Duke Vincentio's disguise as Friar Lodowick illustrates a concept of masculinity as social agency enacted through the conscious adoption of a specific role, thereby integrating "personage" with "person," public ruler with theatrical impersonator. Smith shows that ideas of the masculine in Shakespeare involve complex cross-fertilization of the transcendental, physiological, social, and performative aspects of human identity. A second chapter, drawing upon Elizabethan conduct books and proverb lore, discusses "Ideals" of masculinity and concludes that although Shakespeare's theatre reflected social reality to some extent, it was more notable for inspiring ideals through positive and negative examples (Talbot's heroism, Richard III's villainy). Noting the gradual transition from feudal values rooted in land and titles to more flexible, capitalist ideas of class, Smith points to five types that emerge in Shakespeare as embodiments of masculinity—the chivalrous knight motivated by honor and valor (Troilus, Hector, Pericles, Palamon and Arcite); the Herculean hero with his more independent and self-contained morality (Achilles, Antony, Coriolanus); the humanist man of reason and moderation (Sir Thomas More, Brutus, Vincentio, Prospero); the merchant prince (Baptista, Lucentio, Petruccio, Masters Page and Ford); and the "saucy jack" or upstart knave whose masculinity resides in his assertive wit and in his parodying of more serious models of maleness (Tranio, Bottom, Lancelot Gobbo, Autolycus). If different masculinities are tied to differences in rank, upper- and middle-class notions of exemplary maleness "converge in the gentleman" (58) and are further complicated by "the primacy of male friendship" (61), a value that pits potentially homoerotic attachments against heterosexual love and persists in Shakespeare from *The Two Gentlemen of Verona* to *The Two Noble Kinsmen*.

"Passages," Smith's third chapter, considers the achievement of masculinity as a function of time, as in Jacques's "seven-ages" speech or in Feste's concluding song in *Twelfth Night*. Rejecting Freudian and Lacanian interpretations of ego development with their built-in assumption that such theories are universally valid, irrespective of historical context, Smith shows that Renaissance notions of identity formation depended on belief in correspondences involving Ptolemaic astronomy, Galenic medicine and the four seasons, as well as on rites of passage and Renaissance social customs such as the "breeching" of boys at age seven, the sending them away as teenagers to universities, great houses, or apprenticeships in a tradesman's dwelling, the delaying of marriage, and the sense of selfhood fully attained only when a son replaced his father and assumed his role through inheritance. Rites of marriage and death are most often Shakespeare's focus because of their dramatic importance as points of directional change in life. Almost equally central, especially in the comedies, is the contest between male friendship and companionate marriage with the inevitable struggle to reconcile the high claims of both. Patterns of rise and fall, models of a moral-spiritual "before" and "after," and contrasts between youth and age (all of which can be discerned, for instance, in a play such as *Richard II*), constitute other ways of dramatizing the realization of masculine identity—"something always in the process of being achieved" and therefore "inherently unstable" (99).

In "Others" (one of his best chapters), Smith considers masculine self-definition both as the experience of "various opposites" and as a "fusion of self with others" (104). For the "I" or persona of the sonnets, the "woman coloured ill" illustrates the first situation, the "man right fair" the second. Women, foreigners, social unequals, and sodomites become for Smith the four categories of "others" against whom the masculine "I," as it emerges in Shakespeare, measures and constitutes itself. Women tend to be depicted as dangerous adversaries of manhood (Cleopatra, or Volumnia when she persuades her son to spare Rome), as victims of male conquest (such as Lucrece and Lavinia), or as catalysts in the formation of masculine identity (Beatrice when she instructs Benedick to "Kill Claudio," or Rosalind teaching Orlando how to woo). As for foreigners, the effete French in *Henry V* help to establish the masculinity of the English through contrast, just as the exotic Egyptian queen of *Antony and Cleopatra* helps to define the disciplined masculinity of the ideal Roman. Smith is especially insightful on the complexities of Othello, whom Shakespeare presents both as a racial other and as a vital part of Venetian society—in his death both a Christian (one of us) and a Turk (one of them). Iago exemplifies the double sense of self as defined externally by rank (the ensign's inferiority to his general) and by his essential self (his diabolical capacity to manipulate and dominate a superior): "I am not what I am." Smith shows how separate classes in the theoretically rigid Elizabethan hierarchy tended in practice to blur and overlap, suggesting that the theatre, Shakespeare's medium, became a symbolic agency and prominent site of the new fluidity—a place where servant-actors could portray nobles and kings and where audiences could identify imaginatively with those above and below them on the social ladder. By borrowing Northrop Frye's generic categories (high-mimetic, low-mimetic and mid-mimetic), Smith is able to show how Shakespeare dramatizes differing concepts of masculinity according to the social station of his characters, how royal figures such as Richard II and Henry V project a different sense of the masculine from Jack Cade's rebels and Coriolanus's plebeians, and yet again from citizens on the make such as Petruccio. The section on "sodomites" explores the anxiety, reflected in Shakespeare's works and in the society they portray, about the difficulty of idealizing passionate male friendship (with its homoerotic implications) without condoning a sexual act officially punishable by death and considered by many to embody the ultimate disgrace of unmanning its practitioners. If male friendship at its most intense and admirable could be conceived as a merging of souls (as in Montaigne), the idea of male bodies merged in sexual encounter was problematically difficult to exclude. Thus at one end of the attitudinal spectrum Shakespeare can give us in *Henry V* Exeter's description of Suffolk embracing and kissing the lips of York in a romantic shared death of soldier-lovers, and at the other end in *Troilus and Cressida* make Thersites sneer at Patroclus as Achilles' "masculine whore." Falling somewhere between are the ambiguous quasi-erotic relationships of Antonio and Bassanio in *The Merchant of Venice,* of Antonio and Sebastian in *Twelfth Night,* and of Coriolanus and Aufidius in *Coriolanus.* Shakespeare negotiates the perilous terrain of a subject that could involve extremes of endorsement and condemnation.

A concluding chapter considers how the topics already discussed intersect with and modify each other, leading us to the judgment that "masculinity in Shakespeare's plays and poems seems precarious" (13). Smith's title for this section, "Coalescences," is chosen in an attempt to "avoid the impasse between essentialism and constructionism" (133), though in fact the book handles various critical perspectives and methodologies (new criticism, performance criticism, new historicism, deconstruction, humanist, and post-structuralist approaches) with equal respect and sophistication. Smith is admirably aware of the dangers of oversimplification—of subscribing without due qualification to the theories or doctrines of any one critical school or of failing to address such questions as which conceptions of masculinity are more historically and socially contingent and which are less so. He is equally sensitive to the ambiguities and nuances created by Shakespeare's artistic use of sources, by his tendency to leave difficult questions open and unresolved, and by his balancing of one or more attitudes and outlooks against each other. What we might call Shakespeare's unconformities are refreshingly acknowledged—e.g., Prince Hal's Machiavelian pragmatism versus his chivalric courtesy to Hotspur, Antony's larger-than-life stature as "triple pillar of the world" versus his bungling of suicide, and Hamlet's humanist intellectuality and philosophical indecision versus his rashness in stabbing Polonius.

If I have a hesitant reservation about this fine book, it concerns what sometimes seems like the author's penchant for subordinating all aspects of Shakespearean character to gender, and of tending to take it for granted that "identity" in the plays and poems is necessarily or always subjective, "achieved," and "socially constructed." In Smith's formulation most of the characters who come to successful self-definition are said to "achieve" their masculinity as though gender constituted the totality of self. But some aspects of identity in Shakespeare are surely gender-neutral. Certainly Macbeth and his lady *experience* murder in psychologically contrasted and gendered ways, but both admit the same objective evil into their hearts and can be defined in moral and spiritual terms without reference to their sex. Cordelia's courageous innocence and the brutality of her sisters are dramatically heightened by the fact of their being represented in female form, but the moral contrast inherent in the theme of natural versus unnatural children (as is shown by Edgar and Edmund, their male counterparts in the subplot) has nothing fundamentally to do with gender. The impulse of conscience that causes Cornwall's servant to revolt against Gloucester's blinding is an aspect of his character that could just as well be embodied in a woman, representing, as it does, a humanitarian absolute. To be fair, Smith's topic directs him to the many and important differences between men and women in Shakespeare and Elizabethan culture, not their common humanity; but it is somewhat reductive, at least in effect, to imply by omission or special emphasis that these differences describe the whole of reality or even its most significant features. It must be said, however, that Smith partly anticipates my qualification, even in the realm of moral absolutism, by noting that "With respect to masculine identity, Shakespeare's tragedies mourn the gap between cultural ideals and the human possibility of achieving those ideals" (138).

Smith's documentation is full and accurate except for the Oxford edition of Shakespeare's *Complete Works* (misdated 1989 on page 162, corrected to 1986 on page 165). Charles Laurence Barber's *Idea of Honour* (1957) and Cesar Lombardi Barber's *Shakespeare's Festive Comedy* (1959) are both cited as being by "C. L. Barber" (pages 165 and 169 respectively), a mode of reference suggesting that the two authors are one and the same. Disappointingly, the index excludes the names of modern critics and scholars cited, possibly an unfortunate policy of the series. Useful "Suggestions for Further Reading" are appended.

Shakespeare the Player: A Life in the Theatre, by John Southworth. Stroud: Sutton Publishing, 2000. Pp. xi + 354. Cloth $30.

Reviewer: MICHAEL TAYLOR

The promise of Southworth's book, trumpeted in its blurbs, and repeated by him at intervals in the text, is that here at last, after centuries of academic obfuscation, is the real thing, a work that cuts to the chase, written by someone from the same tribe as Shakespeare, a player like him, and thereby a privileged conduit to his life in the theater. But not just any old player, as the book's acknowledgments, appendices, and notes remind us, but one thoroughly aware of his scholarly obligations to "all those scholars who have toiled so devotedly in the field of research to establish the facts" (xi), even if all those scholars turn out to be, in the main, E. K. Chambers and G. E. Bentley (with contributions from the *Malone Society Collections* and *Reprints,* and *Records of Early English Drama*). It wouldn't matter a jot that Southworth's scholarship, with its narrow notion of what constitutes "facts," jettisons virtually all but a few stalwarts of the old guard of scholars if indeed the promise of his book were kept and his camaraderie with Shakespeare—or William as he chummily calls him—produced insights into the plays, or suggestions for the life, that surprised us, let's say, with the acuity of their cheeky iconoclasm. There is little doubt, to use one of Southworth's favorite locutions (usually introducing something open to considerable doubt), that Southworth would be amazed to learn how receptive these days academic writers on Shakespeare are to writers on Shakespeare who are not academics, especially if these come from the exotic world that Southworth comes from, the world of professional Shakespeare production and acting. Since his scholarship seems to have ground to a halt around 1945 or so, I suppose it is only to be expected that Southworth wouldn't have noticed just how dependent twentieth century Shakespeare criticism has been on the contributions of his colleagues from the theater. You won't find Granville-Barker, Charles Marowitz, Orson Welles or any of their ilk in Southworth's index (although he does mention that he carried a spear in the "definitive" Peter Brook production of *Titus Andronicus* in 1955).

All these absences wouldn't matter either if what Southworth had to say were, to quote from the blurb again, "ground-breaking and contentious." To break new ground in a field as pitted and rutted as Shakespeare criticism would make insignificant all sins of omission. Who cares if over 99 percent of the writings on Shakespeare are neglected here, if the book provides a kernel or two of genuine new insight (or even new information). But the closest the book comes to justifying its blurb's pretentious claims lies in its opening chapters in the hypothesis that Southworth advances that Shakespeare's "missing years" were spent learning the acting profession in the Company of Worcester's Men. He wasn't a schoolteacher in the north of England or broadening his mind in Europe as some have speculated, but spent his formative years learning the actor's trade with a company that toured the provinces. Not being a theater historian myself, I'm uncertain as to this claim's originality but I can see that Southworth's careful attention to the itinerary of Worcester's Men in the late 1570s (which enabled Shakespeare to be with Anne Hathaway on certain crucial occasions) and his common-sense observation that even the Shakespeares of this world don't make "impossible leap[s] to eminence" (23), gives his hypothesis about what Shakespeare was doing in his late teenage years more plausibility than any other I have read. Indeed the general urging of the book that we should think more carefully about Shakespeare as a player throughout his career and look at the plays in the light of his specific, time-bound theatrical resources is persuasive enough. And when Southworth follows his own advice successfully he surprises us with the occasional provocative and acute perception—when he asks us to think about the writing of *Othello* and *King Lear,* for example, as a response in part to the ageing of the leading actors of the King's Men.

There is, however, much less groundbreaking activity in his book than Southworth imagines. It plods muddily after Shakespeare's career, from theater to theater and company to company, recording when and for whom the plays were written, who may have played what parts, what parts Shakespeare may have played, what the plays were, and what happened in them. It's a long time since I have read a book that finds it necessary to give plot summaries of well-known plays such as *The Comedy of Errors, The Taming of the Shrew* or *Richard II,* but Southworth duly trots them out spicing them with lengthy quotations from the plays about which he then has nothing to say. They lie there limply on the page for no other purpose than to mark where we've gotten to in the discussion of plot or character or for no discernible reason other than to add some linguistic spice and typographic variety. And Southworth's *Reader's Digest* prose needs all the help it can get. The book is full of bland, tendentiously "ordinary" judgments expressed in the language of an eager schoolboy: *King John,* we're typically told, "if not in the first division of Shakespeare's plays . . . must be placed near the top of the second" (139), a meaningless judgment made fatuous by the insistence of that "must be." Or consider the naivete and the grammatical confusion of the following: "They [*Macbeth* and *King Lear*] may not be the best of Shakespeare's plays but they are undoubtedly among the very greatest, and more profoundly disturbing" (239). Even if this last remark did come from a real eager schoolboy's essay it would surely require some gentle remonstrance in the margin from its author's English teacher.

Despite Southworth's reliance on the work of all those toiling scholars he so venerates, he makes it clear throughout his book that it's killjoy academic writing that is the real enemy of an audience's or reader's pleasure in Shakespeare. Southworth complains, for instance, that editions of the published text of *Love's Labour's Lost* "are thick with recondite notes in which every quibble and pun is subject to a learned essay" and while this may be all very well for the student it should not be "allowed to smother the spirit of uninhibited fun which, in an unimpeded reading or performance, is the play's dominant mood" (90). He envisages a marriage of true minds between play and reader/ audience that would otherwise be inhibited or impeded by academic explanation, or explanation in general; the play, any play (as long as it's one by Shakespeare), is self-explanatory, self-sufficient, and self-referential, representing "only itself, and we should be more than content with that" (271). Bonded to it osmotically the reader "requires no other justification for its existence than the pleasure it gives" (192) as Shakespeare "weaves his magic in bringing the play's disparate elements into a coherent unity" (267). So if, through this indulgence in adulatory mystification, Southworth denies himself an interpretative or analytic role, what else does he offer to justify the book's hype besides his suggestion in the opening chapters about Shakespeare's early career?

What he's mainly interested in throughout the book is the possibilities of assigning roles in Shakespeare's plays to specific actors from each of the companies Shakespeare wrote for. Much of this information, necessarily conjectural in most cases, can be found, as Southworth acknowledges, in Chambers and Bentley, but it's useful to have it gathered together here in one place. The actor Southworth is obsessed with is Shakespeare himself and as the book wears on he becomes more and more dogmatic as to the characters

Shakespeare must have played, in a manner that Chambers and Bentley would, I suspect, have found reckless. He begins decorously enough with some maybes and probablies; perhaps, he says, Shakespeare played the young king in the first part of *Henry VI*; he probably played Ferneze, Governor of Malta, in Marlowe's *Jew of Malta*; Andrea in Kyd's *Spanish Tragedy*; Erastus in Kyd's (?) *Soliman and Perseda*; the chorus in *Romeo and Juliet*. But even here the probablies and maybes are mixed with more aggressive locutions. There is "little doubt" about Andrea; "it is apparent" that he played Erastus; "I have little doubt that" Shakespeare took on the chorus in *Romeo*. After a while Southworth drops even these slight hesitancies. In *Much Ado About Nothing* "Shakespeare's role is Leonato" (126); "From this time on, Shakespeare and Burbage were to divide the kingly parts between them" (138); "we cannot deny John to Shakespeare" (142); "there can be little doubt that he played it [the role of Julius Caesar] himself" (173); "Shakespeare's part in the play [*The Merry Wives of Windsor*] can only, I think, have been Page" (183). And on and on. The fragility of these exercises in speculation is, for me, exemplified by the bizarre logic of the following: in *Othello*, Southworth tells us, Shakespeare gives us Iago's exact age, twenty-eight, the exactness of which indicates that the part should not be played by Condell or Cook who were approximately the same age as Iago but by someone aged forty, namely Shakespeare himself for, after all, "Why else should Shakespeare have felt the need to state it so precisely?" (235).

Southworth feels the need throughout his book to state things precisely that can only be a matter of conjecture and surmise. And so it's no more than fitting that he should end it with another certainty, that Shakespeare died a Roman Catholic and was, throughout his life, sympathetic to the recusant cause. Of all the hundreds and hundreds of books and articles that argue differently may I recommend a recent one, Huston Diehl's *Staging Reform, Reforming the Stage: Protestantism and Popular Theater in Early Modern England*, for an addition to Southworth's short list of works by toiling scholars? It's never too late to fill in the gaps, however huge they may be.

Shakespeare's Twenty-First Century Economics, by Frederick Turner. New York: Oxford University Press, 1999. Pp. vi + 223. Cloth $35.00.

Reviewer: SCOTT CUTLER SHERSHOW

At bottom, *Shakespeare's Twenty-First Century Economics* is not a serious study of Shakespeare, nor even a work of literary scholarship. Although it is published by a distinguished university press, this book—which lacks either notes or references except of the most cursory kind—is clearly not intended for contemporary scholars and historians of early modern England, whose work it ignores. One might perhaps consider it a work of ideological polemic, although to do so would still overstate its achievement. In the end, I think it should be considered a pop business book, the kind sold in airports for the benefit of commercial travelers. In broad terms, Frederick Turner's book is a sort of fancier version of a genre exemplified by titles such as *Shakespeare in Charge* or *Power Plays: Shakespeare's Lessons in Leadership and Management*: a genre in which some particular instance of world culture is revealed as providing the key for business success.[1] Indeed, if Turner's book had simply been called *Shakespeare C.E.O.*, it could then conveniently take its place on the shelf right between two other recent books: *Jesus C.E.O.* and *Elizabeth I C.E.O.*[2] To speak only a little more seriously and specifically, I would suggest that Turner's book has a close affinity with the work of George Gilder, the former apostle of "supply-side" economics in the 1980s who, in more recent books such as *Microcosm,* has emerged as a kind of corporate futurist or "cyber-libertarian."[3] Both Gilder and Turner strive to provide a transcendental justification for market capitalism with a strange concoction of Christian theology and pop science—to which Turner adds, as an elaborate centerpiece, a bizarre fantasy of Shakespeare as an unfailingly "wise" and universal genius, whose infallible judgment on literally any subject makes him of "extraordinary relevance to present-day economic and psychosocial problems" (62).

Shakespeare's Twenty-first Century Economics has three basic projects, one negative and two positive. The first is to attack Marxism and other modes of contemporary literary theory; the second is to affirm market capitalism as both morally right and "natural" in both a religious and scientific sense; and the third is to extol and celebrate Shakespeare. One can imagine an interesting discussion speculating on the cultural and "psychosocial" reasons as to why this third project should be joined to the first two at all; but one will not, of course, find such a discussion in *this* book. In any case, the first of these projects, the attack on Marxism and theory, never gets beyond the level of invective, because Turner makes no attempt to engage with his opponents' ideas in any substantial way. Essentially, Turner takes Marxism as a set of moral strictures about economic behavior, thus confusing the Marxist critique of historical capitalism with the precapitalist discursive system sometimes known as the "moral economy." In Turner's view, therefore, Marxism is simply a hatred of rich people and a moral outrage about usury and commercial fraud. "The one thing that unites the political Left, from liberals to revolutionary Marxists, is dislike for the rich" (5), he argues.

Turner thus never comes close to grasping that Marxism is precisely *not* a moral vision of saintly workers oppressed by evil capitalists, but rather a structural theory in which individuals are merely what Marx calls the "bearers" of particular economic roles. Turner also seems to think he is being somehow controversial whenever he observes, as he frequently does, that capitalism has done good things across its long history. "Let us be fair," he says, "the Industrial Revolution did in fact liberate a huge moiety of the world's population into a life relatively free of ignorance, famine, disease, and tyranny" (17). By all means; but let us also be fair in observing how Turner recurrently fails to understand the fundamental proposition of Marxist historiography: that capitalism must be grasped dialectically as at once the best and the worst thing that has ever happened to the world: something that did indeed unlock the productive forces of society and did indeed liberate humanity from "the motley ties that bound man to his 'natural superiors,'"[4] even as it also took its place as history's most efficient mode of economic exploitation.

A full list of Turner's misstatements about theory would be a long one. Turner thinks that the Marxist term "consumer fetishism" refers to advertising (31). He claims that Marxist critics read *The Merchant of Venice* "as a condemnation of usury" (68), whereas in fact Marxist critics such as Walter Cohen actually argue that the play "is quite obviously pro-capitalist."[5] Turner thinks that deconstruction is the argument "that all language is ambiguous" (67). While these initial examples seem to indicate genuine confusion or mere ignorance, at other moments it becomes clear that Turner is engaging in what can only be called deliberate misrepresentation. To illustrate this I will need to quote at some length from an even longer passage that reveals Turner's intellectual bad faith at its most extreme:

> The usual academic view [of the early modern period] derives essentially from the thought of Karl Marx. That is, the Renaissance saw the rise of a great perversion in human economic relationships, whereby the owners of the means of production were able to exploit the labor of the workers. . . . All the evils of contemporary civilization followed . . . A devastating indictment. But if it is true, then there can be no question but that we should abolish stock markets, make private corporations illegal, get rid of the practice of taking interest on loans, nationalize all productive enterprise, and either return to the gold standard or find some way to eliminate money as we know it altogether. The world has in the last few decades decisively rejected this policy . . . But intellectuals and artists have tended to go the other way. The poet Ezra Pound, among others, thought it all through in the years following the Great Depression. Usury, he believed, was the source of all evil. . . . Despite the fact that Pound would have been considered a war criminal if he had not been judged insane, most contemporary academics in the humanities and social sciences still believe in some version of his account. In various guises it has been fatally attractive to many fashionable thinkers, including Heidegger, Sartre, Foucault, Benjamin, and Derrida, and is unquestioned at such gatherings as the Modern Language Association (38–39).

So long a quotation is unfortunately necessary to illustrate Turner's characteristic rhetorical strategy, in which each sentence adds another small inaccuracy, another incremental distortion of associative leap of faith, until he has actually managed not only to conflate Marx with Ezra Pound, but even to claim that Pound's economics is somehow a centrally accepted thesis of contemporary philosophy and literary theory! I simply don't know what one can say about such a passage except that in it—as Anne Barton once observed about Dryden's heroic plays—parody recognizes itself.[6]

Turner's second project is to celebrate capitalism, which he tries to do both as a matter of historical fact, and in the most sweeping metaphysical and theological terms. As an example of the first strategy, he argues of "the business company" that "Its worst crimes, mostly in the nineteenth century, consist in the exploitation of child labor, the creation of unsafe working conditions, and the occasional shooting of union members" (6). In such an assertion, it is not merely the appalling moral indifference inscribed in the word "occasional" to which one must object. It is, rather, Turner's willful blindness to the most minimal standards of historical knowledge. Here is a writer claiming to write about the twenty-first century who has apparently never heard of a *maquiladora* factory, nor of the bloody struggles for economic justice that not only filled the *twentieth* century but also continue today, especially in borderland "freetrade zones"—such as (to cite an utterly random example which happens to be available in today's newspaper) the strike at the Mandarin International plant in San Salvador in 1995, in which "guards dragged women out by their hair and clubbed them with guns" and "the factory's owners fired hundreds."[7] This is the real face of what Turner celebrates blandly as "the new age of abundance" (212); and these are the real operations of that global system which, Turner claims, is in tune with "the wisdom of the universe's own vast economy," and to which Shakespeare will "help us connect" (209).

Turner's apology for capitalism merges seamlessly with his third basic project: his celebration of Shakespeare. In this case, his basic approach is strictly circular: he argues that capitalism is great because Shakespeare says so, and Shakespeare is great because he affirms capitalism. Further, the greatness of both Shakespeare and capitalism is grounded in the eternal verities of science and religion. Let's allow Turner once again to speak for himself:

> This book makes three arguments, following Shakespeare. First, that human art, production, and exchange are a continuation of natural creativity and reproduction, not a rupture of them. Second, that our human bonds with one another, even the most ethical and personal, cannot be detached from the values and bonds of the market. And third, that there is a mysterious dispensation according to which our born condition of debt can be transformed into one of grace (14).

The third argument briefly summarized here expresses a kind of idiosyncratic Christian faith or "mystery," and so I will refrain from engaging with it, because, like all faith, it can neither be proven nor refuted. But about the other two arguments, I observe that, far from being what he claims are "refutations" of Marxism, they are in fact entirely faithful to a broadly materialist view, which always seeks to grasp not the *division* from but "the *relation* of man to nature";[8] and which always affirms, in the words of the familiar contemporary formula, that the personal is the political and vice versa. The domain of what Turner refers to as "production," whether material or symbolic, must of course somewhere include the basic human biological encounter with nature; and of course "the market," the basic process of economic exchange, must join other forms of symbolic exchange on a theoretical continuum. In arguing these things, as though they were somehow radical and original, somehow counter to an accepted wisdom, Turner participates in what I have described elsewhere as the massive ideological displacement with which capitalist ideology, over the last century or so, has tried to appropriate the terms of its own critique. For example, Turner frequently deplores that, in contemporary culture, we tend to envision a profound existential division between emotional and financial relationships, between what he calls "personal bonds and hardheaded business transactions." But such a division, as Pierre Bourdieu has argued at length, is itself a "historical product of capitalism."[9] It is not the thought of the Left, but rather capitalist free-market economics, which always "tries to set aside "a 'sacred' island miraculously spared by the 'icy water of egoistical calculation' and left as a sanctuary for the priceless or worthless things it cannot assess."[10]

Nevertheless, I do not doubt that all three of what Turner identifies as his central arguments can, if one tries hard enough, be somehow drawn out of Shakespeare's absorbent and multivocal text. Turner's ultimate point, however, is that Shakespeare can serve as a comprehensive political, intellectual, and spiritual guide to the contemporary world. It is no exaggeration to observe that Turner envisions a Shakespeare who knows everything, who is never wrong about anything, and who anticipates every manner of modern thought. In sonnet 11, Turner claims, "it is quite clear that Shakespeare . . . has already grasped the principle of evolution through natural selection" (25). Cleopatra's reference to the "knot instrinsicate / Of life" (*Antony and Cleopatra* 5.2.304), expresses "the view of present-day biological science" (52). The play *Antony and Cleopatra,* more generally, represents "a remarkably precise scientific analysis (139), for in it, Shakespeare "intuited" the work of "present-day evolutionary biologists" (148). And Turner goes even farther along these lines, claiming not only that Shakespeare had already mastered the technical complexities of postmodern science, but also that he should now be allowed to serve as an ethical guide to our contemporary disputes about the social uses of that science. After a discussion of the famous "art and nature" passage from *The Winter's Tale,* Turner suggests that "As we have followed it, Shakespeare's reasoning endorses the control and re-adaptation of natural processes for human purposes," so that to oppose "the patenting of biomedical processes involving human genes . . . is clearly invalid by Shakespeare's logic" (30). In other words, Turner argues, in all apparent seriousness, that we should allow the human genome to be privatized and commercially exploited because of a particular interpretation of lines written by a seventeenth-century poet!

But even this does not exhaust Turner's endless faith in the Bard. In his account, Shakespeare is not merely the source of modern science but also the fundamental historical progenitor of American democracy. "There is, I believe," Turner argues, "a direct line of political theory running from Shakespeare through Hobbes and Locke to the framers of the American constitution" (111). And if, in the face of this astonishing assertion, one should venture to recall, say, the famous speech on hierarchical order from *Troilus and Cressida,* or otherwise object that Shakespeare's political beliefs were entirely pervaded by the paternalist assumptions of Elizabethan monarchism, then Turner has an answer ready:

> Shakespeare's model [of life] was the then-current medieval and Renaissance idea of the Great Chain of Being . . . The huge and largely unappreciated virtue of the hierarchical model is that it avoids the alienating dualism of the mind/matter dichotomy, providing instead a much more subtly graded set of distinctions, and a universe of fellowship and communication (52).

Given that Turner is here already trying to argue that the Great Chain of Being was a theory of "fellowship," it probably isn't even necessary to observe the more specific historical error of this passage. But I may as well, one more time, observe the obvious. This famous early-modern model of the cosmos not only does not *avoid* the dualism of mind and matter, but is, rather, essentially *grounded* in precisely the basic opposition between what Plato calls the "sensible" and the "intelligible." In this model, mind and spirit are *always* privileged with regard to body and matter; just as gold is privileged over lead, the lion over the lamb, the king over the commoner, and so forth. Whatever else one might want to say about this intricate cosmological fantasy that C. S. Lewis once referred to as "the discarded image," it is hardly a blueprint for American democracy or the world community of the twenty-first century.[11]

As I presume my cited examples have now made sufficiently clear—and to speak at last with a regrettable but necessary frankness—*Shakespeare's Twenty-First Century Economics* is a dunderheaded book. It's hard to imagine that any contemporary scholar of early-modern literature could enter into serious dialogue with it. I suspect, in any case, that the book's real goal is to lend an aura of reflected cultural glamour to the players of contemporary capitalism, and since such a project is specious in the most literal and precise sense of the word, I cannot gauge its potential success or failure. Let me be clear about one thing, however: my complaint about this book is not that its underlying agenda is political and ideological. On the contrary, insofar as this book might be said to move from literary interpretation to broader issues of contemporary politics, I would wish not to bury but to praise it. For although Turner himself joins many other right-wing voices in denouncing the alleged Marxist sympathies of the contemporary academy, the plain fact is that most scholars are politically disengaged. But then, Turner's book is not finally even political in any meaningful sense of that term. It is rather, the product of a kind of solipsism: a bardolatry so excessive that it runs to madness, and without even much method in it.

Notes

1. Full citations for the books mentioned are: Norman R. Augustine and Kenneth L. Adelman, *Shakespeare in Charge: The Bard's Guide to Leading and Succeeding on the Business Stage* (New York: Hyperion, 1999); John O. Whitney and Tina Packer, *Power Plays: Shakespeare's Lessons in Leadership and Management* (New York: Simon and Schuster, 2000).

2. Laurie Beth Jones, *Jesus C.E.O.: Using Ancient Wisdom for Visionary Leadership* (New York: Hyperion, 1992); Alan Axelrod, *Elizabeth I C.E.O.: Strategic Lessons from the Leader who Built an Empire* (Paramus, N.J.: Prentice-Hall, 2000).

3. For Gilder the supply-side economist, see *Wealth and Poverty* (New York: Bantam, 1981); for Gilder the futurist, see *Microcosm: The Quantum Revolution in Economics and Technology* (New York: Simon and Schuster, 1989).

4. Karl Marx and Frederick Engels, "Manifesto of the Communist Party," *The Marx-Engels Reader,* 2nd ed. Robert C. Tucker (New York: W. W. Norton, 1978), 475.

5. Walter Cohen, "*The Merchant of Venice* and the Possibilities of Historical Criticism," ELH 49 (1982): 768.

6. See Anne Righter [Barton], "Heroic Tragedy," in *Restoration Theatre,* ed. John Russell Brown and Bernard Harris, Stratford-upon-Avon Studies 6 (New York: St. Martin's, 1965): 135–57.

7. *New York Times,* Tuesday, 24 April 2001, A10.

8. Karl Marx and Frederick Engels, *The German Ideology, The Marx-Engels Reader,* 165.

9. Pierre Bourdieu, *Outline of a Theory of Practice,* trans. Richard Nice (Cambridge: Cambridge University Press, 1977), 177.

10. Ibid., 178. Throughout the book, Turner also tries to appropriate the terms of a different historical critique of the market, and portray capitalism as the ultimate "gift-economy." In this case, he specifically demonstrates his indebtedness to the work of George Gilder, as I suggested above—see *Wealth and Poverty,* 30. For more on this process of ideological displacement which such arguments exemplify, see Jean-Jo-

seph Goux, "General Economics and Postmodern Capitalism," *Yale French Studies* 78 (1990): 206--24, and Scott Cutler Shershow, "Of Sinking: Marxism and the 'General' Economy," *Critical Inquiry* 27 (Spring 2001): 468–93.

11. See C. S. Lewis, *The Discarded Image: An Introduction to Medieval and Renaissance Literature* (Cambridge: Cambridge University Press, 1964).

Index

Abel, John, 158, 159
Adams, Susan, 153, 158, 160, 181, 182
Allen, Barbara, 139, 140, 164, 171, 172, 174
Andreadis, Harriette, 131
Archer, Ian A., 138, 139, 140, 141, 168, 237, 238
Arden, Katherine, 139, 140, 160, 168, 169, 170, 171, 181, 190–92, 196
Ariosto, Ludovico, 84
Arundel, Thomas, 19, 22, 36
Ashley, Kathleen, 17
Ashley, Sir Anthony, 188
Atkinson, Anthony, 64
Atwood, John, 176, 177

Bacon, Sir Francis, 134
Bale, Johan, 83
Banning, Andrew, 149
Banning, Paul, 144, 149, 158, 159, 160
Barker, John, 64
Barthes, Roland, 79
Bawcutt, Nigel, 253
Baynton, Sir Edward, 171
Beaumont, Francis, 254; and John Fletcher, 92, 93, 94, 107
Beckett, Samuel, 79
Bede, the Venerable, 79, 80
Bedford, Nell, 181, 190, 192, 193
Bedford, Richard, 58
Beier, A. L., 143; and Roger Finlay, 225
Bentley, G. E., 79, 85, 86, 91, 93
Berger, Thomas L., 100; and William C. Bradford Jr., 120, 124–26
Berti, Mauro, 155
Birrell, T. A., 99
Bland, Mark, 100
Blayney, Peter, 63, 80, 86, 88, 89, 99, 101, 110
Bodenham, Richard, 142
Bodley, Sir Thomas, 87

Bradford, William C., J., *see* Berger, Thomas L.
Bradley, Isabel, 191
Braithwaite, Richard, 170, 224
Bratchel, M. E., 154
Breame, Thomasin, 167, 168
Bredgate, Captain, 57
Briscoe, Marianne, 35
Brooke, Henry, 171, 173, 174
Brooke, Sir George, 139, 141, 148, 164, 168, 171–74, 188
Brooke, Sir William, 139, 141, 148, 164, 171, 172, 174
Browne, Magdalen, 174
Brownlow, Thomas, 182
Burbage, Cuthbert, 58
Burbage, James, 85, 103
Burbage, Richard, 58
Burckhardt, Jacob, 79
Burgh, Elizabeth, 172
Burre, Walter, 93, 106
Bury, John, 20
Bywater, Nicholas, 144, 181, 182, 187, 189, 190, 191, 192

Cam, Elizabeth, 190
Carleton, Dudley, 57, 58, 176
Cartari, Vicenzo, 117
Cartwright, William, 252
Cary, Elizabeth, 119
Castelvetro, Giocomo, 152
Cavallino, Antonio, 199
Caxton, William, 79, 80
Cecil, Sir Robert, 252
Cecil, William, 58
Chaldecot, Francis, 142
Chamberlain, John, 57, 58, 64, 176
Chambers, E. K., 252, 256
Chapman, George, 91, 108, 122
Charles I, 134, 251, 257
Charles II, 92

341

Charles V, 186
Chaucer, Geoffrey, 27, 80, 82, 131, 188
Cheeke, Henry, 84
Churchyard, Thomas, 84
Clarke, Richard, 64
Clere, Sir Edward, 144
Clinton, Elizabeth, 231
Clopper, Lawrence, 28
Clowes, William, 166
Cockayne, William, 248–50
Cobham, Henry Lord, 57, 141, 174
Cobham, William Lord, 141, 171, 174
Colwell, Thomas, 90
Compe, Elizabeth, 167
Cootes, Helen, 140, 144–51, 166, 167, 171
Coppinger, Francis, 172
Corsini, Filippo, 154
Coryate, Thomas, 157
Cotton, John, 162, 163, 166, 167
Crispe, Prudence, 177
Crooke, John, 159
Curatory, Francis, 176, 178
Curatory, Mary, 176, 178

D'Avenant, William, 123
D'Avray, David, 24
Daniel, Thomas, 182, 187
Danvers, Sir John, 256
Davies, John, 197
Daye, John, 82
De Baume, Pierre, 24, 29
De Caron, Sir Noel, 249, 250
De Dois, Francis, 188
De Gozzi, Nicolò, 154, 155, 157
De Medici, Catherine, 119
De Padilla, Don Martin, 57
De Rosselli, Giovanni, 152
Dekker, Thomas, 122, 127, 140, 180, 226; and John Webster, 227, 228, 231, 232, 234, 238, 239
Derrida, Jacques, 79
Dethick, Eleanor, 139, 141, 142, 144, 151
Dickenson, John, 144
Dickenson, Margaret, 144
Digby, Mary, 140, 146, 160, 175, 177, 181
Dillon, Janette, 18, 19, 21, 30
Donnolly, Marie, 168
DuBellay, Ronsard, 119

Duckworth, George E., 118
Dutton, Richard, 81
Dymoke, Talboys, 195

East, Gilbert, 161, 164, 169
Eccles, Mark, 28
Eden, George, 147, 148, 149
Edward IV, 20, 249
Edward VI, 80, 184, 237, 249
Eisenstein, Elizabeth, 78, 82, 83, 86
Elias, Norbert, 227, 235, 236
Elizabeth I, 57, 85, 98, 119, 120, 249
Elton, G. R., 194
English, David, 139, 144, 145, 146, 151
Erasmus, Desiderius, 119
Erickson, Amy Louise, 229
Euripides, 84

Fassler, Christopher J., 86
Fenton, Edward, 158, 159
Fey, Elizabeth, 187, 191
Fichte, Joerg O., 17
Fildes, Valerie, 230
Finch, Thomas, 64
Finlay, Roger, see Beier, A. L.
Fitton, Anne, 196
Fitton, Mary, 142, 196, 197, 198
Fletcher, John, 131, 133, 134; see also Beaumont, Francis; Shakespeare, William
Florio, John, 155
Ford, John, 122, 125, 127
Forman, Simon, 172
Foucault, Michel, 78–81, 227, 235, 236
Fowler, Richard, 176
Franciotti, Orazio, 155
Friis, Astrid, 246
Fuller, Jane, 170
Fulwell, Ulpian, 84
Furrow, Melissa, 32

Garrard, Sir John, 185
Gascoigne, George, 84, 85, 125
Gascoigne, Thomas, 20, 35
Gawdy, Philip, 175–78, 195, 196
Genette, Gérard, 101
Gerrard, George, 248, 250
Gill, Roger, 176, 178
Gondola, Paolo, 139, 151, 153–57
Gouge, William, 224–26
Gras, Henk, 198

Gravener, Welgiver, 190
Gray, Cecily, 145–47, 149
Gray, Jane, 147
Gray, William, 146
Greene, Robert, 60, 61, 62, 194
Griffiths, Paul, 138, 139, 141, 168
Gurr, Andrew, 110
Gutenberg, Johann, 82

Halasz, Alexandra, 103
Handford, George, 139, 140, 181, 194, 195
Harington, Lucy, 152
Harington, Sir John, 152
Harridance, Thomas, 64, 69
Harris, Michael, 88
Hart, Percival, 172
Haughton, William, 226
Hawkins, Thomas, 57
Hawkyns, Edward, 142
Hawkyns, Nicholas, 142
Haynes, William, 176
Helmes, Henry, 198, 199
Henry IV, 249
Henry VII, 79, 249
Henry VIII, 30, 88, 186, 237, 249
Henry, Prince of Wales, 194, 195
Henslowe, Philip, 59, 60, 71, 91
Hensman, Bertha, 134
Herbert, Edward, Lord of Cherbury, 253
Herbert, George, 253
Herbert, Philip, fourth earl of Pembroke, 253
Herbert, Sir Edward, 256
Herbert, Sir Henry, 134, 243, 253, 254, 256
Herbert, William, third earl of Pembroke, 196, 253
Hesiod, 117, 118
Hewett, Anne, 149
Heywood, John, 83
Heywood, Thomas, 107, 109, 131, 238
Hill, Lawrence, 181
Hoby, Margaret, 172
Hoby, Sir Edward, 172
Holcrafte, John, 144
Holcrafte, Mary, 144
Holland, Elizabeth, 177, 178, 181
Hollyngbryg, John, 176
Homer, 117, 118
Honigmann, E. A. J., 106, 174

Hotson, Leslie, 174, 196, 197, 199
Hudson, Anne, 20
Hunter, G. K., 131

Ingeland, Thomas, 84
Inman, John, 176, 178

James I, 98, 105, 183, 184, 248, 249, 251, 256
James, Thomas, 87
Jeayes, Isaac Herbert, 176
Jeffrey, Violet, 131
Johnson, Samuel, 82
Jones, Inigo, 252, 253
Jones, Richard, 103
Jonson, Ben, 81, 85, 87, 91, 93, 94, 98, 105, 107–9, 121, 126, 127, 168, 170, 174, 227, 246, 248, 249, 252–54

Karras, Ruth Mazo, 138, 237
Kevile, John, 143, 194
Kinwelmershe, Francis, 84
Kirkham, Elizabeth, 169
Kirkman, Francis, 92
Knollys, Sir William, 196, 197
Korda, Natasha, 225, 228

Lacke, William, 144
Langland, William, 27
Langley, Francis, 188
Lapides, Fred, 44
Layton, Richard, 179, 180
Lea, Katherine M., 118
Leasing, John, 64
Leighton, Sir Thomas, 58
Lesser, Zachary, 106
Leveson, John, 172
Lewis, Eleanor, 189, 190
Loewenstein, Joseph, 94, 108, 110
Long, William B., 85, 86
Love, Nicholas, 19, 20, 35
Lucan, 119
Lucas, C. P., 251
Lucas, Thomas, 172
Luther, Martin, 30
Lyly, John, 127, 130, 131

Magdalene, Mary, 193
Magno, Alesandro, 178
Manelli, Alesandro, 155
Manzione, Carol Kazmierczak, 139

Marini, Tomas, 139, 151–54, 157, 166, 182, 187
Markham, Gervase, 224
Marlowe, Christopher, 104, 105, 121, 125
Marotti, Arthur, 100 ·
Marston, John, 108, 109, 125, 126, 128
Martin, Richard, 197, 199
Mary I, 80; and Philip, 249
Massinger, Philip, 120, 133
Masten, Jeffrey A., 78
May, Thomas, 121
Maye, James, 167
McGann, Jerome, 99
McKeen, David, 174
McKenzie, D. F., 88
McLaren, Dorothy, 230
McLuhan, Marshal, 90
McMillin, Scott, 77, 94
Medwall, Henry, 82, 83
Melchiori, Georgio, 44, 52
Menander, 118
Middleton, Thomas, 120, 127
Miller, Anne, 139, 141, 158
Minois, Georges, 118, 119
Mirk, John, 17, 24, 27, 28
More, Sir Thomas, 30
Morgan, Ann, 167
Morgan, Luce, 160, 181, 198, 199
Morgan, Lucy, 140
Mosley, Humphrey, 92, 93
Mountjoy, Christopher, 164
Mowdler, Paul, 168
Myers, Robin, 88

Nashe, Thomas, 140, 174
Negro, Lucy, 198
Neuss, Paula, 17
Newborough, George, 140, 142, 143, 183, 198
Newborough, Mary, 139, 140, 142, 144, 146, 147, 149, 150–54, 156–61, 164–68, 170–72, 175–82, 187–95, 197–99
Newborough, Roger, 142
North, Marcy, 77, 78, 80, 83
Norton, Thomas, 84, 85, 129

O'Donoghue, Edward Geoffrey, 182
Offley, John, 149
Offley, Robert, 149, 159, 166
Okeover, Philip, 188

Oldcastle, Sir John, 174, 175
Orgel, Stephen, 252
Orlin, Lena Cowen, 225
Orsino, Don Virgino, 197
Osborne, Anne, 149
Osborne, Sir Edward, 149
Otes, Richard, 64
Overbury, Elizabeth, 179
Ovid, 119, 127

Palavicino, Horatio, 168
Panciatichi, Gualtieri, 153, 154, 156, 157
Partridge, Alice, 172, 173
Pask, Kevin, 80
Paster, Gail, 231
Pecham, John, 24
Pecock, Reginald, 18–22, 24, 27–29, 33–36
Pembroke, Philip, fourth earl of, see Herbert, Philip, fourth earl of Pembroke
Pembroke, William, third earl of, see Herbert, William, third earl of Pembroke
Peters, Julie Stone, 93
Philip II, see Mary I
Philip III, 57
Phillip, John, 84
Pikeryng, John, 84
Plato, 79
Plautus, 118
Plutarch, 132
Popham, Sir John, 142–44, 157, 175, 183, 184, 186, 187, 191–93, 197, 198
Porter, Henry, 123
Powell, Dorothy, 151
Preston, Thomas, 84
Prynne, William, 87

Reignoldes, Edmond, 161
Reignoldes, Elizabeth, 139, 140, 158, 159, 161–67, 169, 170, 196
Repingdon, Philip, 26
Ro, Henry, 69
Roberts, James, 60
Rowley, William, 120, 122, 127

Sackville, Thomas, 84, 85, 128
Saeger, James P., 86
Sanders, Eve, 229
Seneca, Lucius Anneus, 84, 85, 90, 91, 119

Shakespeare, William, 80, 82, 83, 87, 91, 93, 94, 100, 101, 106, 121, 124, 129, 132, 134, 143, 155, 174, 175, 196, 197, 253; works: *All's Well that Ends Well*, 132; *As You Like It*, 63; *Comedy of Errors*, 132; *Hamlet*, 72; *1 Henry IV*, 93, 123, 141; *2 Henry IV*, 59; *1 Henry VI*, 93, 130; *2 Henry VI*, 93, 130; *3 Henry VI*, 93, 130; *Henry V*, 59, 63, 93; *Henry VIII*, 124, 126; *Julius Caesar*, 66; *King John*, 124; *Macbeth*, 129; *Merry Wives of Windsor*, 123, 175; *Midsummer Night's Dream*, 61, 119; *Much Ado About Nothing*, 59, 63; *Othello*, 106, 107; *Pericles*, 132; *Rape of Lucrece*, 101; *Richard II*, 123, 124; *Richard III*, 93, 124; *Romeo and Juliet*, 93, 125; *Sonnets*, 101, 199; *Titus Andronicus*, 68, 93, 101, 125; *Troilus and Cressida*, 106; *Twelfth Night*, 139, 195–99; *Venus and Adonis*, 101; *Winter's Tale*, 132; and John Fletcher, 129
Shelton, Philippa, 189
Shirley, James, 108
Shugg, Wallace, 138, 237
Sidney, Philip, 100
Simonelli, Giuseppe, 155
Sixtus IV, Pope, 20
Slights, William, 108
Smith, Robert, 189
Soame, Sir Stephen, 147, 185
Spencer, H. Leith, 31
Spenser, Edmund, 100
Stanhope, Sir John, 65
Stanley, Thomas, 182–84, 186–89, 197
Stansby, William, 93
Stapleton, Elizabeth, 140, 146, 147, 150, 151, 166
Stow, John, 57, 64, 176
Stubbes, Philip, 163
Sutton, Henry, 89

Targoff, Ramie, 104
Tatham, John, 92
Terence, 118
Thibaud, Adrian, 150
Thibaud, Christian, 150, 151
Thirsk, Joan, 225
Thomas of Chobham, 24
Thomas, Joan, 192
Thoresby, John, 24
Townshend, Aurelian, 243, 249, 251, 252, 254, 256, 257
Trosse, Jane, 191, 192
Truelove, Anne, 191
Trumbull, William, 252
Turberville, Robert, 142
Tusser, Thomas, 224, 226, 231, 235

Vaughan, Richard, 64

Wager, Lewis, 194
Wager, W., 84
Walkley, Thomas, 106, 107
Wall, Wendy, 82
Walley, Henry, 106
Wapull, George, 85
Watkins, John, 32, 35
Webster, John, 109, 124; *see also* Dekker, Thomas
West, Richard, 162
Wilkinson, Agnes, 139, 141, 164, 171, 172
Wilkinson, Michael, 171, 174
William I, 174
William of Ockham, 24
Williams, Katherine, 168
Wilson, John Dover, 196
Winnicombe, Bridget, 190, 191, 192
Woodstock, Alice, 139, 140, 164, 173
Wright, James, 189
Wriothesley, Henry, 101
Wyclif, John, 22